American Business History

CASE STUDIES

Arthur S. Link
Princeton University
GENERAL EDITOR FOR HISTORY

American Business History

CASE STUDIES

Henry C. Dethloff
Texas A & M University

C. Joseph Pusateri
University of San Diego

EDITORS

HARLAN DAVIDSON, INC.
ARLINGTON HEIGHTS, ILLINOIS 60004

Copyright © 1987
Harlan Davidson, Inc.
All Rights Reserved

This book, or parts thereof, must not be used or reproduced in
any manner without written permission. For information, address the publisher, Harlan Davidson, Inc., 3110 North
Arlington Heights Road, Arlington Heights, Illinois 60004–
1592.

Manufactured in the United States of America

Library of Congress Cataloging-in-Publication Data

American business history.

    1. Corporations—United States—History—Case
studies. 2. Business enterprises—United States—
History—Case studies. 3. United States—Industries—
History—Case studies. 4. Entrepreneur—History—
Case studies. I. Dethloff, Henry C. II. Pusateri,
C. Joseph.
HD2785.A76 1987   338.7′4′0973   86–16651
ISBN 0-88295-845-3

Cover illustration: A Texas oil field, early 1900s, (Courtesy
William Owens Papers, Texas A&M University
Archives)

91 90 89 88 87 1 2 3 4 5 6 7 EB

ACKNOWLEDGMENTS

Any work of this type is necessarily the product of the efforts of many different contributors, and they deserve to be properly acknowledged. The editors wish to first express their appreciation to those periodicals and publishers who gave permission for the reprinting here of previously issued materials. A very particular thanks is also due five scholars who prepared original studies specifically for this casebook. They are, in alphabetical order:

Jimmy Anklesaria, University of San Diego
Maurice P. Brungardt, Loyola University (New Orleans)
Harry C. McDean, San Diego State University
Philip T. Rosen, University of Alaska (Anchorage)
Larry Schweikart, University of Dayton

It was a suggestion by the late Harlan Davidson, Sr., that originally brought the two editors together to work on this project. To him and to Harlan Davidson, Jr., who continued support for the project, the editors are pleased to extend sincere appreciation. As always, the consistent encouragement, invaluable advice, and welcome oversight of Maureen Hewitt, editor-in-chief of Harlan Davidson, Inc., was of critical importance in bringing the eventual book to life. It should be noted too that the readability of the manuscript was greatly improved by the skill of Patricia K. Kummer, who carefully edited the copy.

Finally, the editors believe any listing of acknowledgments would be entirely incomplete without a grateful bow in the direction of the Dethloff and Pusateri families. Four hundred years ago, Francis Bacon wrote: "He that hath wife and children hath given hostages to fortune; for they are impediments to great enterprises. . . . " Bacon was never more wrong.

Henry C. Dethloff
C. Joseph Pusateri

CONTENTS

ILLUSTRATIONS

TABLES

1

Introduction

The editors of *American Business History: Case Studies* have also written textbooks on American business history, which are perhaps not inappropriately published by competing companies.* As textbook writers and as teachers, both editors realize that business history requires an approach different from the usual narrative survey of history. Given the individualistic and dynamic nature of business enterprise, the business history classroom should seek to recapture the kinds of experiences that are crucial to a better understanding of the social and personal forces involved in business activities and decisions.

This book is organized chronologically. After a brief statement about the use of case materials, the initial case is an overview of the character of American entrepreneurship. The cases that follow then trace the historical evolution of business enterprise in the United States and explore some of the key issues and controversies that have surrounded its development. But while the specific economic, structural, and socio-political contexts in which business decisions have been made may have sharply varied, the fundamental decision-making process has not. Business managers in the 1980s still

*C. Joseph Pusateri, A *History of American Business* (Harlan Davidson, Inc., 1984); Keith L. Bryant, Jr., and Henry C. Dethloff, A *History of American Business* (Prentice-Hall, Inc., 1983).

grapple with some of the same basic questions as their counterparts two hundred or more years before, and they still must seek their profits in a risky, capitalistic environment.

Some Suggestions for Using Case Studies in Business History

Business history is at heart the study of how individual firms and profit-seeking private enterprises operate. The study of business history lends itself particularly to the case study method. The majority of the selections in this book are cases or accounts of how the owners and/or managers of specific American business organizations conducted the affairs of their respective companies at certain times during the nineteenth and twentieth centuries. These cases are intended to illustrate some of the important events, problems, or issues in the unfolding story of the growth of American economic institutions.

When properly approached, case studies can provide a vital bridge between abstract theory and the experience of real people in actual situations. For many students, the case study method will already be a familiar one. Both business and legal education have long employed it as a fundamental teaching tool for intensive analysis. For those other students, however, whose exposure to case studies has been minimal, some suggestions regarding the effective use of case studies follow.

Basic to the successful use of case studies in any field is recognizing that the case, besides simply describing an interesting episode, is meant to generate a thoughtful and productive classroom discussion. Hence, concentration on the simple memorization of the situation's facts is discouraged. Instead, the situation's facts should be used to form observations and conclusions about the issues or problems upon which the case focuses. To aid in that process, the editors have included at the end of each case or group of cases, a series of possible discussion questions. Naturally, each instructor will want to formulate questions of his or her own to supplement or to replace those included in the text.

To adequately prepare for dealing with the discussion questions posed either in the text or by the instructor, the obvious first step is to read the case thoroughly, thus becoming familiar with all the facts and data contained within it. A single reading is never sufficient. At least two, and possibly three, readings are generally required. The first reading may be rather rapid and done primarily to grasp the general outline of the material and to recognize its basic details. The second and third readings are intended to be response building. By then the events being described should be so familiar that they can be visualized as a forest and not just as a series of individual trees.

At that point, the root issue in the case—what actually makes the case worth studying at all—should also be identifiable. Moreover, informed observations should then be possible about how the situation embodying the root issue could have arisen, what causal factors produced it, and how disastrous consequences might have been prevented. The concern with effects, both good and bad, can move the discussion into the area of alternative strategies, in effect choosing between different courses of action.

The case study method is at its most challenging when the discussion is drawn to the point of making a decision based on the careful evaluation of available evidence. However, in most cases, there is no single, right answer for the questions that have been asked. All the pertinent information that is necessary to reach a comfortable conclusion or decision is rarely present. But that is a true reflection of the real world. Decision makers in business are faced more often than not with incomplete information, uncertainty, and thus tough calls.

But unlike the real world, the answers ultimately arrived at through a case study discussion are not as important as the reasoning pathway that was followed to reach those answers. A case study discussion should be viewed as a laboratory in which to test general and specialized knowledge by thinking through a complex problem to what seems to be its most reasonable conclusion. The case study method is especially valuable because it affords practice in critical reasoning and expands the body of decision-making experience that one can draw upon in the future when choices have consequences with which one actually will have to live.

Henry C. Dethloff and
Keith L. Bryant, Jr.

ENTREPRENEURSHIP

Henry Ford and John D. Rockefeller were highly successful entrepreneurs, but J. P. Morgan was not an entrepreneur at all.

Thomas Edison was both an extraordinary inventor and an imaginative entrepreneur, but inventor Samuel F. B. Morse proved to be a business failure.

The difference between an entrepreneur and a business person is not measured in success or failure, but in an individual's creative approach to the development, production, or marketing of an object or a service.

An awkward French adjective, *entrepreneur* is a most difficult word to define.

The entrepreneur is a person who formulates a new idea or concept and carries it successfully into the economic order.

The entrepreneur becomes aware of a need, be it for a product or service, and creates a business enterprise to fulfill that need. The entrepreneur seizes upon opportunities presented by our national economy and begins to do things that were generally not done in the traditional business routine.

Those individuals whom we call entrepreneurs have made capitalism in the United States a success. Over time, entrepreneurs have become the central fig-

Henry C. Dethloff and Keith L. Bryant, Jr., *Entrepreneurship: A U.S. Perspective*, Series on Public Issues No. 5 (College Station, Texas: Center for Education and Research in Free Enterprise, Texas A&M University, 1983), 1–22.

ures in our modern economy, for they add the innovative element that alters previous business practices.

Entrepreneurs usually unite the major aspects of production—labor and capital—to create an object or render a service at a price that produces a profit for themselves and their investors. Such undertakings require good judgment, perseverance, and knowledge. The entrepreneur must estimate probable importance of the product or service, consumer demand for it, and the means of manufacture and delivery. They must employ labor, purchase raw materials, and find customers. And in the midst of these activities, the entrepreneur must be concerned with orderly process and economy.

Thus, the entrepreneur combines traits of inventor or innovator, superintendent, administrator, and marketer. Is it any wonder that the rate of success is relatively low or that we marvel at those whose success is extraordinary—an Andrew Carnegie, Henry Kaiser, or Herbert Land?

The elements of innovation, management, and adjustment to external forces are critical to entrepreneurship. The decision-making process determines the success of entrepreneurs who seek a positive advantage within the market for their product or service. Their purpose is to minimize risk and uncertainties—and to gain necessary profits. While those who provide only capital can be called investors, financiers, or capitalists, and those who simply keep the organization functioning day-to-day can be called managers, only the entrepreneur has the vision, courage, ideas, and creativity to develop a new business concept and carry it to success.

An Entrepreneurial Environment

The entrepreneurial spirit permeates the history of the United States. From colonial times to the present, our society and the laws it created encouraged the rise of entrepreneurs. Society encouraged the exploitation of resources and the manipulation of markets, within certain limitations. The virtually unregulated economy allowed for the emergence of individual talents and dynamic personalities. Entrepreneurship found a comfortable home in our capitalist society.

Without private property, entrepreneurship cannot function. English Common Law, the Declaration of Independence, the U.S. Constitution, and subsequent state constitutions became a vast legal framework in which the entrepreneur could operate. The right to own land became the right to own factories and distribution systems. Laws made it possible to buy or sell real property, such as land and houses, and intangible property, such as stocks or bonds. The states made incorporation of enterprises easy, and sales of stocks and bonds began to flourish early in the nineteenth century. The sale of securities, in turn, gave entrepreneurs access to capital to carry out their schemes. In no other country were entrepreneurs so well protected and encouraged as they were in the United States.

Ironically, in 1776, just as the colonists sought political independence from England, Adam Smith, a British economist, wrote a book arguing that government should not attempt to direct or control economic activity. He believed that competition and a free market encouraged economic growth. Smith not only revolutionized economic thought, but also suggested the basis upon which the new nation should establish its economic order; that is, individual initiative and little or no governmental intervention. Smith envisioned a system based on a free market, and the new American nation adopted his views.

Adventurous men and women found incentives for exercising entrepreneurial skills in a society that protected and encouraged profitable enterprise. The search for profit came to dominate the political, religious, and educational sectors. Their success made capitalism, with all its obvious advantages and defects, believable to each succeeding generation of Americans.

The cultural environment is a key element for the entrepreneur. The entrepreneurial personality type is present in all societies, but only in a few nations can these individuals exercise such traits. Some societies reject acquisition. Others exert governmental controls to preclude profit making. The absence of legal protection for private property makes successful entrepreneurship almost impossible.

American culture provided an environment conducive to entrepreneurship. Society emphasized the individual and the right of self-determination. Americans believed that they had the ability to control their society and even the forces of nature. Society, they concluded, should be equalitarian, and economic opportunity should be open to all. The culture stressed the importance of progress, particularly when progress was measured by the physically spectacular, such as a factory or a skyscraper. And finally, Americans assumed that change was normal, indeed inevitable, and represented progress. In such an environment, entrepreneurial activities would be cultivated, encouraged, and rewarded.

The Entrepreneur

While economists, business historians, and sociologists may argue about a clear definition of entrepreneurship, they agree that not all individuals have the traits needed to become successful entrepreneurs. They also agree that these individuals are central to the well-being of our economy, and that these individuals must be creative and innovative. And they agree that society exerts both positive and negative influences on the entrepreneur.

The restless innovators, then, occupy the center stage and are both the principal actors and the directors. They are changed by society, but they also influence or alter their social environment. A merchant in a Middle Eastern bazaar who simply buys and resells traditional goods is not an entrepreneur, but the occupant of the next stall who acquires new products, studies the local consumers, and introduces fresh marketing techniques is truly as much an entrepreneur as A. T. Stewart, who created the American department store in the nineteenth century.

Entrepreneurs do new things or do old things in a new way and thereby alter the business system. Some would characterize them as the "movers and the shakers" in our economic life. They possess managerial expertise, insight, and sheer force of character. Each entrepreneur determines the goals and objectives of his or her enterprise and seeks adequate capital to carry out those goals. They establish the strategy to produce and market a commodity or service while anticipating shifts in patterns of consumption and the rise of competition.

All the while, the entrepreneur seeks good relations with labor, government, and the public. But not all successful entrepreneurs engage in all these activities to the same extent. They enter the world of entrepreneurship in a variety of ways.

Some entrepreneurs emerge from the world of invention, while others pioneer in the areas of marketing or management. And some create new administrative structures to carry out business projects or introduce new products. The inventor who devises a marketable object and then sells the patent is not an entrepreneur. The marketer who accepts a product developed by another and sells it in a "tried and true" method does not innovate. The manager who accepts the routine in which he or she functions with no effort to be creative is not an entrepreneur.

The Inventor as Entrepreneur

The old adage that necessity is the mother of invention has some validity, but it is not simply necessity that leads to invention. Rather it is a combination of social conditions and individual insight, often called genius.

Everyone is more or less a participant in the creation of new products. We can be exposed to the same ideas, thoughts, and knowledge, but as unique individuals, we absorb differing portions of that knowledge and gain different insights. This marks the first step in invention. Because of the information gained, an individual senses that something is missing, or that there is an unfulfilled need.

For example, James Watt, the English mechanic, did not invent the steam engine, but he did devise a condenser that helped perfect and improve the steam engine. Watt was a mechanic trying to repair a steam engine built by Thomas Newcomen in about 1712. The engine had a cylinder 21 inches in diameter, and a 7-foot, 10-inch piston. The piston made twelve strokes per minute and developed about seven horsepower. Live steam injected into the top of the cylinder pushed the piston down, and the depleted steam was slowly ejected. The machine was slow, bulky, and powerless. Watt's condenser enabled steam to be injected at either end of the cylinder, thus doubling the power stroke, and he improved the system for ejecting the steam more rapidly, making it possible to have more strokes per minute.

Watt obtained patents and financial backing and began manufacturing his greatly improved engine in 1769.

Watt not only had absorbed the basic technology of the steam piston, but also saw a real weakness in the system, and by a fortunate combination of information, devised a way to solve the problem. The solution, injecting live steam at both ends of the cylinder and using the condenser for the rapid injection of live steam and the ejection of "dead" steam, marked the moment of invention. By obtaining funding for production, and in refining his product and marketing it, Watt became an entrepreneur rather than simply an inventor.

The final phase of invention is essentially an entrepreneurial function: the final revision and adaptation for the marketplace. The inventor-entrepreneur steps beyond the role of inventor to market his invention, bringing a change in consumption patterns and in the quality of life.

The experiences of Cyrus McCormick provide another good example of the inventor as entrepreneur. Born in 1809 on a farm in Rockbridge, Virginia, McCormick grew up watching his father attempt to develop a machine to cut wheat. At that time wheat was harvested by hand using a cradle, a scythe or blade with a wooden frame to catch the wheat sheaves. One man with a cradle could harvest almost three-quarters of an acre of wheat a day, for wages of $1 to $3.

Despite continuing efforts, McCormick's father failed to develop a workable harvesting machine. After his father's final failure in a field trial of harvesting machines, the elder McCormick turned the project over to Cyrus. He had absorbed his father's mechanical information and skills, and was well aware that here was a serious agricultural problem that needed a solution.

After some experimenting, he hit upon the right combination of tools. He substituted a saw-toothed cutting bar for the straight knife-like bar his father used. Instead of "beaters," Cyrus substituted a revolving reel which pushed the stalks across the cutting bar. He continued to perfect and improve his harvester, and obtained a patent in 1834. But he was not yet an entrepreneur because he had made neither an effort to produce or sell his machine, nor did he turn it over to someone who would.

Curiously, Cyrus McCormick parked his harvesting machine in a barn and turned his hand to farming and the operation of an iron foundry. In 1838 his iron business failed, and hard times forced him to attempt to sell his reaper. He sold the first machine in 1840 and built additional harvesters he personally demonstrated to neighboring farmers. By 1844 he had sold fifty reapers, all of which he built in his own workshop. The inventor had become an entrepreneur, if on a relatively small scale.

In 1847 he contracted with a Chicago firm for the manufacture of his reaper and by 1850 had become the sole owner of his own manufacturing plant. But by then Cyrus McCormick was only one of thirty companies manufacturing reapers, many of which had borrowed or stolen his design. McCormick's skill in manufacturing and marketing in many ways exceeded his inventiveness. His success came from the production and mass marketing of the reaper, rather than from patents or royalties on his invention.

By 1856 his Chicago plant could produce 4,000 reapers per year. He sold the machines by advertising nationally at a time when advertising was a novelty. He challenged competitors to field trials, matching his machine against theirs in a public contest. McCormick offered prospective buyers easy credit terms at a time when buying on credit was unknown.

Farmers anywhere could buy a reaper for a $35 down payment, plus freight costs from Chicago, with the balance of $125 due December 1. Despite the constant entry of new competitors and new kinds of machinery, McCormick was able to dominate the reaper market until almost 1870, when the improved Marsh harvester came on the market. McCormick had learned a basic principle of large successful business— to diversify products and market lines. He began producing plows, hay balers, and other implements, creating marketing wars between McCormick's Harvesting Company and Deering Plow Company. These ended only with the creation of McCormick-Deering International Harvester Company in 1903.

In some respects, the career of Thomas Alva Edison parallels that of McCormick. Edison not only invented electric lights, generator systems, phonographs, storage batteries, dictating machines, the mimeograph, and moving-picture projectors, but he also perfected, produced, and marketed his inventions. Edison always was interested in the commercial possibilities of his devices, as most inventors are, but he seemed to be unusually adept at establishing businesses to manufacture and market them.

Born in 1847 in Milan, Ohio, Edison had little formal education. At age 12 he was hawking newspapers and candy on a passenger train. He became a telegraph operator in 1863 and was always an inveterate tinkerer and experimenter. He patented his first inventions, a vote recorder and a stock ticker, in 1869, and began to manufacture both the stock ticker and a telegraph transmitter that could send four messages at once. Both products proved profitable. In 1876 Edison organized the first commercial research laboratory in the United States at Menlo Park, New Jersey. Within a few years he developed a carbon telephone voice transmitter, the phonograph, and the carbon filament light bulb.

Edison needed $500,000 in capital to improve and market his light bulb. Bulbs without electric transmission and generating systems were useless. He obtained financial backing from J. P. Morgan, built generators and transmission lines, and in 1882 turned the switch lighting the Morgan offices in New York City with incandescent lights. Edison's lighting systems were not only better, but also less expensive than the prevalent gas lights. Within a decade gas lighting had given way to electric.

Edison Lamp Company manufactured the bulbs and Edison Electric Light Company built the generators, laid the underground cables, and installed the wiring in buildings. In 1889 these firms combined to form Edison General Electric, and Edison retired to his laboratory at Menlo Park.

In 1892 Thompson-Houston Company, organized by two high school science teachers, Elihu Thompson and E. J. Houston, to build improved electrical generators, merged with Edison General Electric to become General Electric Company. Charles A. Coffin became president of the new company, which soon became involved in a bitter rivalry with Westinghouse Electric Company. The contest, but not the competition, ended in 1896 when Westinghouse and General Electric organized a "patent pool" from which both could share rapidly changing technology. Edison, meanwhile, withdrew completely from the management of the company.

More recently, Herbert Edwin Land, born in 1909 in Bridgeport, Connecticut, has tread much the same entrepreneurial path as Edison, but in a different industry. Land attended Harvard University, where he became interested in the polarization of light. He developed a plastic sheet that would not produce a flare or bright reflection, and in 1933 in a basement laboratory he began to manufacture anti-glare plastic sheets and camera filters. In 1936 he organized American Optical Company to manufacture sunglasses using the new plastic lens. The following year he organized Polaroid Company and obtained patents on his plastic and its processes of manufacture.

Land next developed a new film process that made "3-D" movies possible. Although Polaroid did well financially, Land's most important development was the invention of a one-step photographic process that allowed a picture to be instantly developed. Polaroid began production of the revolutionary Polaroid Land Camera in 1949, and followed with the production of color cameras in 1969. Land's new process competed directly with the giant Eastman Kodak Company, which had enjoyed a virtual monopoly on photographic processing since the 1880s. By

1973 Polaroid was manufacturing 25,000 cameras a day, . . . Land, as Edison, retired from active management of the company and returned to his labs.

The Owner-Manager as Entrepreneur

While an Edison or a Land might retire to the laboratory once their enterprises had been launched, other entrepreneurs manage their creations. They continue to be active in designing new products, in devising new marketing strategies, and in meeting the inevitable competition that emerges when a profitable sector of the economy is created. Often the firm becomes an extension of the owner-manager's personality. An excellent example is Mary Kay Ash and Mary Kay Cosmetics.

Personal enterprise and personal involvement are the essence of these entrepreneurs because they place their own capital at risk, as Mary Kay Ash did. She formed Mary Kay Cosmetics in 1963 with $5,000 in capital, and by 1979 the firm had sales exceeding $90 million and a net income of more than $9 million. She produced a line of cosmetics sold by sales representatives whom she called "beauty consultants." By 1980 she had 70,000 consultants who marketed the firm's five basic, pink-packaged products.

Unlike firms such as Avon, which had a wide variety of products in their catalogues, Mary Kay Cosmetics sold a limited line, most of which it manufactured. The consultants held "beauty shows" for small numbers of women in private homes where the products were demonstrated. They had no territories and no franchises. Mary Kay Ash motivated her sales force with an almost evangelistic fervor, and some of the "consultants" had yearly earnings in excess of $100,000.

The secret of her marketing success was the mobilization of female sales personnel. Mary Kay Cosmetics took advantage of the changing role of women in the 1970s and an untapped labor pool to develop a unique approach to marketing.

An annual convention would attract as many as 8,000 consultants who received pink cars, vacations, jewelry, and mink coats as rewards for successful sales. They sang "Mary Kay Enthusiasm," and attended sales seminars led by Mary Kay herself. The absence of territories allowed her consultants to transfer their work when their husbands moved. They paid for the cosmetics in advance so there were no accounts receivable. Until recently, there was very limited national advertising. As the consultants enthusiastically sold their line, they were taught goal setting and self-motivation and were given public recognition for their achievements.

While Mary Kay Ash perfected new marketing systems for cosmetics, Ray Kroc transformed a small hamburger chain in California into the truly golden arches of McDonald's Corporation through innovative marketing techniques. As a young man Ray Kroc became a successful salesman and regional sales manager for Lily-Tulip Cup Company. In 1937, after seventeen years of service, he left Lily and became the exclusive distributor for the Prince Castle Multimixer, a machine that could mix six milkshakes at once. In 1952 Kroc was intrigued and puzzled by an order for eight multimixers for a single restaurant in San Bernardino, California.

Kroc flew to California and met Richard and Maurice McDonald. Their hamburger drive-in restaurant stressed cleanliness, efficiency, and an assembly-line process of cooking low-priced hamburgers that were served minutes after being ordered. The original drive-in also featured the famous golden arches. Kroc was impressed. He obtained a contract from the McDonalds giving him exclusive franchise rights for the restaurants. Kroc was to receive $350 from each franchiser and 1.9 percent of gross receipts, of which 1.4 percent went to Kroc and .5 percent to the McDonalds.

In 1957 he had 37 franchised restaurants. By 1959, over 200 were in operation. In the 1960s, eager franchisers clamored for McDonald's sites. Kroc bought out the McDonalds' interest in the operation for $2.7 million, and in 1963 sold McDonald's stock to the general public. The stock, which was offered at $22.50 per share, quickly rose to $50. By 1980 McDonald's had become an international household word, and young Americans were literally being weaned on McDonald's hamburgers. Sales exceeded $6 billion annually.

While Kroc had not created or invented the McDonald's "system," he assumed control and converted a small family enterprise into the largest and most successful fast-food business in America. In so doing, he helped to alter our eating habits and those of millions abroad. Ray Kroc is a good example of the owner-manager as entrepreneur.

The Manager As Entrepreneur

While managers as entrepreneurs do not often have a personal style as dramatic as a Henry Ford or a Mary Kay Ash, their contributions can have a significant impact on business administration, structure, and marketing techniques. The entrepreneurial manager is not a "man in a grey flannel suit" who simply aids the flow of paperwork and participates in group decisions.

In modern, large-scale firms there can be many executives and managers who seek and find ways to develop creative responses to problems of design, manufacture, sales, and distribution. In effect, these individuals have managerial responsibilities and find entrepreneurial opportunities which they exercise. They can exercise their entrepreneurial talents only in a favorable atmosphere, which can be created by the chief executive officers of the firm. There must be a system of rewards for these managers, and there must be a promotional structure which allows upward mobility through the corporate structure. Unlike earlier managers who were entrepreneurs, the present occupants of these positions must command more facts, synthesize more advice, be aware of the much greater impact of their decisions, and often make those decisions in a much shorter time.

While decision making in a vast enterprise is often plural, it remains the critical operation in entrepreneurship. Successful professional managers are generally not large security holders in their firms, but their decisions can have an immediate effect on millions, indeed billions, of dollars in capital invested by others. The significance of the manager as entrepreneur can be seen clearly in the transportation sector of the economy through the experiences of Daniel Willard (railroading), Alfred Sloan (automobiles), Juan Trippe (aviation), and Lee Iacocca (automobiles).

The railroads were the nation's first large businesses, and as such became the models for administrative structures used in steel, petroleum, and other industries. The many complexities involved in moving tens of thousands of cars of freight over hundreds of miles of track to dozens of destinations required a business structure that was efficient and effective.

A hierarchy was established with clearly assigned tasks given to managers and workers alike. New operating and accounting procedures had to be devised and the routinization of work had to be established based on rigidly enforced time schedules. Thousands of young men entered the railway industry, which offered opportunities for advancement. Many would later leave railroading to apply their acquired managerial skills in another business.

Others, like Daniel Willard, made railroading their life-long profession, and developed entrepreneurial techniques to make the railways even more efficient arteries of commerce. Unlike the unsavory Jim Fisk, Daniel Drew and Jay Gould, and other so-called "Robber Barons," the manager-entrepreneurs operated the railways for profit, not for the purpose of manipulating their securities.

Born in Vermont, in 1861, Willard grew up on a farm, and at age 18 went to work on a section gang on the Vermont Central Railroad. He moved on to other lines, advancing to fireman, engineer, trainmaster and division superintendent. An excellent manager, Willard became vice president of the Chicago, Burlington and Quincy. On that line Willard created a new personnel system that used demerits rather than harsh discipline. The result was a high degree of morale on the CB&Q.

Willard's work led the management of the Baltimore and Ohio to offer him the presidency of that company, a post he would hold for several decades.

He rebuilt and re-equipped the railway, and soon the B&O was one of the industry's leaders. Willard established good relations with the employees and was

sympathetic to the grievances. After all, he had been one of them. A "cool" nego-
tiator, he won their respect, and when the depression of the 1930s forced Willard
to ask them to take a 10 percent wage cut, they agreed. He reduced his own salary
from $150,000 per year to $60,000. His company weathered the depression, and
Willard's creative management became a model for other lines.

Even as the railways served as the basis for industrial organization in the nineteenth century, Alfred P. Sloan made General Motors Corporation the model for
industrial organization in the twentieth century. Sloan created for GM a highly
innovative administrative structure that gave other managers opportunities to exercise their entrepreneurial talents. It took all of Sloan's skills to salvage GM,
which was on the brink of bankruptcy.

General Motors had been created in 1908 by the colorful William C. Durant.
Bill Durant decided to bring together many of the hundreds of car manufacturers
in one company which would produce cars in all price ranges and would include
its own parts suppliers. He brought together Buick, Cadillac, Oldsmobile,
Oakland, and eventually Chevrolet. But Billy overextended GM, and even massive investments by the DuPont family could not save the firm. The board of
directors ousted Durant, and brought Alfred Sloan, head of Hyatt Roller Bearing
Company, into GM's management.

An organizational genius and creative manager, Sloan devised a plan to
restructure GM in 1920. Where Durant's erratic management had driven out
young executives like Charles Nash and Walter P. Chrysler, Sloan tried to develop a structure that encouraged young talent. He made GM a single coordinated
enterprise with a general office that formulated broad corporate goals and policy
for the operating units. He gave the operating divisions autonomy to encourage
innovation and initiative. While some activities would be coordinated at the top,
the general office would not be concerned with details. There were clear lines of
authority and responsibility, and each operating unit had to establish actual cost
and profit figures for review by the corporate executives. The corporate management would do marketing forecasts for the operating divisions and estimate future
economic conditions.

Sloan assigned each division a specific function; Chevrolet competed directly
with Ford, which Cadillac would be the prestige line. His plan emphasized the
crucial role of the entrepreneur in management and had an impact far beyond
GM. Even Henry Ford would reluctantly accept the Sloan concept and employ
it. The basic concepts Sloan developed would be utilized by many major corporations and become the basic structural device in American industry.

The manager-entrepreneur's decisions about allocation of resources for new
ventures represents a serious risk of the capital of others, indeed even the future of
the enterprise.

But individuals such as Juan T. Trippe took the risk and altered their entire industry. In Trippe's case, the aviation industry would reflect his foresight and courage several times. An aviation pioneer, Trippe invested in several airlines in the 1920s, and in 1927 won an airmail contract to Cuba. He bought huge multi-engined flying boats in the 1930s, and his Pan American Airways expanded over the Caribbean, then to Europe and across the Pacific. He had Charles Lindbergh find the most feasible routes for the fleet of "Clippers" which soon linked the United States with England and even China. The federal government encouraged Trippe to expand in Latin America before World War II to counter the German and Italian airlines in that market.

He constantly sought better aircraft capable of longer flights with more passengers. With mail subsidies from the government and technological advances from Boeing and Martin, Pan American became America's primary international airline.

The intervention of the war and the growth of other international carriers put great pressure on Trippe's firm. Thus, he decided that what was needed to meet competition was a giant, efficient airliner, and between 1965 and 1970, Pan American and the Boeing Company risked over $2 billion in capital on the development of the Boeing 747.

Trippe sought a plane that could carry passengers and freight over great distances at low costs. He projected a massive increase in international air travel and wanted a plane that could outdistance his competitors. Boeing wanted to produce an aircraft that would put it in the forefront—ahead of Douglas, Lockheed, and the European plane builders.

Pan American had to invest $500 million before the plane could even be tested. For four years the process continued with changes in designs and engines. But the gamble paid off. The 747 is an excellent plane, Pan American got a head start through its initial order, and Boeing would sell hundreds of the model, pushing Lockheed out of the passenger plane business. Trippe helped to create an entirely new concept in long-distance air travel, but at a monumental financial risk to his firm.

Courage and perseverance are indeed traits of the manager-entrepreneur, as Lee A. Iacocca's career demonstrates. The son of Italian immigrant parents, Iacocca was born in Allentown, Pennsylvania, in 1924. His father made a considerable fortune in real estate, but the Great Depression took much of his wealth.

One of his businesses included car rentals, mostly Ford cars, and young Lee, originally named Lido, determined that his life's goal was to become a Ford Motor Company executive. After receiving his bachelor's degree from Lehigh University in 1945, he joined Ford's executive training program and then went to Princeton for a master's degree in 1946. He became a district salesman for Ford in Pennsylvania, and by 1960 had become general manager of the Ford division of the company.

A brash, colorful, outspoken executive, his success in developing sales campaigns brought him to the attention of Robert McNamara, one of Ford's "bright young men," and Henry Ford II. As head of Ford division, Iacocca determined to develop a new, "sportier" Ford and spent $50 million creating the Mustang, which appeared in 1964. The car was a brilliant success, and Iacocca joined the board of directors of Ford in 1965. During the next fifteen years he moved up in the corporate structure of Ford to become Chairman of the Board and Chief Operating Officer in 1979. It was assumed in Detroit that he was Henry Ford's heir apparent, but the founder's grandson fired Iacocca. He then took over the ailing Chrysler Corporation.

In 1980 Chrysler Corporation was an industrial disaster. Never fully recovering from World War II, its dealer network a weak third to GM and Ford, Chrysler had been in trouble for more than a decade. Its cars were not stylish and often were not well built. Losses in 1974–1975 led to cutbacks in research and development, and a massive overseas investment program proved to be a gross error. The company lost $205 million in 1978 alone.

Iacocca devised a grand strategy to save the corporation. He closed plants and cut the labor force from 140,000 to 79,000. He convinced the United Automobile Workers union to take pay cuts, but put union representatives on the Chrysler board of directors. Iacocca went to Washington and arranged for $1.5 billion in federally guaranteed loans against considerable political opposition. Chrysler creditors and suppliers had to accept reductions in debts and prices to keep the company alive. Subsidiaries, such as the tank manufacturing division, were sold to raise cash.

But more dramatically, Iacocca went on television himself to sell Chrysler products and to preach the survival of the firm. He emphasized the quality of the new K-cars and his determination to save Chrysler. While cutting costs by $1.2 billion between 1981 and 1983, he also introduced new styles of cars, including a production-line convertible.

The recession of 1981–1982 made all these efforts questionable. Indeed, an issue of *Fortune* in February 1981 said the future of Chrysler was "bleak." But the breakeven point had been cut by half, Chrysler's market share rose to more than 10 percent, and increasing sales in 1983 produced profits. This allowed Iacocca to pay off the federally guaranteed loans far ahead of schedule.

Barring a return to the deep recession days of 1981–1982, Chrysler looks like a major automobile firm again. National news magazines have even suggested that Iacocca's next presidency might be located at 1600 Pennsylvania Avenue in Washington. His dramatic flair, perseverance, and bold initiatives demonstrated that opportunities for managerial entrepreneurship still exist in our economy in the 1980s.

The Modern Entrepreneur

Historians often trace the entrepreneurial spirit to the frontier. During the rapid expansion of the United States from the Atlantic to the Pacific Ocean, the frontiersmen, trappers, miners, and farmers initiated social and economic changes. They settled new lands, opened mines, established trade routes, and poured forth an abundance of agricultural crops. They operated in an almost pure, free-market economy largely beyond the influence of government. As the society matured and expanded, government began to constrain and regulate the frontiersman. An inherent conflict between the entrepreneurial spirit and government regulations began.

America's industrial revolution created a different kind of entrepreneurship, one primarily engaged in technological innovation and in the organization and arrangement of new business structures. The corporate form provided an exciting and dynamic instrument for economic opportunity.

Elias Howe, John Deere, Cyrus McCormick, and Samuel Colt are among the innovators, technicians, and entrepreneurs who paved the way for the advent of the industrial giants, led by men such as John D. Rockefeller of Standard Oil and Andrew Carnegie of Carnegie Steel. In turn, the vast corporate wealth became organized into trusts or monopolies in petroleum, farm machinery, sugar, flour, tobacco, and many consumer products.

As the economy became more complex and the power and influence of the private corporations grew, demands for government intervention on behalf of individual liberty and property rights became louder. The results were the reforms of the late nineteenth and early twentieth centuries that brought government into essentially "nonmarket" control in certain areas. In other words, government began to influence economic decisions, but not as a consumer or as a seller in the marketplace, but rather as a regulator or rule-maker.

For example, the Interstate Commerce Act of 1887 created the Interstate Commerce Commission, which was authorized to review rates charged by railroads to see if they were reasonable and just. The act was largely ineffective until additional legislation broadening the powers of the ICC was passed by Congress after 1900.

Similarly, the Sherman Anti-Trust Act of 1890 was supposed to prevent monopolistic practices. The Meat Inspection Act and the Pure Food and Drug Act of 1906 required government inspection and certification of meat, food, and drug products. The Clayton Anti-Trust Act of 1914 established broader controls over corporations, prohibited interlocking directorates (by which officers of one company controlled or influenced other companies by having membership on their boards of directors), and forbade giving one customer lower prices than another or giving contracts only to preferred customers.

The Federal Reserve Act of 1916 created a new government-controlled national banking system, and the Sixteenth Amendment to the Constitution established the graduated income tax, which clearly affected economic decision making. Thus, in the twentieth century the political and economic environment in which the entrepreneur operated changed markedly from that of the frontiersman.

But by no means did entrepreneurship die. On the contrary, the early twentieth century witnessed the formation of many new businesses and the development of new technology, particularly relating to the automobile and the expansion of electrical power in industry and in the home.

The depression of the 1930s, the New Deal, and World War II again altered the relationships between government and the private economy. Large-scale public spending, welfare programs, tax incentives, business subsidies, and the proliferation of regulatory agencies became commonplace.

Increased regulation by the state and federal governments—especially the latter—limited the range of choices open to entrepreneurs. Even as the federal government enacted additional laws regulating the economy in the areas of labor, safety, environmental protection, and foreign trade, it created quasi-federal corporations (Conrail), guaranteed the loans of firms in financial trouble (Lockheed and Chrysler), and entered the railway passenger business (Amtrak).

In the decade of the 1970s alone, the budgets of the federal regulatory agencies increased from $660 million to more than $5.5 billion. The employees of those agencies grew from 27,000 to 87,000. It is estimated that the annual cost of federal regulations reached $90 billion by 1980, when such restrictions added an average of $600 to the cost of an automobile and seven cents to the price of a pound of hamburger.

A growing negative response to the proliferation of these agencies and intervention by government in the economy led to demands for "decontrol" or "deregulation" of the airlines, petroleum prices, railways, trucking, banking, and other enterprises. One reason for the reversal of almost 80 years of growing regulation was the concern that entrepreneurship was being diminished and the total economy was being grievously harmed.

Despite the fears of many economists that innovation, invention, and entrepreneurship are discouraged, institutionalized, or destroyed by government regulation, such regulation has created new opportunities, such as the manufacture of pollution control devices, seat belts for automobiles, and national chains of tax consultants to help the taxpayer deal with the mass of government regulation. For example, insurance companies now offer insurance against an Internal Revenue Service income tax audit. But for the most part, the entrepreneur had already left the government and its regulations behind, and was moving into new and largely unregulated territory.

Computers spawned a host of new entrepreneurs engaged in equipment design and programming. Modern electronics created cable television companies which now compete with satellite "dish" receivers. Cordless telephones, stereophonic equipment, word processors, and microcomputers all are fast moving frontiers for the entrepreneur. Indeed, the entrepreneur both creates change and thrives on change. Rapid change generates new problems, new needs, and new opportunities. This has been especially true in the computer industry.

Computers and Hi-Tech Entrepreneurs

Early computers, using the old-style vacuum tubes, were massive, terribly expensive, and prone to constant breakdowns. The problem of keeping such systems physically cool so that they did not burn out was great. The systems used by NASA at Cape Canaveral, Florida, during the early days of space flight, the not-so-long-ago 1960s, occupied buildings the size of a city block.

In 1948 Dr. William Shockley and his associates at Bell Laboratories developed a solid-state transistor to replace the cumbersome vacuum tube. It soon became possible to build computers with enormous capability and memory in desk-size units. Miniaturization created opportunities for startling developments in electronic components of every kind. In 1954 the silicone transistor, which could store far larger bits of memory, was developed by Gordon Teal, an associate of what was then a relatively small electronics firm, Texas Instruments. Between 1954 and 1960, as transistors came into widespread use in almost every industry from auto manufacture to missiles, Texas Instruments sales rose an average of 40 percent a year.

Over the next 20 years, sales continued to increase an average of 30 percent each year. Almost none of the products manufactured by Texas Instruments today, which generate almost $2 billion in yearly sales, existed before World War II.

Just as Texas Instruments in the 1960s and 1970s brought innovative new products and techniques to the computer and electronics market, a number of minicomputer firms in the past decade have brought almost revolutionary changes in the "personal computer" industry. Apple, Atari, Intel, and Commodore have created a personal or home computer industry where there was none a decade ago. Thanks to enterprising entrepreneurs such as the two "Steves," Steven P. Jobs and

Stephen G. Wozniak, the founders and creators of Apple computers, computers have moved from industry to the farm and home.

Jobs and Wozniak graduated from Homestead High School in Santa Clara, California, in the heart of the developing "Silicon Valley." They were self-taught computer whizzes who began to work together at the Home Brew Computer Club in Palo Alto, where they were employed by various electronics companies. The two Steves decided that a small multi-use, essentially portable computer was badly needed. They worked together in Jobs' parents' home designing the computer, and then proceeded to build one in the garage. They were so satisfied with what they built that they took it to a local computer store owner who ordered twenty-five of the computers. Jobs and Wozniak, then in their early twenties, proceeded to personally build and fill the orders even as demand soared. The business quickly outgrew the two Steves.

At this critical juncture, A. C. Markkula, a marketing manager with Intel Corporation, which manufactured integrated circuits, offered his financing and marketing expertise. He invested $91,000, obtained additional credit, and soon attracted $600,000 from other investors. Markkula became chairman of the Board of Directors in May 1977, and in June 1977, Michael Scott became president of Apple Computers.

Markkula is an excellent example of the modern manager-entrepreneur who directed the firm from a fledgling operation into a giant enterprise. One of his great innovations was, with the aid of the public relations firm of Regis McKenna, to market the Apple as an inexpensive "home personal computer," rather than an expensive minicomputer. The idea was that one day there would be, or should be, a computer in every home, just as there was a car in every garage, or a television set in every den.

Expanding sales and production required new capital, and in 1980, Apple Computers sold stock to the public. Shares were offered at $22 and quickly rose to $29 and later to $33 per share. In that year, Apple sales were $117 million with earnings of $11.7 million. It was estimated at the time that Steven Jobs, then 25, held stock worth $165 million; and Markkula and Scott held shares valued at $154 and $165 million, respectively.

But the Apple story was not one of unblemished success. The standard Apple II computer was supplemented, too hastily it appeared, with the production of the more sophisticated, but less reliable Apple III. In mid-1981, Scott resigned the presidency, and Markkula stepped in until 1983, when he turned the leadership position over to John Scully, a former president of Pepsi-Cola Company and a marketing expert.

Computers are used in banking, business, publishing, education, robotics, recreation, construction, manufacturing, space, and defense, to mention only a few areas of application. Indeed, the possibilities appear almost infinite, thus creating a veritable playground for the entrepreneur.

One important facet of the industry that particularly attracts the enterprising entrepreneur is "software." In computers, the "hardware" is the electronic unit, the "software" is the program which makes the equipment perform assigned tasks in a designated way. A host of young people have earned reputations—and fortunes—by designing computer programs for games and various tasks. For example, Daniel Bricklin discovered that solving problems on his calculator at the Harvard University Graduate School of Business Administration was awkward and often frustrating. He designed Visicalc, a program which has become one of the most popular for use by executives, accountants, and home owners. In 1978 he and a friend, Robert Frankston, invested $16,000 in their Software Arts firm which markets Visicalc and other programs. Visicalc has sold over 100,000 copies at $200 each.

Similarly, Seymour Rubenstein organized Micro-Pro International in mid-1978, and with John Barnaby, developed and marketed one of the most successful word processing programs called WordStar. Sales of WordStar and DataStar, which handles tabulations, problems, and columns of figures, have exceeded $10 million. Bill Gates and Paul Allen designed and successfully marketed over 500,000 copies of the widely used Microsoft Basic, which has generated over $4 million in earnings for their company.

While the "hardware" and "software" aspects of the computer industry continue to experience rapid change and development, one of the most recent spin-offs has been the emergence of yet another industry—robotics—which holds exciting possibilities for the entrepreneur.

Although the "high technology" industries appear to constitute the frontier in entrepreneurship, for every "hi-tech" innovation there have been several in traditional business pursuits. There always seems to be a better way to prepare and market hamburgers or pancakes. The old frontier spirit is still very much alive in the modern entrepreneur.

QUESTIONS FOR REVIEW AND DISCUSSION

1. Explain entrepreneurship and its relation to the business system.
2. What are distinctive traits of character or aptitude, if any, that might be used to describe an entrepreneur?
3. Identify persons now living, on the national or local scene, whom you would describe as entrepreneurs. Why does the label fit? Compare them to other nationally prominent or local business people whom you would *not* identify as entrepreneurs.

4. Can you identify an entrepreneur whose major innovations or contributions have been in the areas of management, invention, finance, marketing, or manufacture?
5. How does the entrepreneur ascertain a business opportunity?
6. Having once ascertained an opportunity, what might be the subsequent initiatives of the business entrepreneur?
7. Is an inventor by definition an entrepreneur?
8. In group discussion or "brain-storming" sessions, identify areas of "business opportunity," and discuss possible initiatives for creating profitable new businesses.
9. What "external" factors might promote or discourage entrepreneurship?

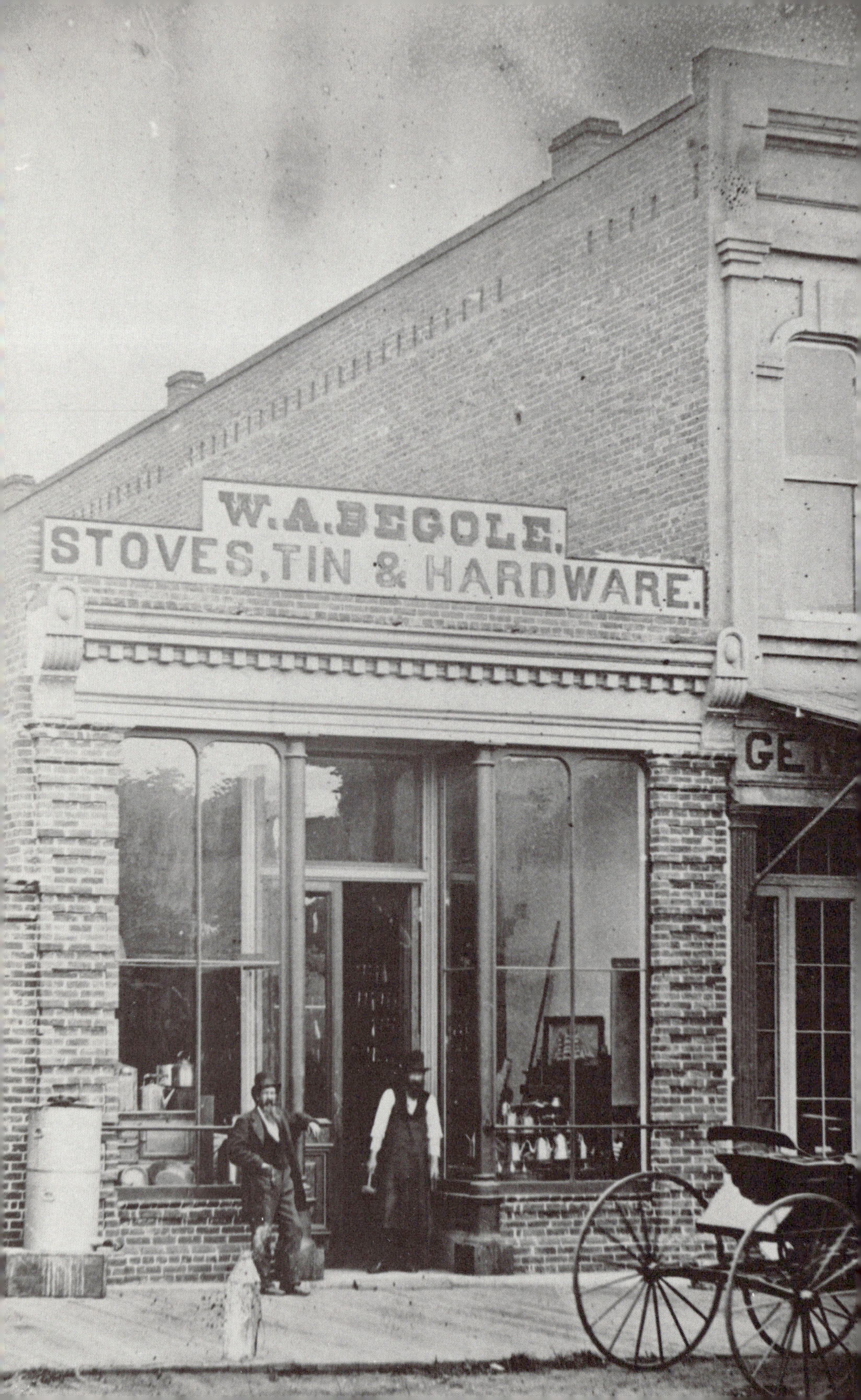
W. A. BEGOLE.
STOVES, TIN & HARDWARE.
GE

2

Marketing: The Essence of Business Enterprise

In *Marketing Efficiency, 1790–1840*, Stuart Bruchey examines what is meant by marketing and how marketing efficiency is achieved. Marketing is more than the flow of goods and services regulated by laws of supply and demand. Marketing also involves making decisions about where goods and services shall flow. Before a marketing decision can be made, the numerous elements of marketing must be organized to initiate and consummate the flow of goods or services. Pricing, packaging, shipping, financing, paying, insuring, storing, and advertising are some elements that make up marketing decisions.

A correct marketing decision reduces costs and maximizes profits. This is known as marketing efficiency. Marketing efficiency is the primary motivation for the inception and development of new businesses and for the reorganization or redirection of existing businesses.

Marketing decisions are based on information or knowledge about such factors as prices and rates of exchange. In the early days of merchant capitalism, gaining such information was a highly individual effort. Thus marketing efficiency was precarious. Improved methods of communication and the formation of partnerships, agencies, and commissions provided opportunities for marketing efficiency. Knowing the price of various goods or commodities in different places and knowing the kinds of goods and services that were most in demand in those places improved the opportunity for making a better marketing decision and thus for marketing efficiency.

Bruchey raises many questions about marketing and the development of a business society in the United States. Some of these questions remain unanswered because hard data for this early period (1790–1840) are elusive. However, Bruchey's ability to raise the right questions provides a starting point for understanding the concept of marketing efficiency and the nature of marketing decisions. This is essential for comprehending the dynamics of the American business system in any period of time.

Although data on specific business activities are particularly elusive for the period before 1869, a number of tables and charts, which are placed at the end of this case study, offer some additional insights into the growth and development of American business activity through 1880. Table 2–1 illustrates the balance of international payments that in turn indicates the flow of goods and services. As a developing nation, the United States drew heavily upon England and Europe for much investment capital and for goods and services throughout the nineteenth century. In 1876, however, the balance of trade seemed to shift permanently in favor of the United States—that is, until recent decades. Table 2–2 shows the land acquired by the United States between 1803 and 1853. These acquisitions suggest economic expansion. Finally, Table 2–3 gives the number of rail miles in the United States. Railway construction provides a sense of business activity and economic well being, as does present-day highway construction.

Questions then to keep in mind throughout this case are: What is the nature of American business activity? What elements provide the basis for making a marketing decision? What are the consequent marketing efficiencies that may be derived from a marketing decision?

Stuart Bruchey

MARKETING
EFFICIENCY, 1790–1840

One of the oldest and most honored theorems in economics is Adam Smith's principle that the division of labor is limited by the extent of the market. In a classic exegesis of the theorem in 1951 George J. Stigler noted how, with the expansion of an industry, the magnitude of functions subject to increasing returns "may become sufficient to permit a firm to specialize in performing it." With continued expansion the number of firms supplying the function would increase, the new industry become competitive and, in turn, possibly abandon parts of the function to a new set of specialists. . . . [1] For centuries the merchant in foreign trade had been a generalist, a jack-of-all trades, shipowner and provider of common carriers for others (and sometimes shipbuilder besides), trader on his own capital as well as commission merchant, exporter as well as importer, wholesaler as well as retailer, money lender and insurer of maritime risks. The market for any one of these services had been too limited to permit much concentration of effort or other investment on it. Now the old order was passing and the many functions of the generalist were splitting up. In the words of George Rogers Taylor, presently "exporters would ship abroad by common carriers rather than in their own vessels, banking and insurance functions would be more and more taken over by corporations organized for those purposes, and

Stuart Bruchey, "The Business Economy of Marketing Changes, 1790–1840: A Study of Sources of Efficiency," *Agricultural History* 46 (January 1972), 211–216.

manufacturing would be carried on by industrialists who, concentrating on fabricating or processing, would leave the problems of transporting, financing, and marketing to others.[2] The question naturally arises how this increasing tendency towards specialization affected the marketing of agricultural commodities, especially the efficiency with which those processes were conducted.

Before we can examine these questions it will be necessary to make clear what we mean by marketing and to issue a word of warning. The warning is this: while efficiency tends to vary directly with the degree of specialization it does so only within limits. The upper limit is passed when the degree of subdivision has given rise to operations so minutely specialized as to be beyond effective managerial control. Here "savings" at one end have generated increased unit costs at the other, and it is the development of this situation that gives rise to vertical integration. The lower limit is that point at which the volume of demand for a good or service is just enough to warrant the introduction of specialization, the point at which Smith's principle first becomes operative. As Henry George reminds us in *Progress and Poverty*, in general the "rude devices of production and exchange which obtain among the sparse populations of new countries, result not so much from the want of capital as from inability to profitably employ it."[3] And, just as a "canoe is a better instrument than a steamboat" to occasionally carry two or three passengers, so "capital" in the form of a more minutely subdivided marketing organization than is warranted by the volume of goods seeking market will increase rather than lower the unit cost of handling those goods.

But precisely what do we mean by marketing? The problem of definition, it must be acknowledged, is not an easy one. According to Reavis Cox, "someone whose basic interest lies in the whole complex of relations between farmers and the rest of the economy . . . is likely to say that marketing includes everything that happens to farm products after they have been harvested." Definitions, he emphasizes, vary widely. However, the American Marketing Association has for many years tried to persuade its members to define the term as "the performance of business activities directed toward and incident to the flow of goods and services from producer to consumer or user"[4] and this seems to me a useful starting point.

In the first place, it distinguishes between flows of goods and flows of services. The latter include such functions as packing and sorting, insuring and storing, shipping, financing, and advertising. Without these services there would be no flow of goods at all, although obviously the importance of some of them varies with circumstances. Yet all of them ought to be regarded as ancillary services for this reason: they depend upon a service of even more fundamental importance, namely, that of organizing the flow of goods and services.

To organize the flow means, above all, to make market decisions, decisions concerning when and where the goods shall flow, and sometimes, at any rate, their packaged form and assortment. Deciding where means choosing among alternative markets; deciding when is obvious, although it may be less obvious that it implies a need to provide or arrange for storage and perhaps insurance as a precondition of time selection. Organizing the flow also means either providing the necessary ancillary services or arranging to have them provided by others. The more highly specialized the individual or firm the fewer the services it provides itself, the greater its dependence upon outside specialists to provide them. In the period 1790–1840, however, as during the regime of the generalist, occupational differentiation among firms organizing the flow was nowhere complete: all appear to have provided some services themselves. Nevertheless, it is important to ask whether the degree of occupational differentiation was greater in this period than it had been, and also whether it was greater in some regions and trades than in others.

While, as we have seen, we may assume that within limits specialization increases efficiency, it is not self-evident how this principle applies to specialization in the making of market decisions. The application will be clear if it is stressed that market decisions can only be made on the basis of market information, information about prices, volumes of competing goods gone or going to alternative markets under consideration, the credit-worthiness of prospective buyers, exchange rates where pertinent, and so on. But information is not a free good. Rather, it belongs among the operating costs of business, and since this is so, a reduction in the real cost of acquiring it necessarily increases efficiency. To express the thought in another way: organizing the flow of goods and services requires the making of market decisions; these decisions require market information; information is an economic good that requires resources to produce, and therefore anything that reduces these requirements per unit of output reduces the real costs of making market decisions—such a reduction being the meaning of efficiency. Now I must make it plain at the outset that the difficulties in the way of discussing this question in terms of real resources seem to me hopelessly complex, and also that, as I shall say at more length later on, even the use of prices as a proxy is almost as difficult. All I can offer are some suggestions which I hope may prove conceptually valid and useful and some impressions which appear to support them.

I shall commence with a brief discussion of foreign trade and try to trace the sources of increased efficiency in that sector. I shall then sketch the origins of marketing mechanisms in domestic trade, beginning, for reasons that will later be clear, with colonial tobacco, and try to do the same for that sector. In order to fit the task to the available time and space I shall confine my attention to southern cotton and western grain. Finally, I shall have a few words to say about problems of measuring efficiency and raise the question of its impact on agricultural incomes.

As a rule, the merchant engaged in foreign trade in 1790 was still a generalist rather than a specialist, a man of numerous investment interests rather than a member of an occupation specializing in the making of market decisions. He would not do the latter until exporting and importing had gone their separate ways, which they were increasingly to do in the years ahead. In 1790 the conduct of foreign trade was beset by inefficiencies of many kinds, some of them pertaining to the process of decision making, others to the provision of ancillary services. While I think it is possible to overstress the difficulties under which the merchant labored, many scholars point out that he did not accompany his goods to market and was therefore dependent upon decisions made on the spot for him by various agents—ship captains, supercargoes, and resident merchants. They stress the difficulties in guiding the path of these agents at a distance, the uncertain quality of market information that reached him weeks or months after its dispatch, the small and easily glutted markets, particularly those of the vital West Indies, the irregularity and unpredictability of departure and arrival times—in a word, the uncertainties of making market decisions in an age of sail. Although past profit-and-loss experience sometimes counted for something, it is true that as a rule it mattered far less than the freshest obtainable reports on commodity prices and exchange rates and on known arrivals or rumored departures of competing cargoes, especially from ports other than the merchant's own.[5]

Both technological and commercial considerations bear upon the question of the degree of regularity enjoyed by these information flows. The former concern the impact of wind and tide on sailing ship movements between home and foreign ports, and the latter the nature of the arrangements made for the sale of exported cargoes and the purchase of returns—arrangements which decisively affected, although they did not wholly determine, the length of time spent in foreign waters (cargoes, after all, had to be loaded and unloaded). Whether vessels were so buffeted by the elements as to make unpredictable their transit times on the ocean is a question on which historians are not agreed. Carl C. Cutler emphasizes the "fitful, changeable character of the North Atlantic gales," but Herbert Heaton subscribes to a less romantic view: "Much has been said about the 'maddening uncertainty' of sailing ship movements," he writes. "Yet the dates of arrivals of vessels [from England to American ports] do not vary greatly from year to year." At least some contemporary testimony is also available. A voyage from Baltimore "to the West Indies and back," a merchant of that city remarked in 1797, "is often performed in 6 or 7 weeks." He observed in 1808 that his schooners "generally completed their voyages [to Vera Cruz and back] in 60 days." I have examined his accounts and find that the average time required for twenty such voyages in the years 1805–1807 was 62½ days. On the other hand, the same merchant reported in 1802 that one of his vessels "had forty nine days passage to St. Croix which should not have exceeded 15."[6]

That New England vessels as well as those of Baltimore may have enjoyed a greater degree of regularity than often believed is indicated by the experience of the Pepperells of Pascataqua. William Pepperell does not appear to have been at the mercy of the elements: he "seems to have counted on Barbados sugar, molasses, and rum being ready in March, since four of his seven spring sailings between 1717 and 1724 arrived in Barbados during that month." The other three arrived in February or earlier. It was not uncertainty with regard to the elements, but with regard to the market, together with William's "positive assurance that he could depend upon Thomas Kerby, his correspondent at Antigua, to accept goods whenever available and hold them for the arrival of one of William's vessels," that explain the "irregularity of his Antigua sailings."[7] Obviously, statistics on departure and arrival times for as many ports as possible need to be assembled. Pending that, one can acknowledge the existence of irregularity in ocean travel without going overboard.

The commercial arrangement making for the highest degree of irregularity in time spent abroad was that under which the stay-at-home merchant engaged his ship captain or supercargo to sell the outward cargo and purchase returns; the engaging of a merchant resident at a particular port to serve as agent made for the least. Stay-at-home merchants consigned their cargoes to captains because of market uncertainty, and a principal reason for that uncertainty was the shallowness of demand, especially in the West Indies. With the consignment in his charge the captain could wander from port to port in search of the best market, a procedure costly in time and in numerous other ways. Richard Pares thinks that "much less than half" of American shipments to West Indian ports before the Revolution went to resident agents.[8] Obviously, any development making it possible to reverse these proportions in favor of resident agents would place in the hands of the stay-at-home merchant the power of choosing his markets, and this would not only increase his efficiency in decision making but also enable him to save on wages, insurance, and other ancillary service costs. He would be able to save on these costs because resident agents almost always were willing to advance from two-thirds to three-quarters of the value of the cargo pending its sale, which permitted the vessel to get home with a return cargo with dispatch.

My impression is that these proportions were indeed reversed in the period of our concern and that the reason for it was the increasing width of markets in many parts of the world. At least in the short run West Indian markets widened dramatically because the exigencies of the Continental Wars made American neutral vessels the leading carriers of the world. Previously they had supplied the island ports with timber and fish, bread and flour, and other native products. Now they carried a broader range of goods. Speaking of the Baltimore market the firm of Robert Oliver & Brothers wrote in 1800: "One cargo of German linens was formerly a large supply for a year's consumption and we have now a demand for more than fifty cargoes. The consumption of East India Goods has also increased astonishingly." A few months before the firm had made clear that the reason for much of the increased demand was "Our West India trade on which we chiefly depend for the Sale of Linens."[9] According to Tyler Dennet "One hears very little" of the supercargo after 1815 in American trade with the Far East. His place, Dennet says, was taken "by the resident commission agent."[10] One hears equally rarely of cotton consignments to ship captains in the antebellum period. The overwhelming majority seem to have been addressed to a named American house, or one in Europe, especially in Liverpool, of course.

The period 1790–1840 also saw other important contributions to efficiency in foreign trade, some of them pertinent to the making of market decisions as well as to the ancillary services of marketing. The organization of packet lines to Liverpool and other ports soon after the War of 1812 made for greater speed and regularity and by quickening the flow of information undoubtedly contributed to the efficiency with which decisions were made. An important recent article by Douglass North points to additional sources of raising productivity in shipping itself, namely, a substantial increase in the size of vessels between 1820 and 1850, with consequent lowered unit costs, and a steady decline in the size of crews. He attributes to the growing size of markets a reduction in time spent in port, with consequent increases in the number of round trips made by vessels during the course of a given year.[11] As I see it, the achievement of greater efficiency in the ancillary service of transportation, now increasingly provided by firms belonging to a separate and specialized occupation, yielded external economies to exporting firms utilizing that service.

When we view the domestic trading scene in 1790 we already see early signs of specialization, although Fred M. Jones concluded more than thirty years ago that there was not much of it even in 1800. Part of the evidence of its beginnings is the presence in coastal cities of factors, brokers, and auctioneers, as well as merchants trading on their own account, some as exporters and others as importers, with some in each group giving their attention to one line of goods. Public markets and retail stores complete the scene, the latter being located not only in coastal cities but also in the interior.[12]

Back-country stores trace their origins at least as far back as the early decades of the eighteenth century. One finds them in the North as well as the South, as Glenn Weaver's study of Jonathan Trumbull, storekeeper at Lebanon, Connecticut, in the 1730s and 1740s, reveals. Trumbull bartered a wide variety of European merchandise for no less a variety of hogs, flaxseed, grain, and other "country pay," personally selling the latter and buying the merchandise with cash and provisions in Boston and Norwich. Cattle and hog drover, meat packer, and farmer, Trumbull also operated a flour mill, fulling mill, malt house and brewery, matching in the North Aubrey C. Land's vignettes of the diversified planter-storekeeper of Maryland and Virginia.[13] In Virginia, back-country stores owed much to Scottish and other outport challenges to the dominance of the tidewater tobacco trade by factors or commission merchants representing English mercantile houses. Firms in Glasgow sent factors into the interior to establish stores at convenient points to purchase tobacco and supply merchandise on credit of nine months or more. Later some of these became the nuclei of such towns as Baltimore, Georgetown, Alexandria, Fredericksburg, Richmond, Petersburg, Washington, and Edenton. Then "when settlement spread back to the Blue Ridge and entered the Valley," to cite the words of Lewis C. Gray, "it was no longer convenient for the back-country planter or farmer to come to one of the towns on the fall line to purchase his supplies and market his crops. The result was a tertiary mechanism of commerce developed in the form of numerous local stores, which shipped products and purchased supplies on long credit from larger firms in towns at the head of tidewater. In still more remote districts peripatetic merchants, or peddlers, went about in wagons trading various commodities for farm produce." However, tidewater planter-storekeepers like Colonel William Fitzhugh of late seventeenth-century Virginia continued to consign their tobacco direct to England: when an English vessel arrived at his plantation landing on the James, he saw to it that his tobacco, which included parcels purchased or received on consignment from smaller neighbors, was loaded on board for the return trip. He then retailed the imported merchandise from his two local stores or from small boats sent upriver to other planters in the area. As Gray makes plain, the feasibility of shipping tobacco from the planter's own wharf enabled the practice of direct consignment to predominate in the tidewater till late in the colonial period.[14]

I have glanced at the origins of these institutions and practices because of their continued importance in the early decades of the period of our concern. Some of them continued to be important throughout the antebellum period. Clarence Danhof has recently made the point that for the majority of northern farmers the country merchant, that is to say storekeeper, was before 1820 "the principal and sometimes sole contact with markets." In New England before 1820 there were one or two storekeepers in every country town, "and much the same was true throughout the older settled areas." They "appeared in the West," Danhof adds, "as members of the earliest wave of settlement."[15] Not only in the North but also the South, as both Lewis Atherton and Harold Woodman have emphasized, they served the needs of the small farmer.[16] So too did the peddler, but after the first decades of the nineteenth century he is a figure that is increasingly rare. The country store can handle better than he can even the marginal commercial output of the small farmer. He has no storage space; and besides, the farmer needs the credit which the country store provides.

In the cotton trade other early practices also survived into the first decades of the nineteenth century. Some tidewater planters, like a number of large planters in Natchez throughout the prewar years, continued to deal directly with English houses.[17] "But it is not believed that this method," Norman S. Buck wrote many years ago, "was ever very general, or very significant."[18] In some cases farmers and planters who had moved further inland themselves hauled their cotton to the coast and supervised its sale.[19] But these were dying practices. In cotton, if not, as we shall see, in the early grain trade, the main part of the story belongs to a more long-lived survivor of the colonial tobacco trade.

That survivor, of course, was the factor, or commission merchant. A specialist in cotton, just as factors handling other southern staples in the larger markets specialized in sugar, rice, and tobacco, it was he who was the chief organizer of the flow of marketing services in the antebellum period. His main marketing service was to convert superior sources of information into judgments concerning where and when to sell. In addition, he used his expert knowledge of the product to classify, grade, and sample it prior to sale. As Harold Woodman has recently expressed it, "A factor was expected to have the skill, experience, and sources of information that would make his judgment superior to that of the planter."[20]

Most factors operated from the coastal ports, especially those on the Gulf, where the bulk of the cotton sales were made to agents or resident partners of northern or European merchants and manufacturers. There were other bidders too, including speculators and brokers, the latter in numbers difficult to determine. In addition to competing with factors in bringing together buyers and sellers, brokers sometimes also acted as consultants in questions of quality. Here in the coastal cities the degree of specialization was most pronounced and the competition between buyers sharpest; here the factor provided links between the planter and an "intricate worldwide marketing system." As production mounted in the interior, increasing numbers of factors, only a minority of whom were specialized because of the smaller volume of business they handled, settled in such fall-line towns as Augusta, Macon, Atlanta, Montgomery, Nashville, Memphis, and Shreveport.[21] Their locations marked the extreme western or northern points accessible to ocean-going vessels and their services as warehousing and forwarding agents were indispensable. As the records of William Bostwick of Augusta intimately reveal, they served planters, farmers, and storekeepers able to cart their cotton by land or float it on the upper reaches of such rivers as the Savannah to inland markets, where it was sometimes sold on the spot, sometimes before being unloaded, or warehoused to await the factor's subsequent exercise of judgment. That judgment might dictate a sale in the interior, shipment to a coastal city, or export to Europe via the intermediation of a coastal correspondent.[22] Cotton was a product low in value relative to its weight and partly for this reason and partly for the sake of merchandise advanced on credit remotely located farmers had no alternative but to dispose of their small crops in barter sales to village storekeepers. The channels of distribution thus ran from the frontiers of commercial agriculture, where specialization was not at all in evidence, to the textile mills of first England and then the northern United States.

In contrast to the existence in the South of what Woodman and North pronounce an efficient institutional structure for cotton marketing[23] stands the mechanism of western grain, especially during the early years of the period, and most especially that of the grain trade of the Mississippi. That this should have been so is not surprising in view of the findings of the most recent student of the subject. "The change to commercially oriented farming," Clarence Danhof writes, "took place slowly, was not without protest, and suffered from the instability of the market structure." Not until the 1850s, he adds, was "market-oriented agriculture . . . firmly established as the dominant type, clearly distinguishable from the semisubsistence approach."[24] Semisubsistence meant market production on a small scale, and this, together with early transport difficulties that both encouraged and reflected it, helps account for delay in the development of an efficient marketing system. Yet even after 1830, when the steamboat achieved predominance on the western rivers,[25] farmers themselves continued to play a direct and active role in the grain trade of the Mississippi, constructing flatboats and personally accompanying their produce to market, some of them stopping at the head of steamboat navigation and consigning their goods to a steamboat captain, others, making sales en route wherever possible, continuing on to New Orleans. They did so until well into the 1840s. Clearly, these farmers were less organizers of the flow than part of it, and they complained about a system whose costs constituted a charge upon the efficiency of agriculture.[26] While flatboats afforded an efficient system of *transport* for a volume of grain (especially wheat and flour) that was relatively small before the 1830s, it was that very smallness of volume that principally explains the slowness with which a more efficient marketing system developed. The latter required specialization, a separation of the roles of farmer and marketer.

That numerous farmers on inaccessible small streams should have undergone these hardships and taken the risks of forced sales on glutted markets is understandable, although many were able through the antebellum period to find markets nearer home in village stores or in sales to millers or newcoming migrants. But others appear to have done so as well. Thomas D. Odle thinks that "regular dealers were discouraged from entering the produce business on the river because of the ease with which irregular dealers could compete with them," but there is some evidence that regular dealers were also discouraged because of the short period of the spring rise of western rivers. Nevertheless, according to Odle "the development of shallow-draught steamboats on the upper Ohio" enabled them to compete. "The owners and agents of these boats became regular dealers in Agricultural commodities and in the 1840s this method of marketing began to replace the flatboat trade on all the rivers of the Mississippi system."[27]

One should add to this explanatory complex, I think, the probability that a mounting commercial production encouraged by the burgeoning demand of eastern cities—larger southern plantations being substantially self-sufficient in foodstuffs—simply could no longer be handled either by travelling farmer-merchants or storekeepers. What John G. Clark calls the "pioneer stage in the grain trade" was ending with the result that forwarding and commission merchants multiplied in all the larger towns along the Mississippi and Ohio rivers. These firms, Clark says, handled grain for both farmers and storekeepers, "provided storage facilities, found the most efficient transportation, and made an effort to sell at the dearest market." Clear counterparts of the southern factor, they gradually "adopted the policy" of extending cash advances to country storekeepers "with whom they had consistently dealt" and this enabled the storekeeper in turn "to offer increased credit facilities to the consumer."[28] An additional difference between the cotton and grain trades was that the former was principally financed by northern and English capital while the latter, of comparatively little moment in foreign markets—only 4 percent of the products of northern farms being exported even as late as 1870[29]—drew upon domestic resources, first those of New Orleans and later those of such larger grain markets as Chicago and Milwaukee.[30]

If we complete the western scene with a glance at the grain trade of the various canal systems connecting with the Great Lakes it becomes clear that the relatively greater cost of constructing a canal boat discouraged farmers from playing a direct role in marketing. In consequence, commission and forwarding merchants regularly engaged in the produce business much sooner than was the case on the Mississippi route. Harry N. Scheiber provides us with a clear picture of their functions on the Ohio canals:

> The forwarders were the men engaged in the transportation business only, including small-scale operators of one or two boats as well as the owners of large fleets, maintaining regular through-freight arrangements with Erie Canal, Pennsylvania Mainline, and river boat lines. The merchants were the men who performed the critical middleman functions in Ohio's far-flung trade with the East and overseas markets: they owned warehouse facilities, extended credit to millers and farmers, and—through arrangements with "correspondent" houses in the coastal cities—arranged for the sale of Ohio

produce, and for the purchase and shipment of merchandise from the seaboard to Ohio retail stores.[31]

According to Odle, the marketing process was also handled by so-called canal boat "lines," business affiliations of the owners of the boats. The agents of these affiliations located at various points along the Erie Canal, for example, and "offered a through marketing and transportation service for the entire length" of the Canal.[32] To some extent, therefore, marketing and transportation functions in the grain trade of the canals and Great Lakes were combined rather than handled separately, and presumably this was a less efficient arrangement than specialization would have provided. If the presumption is valid this lesser degree of efficiency, in combination with the more certain inefficiency of the farmer-marketer on the Mississippi, makes it difficult to avoid the impression that the marketing mechanism for grain in this period was less efficient than that for cotton.

Impressions, however, are poor substitutes for measurements. Ideally we should have statistics, in monetary units and units of work done, broken down by firms, commodities, geographic areas, and time periods. These should make it possible to compare units of expenditure with specific revenues. Unhappily, the statistics do not appear to exist; furthermore, given the accounting practices of the period they will be difficult to extract from the records of firms. Briefly, this is because numerous costs are not associated with the investments giving rise to them; nor did accounting theory acknowledge as costs functions recognized by both this age and that as central to marketing, most particularly the cost of acquiring market information. A number of those that were so recognized were placed in generalized expense accounts, and elsewhere, and they are sometimes impossible to locate. Expense and investment accounts were closed to profit and loss independently of each other, with investment accounts often being permitted to run on unclosed for years. While everything came out in the wash of the capital account, what we would like to know are the effects on specific revenues of reductions in units of expenditure.[33] In short, we would like a quantitative measure of the changing relationship between output and units of input. This we do not have.

I can offer, then, only my impression that the marketing system for western grain was less efficient in this period than that for southern cotton. In the 1840s, however, as a splendid recent article by Morton Rothstein makes clear, the adoption of elevating mechanisms, drying and fanning machinery, and other devices for the handling of grain, together with the advance of specialization to an even further degree of refinement as receivers, warehousemen, brokers, commission agents, and shippers concentrated on those particular functions, notably improved the efficiency of grain-marketing.[34] Cotton's marketing system was also to undergo a remarkable change, especially in the postwar years, with the development of railroads and through bills of lading, the advent of improved cotton compresses in the interior, and of the telegraph and transatlantic cable. Merchants in every market could now be in almost instantaneous touch with one another and cotton marketing could move inland away from the coast. At numerous newly opened interior markets cotton could be sampled, graded, and compressed, and then ordered shipped to New York, with a through bill of lading permitting the transfer of cotton from railroad to ship. The factor's services were no longer needed. In Woodman's words, "The seller had no need of the expert advice of the factor concerning possible price movements and other market information. In the interior statistics were received regularly and posted for all to see and judge."[35]

In marketing, efficiency is always relative, whether to some earlier or later system, or to the possibilities defined for a given system by economic geography, the state of the arts, and the quality of the entrepreneurial stock. That the technological developments which altered the "givens" of a later period enabled cotton to be marketed more efficiently by cutting out the expenses of factorage I have no doubt. Whether its marketing was as efficient as it might have been within the framework of its "givens" during the period 1790–1840 is extremely difficult to say, although I am inclined to accept Woodman's judgment that "it would be difficult to conceive of a less expensive means to market the crop."[36] While I recognize the contribution of the southern river system to the efficiency of the ancillary services connected with cotton marketing, it should be remembered that the Mississippi was also the way to market for less efficiently marketed grain and flour. Certainly it is easy to believe that the passing down of an institutionalized experience in tobacco marketing provided an important margin of regional difference.

Yet I strongly suspect that cotton was marketed more efficiently than colonial tobacco had been. In the first place, tobacco was enumerated, required by law to be shipped to Great Britain. In consequence, even when a planter consigned his tobacco it was a British commission merchant that made the sale, either in England or on the continent. Specialization in marketing therefore occurred on the European side rather than the American. In the second place, decreasing proportions of the crop were shipped on consignment—by the eve of the Revolution only an estimated one-fourth of Virginia's tobacco was so shipped. The great bulk of it was purchased outright at backwoods stores or by ships laboriously proceeding from plantation to plantation, although the adoption of a public warehousing and inspection system in Maryland and Virginia in the early eighteenth century reduced the amount of the latter.[37] In the third place, the volume of cotton produced and exported in the later years of the period 1790–1840 exceeded by far the largest recorded volume of colonial tobacco exported.[38] One has the sense, in sum, of far more competition between buyers, a far broader range of alternative markets, and a higher degree of specialization in the case of cotton. For example, I find no evidence of brokers in the colonial tobacco trade.

While increased specialization enhanced efficiency it is also possible that the appearance and multiplication of urban newspapers, increasingly rich in price and market news, yielded external economies to marketers. Nor should the beginnings of specialization in credit-rating be overlooked. Surely no external economy compares in importance with that provided by the well-known decline in internal transport costs.

One question remains to be raised: were the economies bestowed on marketers passed on to farmers and planters? The question is an important one, for as Stigler has noted, "it is no longer a foregone conclusion that such economies will be shared with the buyers."[39] The answer depends on the structure of the market of the "industry" producing the services purchased by the buyers—the planters and farmers—and also of the price elasticity of demand for those services. These are related considerations: the higher the degree of competition within the industry the greater the likelihood that an increase in "prices" charged by marketers for their services will result in a proportionately larger loss of business to a rival. The "prices" we are discussing are not commission rates, which seem to have been uniformly 2.5 percent on cotton sales, but rather interest rates on advances and charges concealed in prices of merchandise supplied planters on credit. In the case of the country store a strong element of monopoly is present, but in the far more important segment of the "services industry"—if I may call it that—represented by cotton factors, competition appears to have been not only more pronounced but increasingly so. The degree must have varied with ease of access to market and have risen markedly with improvements in transportation. Woodman is convinced that "vigorous competition" for the planter's business existed. Nor did indebtedness abridge the freedom of planters and farmers to select alternative providers of marketing services. In Woodman's words: "The thesis that the cotton factor held the planter in debt bondage and was the real power behind the throne of King Cotton is unfounded." He assigns to the postwar period the "penalty commission clause" that historians once believed to have been a phenomenon of antebellum years.[40]

A final thought: the impact on economic growth of productivity change in marketing appears a possibility of sufficient importance to warrant efforts to find a place for it in growth theory.

Table 2-1. Balance of International Payments: 1790 to 1970. [In millions of dollars. For fiscal years, 1790–1900; thereafter, calendar years.]

| | | Exports of goods and services[1] | | | Income on investments abroad | |
| | | Merchandise, adjusted[2] | Transportation | Travel | Private[3][4] | Government |
Year	Total					
	1	2	3	4	5	6
1970	62,870	41,963	3,627	2,319	10,517	909
1969	55,502	36,417	3,112	2,058	9,607	932
1968	50,603	33,576	2,948	1,775	8,468	765
1967	46,177	30,638	2,792	1,646	7,672	638
1966	43,277	29,287	2,609	1,590	6,988	593
1965	39,408	26,438	2,415	1,380	6,583	509
1964	37,281	25,478	2,317	1,207	5,943	456
1963	32,603	22,252	2,103	1,015	5,041	498
1962	30,507	20,779	1,955	957	4,748	471
1961	28,772	20,107	1,803	947	4,223	381
1960	27,490	19,650	1,782	919	3,591	348
1959	23,652	16,458	1,646	902	3,237	349
1958	23,217	16,414	1,638	825	2,980	307
1957	26,653	19,562	1,967	785	3,058	205
1956	23,772	17,556	1,617	705	2,906	194
1955	19,948	14,424	1,406	654	2,543	274
1954	17,889	12,929	1,171	595	2,283	272
1953	17,078	12,412	1,198	574	1,963	252
1952	18,122	13,449	1,488	550	1,916	204
1951	18,864	14,243	1,556	473	1,956	198
1950	13,893	10,203	1,033	419	1,730	109
1949	15,834	12,213	1,238	392	1,517	98
1948	16,861	13,265	1,317	334	1,451	102
1947	19,819	16,097	1,738	364	1,237	66
1946	14,792	11,764	1,383	271	957	21
1945	16,273	12,473	1,308	162	572	17
1944	21,438	16,969	1,306	117	556	17
1943	19,134	15,115	1,110	84	497	12
1942	11,769	9,187	689	82	496	18
1941	6,896	5,343	562	70	535	9
1940	5,355	4,124	402	95	561	3
1939	4,432	3,347	303	135	539	2
1938	4,336	3,243	267	130	583	2
1937	4,553	3,451	236	135	576	1
1936	3,539	2,590	158	117	567	2

		Imports of goods and services					
Other trans-actions[5]	Total	Mer-chan-dise, ad-justed	Trans-porta-tion	Travel	Direct military expendi-tures	Income on foreign invest-ments in U.S.[6]	Other trans-actions[5]
7	8	9	10	11	12	13	14
3,536	59,307	39,799	4,034	3,973	4,852	5,167	1,484
3,376	53,591	35,796	3,547	3,407	4,856	4,564	1,422
3,071	48,178	32,964	3,258	3,030	4,535	3,013	1,377
2,791	41,041	26,821	2,994	3,207	4,378	2,423	1,217
2,210	38,108	25,463	2,922	2,657	3,764	2,206	1,095
2,083	32,310	21,496	2,675	2,438	2,952	1,797	952
1,880	28,715	18,647	2,462	2,211	2,880	1,524	991
1,695	26,646	17,011	2,316	2,114	2,961	1,386	860
1,598	25,382	16,218	2,128	1,939	3,105	1,167	827
1,310	23,173	14,519	1,943	1,785	2,998	1,050	878
1,201	23,383	14,744	1,915	1,750	3,087	1,098	789
1,060	23,342	15,310	1,759	1,610	3,107	860	696
1,053	20,861	12,952	1,636	1,460	3,435	703	675
1,076	20,752	13,291	1,569	1,372	3,216	675	629
794	19,627	12,803	1,408	1,275	2,949	606	586
647	17,795	11,527	1,204	1,153	2,901	520	490
639	15,930	10,353	1,026	1,009	2,642	443	457
679	16,546	10,975	1,081	929	2,615	483	463
515	15,766	10,838	1,115	840	2,054	445	474
438	15,047	11,176	974	757	1,270	434	436
399	12,001	9,081	818	754	576	379	393
376	9,616	6,874	700	700	621	342	379
392	10,343	7,557	646	631	799	291	419
317	8,202	5,973	583	573	455	256	362
396	6,985	5,067	459	462	493	222	282
1,741	10,232	5,245	420	309	2,434	231	1,593
2,473	8,986	5,043	399	225	1,982	161	1,176
2,316	8,096	4,599	343	173	1,763	155	1,063
1,297	5,356	3,499	263	155	953	158	328
377	4,486	3,416	343	212	162	187	166
170	3,636	2,698	334	190	61	210	143
106	3,366	2,409	367	290	46	230	24
111	3,045	2,173	303	303	41	200	25
154	4,256	3,181	366	348	41	295	25
105	3,424	2,546	247	297	38	270	26

(*continued*)

Table 2–1. Continued

Year	Exports of goods and services[1]				Income on investments abroad	
	Total	Merchandise, adjusted[2]	Transportation	Travel	Private[3][4]	Government
	1	2	3	4	5	6
1935	3,265	2,404	139	101	521	
1934	2,975	2,238	133	81	437	
1933	2,402	1,736	108	66	417	20
1932	2,474	1,667	171	65	460	67
1931	3,641	2,494	247	94	674	92
1930	5,448	3,929	325	129	876	164
1929	7,034	5,347	390	139	982	157
1928	6,842	5,249	372	121	922	158
1927	6,456	4,982	360	114	821	160
1926	6,381	4,922	370	110	793	160
1925	6,348	5,011	318	83	752	160
1924	5,911	4,741	315	77	602	160
1923	5,494	4,266	302	71	676	164
1922	4,954	3,929	286	61	544	126
1921	5,505	4,586	394	76	405	40
1920	10,264	8,481	1,119	67	588	8
1919	10,776	8,891	1,109	56	544	175
1918	7,272	6,432	346	44	450	
1917	7,072	6,398	290	34	350	
1916	6,029	5,560	197	22	250	
1915	3,948	3,686	38	24	200	
1914	2,445	2,230	31	39	145	
1913	2,816	2,600	29	50	137	
1912	2,738	2,532	34	49	123	
1911	2,405	2,228	22	41	114	
1910	2,160	1,995	19	38	108	
1909	2,013	1,857	15	41	100	
1908	2,022	1,880	14	39	89	
1907	2,192	2,051	19	35	87	
1906	2,052	1,921	18	27	86	
1905	1,859	1,751	14	18	76	
1904	1,657	1,563	11	13	70	
1903	1,663	1,575	12	9	67	
1902	1,550	1,473	11	9	57	
1901	1,651	1,585	11	8	47	

		Imports of goods and services					
Other trans-actions[5]	Total	Mer-chan-dise, ad-justed	Trans-porta-tion	Travel	Direct military expendi-tures	Income on foreign invest-ments in U.S.[6]	Other trans-actions[5]
7	8	9	10	11	12	13	14
100	3,137	2,462	206	245	41	155	28
86	2,374	1,763	196	218	34	135	28
55	2,044	1,510	154	199	41	115	25
44	2,067	1,343	255	259	47	135	28
40	3,125	2,120	366	341	48	220	30
25	4,416	3,104	477	463	49	295	28
19	5,886	4,463	509	483	50	330	51
20	5,465	4,159	460	448	44	275	79
19	5,383	4,240	417	400	38	240	48
26	5,555	4,500	415	372	43	200	25
24	5,261	4,291	391	347	39	170	23
16	4,560	3,684	361	303	36	140	36
15	4,652	3,866	332	260	33	130	31
8	3,957	3,184	341	243	42	105	42
4	3,383	2,572	334	200	65	105	107
1	6,741	5,384	848	190	123	120	76
1	5,908	3,995	818	123	757	130	85
	4,814	3,103	510	83	1,018	100	
	3,597	3,006	391	100		100	
	2,927	2,423	263	123		118	
	2,200	1,813	91	160		136	
	2,389	1,815	102	272		200	
	2,442	1,829	92	311		210	
	2,481	1,866	112	306		197	
	2,131	1,576	76	289		190	
	2,114	1,609	68	265		172	
	1,987	1,522	50	251		164	
	1,595	1,159	44	232		160	
	1,896	1,469	60	214		153	
	1,756	1,365	52	191		148	
	1,561	1,215	41	160		145	
	1,378	1,062	35	140		141	
	1,323	1,019	38	127		139	
	1,292	996	35	124		137	
	1,213	912	36	130		135	

continued

Table 2–1. Continued

Year	Total	Merchandise, adjusted[2]	Transportation	Travel	Income on investments abroad	
					Private[3][4]	Government
	1	2	3	4	5	6
1900[7]	1,686	1,623	17	8	38	
1900[8]	1,578	1,534	23	19		
1899	1,400	1,363	19	17		
1898	1,340	1,304	19	16		
1897	1,173	1,136	21	15		
1896	1,082	1,048	18	15		

Exports of goods and services[1]

Year	Total	Merchandise, adjusted[2]	Transportation	Travel	Other transactions
	1	2	3	4	7
1895	888	855	18	14	1
1894	981	943	17	20	1
1893	1,021	974	20	26	1
1892	1,122	1,084	23	14	1
1891	1,035	997	24	13	1
1890	960	921	23	15	1
1889	880	841	23	14	1
1888	786	750	22	14	1
1887	810	774	21	14	1
1886	817	781	20	15	1
1885	830	792	20	17	2
1884	862	822	23	15	2
1883	915	875	25	13	2
1882	859	824	26	7	2
1881	971	936	26	6	2
1880	963	929	25	7	2
1879	813	784	22	5	2
1878	813	780	26	4	3
1877	716	687	24	3	3
1876	654	620	26	4	4
1875	623	590	26	3	3
1874	707	669	31	3	4
1873	675	631	39	2	4

			Imports of goods and services				
Other transactions[5]	Total	Merchandise, adjusted	Transportation	Travel	Direct military expenditures	Income on foreign investments in U.S.[6]	Other transactions[5]
7	8	9	10	11	12	13	14
	1,179	869	53	120		137	
1	1,149	894	30	98		114	13
1	973	735	26	77		124	11
1	896	653	25	76		133	10
1	1,041	803	30	69		127	12
1	1,048	816	26	71		122	13

	Imports of goods and services				
Total	Merchandise, adjusted	Transportation	Travel	Income on foreign investments in U.S.[6]	Other transactions
8	9	10	11	13	14
1,015	774	28	75	126	12
883	692	22	45	113	10
1,140	898	26	62	139	15
1,142	888	28	69	143	14
1,124	875	31	69	134	15
1,109	866	36	68	125	15
1,046	817	35	62	118	14
1,013	791	34	67	107	14
967	759	31	65	98	14
894	698	30	60	93	13
818	635	28	58	86	12
921	730	31	56	90	14
927	748	31	45	89	14
915	747	30	39	84	14
834	672	27	34	88	12
848	694	28	35	79	13
612	469	20	36	78	8
595	462	20	29	76	8
614	475	21	23	86	9
634	478	23	29	96	9
722	556	26	30	99	11
767	593	31	30	102	12
856	683	36	25	99	13

(continued)

Table 2-1. Continued

Year	Total	Merchandise, adjusted[2]	Transportation	Travel	Other transactions
		Exports of goods and services[1]			
	1	2	3	4	7
1872	578	539	31	4	4
1871	603	564	29	6	4
1870	507	473	27	3	4
1869	395	365	24	2	3
1868	428	395	28	2	4
1867	401	369	27	1	4
1866	481	446	29	1	5
1865	279	261	16		2
1864	304	288	14		2
1863	313	287	19	1	7
1862	272	248	20	1	4
1861	303	261	36	1	5
1860	438	401	35	2	
1859	384	358	25	1	
1858	350	326	23	2	
1857	385	366	18	2	
1856	359	329	27	2	
1855	303	279	22	2	
1854	314	281	28	4	
1853	258	231	23	4	
1852	232	211	17	4	
1851	251	219	28	4	
1850	166	153	9	4	
1849	166	146	16	3	
1848	174	155	17	2	
1847	181	160	19	2	
1846	133	114	17	2	
1845	135	115	19	1	
1844	126	112	14	1	
1843	101	85	15	1	
1842	119	105	13	1	
1841	136	122	13	1	
1840	160	133	27	1	
1839	135	121	12	1	
1838	128	109	19	1	

	Imports of goods and services				
Total	Merchandise, adjusted	Transportation	Travel	Income on foreign investments in U.S.[6]	Other transactions
8	9	10	11	13	14
824	662	30	32	86	13
704	557	24	28	84	11
608	475	22	22	80	9
567	450	23	17	69	9
505	382	22	26	67	8
550	430	29	25	58	9
572	459	27	25	51	10
343	256	15	22	45	5
418	339	21	17	34	7
328	260	13	15	31	9
272	211	11	14	30	5
406	344	17	15	24	6
438	376	17	20	25	
416	352	14	26	23	
334	293	8	17	15	
416	375	10	16	15	
378	327	9	19	23	
325	272	8	23	22	
377	316	15	25	20	
333	279	13	25	16	
265	221	9	20	15	
271	225	10	23	13	
210	185	5	8	12	
173	154	6	2	12	
188	161	6	2	12	[98]
178	151	7	4	9	[98]
143	126	5	3	9	
138	120	5	4	9	
126	111	4	5	7	
81	66	6	3	7	
119	102	4	5	8	
148	130	4	6	8	
134	109	7	6	12	
188	165	4	5	14	
135	116	5	5	10	

(continued)

Table 2–1. Continued

Year	Total	Merchandise, adjusted[2]	Transportation	Travel	Other transactions
		Exports of goods and services[1]			
	1	2	3	4	7
1837	133	118	13	2	
1836	141	129	11	2	
1835	132	122	9	1	
1834	116	105	10	1	
1833	101	90	9	1	
1832	101	88	12	1	
1831	97	82	14	1	
1830	86	74	11	1	
1829	83	73	10		
1828	84	73	10	1	
1827	98	83	14		
1826	91	78	13		
1825	112	100	12		
1824	90	77	14		
1823	89	75	14		
1822	83	73	10		
1821	76	66	11		
1820	84	70	14		

	Exports of goods and services[1]			Imports of goods and services			
Year	Total	Merchandise, adjusted[2]	Transportation	Total	Merchandise, adjusted	Transportation	Income on foreign investments in U.S.[6]	Other transactions
	1	2	3	8	9	10	13	14
1819	91	72	19	105	94	4	6	2
1818	116	95	20	141	128	4	6	3
1817	103	89	14	113	102	3	7	2
1816	105	84	21	163	151	4	5	3
1815	81	55	26	96	85	5	4	2
1814	11	8	3	20	16	1	3	
1813	45	32	13	30	22	3	4	
1812	75	39	36	96	83	7	3	3
1811	114	63	51	78	61	10	5	2

	Imports of goods and services				
Total	Merchandise, adjusted	Transportation	Travel	Income on foreign investments in U.S.[6]	Other transactions
8	9	10	11	13	14
161	144	4	4	9	
209	194	4	4	9	
166	153	3	3	7	
140	129	3	2	6	
119	110	3	1	5	
112	103	4	1	5	
112	103	4	1	4	
79	71	3	1	5	
83	75	3	2	5	
97	89	3	2	4	
90	80	3	2	5	
95	85	3	2	5	
106	96	3	2	5	
90	81	3	1	5	
87	78	3	1	5	
92	83	3	1	5	
72	63	3	2	5	
84	75	3	2	5	

	Exports of goods and services[1]			Imports of goods and services				
Year	Total	Merchandise, adjusted[2]	Transportation	Total	Merchandise, adjusted	Transportation	Income on foreign investments in U.S.[6]	Other transactions
	1	2	3	8	9	10	13	14
1810	117	68	49	110	91	10	6	4
1809	88	55	33	76	61	7	6	2
1808	55	26	29	71	58	6	5	2
1807	162	109	53	167	146	11	5	6
1806	148	105	43	155	137	9	4	6
1805	134	97	37	144	128	7	4	5
1804	114	81	34	102	87	7	5	4
1803	88	59	30	80	67	6	4	3
1802	98	75	23	91	78	5	5	3

(continued)

Table 2-1. Continued

Year	Exports of goods and services[1]			Imports of goods and services				
	Total	Mer-chan-dise, ad-justed[2]	Trans-porta-tion	Total	Mer-chan-dise, ad-justed	Trans-porta-tion	Income on for-eign in-vest-ments in U.S.[6]	Other transac-tions
	1	2	3	8	9	10	13	14
1801	134	95	39	132	114	8	5	5
1800	107	74	33	108	93	7	5	4
1799	111	80	30	96	81	6	6	3
1798	83	62	21	84	72	4	6	3
1797	79	57	21	90	77	4	5	3
1796	94	67	27	97	84	5	5	3

Source: *Historical Statistics of the United States, Colonial Times to 1970*, pp. 884–886, 897–899.

Table 2-2. Expansion of Public Domain, 1800–1860 (Area in Acres).

	Land	Water	Total	Cost
Louisiana Purchase (1803)	523,446,400	6,465,280	529,911,680	$ 23,213,568
Basin of the Red River of the North	29,066,880	535,040	29,601,920	
Cession from Spain (1819)	43,342,720	2,801,920	46,144,640	6,674,057
Oregon Compromise (1846)	180,644,480	2,741,760	183,386,240	
Mexican Cession (1848)	334,479,360	4,201,600	338,680,960	76,295,149
Purchase from Texas (1850)	78,842,880	83,840	78,926,720	15,496,448
Gadsden Purchase (1853)	18,961,920	26,880	18,988,800	10,000,000
TOTAL	1,208,784,640	16,856,320	1,225,640,960	$131,679,222

Source: U.S. Department of the Interior, Bureau of Land Management.

Table 2-3. Railway Mileage in the United States.

1830	23	1880	93,267	1930	249,052
1840	2,808	1890	163,597	1940	233,670
1850	9,021	1900	193,346	1950	223,779
1860	30,626	1910	240,439	1960	217,552
1870	52,922	1920	252,845	1970	205,782

Source: Interstate Commerce Commission.

| Year | Exports of goods and services[1] | | | Imports of goods and services | | | | |
	Total	Mer-chandise, ad-justed[2]	Trans-porta-tion	Total	Mer-chandise, ad-justed	Trans-porta-tion	Income on for-eign in-vest-ments in U.S.[6]	Other transac-tions
	1	2	3	8	9	10	13	14
1795	72	48	24	85	73	5	4	3
1794	55	36	19	46	36	4	5	1
1793	43	28	15	42	33	3	5	1
1792	32	23	9	40	33	2	4	1
1791	29	21	8	37	31	2	4	1
1790	29	21	7	30	24	2	4	1

Notes

1. George J. Stigler, "The Division of Labor is Limited by the Extent of the Market," *Journal of Political Economy* 59 (June 1951): 188.

2. George Rogers Taylor, *The Transportation Revolution, 1815–1860*, The Economic History of the United States, vol. 4 (New York: Holt, Rinehart and Winston, 1951), 11.

3. Henry George, *Progress and Poverty* (New York, 1887), 76.

4. Reavis Cox, Charles S. Goodman, and Thomas C. Fichandler, *Distribution in a High-Level Economy* (Englewood Cliffs, N.J.: Prentice-Hall, Inc., 1965), 13.

5. Stuart Bruchey, *Robert Oliver, Merchant of Baltimore, 1783–1819*, Johns Hopkins University Studies in Historical and Political Science, vol. 74, no. 1 (Baltimore: Johns Hopkins Press, 1956), chap. 3; Stuart Bruchey, "Success and Failure Factors: American Merchants in Foreign Trade in the Eighteenth and Early Nineteenth Centuries," *Business History Review* 32 (Autumn 1958): 22–92; for emphasis on mercantile difficulties see William T. Baxter, *The House of Hancock: Business in Boston 1724–1775* (Cambridge: Harvard University Press, 1945), 302; James B. Hedges, *The Browns of Providence Plantations: Colonial Years* (Cambridge: Harvard University Press, 1952), 28; and Byron Fairchild, *Messrs. William Pepperrell: Merchants at Piscataqua* (Ithaca: Cornell University Press, 1954), 51.

6. Bruchey, "Success and Failure Factors," 284–85.

7. Fairchild, *Messrs. William Pepperrell*, 52.

8. Richard Pares, *Yankees and Creoles: The Trade Between North America and the West Indies before the American Revolution* (Cambridge: Harvard University Press, 1956), 77.

9. Bruchey, *Robert Oliver*, 80, 190, 194–95.

10. Tyler Dennet, *Americans in East Asia: A Critical Study of the Policy of the United States with Reference to China, Japan and Korea in the Nineteenth Century* (New York: Macmillan Co., 1922), 71.

11. Douglass C. North, "The Role of Transportation in the Economic Development of North America," in *Les Grandes voies maritimes dans le monde, xvi–xix siècles* (Paris: SEVPEN, 1965), 209–46. The paper was originally presented at The International Congress of Historical Sciences, Vienna (August 1965).

12. Fred M. Jones, *Middlemen in the Domestic Trade of the United States, 1800–1860*, Illinois Studies in the Social Sciences, vol. 21, no. 3 (Urbana: University of Illinois Press, 1937), 9–10, 19–20.

13. Glenn Weaver, *Jonathan Trumbull, Connecticut's Merchant Magistrate, 1710–1785* (Hartford: Connecticut Historical Society, 1956), chap. 2; Aubrey C. Land, "Economic Behavior in a Planting Society: The Eighteenth Century Chesapeake," *Journal of Southern History* 33 (November 1967); and Aubrey C. Land, "Economic Base and Social Structure: The Northern Chesapeake in the Eighteenth Century," *Journal of Economic History* 25 (December 1965): 639–54.

14. Lewis C. Gray, *History of Agriculture in the Southern United States to 1860*, Contributions to American Economic History, 2 vols. (1933; reprint ed., Gloucester, Mass.: Peter Smith, 1958), 1:417–27; and Stuart Bruchey, ed., *The Colonial Merchant: Sources and Readings* (New York: Harcourt, Brace and World, 1966), 120–1, 126–34.

15. Clarence H. Danhof, *Change in Agriculture: The Northern United States, 1820–1870* (Cambridge: Harvard University Press, 1969), 29.

16. Lewis E. Atherton, *The Southern Country Store, 1800–1860* (Baton Rouge: Louisiana State University Press, 1949), 13–14; and Harold D. Woodman, *King Cotton and his Retainers: Financing and Marketing the Cotton Crop of the South, 1800–1925* (Lexington: University of Kentucky Press, 1968), 83.

17. Woodman, *King Cotton*, 15–16; and Morton Rothstein, "The Antebellum South as a Dual Economy: A Tentative Hypothesis" *Agricultural History* 41 (October 1967): 373–82.

18. Norman S. Buck, *The Development of the Organization of Anglo-American Trade, 1800–1859* (New Haven: Yale University Press, 1925), 91.

19. Woodman, *King Cotton*, 10.

20. Ibid., 15, 21–26, 81–82, 274.

21. Ibid., 6, 15–16, 25–29, 81–82, 272.

22. Stuart Bruchey, ed., *Cotton and the Growth of the American Economy 1790–1860* (New York: Harcourt, Brace and World, 1967), 230–32, 245–63.

23. Woodman, *King Cotton*, 186; and Douglass C. North, *The Economic Growth of the United States 1790–1860* (Englewood Cliffs, N.J.: Prentice-Hall, 1961), 125–26.

24. Danhof, *Change in Agriculture*, 21.

25. Taylor, *Transportation Revolution*, 65.

26. John G. Clark, *The Grain Trade in the Old Northwest* (Urbana: University of Illinois Press, 1966), 41; and Thomas D. Odle, "The American Grain Trade of the Great Lakes, 1825–1873: Part V," *Inland Seas: Quarterly Bulletin of the Great Lakes Historical*

Society 8 (Winter 1952): 248–50. Odle emphasizes their dissatisfaction: "The farmers of Knox County, in southern Indiana, who shipped their products to market on the Wabash River, summed up thier complaints in 1844 as follows: 'The uncertainty of the time of shipment, and the short period during each season [of the spring rise of the Wabash River], have prevented the merchants of this country embarking as regular dealers in the produce business. The consequence has been, the farmers have, much to their injury, been compelled to ship their own products . . . and too often does it happen that they loose one year's cropping in disposing of the cropping of the previous year, and that, too, at a ruinous sacrifice, both in their health and their fortunes'." Odle goes on to say that the "slowness with which a regular marketing system was developed on the Mississippi route and the inadequacies of this system fostered the diversion of trade to the Great Lakes-Erie Canal route."

27. Odle, "Grain Trade on the Great Lakes," 248.

28. Clark, *Grain Trade*, 41–43.

29. Danhof, *Change in Agriculture*, 9–11.

30. Clark, *Grain Trade*, 43.

31. Harry N. Scheiber, *Ohio Canal Era: A Case Study of Government and the Economy, 1820–1861* (Athens: Ohio University Press, 1969), 252. Presumably this description applies to the 1830s and 1840s (ibid., 252–53) although I should think, in view of data cited by Morton Rothstein (see n. 34), that it is particularly applicable to the latter decade. . . .

32. Odle, "Grain Trade of the Great Lakes," 251–52.

33. Bruchey, *Robert Oliver*, 135–39; and Stuart Bruchey, "Robert Oliver and Mercantile Bookkeeping in the Early Nineteenth Century," (Master's thesis, Johns Hopkins University, 1944).

34. Morton Rothstein, "Antebellum Wheat and Cotton Exports: A Contrast in Marketing Organization and Economic Development," *Agricultural History* 40 (April 1966): 91–100.

35. Woodman, *King Cotton*, 272–74.

36. Ibid., 186.

37. Gray, *History of Agriculture in the Southern United States*, 1: 227–28, 246, 250, 252, 262.

38. *Historical Statistics of the United States, Colonial Times to 1957* (Washington, D.C.: GPO, 1960), 547 (cotton), 765 (tobacco).

39. Stigler, "Division of Labor," 186.

40. Woodman, *King Cotton*, 184, 64n, 174, 174n. Strictly speaking, the question of economics does not arise in the case of country stores, which were not specialized.

QUESTIONS FOR REVIEW AND DISCUSSION

1. What is *marketing?*
2. What elements affect a marketing decision?

3. How does a marketing decision affect *efficiency?*
4. Identify and discuss sources of marketing efficiency in foreign trade. Do these sources of efficiency obtain more or less profits today than they did in the first half of the nineteenth century?
5. Illustrate ways in which technology has affected marketing decisions.
6. How does *organization* affect marketing efficiency?
7. Why does Bruchey believe that the marketing system for western grain was less efficient than that for southern cotton?
8. During the first half of the nineteenth century, were savings or marketing efficiencies retained by the marketing decision maker or were they passed on to a supplier or to consumers?

3

Ownership and Management

Most early American businesses were owned and operated by (1) a single individual or proprietor, (2) a family unit that usually included the head of the household as the key decision maker, or (3) a partnership or association of individuals that usually included a senior partner. Joseph Schumpeter stressed the concept of creativity in defining the classical businessperson or entrepreneur. For Schumpeter the business leader is a person who challenged the status quo and who commercially utilized a new idea or invention. Business historian Arthur H. Cole, on the other hand, stressed the continuing purposeful activity that maintains a profit-making enterprise for the distribution of goods or services. Schumpeter and Cole have essentially differentiated between the innovative role and the managerial role of the businessperson. Even among similar kinds of business organizations—single proprietorships or partnerships—the style and effectiveness of management can and does vary widely. Although the organization of businesses as corporations in the early nineteenth century facilitated the separation of ownership and management, it was not until later in the nineteenth century that management characteristically became separated from ownership.

The development of manufacturing enterprises such as the textile mills of Samuel Slater and Francis Cabot Lowell provide excellent examples of the innovative and creative role of the businessperson and of contrasts in management styles and organization. Slater, an Englishman, incorporated in his American textile mills the new technology of Richard Arkwright, who obtained patents in Britain in 1769. Slater improved upon Arkwright's designs of the water frame and the power loom, but his basic contribution was bringing the Arkwright mill to America, thus eluding the British restrictions on the transfer of technology outside of England. Moses Brown of Providence, Rhode Island, and members of the Wilkinson family of Pawtucket, Rhode Island, provided capital for the establishment of Slater's first mill in 1790. A new combination of partners, Almy, Brown, and Slater, opened a second mill at Pawtucket in 1793. By 1829 Samuel Slater is estimated to have accumulated a personal fortune of almost $700,000. But it was Francis Cabot Lowell, rather than Slater, who established the more lasting and successful production processes and forms of management.

Lowell, as did Moses Brown, came from successful New England merchant-shipowner families. The American Revolution and the following Napoleonic Wars severely disrupted the traditional shipping and export business. Manufactured goods, such as cotton and woolen textiles, became increasingly difficult to obtain in America. After touring British textile manufacturing plants in 1810, Lowell returned to the United States and convinced a number of people, notably Nathan Appleton and Patrick Tracy Jackson, to join him in constructing a textile mill that used the latest technology. The latest invention at that time was the Cartwright power loom, which Lowell copied from memory and improved upon considerably. Whereas the spinning, weaving, dyeing, and printing processes were usually performed by separate firms in England, Lowell incorporated all of these processes within one plant. However, he organized each special function in its own department. Lowell's laborers, usually women, were assigned specialized tasks within the departments. He also introduced a cost-accounting system and systemized the purchase of raw cotton by using his own agents. Moreover, he was inclined to employ a plant manager or supervisor. Lowell's method became known as the "Waltham system."

Lowell died in 1817. In that same year, his associates incorporated the Merrimack Manufacturing Company and began the construction of a new plant along the Pawtucket Falls area of the Merrimack River. This same group purchased the Locks and Canals Company and 400 acres of adjoining farmland to create what essentially became an industrial park, which included the waterway as a power source. By 1845 the Merrimack Company operated five textile mills and was capitalized at $5 million. In 1825 the Merrimack Company organized its machine shop, which provided parts and service for the textile mills, into an independent machine-tools operation that began to provide machine components for other manufacturers in the area. The ability to mass produce machine components made possible the creation of mechanical devices of an endless variety and effectively initiated the industrial revolution in America.

Expansion in iron manufacturing and in transportation industries, particularly steamship and rail transportation, complemented the growth of American manufacturing enterprises. Generally, manufacturing enterprises, such as railroads, required larger sums of capital and more investors. The traditional proprietorship and partnership arrangements proved increasingly inadequate for the requirements of modern business. The corporation as a form of business organization accommodated the changing role of business management, but it did not in and of itself solve the problem of management.

The experiences of Lowell and Slater provide a sense of management styles and procedures that are true for any period of time. Barbara M. Tucker's study of Samuel Slater and the biographical sketch of Francis Cabot Lowell and contemporary descriptions of manufacturing around Lowell, Massachusetts, by Henry A. Miles offer special insight into the dynamics of the developing industrial revolution in the United States.

Barbara M. Tucker

FORMS OF
OWNERSHIP AND
MANAGEMENT

---

c. Sam. Slater.

From Pawtucket the factory system spread throughout
Rhode Island, Connecticut, Massachusetts, Pennsylvania, and New York. At
first, growth was slow. It has been estimated that by 1808 only fifteen spinning
mills were operating in the United States and that almost half of them belonged to
Samuel Slater, William Almy and Obadiah Brown, or one of Slater's former employees.[1] Some manufacturers and their associates feared that the local market
could not absorb any increase in yarn production. Writing to his children in the
fall of 1810, Moses Brown urged caution in the expansion of their business: "Our
people have 'cotton mill fever' as it is called. Every place almost occupied with
cotton mills; many villages built up within 16 miles of town and spinning yarn and
making cloth is become our greatest business. We were first to get into it. Samuel
Slater has sold out one half of one mill and I should be pleased my children could
do, with their four, in part as he has done."[2] While Brown exaggerated the situation, his concern had merit. British competition, a limited national market for
domestic yarns, and, of course, increasing competition from other manufacturers
were considerations. But none of these factors curbed the "cotton mill fever."

Barbara M. Tucker, *Samuel Slater and the Origins of the American Textile Industry, 1790–1860*
(Ithaca, N.Y.: Cornell University Press, 1984), 89–110, 123–124. Used by permission of the publisher, Cornell University Press. Some footnotes have been renumbered.

When the Embargo and the War of 1812 effectively cut off the supply of British yarn and cloth goods, the American industry boomed. Potentially profitable outlets for capital were scarce during the war years, and merchants, traders, and professional men began to invest in the emerging textile industry. One of the most innovative and enterprising men to enter the industry was Francis Cabot Lowell, a Boston merchant. He introduced an industrial system that was characterized by innovative technology, the integration of spinning and weaving, corporate ownership, professional management, and the use of a female labor force. Rather than manufacture yarn exclusively, Lowell perfected a power loom and produced sturdy, inexpensive coarse cloth for the Western trade. Successful and especially profitable, this system achieved worldwide recognition for its novel approach to industrialization. Historians have claimed that the Lowell system "was the most important thing which could have happened to the cotton industry," for it was "taken up by men with the best business imagination in the land, unhampered by its traditions, concerned with making fortunes and building states, not with manufacturing cotton cloth."[3] Yet in 1813 and 1814 the full implications of the Lowell system remained to be seen. Lowell was only one of many men who took advantage of the temporary dislocation in the textile industry and tried to capture a part of the local market.[4] By 1814 Tench Coxe estimated that 243 cotton mills operated within fifteen states; Pennsylvania, Massachusetts, Rhode Island, and New York led the way with 64, 54, 28, and 26 mills, respectively.[5]

At the war's end, however, the boom collapsed and British goods flooded the market; many American firms shut down. The *Niles Weekly Register* reported in November 1816 that "the importation of British goods is yet enormous, and they are selling at prices insufficient to pay costs and charges—the pound sterling of the invoice is often, it is said, fairly sold for the pound currency at New York; and all, or nearly all, of our large manufacturing establishments have more or less suspended business."[6]

Costs had to be cut. Robert Zevin believed that it was during this crisis that American textile manufacturers turned increasingly to the power loom. Two looms were on the market; one made at Waltham sold for about $125, and a second machine, developed by William Gilmore, cost $70. No patent limited the spread of the Gilmore loom, and soon owners of the Lyman Mills in North Providence and the proprietors of the Coventry factory several miles away introduced a version of this machine. Dexter Wheeler, who was associated with the Fall River Manufacturing Company, copied this pattern, and the machine spread throughout southern New England. The Waltham and the Gilmore looms were immensely beneficial to the textile industry. Savings of 4, 6, and 9 cents a yard could be achieved through the introduction of a power loom. Many mills that formerly had been engaged in yarn production switched to the new loom and combined spinning and weaving in their factories.[7] In Massachusetts, Rhode Island, and Connecticut, integrated factories with power looms numbered eleven, fifteen, and eleven, respectively, by 1820.[8] Cloth output soared: Zevin estimated that between 1816 and 1833 cloth production increased at a compound annual rate of 39 percent.[9]

Further reductions in the cost of production were achieved as the price of raw cotton declined throughout the era. For upland cotton, which sold in the New York market, manufacturers paid approximately 31 cents a pound in 1818 and about 10 cents a pound in 1832.[10] Cloth prices reflected these changes. Prices charged for goods manufactured by the Boston Manufacturing Company, for example, were almost cut in half between 1823 and 1833. Other manufacturers had to scramble to keep pace with these prices; they tried to cut costs where they could.[11]

Factories and Firms

Samuel Slater participated in the phenomenal growth of the industry. His career was an eminently prosperous one, and at his death in 1835 he was operating in three states. At one time he either owned or held an interest in at least thirteen textile mills, two machine shops, and a wholesale and commission firm (see Table 3–1). Slater's factories and firms served as the models for hundreds of would-be manufacturers throughout the United States.

Slater formed his first factory independent of Almy and Brown in 1799, the year his Providence partners bought the Warwick Spinning firm. With the financial support of Oziel Wilkinson, William Wilkinson, and Timothy Green, all related to him through marriage, Slater formed Samuel Slater and Company and built the "White Mill" on the Massachusetts side of the Pawtucket River, at Rehoboth. This two-story spinning factory measuring 49′ by 26′ resembled the "old mill" at Pawtucket in size, appearance, and the type of goods manufactured. Slater continued in partnership with Almy and Brown. For years he shuttled between Pawtucket and Rehoboth to supervise operations at both mills.[12] From the outset the two firms were run as one. This decision received the wholehearted support of Slater's several partners. As Moses Brown explained: "You may well think that the Erection of that mill [Samuel Slater and Company] was not agreeable to my Ideas but after it was determined on . . . in order to save the business from Immediate ruin We thought best, to so far unite so as not to interfere with each other in Workmen nor wages."[13] This attitude carried over into the prices proprietors charged for goods. To New York agent Gilbert Everingham, Almy and Brown wrote: "Slater is connected with us in the business & we unite in our prices of yarn & they are exactly conformable to theirs."[14] It should be noted also

Table 3-1. Firms founded, purchased, or partially owned by Samuel Slater, 1790-1835

Firm	Date acquired
Almy, Brown, and Slater	1790
Samuel Slater and Company	1799
Almy, Brown, and the Slaters	1806
Slater and Tiffany*	1811
Slater and Howard†	1815
Providence Iron Foundry	1815
Jewett City Factory	1823
Phoenix Thread Company*	1824
Amoskeag Manufacturing Company	1825
Slater and Wardwell	1827
Slater and Kimball*	1827
Steam Cotton Manufacturing Company	1827
Central Falls Mill	1829
Sutton Manufacturing Company	1832
S. &. J. Slater	1832
Providence Machine Company	1834

*Succeeded by Union Mills.
†Succeeded by Dudley Manufacturing Company and later by Webster Woolen Company.

that the firms pooled their resources when they purchased cotton. The Rehoboth factory was only one of Slater's many successful business ventures.[15]

In 1806 Almy, Brown, and Slater settled some of their outstanding differences, and the three partners joined forces with John Slater, Samuel Slater's brother, to purchase 122 acres of land on the Mohegan River in upstate Rhode Island and construct another yarn-spinning mill. John Slater managed the factory and planned the community of Slatersville, which developed around it. The Slater brothers continued to invest in the region, and eventually they purchased Almy and Brown's share in the enterprise. By the 1830s S. & J. Slater, as their firm was called, ran at least four factories, operated 9,500 spindles, and provided employment for 66 men, 109 women, and 169 children. In addition to the factories, the outbuildings, and the company cottages, the Slater brothers acquired more than 1,200 acres of land in the Slatersville area.[16] Throughout the period the management of Slatersville remained the responsibility of John Slater.

By the first decade of the nineteenth century, Samuel Slater held part ownership in three factories in Massachusetts and Rhode Island. With management of the Pawtucket and the Rehoboth factories weighing him down, he sold his interest in the Rehoboth factory in 1810 and invested immediately in another Massachusetts concern.[17]

Samuel Slater wanted to strike off on his own. He entered into a partnership in

1811 with Bela Tiffany, a former employee and a family friend, to purchase almost 270 acres of land and water privileges in Oxford Township, in south-central Massachusetts. Slater and Tiffany probably began operations a year later.[18] Although Tiffany, who held a one-sixth share in the enterprise, managed this factory, Slater retained a keen interest in the venture. Independently of his partner, he increased his holdings in the region to include a woolen mill, a dye and bleach house, a saw- and gristmill, sixteen dwellings, and 700 acres of land.[19] Of these investments the woolen factory was the most important. With fellow Englishman and friend Edward Howard, Slater built a small woolen mill near the Slater and Tiffany factory in 1815 and rebuilt it after it was destroyed by fire in 1820. A notice published in the *Massachusetts Spy* on January 15, 1823, declared the new factory open for business:

> The Subscribers hereby give notice, that they have formed a Copartnership, for the purpose of manufacturing Woollen Goods, under the Firm of SLATER & HOWARD.
>
> The business will be carried on as usual, in all its branches.[20]

Initially, Howard managed the business. The Slater and Tiffany mill together with the Slater and Howard factory formed the nucleus of a new community. The area was known as Oxford South Gore until it was incorporated as Webster in 1832. To avoid confusion, the name Webster will be used to designate this factory colony throughout the remainder of this [case].

Next Slater turned his attention to Connecticut. He formed a second partnership with his brother in 1823, and together they purchased for $17,000 a small mill in Jewett City, New London County. Once again management fell to John Slater, who built up the site by constructing a small woolen factory, a saw- and gristmill, and several dwellings. While the area was being developed, Samuel Slater remained in the background, and in 1831 he sold his interest to his brother.[21]

Slater continued to expand. Interest in a New Hampshire firm, the celebrated Amoskeag Manufacturing Company, coincided with his involvement in the Jewett City venture. Although inquiries were initiated earlier, by 1825 it appeared that Slater, together with Oliver Dean, Lyman Tiffany, Willard Sayles, Larned Pitcher, and Ira Gay, had secured property and an unfinished mill in Manchester, New Hampshire. But Slater's involvement in this factory was negligible, and his interest and activities shifted again to the southern part of the region.[22] Between 1827 and 1831 Slater built, bought outright, or acquired an interest in several other factories, including the Central Falls Mill in Smithfield, the Sutton Manufacturing Company in Wilkinsonville, Massachusetts, and the Steam Cotton Manufacturing Company in Providence, Rhode Island. Of the

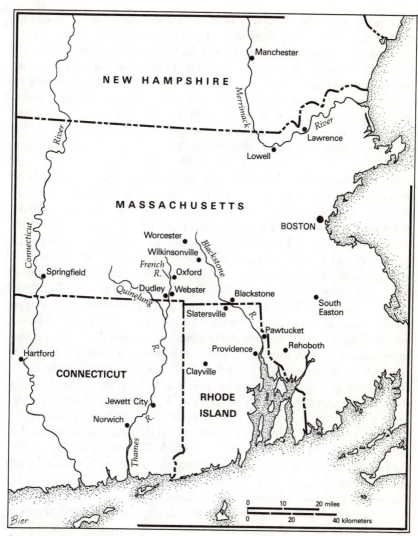

Southern New England

three factories, the Steam Cotton Manufacturing Company was the most note-worthy because of the novel mode of power employed there. Steam engines operated the 4,344 spindles, 18 mules, and 100 new power looms the mill used to manufacture fine-quality sheeting and shirting. The size and scale of the new factory can be estimated from entries in the company's daybooks concerning its construction. Built of stone and plated with brick, this two-story factory, measuring 30' by 43', was similar in size to Slater's earlier mills in Pawtucket and Rehoboth. A stone furnace was added to it soon after the factory was built.[23] This mill was one of three in Rhode Island in the 1820s and early 1830s to use steam power.[24]

Slater's business enterprise was not confined to textile mills. In the 1820s he began to diversify. To circumvent the customary commission house system and thereby to avoid the fees paid to wholesalers, shopkeepers, and other agents, Slater purchased an interest in George Wardwell's Providence wholesale firm and instructed Wardwell to sell part of his cloth, yarn, and thread through this outlet. Although Wardwell objected to the scheme and argued that "after making particular inquirie respecting the sale of woolen goods at this place . . . I think it best for us to relinquish the idea of attempting the business at present," Slater persisted with his plans.[25] Within a month Slater and Wardwell sold not only woolen goods but also satinets and cotton goods of all descriptions. But Wardwell lacked the knowledge to market such competitive products successfully. In the fine and fancy goods market, British, not American, manufacturers determined "what *is* and what *is to be* 'the go.'"[26] Style, fashion, and color followed British and European trends, and American manufacturers had to keep pace with the latest changes if they hoped to compete successfully. When Wardwell proved to be incapable, Slater reverted to commission agents in New York, Boston, New Orleans, Philadelphia, Baltimore, Providence, and Hartford to sell his cloth. But the Slater and Wardwell firm had set a precedent. This was the first but not the last time Slater and, later, his sons would try to sell their products without the aid of middlemen.[27]

Diversification was not limited to marketing. When Samuel Slater built the Steam Cotton Manufacturing Company in 1827, he organized a machine shop on the first floor of the factory and hired Thomas J. Hill to take charge of it. Four years later the two men entered a partnership and formed a new firm, the Providence Machine Company. This enterprise supplied not only the Slater factories but also manufacturers throughout New England with doublers, mules, spreaders, stretchers, dressers, and lappers.[28] Most of the iron used in the construction of the equipment was purchased from another Slater venture, the Providence Iron Foundry, a partnership formed with his brother-in-law, David Wilkinson, and five other men. In 1847 Hill purchased the Slater interest in the machine company for almost $50,000 and relocated the business.[29]

The Slater System

The Slater factories shared certain features: the type of product manufactured, the technology employed, the partnership form of ownership, and personal management. These characteristics became the hallmark of a model of production which was adopted by hundreds of manufacturers throughout the country. During his life Samuel Slater remained at the vanguard of the system that came to bear his name.

Throughout much of his career, Slater confined the products of his spinning factories to fine yarn, thread, and twine. In this emphasis on yarn spinning, Slater differed from many of his contemporaries. He was also unlike many other factory owners in his slowness to introduce the Gilmore power loom. Slater ignored the mechanical device until 1823, when he installed it in the cotton mills; later he mechanized the woolen branch of his business. Although the cotton power loom had been adapted successfully to woolen cloth weaving following the War of 1812, Samuel Slater did not introduce this equipment until 1829–30. The delay cost Slater dearly.[30]

During the transition in the woolen mills, Slater kept a ledger of the costs involved in weaving woolen goods both by hand and by the new loom. A comparison of the costs showed vividly the savings that could be effected by the new machine. In August 1829 Samuel Slater employed twenty-two male hand-loom weavers at his Webster woolen factory, and he paid them between $0.14 and $0.20 a yard for weaving various types of broadcloth and $0.06 a yard for weaving kersey. Those who worked steadily earned between $24.00 and $30.00 that month. William Archer, for example, wove slightly more than 201 yards of steel mountain, claret, and olive broadcloth at $0.14 a yard for a total income of $28.21. Earlier in the year the firm had installed power looms, had employed young women to operate them, and had begun to manufacture various types of broadcloth. By August of 1829, thirteen women worked in the new weaving room, and they received $0.08 per yard for their cloth. A woman operating a power loom could produce roughly the same amount of cloth as a hand-loom weaver. The company records over the next ten months show a gradual decline in the number of hand-loom weavers employed at this factory. By June 1830 only six of them remained on the payroll. While they continued to receive high piece rates of between $0.12 and $0.20 a yard for their cloth, they worked fewer and fewer hours each month. During the same period, the number of power-loom operators rose to sixteen, and they worked steadily. All received $0.06½ a yard for their fabric. By adopting the power loom, the Slater family had cut weaving costs by one-half or more.[31]

Slater's reluctance to adopt the new equipment was not due to the cost of conversion; expenses were not exorbitant. Explanations lie elsewhere. Workers could have opposed the introduction of new technology and delayed its adoption. The power loom was operated largely by single, itinerant women, and Slater employed entire families in his mills. To recruit workers he would have had to look beyond the kinship network. Or Slater may have been content not to develop his market further. By the 1820s Slater's name was synonymous with quality yarn, thread, and hand-woven cloth, and he shared the market for these goods in part with British producers. Or perhaps Samuel Slater was less cost-conscious than his competitors. Committed to a system of cloth production which had served him well for decades and which provided employment for hundreds of people in and near his factory colonies, he saw few reasons to change. Wholesale adoption of the power loom occurred when his sons assumed control of the family business in 1829.[32]

Technological innovation proceeded slowly in other areas as well. With the exception of the Steam Cotton Manufacturing Company, almost all of Slater's firms relied primarily on water power to operate equipment. His factories were located in rural areas of Rhode Island, Massachusetts, and Connecticut where water resources were available. His preference for water power could be seen in his largest and most highly developed factory colony, located in Webster, Massachusetts. There in 1812 Slater constructed his first factory near Chaubunagungamaug Pond, a large body of water that empties into the French River. From its origin near Leicester, Massachusetts, the French River drains an area of fifty square miles above this region. This drainage basin, together with the natural ponds and later the artificial reservoir built to hold back the water and to regulate its flow throughout the year, made the Oxford South Gore area an ideal site for water-powered factories. All of Slater's factories there were powered by huge breast-type water wheels.[33] In the initial stage of factory operations at Webster, sufficient water flow allowed for easy expansion of the factories. Water power also was cleaner and probably was cheaper than steam power. Expenses for steam power included the purchase of coal, transportation of the coal to an inland location, and the employment of a person to supervise the engine and the boiler room.[34] In most of the Slater mills, steam engines were not introduced until the Civil War, and then they served primarily as a reserve, emergency power source and not as the main mode of power.[35]

In all of Slater's factories, ownership and management went hand in hand. Adopted first at Pawtucket, the partnership form of ownership was retained by

Slater despite the advantages of incorporation, an ownership form that had become popular during the War of 1812. If granted a special incorporation charter by the state, firms were guaranteed perpetual life, limited liability, and the right to accumulate capital. Through their charters, businessmen also received special concessions, monetary grants, and other privileges. By the war's end, seventy-five textile firms had received state charters, but Slater's was not among them.[36] He was not persuaded to adopt this form of ownership; he preferred traditional partnership agreements or single proprietorships.

For Slater's enterprises capital requirements were limited: one or two partners usually supplied the funds necessary to construct a factory. By reinvesting his profits, Slater could expand operations.[37] This was common practice throughout much of the industry. Zachariah Allen, for example, rejected offers of outside capital when he established his factory and wanted to expand. In a letter to Francis C. Lowell II, a prospective investor, he explained: "I commenced my works about four years since with the intention of extending them no farther than my own capital would allow without inconvenience, I still think it would be preferable to continue in the course I have adopted."[38]

In the selection of suitable partners, only kin, close family friends, and business associates—all considered trustworthy individuals—proved acceptable to Slater. David Wilkinson, a partner in several Slater enterprises, was his brother-in-law; John Slater, his Slatersville and Jewett City partner, was his brother; Thomas Hill and Bela Tiffany, respectively partners in a machine shop and a cotton mill, were former employees; George Wardwell and Edward Howard, both close family friends, were partners in a commission business and in several factories. Much of his property came to be held by Samuel Slater and Sons, a closed family partnership formed with three of his sons, George, John II, and Horatio Nelson Slater.[39]

Slater's preference for the partnership form of ownership probably had more to do with his attitude toward management than with concern over costs. With the partnership form of ownership, a simple line of organization could be adopted to manage the firms: proprietors not only owned the concern but also usually managed it, often working alongside laborers on the factory floor. Like his Pawtucket partners, Slater came to distrust outsiders and believed that a business failed when its owners, "who themselves engaged in other pursuits, have invested the net profits of their business in manufacturing and left the latter to the superintendence of others," for "it is in this triple capacity of money lender, employer and laborer that our most successful manufacturers have succeeded."[40] He preferred to superintend the factories himself or to entrust the task to one of his partners or sons.

Slater's management policies worked well for a number of years. Problems arose, however, when the partners wanted to resign and leave the firm. Where could

Slater secure a competent, trustworthy, knowledgeable supervisor? Not willing to entrust responsibility to paid professional agents, he turned to his family for assistance, and he increasingly drew his sons into his business activities. The factories at Webster became a training ground for his children, who one day would control the family business. For his sons, this was not an easy apprenticeship.

Family Management

Although Slater's interest in Webster dated from the War of 1812, it was not until the end of the decade that Slater began to focus attention on the area. Beginning in 1818 he acquired full ownership of the Slater and Tiffany factory, bought the Slater and Howard mill, and then built a third factory, the Phoenix Thread Mill. Repeatedly these factories were enlarged, first in 1822, then in 1826 and 1827, and again in 1828.[41] His early partnerships with Tiffany and Howard had been a necessary expedient that had allowed him to limit capital outlay, to secure the services of a factory manager, and to see if local labor resources, transportation networks, and water power could support large-scale production. Convinced that the area had potential, he began to acquire ownership of the various enterprises in the region, but these acquisitions brought problems. With the retirement of Tiffany and later of Howard, Samuel Slater assumed responsibility for managing the mills. He still supervised directly the old mill at Pawtucket and tried to assist his brother in the management of the Slatersville concerns. He found he could not do it all. Traveling the almost seventy miles between Pawtucket and Webster taxed his strength, and supervision of the Webster property presented special problems. At Pawtucket the division of labor initiated among the partners relieved Slater of responsibility for the purchase of supplies, the marketing of manufactured goods, and the supervision of the putting-out system: Almy and Brown managed these operations and left Slater in charge of the factory. This was not the case at Webster, where Slater had to oversee the factory, recruit and discipline an industrial labor force, plan and design a community for his workers, purchase supplies and sell products, and supervise a vast putting-out network.

In the early years at Webster Slater employed more than five hundred part-time hand-loom weavers. While some of the weavers were the parents of the children who worked in his factory and lived nearby, most of them lived in the surrounding towns of Thompson, Dudley, Oxford, and Charlton and periodically traveled to the Slater mills to collect materials. When Samuel Slater dispensed yarn, he provided outworkers with detailed instructions on how the cloth was to be woven. In part, the weaver's ticket read: "Weavers must return the Yarn left of a piece, with the cloth—Cloth must be trimmed, wove as thick at the ends as in the middle, and returned free from stains and dirt and if it is made too sleazy, or damaged in any way, a deduction will be made from the weaving."[42] The threat was not an idle one, for Slater examined thoroughly every piece of cloth. If weavers took more than four months to complete their work, they were docked a half-cent a yard on the cloth returned, and if they failed to return all of the yarn given out, they were charged for it and dismissed.[43] This procedure proved burdensome, to him, and in the early 1820s Slater began to employ subcontractors to handle it.

"Merchant Weavers attend!" began a notice placed in the *Massachusetts Spy* (Worcester) on January 8, 1823. "A few yards good YARN will be furnished to WEAVE on reasonable terms, on application to the Subscriber at his Factory in Oxford [Webster]."[44] To men who answered this advertisement, usually shopkeepers who operated putting-out systems as sidelines to their regular retail trade, Slater transferred the burden of finding weavers and supervising their work. Merchant weavers now collected yarn from the factory, distributed it to country weavers, checked their work for quality and regularity of weave, paid them in cash or, more frequently, in store goods, and then returned the finished cloth to Slater.[45] Several years later Slater went a step further and converted to the power loom and thus integrated his Webster mills. Yet even with this modification, Slater could not manage easily both the Pawtucket and the Webster factories. Rather than seek another partner or hire a professional manager to operate one of them, Samuel Slater turned to his family for assistance. He was determined that his sons should follow him into the family business.

In 1791 Samuel Slater had married Hannah Wilkinson, daughter of a Pawtucket iron manufacturer, and they had nine children, two girls and seven boys. Eight of the children survived infancy.[46] Shortly after Tiffany's retirement in 1818, Slater employed the adolescent Samuel Slater II, but the boy was frail, and he died. Effective supervision of the Webster property once again reverted to Samuel Slater, who subsequently wrote to his son John Slater II, recently turned sixteen: "You will have to make your appearance at Oxford [Webster] or here in one of the stores as per conversation with you some time past. It is highly important that one or more of my sons was learning the business so as to in some measure relieve me from the close attention which I have to attend."[47] The boy was taken out of school and sent to the old "Green Mill." John Slater II served a long apprenticeship under his father. Although Samuel Slater was fifty-three years of age and suffered from rheumatism, he did not allow his son appreciable discretion in the actual operation of the factory. Through numerous personal visits to Webster and frequent detailed correspondence, he supervised John and, indirectly, the factories. In March 1826, for example, he wrote: "You observed that the hands were anxious to know about working another year. You can state to them that I am willing to give them what they had last year and probably in a few instances I will be willing to allow some of the children a little more for the ensuing year."[48] All details would be sorted out after his arrival. Two years later he was still offering advice on this subject: "As days are now short and cold and much time is taken up by those people who do not like work very well in thrashing their hands therefore under these circumstances you will discontinue all you can."[49]

Although supervision of the Webster property absorbed his time, Slater preferred this method to the employment of an outside manager who might prove dishonest, inefficient, or lazy. Besides John, two other sons, George Basset and Horatio Nelson, served long apprenticeships under their father.

Slater completely dominated his sons. If they wanted a share in the family business, his sons had to obey his orders, including those pertaining to their education, marriage, and career choices. None of the Slater children attended college; all worked for their father. Successful manufacturers, Slater believed, "employed their families in the labors of the business, and, to the extent of this savings of the wages of superintendence and labor, realized the gross profits of manufacture."[50] George, John, and Horatio Nelson Slater did not exercise significant authority in the business until 1829, when Samuel Slater formed a family partnership, Samuel Slater and Sons.

Decline of the Slater System

Weaknesses within the Slater system became increasingly apparent in the 1820s. The Slater business network included cotton factories, woolen mills, commission firms, foundries, machine shops, and real estate in several states. The business grew in a topsy-turvy manner, and scant attention was directed toward coordinating and integrating the various concerns. The administration of these units presented another set of difficulties. In some cases Samuel Slater tried to exercise personal oversight of operations, especially at Webster and Pawtucket. Unwilling to delegate authority, he made most of the decisions, including those concerning day-to-day operations. This form of administration occasioned delay and proved inefficient and troublesome. When Slater did delegate responsibility, it was to men he had chosen on the basis of friendship or kinship rather than ability.

Several years before his death, Samuel Slater recognized that his values and his way of doing business were out of step with the practices of those around him. The panic of 1829 highlighted these differences. During the 1820s the textile industry had boomed. "THE COTTON MANUFACTURE is increasing at a wonderful rate in the United States," boasted the *Niles Weekly Register* in 1828. "Many of the old mills are worked to their utmost production, and new ones are building or projected, in all parts of our country. The more the better."[51] But this optimism was premature. Many of these new firms were poorly equipped and improperly managed by agents and owners, and during the economic downturn in 1829, some of them went under while others were forced temporarily to suspend operations. Banks closed, money was in short supply, and credit dried up. A spate of bankruptcies ensued.[52] Even the most successful firms, such as those owned by Samuel Slater, were not immune. In January 1829 Slater acknowledged: "It is rather a pinching time here for money; . . . I have a very heavy load on my back, &c. It is true. I am on two neighbours' paper, but am partially secure, and hope in a day or two, to be fully secured against an eventual loss."[53] The expected upturn did not come, however, and by the early summer recovery appeared remote. Slater found himself stretched to the limit. The two neighbors referred to were David Wilkinson and a family friend, John Kennedy. He had endorsed their notes (which totaled about $300,000), and when the two men failed, he fell liable for their debts. To a group of fellow businessmen he wrote: "D. W. [David Wilkinson] has gone down the falls. His failure is a serious one, and it affects my mind and body seriously, and purse too for the present, but hope eventually to meet with but little loss."[54] This hope was in vain. Debts mounted as another transaction went sour. To a former employee, Olney Robinson, Slater had lent between $4,000 and $5,000 to construct a factory; Robinson failed.[55] Unable to raise the funds he required immediately, Slater was forced to issue thirty notes against his vast business network, including claims against his factories. He did not come away from the crisis unscathed. Shares in several factories were sold.[56]

Although these financial losses proved temporary, Slater feared the future. Friendship, kinship, and trust had been the basis for several loans made by Samuel Slater, and when his associates went bankrupt, Slater's confidence in himself as a businessman was shaken. Personal favors for friends almost ruined him. The values that had guided his decisions and policies for decades meant little in the financial marketplace. Indeed, many of Slater's associates deserted him. When he needed money, for example, he approached William Almy, a partner and an associate for almost four decades, for a loan; but for William Almy, friendship proved insufficient collateral for a loan. In fact, Almy recognized that Slater was vulnerable and seized the opportunity to acquire both the Pawtucket and the Slatersville property. Although later Slater bought back the Slatersville property, his active participation in Pawtucket ended. Slater was out of step with the rest of the business community; competition had replaced personal relationships and cooperation.[57]

George White noted significant changes in the man after 1829. Unaccustomed to failure, Slater "never before knew what it was to be unable to meet every demand, and could generally anticipate calls. He said to me 'I felt the more, because I had never been used to it.' He felt his dignity as a businessman hurt."[58]

The years following the panic caused further alarm, and when business conditions took another downturn in 1834, Samuel Slater considered closing his factories.[59]

Samuel Slater could not adapt easily to a new business morality; nor could he cope with the changes evident in the economy. Between 1790 and 1835 a market economy had emerged. According to Karl Polanyi, "a market economy is an economic system controlled, regulated, and directed by markets alone."[60] In order for the economy to function efficiently in the early nineteenth century, markets had to be developed for all elements of industry, including labor, land, and money. "In a commercial society their supply could be organized in one way only; by being made available for purchase. Hence, they would have to be organized for sale on the market—in other words, as commodities."[61] Labor, for example, would have to be transformed into a commodity and be offered for sale. Market value would dictate the prices paid for this commodity. This trend represented a reversal of traditional relationships between the economy and society. "Instead of economy being embedded in social relations, social relations are embedded in the economic system."[62]

Samuel Slater thought of the world and his relationship with fellow business associates and laborers in different terms from those demanded by the growing market economy. He was no cost-conscious factory master who treated friends and laborers as commodities. Pecuniary interests alone did not dictate his actions. Yet economic survival in Jacksonian America required that costs be calculated and reduced. The near collapse of the business in 1829 suggested that there might be other weaknesses. If Samuel Slater would not institute cost-saving cuts, his sons would. When George, John, and Horatio Nelson Slater gained control of the family business, they directed it along a new path. While their father lived, they proceeded slowly, for Slater relinquished power only reluctantly. Full economic independence for his sons came only with his death in April 1835. At that time his sons ranged in age from twenty-seven to thirty-one. While on vacation in St. Croix, John Slater II died in 1838. Five year later, George B. Slater died of tuberculosis.[63] Horatio Nelson Slater became the architect of a new system. Based on the model established by his father, it nevertheless represented a pragmatic response to contemporary economic problems. . . .

In the nineteenth century the Lowell and the Slater systems represented two different approaches to industrialization. By the 1830s economic self-interest and indeed a rising sense of individualism came to characterize Lowell-style firms. Ownership and management were separated. Lowell stockholders viewed their relationship to the business largely in economic terms. While economic self-interest was evident in the Slater system as well, Slater emphasized close product-family identification, family participation and control, and slow, steady long-term growth.

What prompted Slater to adopt this business scheme? Despite his voluminous business correspondence, his public addresses and publications, and the numerous books and articles that have been published about him, Slater remains an enigmatic figure. He was ambitious, determined to succeed, hard-working, and frugal, but these characteristics explain only partly the man's complex nature. Scholars have attributed many of his business decisions to "entrepreneurial conservatism," to economic dislocations in the industry, or even to a desire to preserve his reputation for producing quality goods.[64] These factors do not adequately explain his actions. Although he was one of the most important businessmen in America and one of the most successful manufacturers of the time (by the 1830s his property, buildings, and equipment in Webster alone were valued at $242,000), throughout his long career Slater was bound by traditional or preindustrial values that influenced his actions and decisions. Traditional notions of authority and responsibility were reflected in his business organization and in his labor-management relations.[65]

Slater monopolized power. He not only made all the strategic choices concerning finance, diversification, marketing, and the introduction of new technology, but also remained involved in day-to-day operations. Personal ownership and management could be effective primarily on a small scale. Personal control of dozens of widely dispersed enterprises proved impossible. While the growth of his business empire necessitated new attitudes toward management, Slater could not break with past practices. He could not delegate authority to outsiders.

In the Slater firms, loyalty, trust, kinship, and friendship ties meant more than merit in the choice of partners and managers. This was obvious when Slater sent children, his sons, to supervise other children at the Webster property. Neither Samuel Slater II nor John Slater II had technical or managerial experience, and hence neither could fulfill his obligations.[66] This was a family business meant to be handed down to the next generation. Growth and profits ranked behind other, personal considerations.

Slater's commitment to traditional values could be observed not only in ownership and management policies, but also in the type of labor he employed in his factories and in the industrial colonies he established. Family labor predominated, and the communities he planned and built served to attract and retain this form of labor. Through advertisements placed in the *Massachusetts Spy* (Worcester), in the *Plebeian and Millbury Workingman's Advocate*, and in the *Manufacturers' and Farmers' Journal and Providence and Pawtucket Advertiser*, Slater sought to attract people to his factories. Advertisements assured them that they would be provided for and that they would be given steady, honorable forms of labor if they accepted industrial employment. Many New England householders responded to the advertisements, leaving their farms, their jobs, and their communities in search of a better life in the factory towns. On arrival many of them found a style of life and a set of work patterns similar to those they recently had left behind. Within the context of the factory system, Samuel Slater recreated the traditional New England village.[67]

Henry A. Miles

LOWELL, AS IT WAS, AND AS IT IS

We begin with Francis Cabot Lowell, of whose name and memory our city is a monument. His connection with the manufacturing business will not be understood, without some brief sketch of the progress of that business in New-England.

The "Beverly Cotton Factory" was the first company in this country to engage in the manufacture of cotton. It was organized in 1787, with a capital of ninety thousand pounds sterling. The Messrs. Cabots, Thorndike, and Fisher, of Beverly, and Henry Higginson, of Boston, were its chief proprietors. John Cabot and Joshua Fisher were appointed agents for the management of its concerns. It continued in operation upwards of fifteen years, making corduroys, bed-tickings, cotton velvets—durable and approved fabrics; yet the business was not profitable, the loss having been as great as ninety cents on the dollar.

Mr. Samuel Slater came from England in November, of 1789. In December, 1790, he established a small factory at Pawtucket, near Providence, R.I. In 1793, another factory was built by Messrs. Brown, Almy, and Slater, in Pawtucket, in which they set in motion, July 12th, of that year, seventy-two spindles. For many years the progress of the business was extremely slow, and as late as January,

Henry A. Miles, *Lowell, As It Was, and As It Is*, (Lowell, Mass.: 1846). Reprinted from a copy in the State Historical Society of Wisconsin Library (New York: Arno Press, 1972), 21–32, 45–58, 217–224.

1807, there were but four thousand spindles in operation in Pawtucket and its neighborhood. These supplied yarns for handweaving, and the cloth that was made was almost entirely of family manufacture. At that time the country received nearly all its cotton cloth from Great Britain, and the East Indies. In 1807 and 1808, there were imported from Calcutta fifty-three millions of yards, principally of coarse cotton goods, and worth, as prices then were, over twelve millions of dollars. In 1810, there were made in all the factories in the United States, as appears by returns made by order of Mr. Gallatin, then Secretary of the Treasury, only eight hundred and fifty-six thousand six hundred and forty-five yards of cotton cloth, viz.—

In Rhode Island,	735,319
Massachusetts,	36,000
Vermont,	2,500
New-Jersey,	17,500
Pennsylvania,	65,326
Total,	856,645

This is not so many yards as four of the establishments in Lowell can now turn out in one week. The whole number of yards made in the United States in that year, was sixteen million five hundred eighty-one thousand two hundred and ninety-nine. Of this, fifteen million seven hundred and twenty-four thousand six hundred and fifty-four yards were of family manufacture, so imperfect was the machinery then in use. The weaving of the yarn alone cost double the whole process of making the fabric, after the introduction of the power-loom, in 1815.

Francis Cabot Lowell, son of Hon. John Lowell, LL. D., and grandson of the Rev. John Lowell, of Newburyport, was born in that town, in 1774. He was graduated at Harvard College, in 1793.

In a Memoir of Mr. Lowell's son, John Lowell, Jr. the founder of that course of lectures in Boston, known as the Lowell Institute, Mr. Edward Everett thus writes:—"In 1810, Mr. Francis Cabot Lowell was induced to visit England with his family, on account of the state of his health. The vast importance of manufacturing industry, as a source of national wealth, was no doubt impressed with new force upon his mind, in consequence of his observations in that country, and some branches of manufactures were examined by him with care; but it is not known that he paid particular attention to that of cotton. On his return home, and shortly after the commencement of the war of 1812, Mr. Lowell was so strongly convinced of the practicability of establishing that manufacture in the United States, that he proposed to a kinsman and friend (Mr. Patrick Tracy Jackson) to make the experiment on an ample scale. The original project only contemplated the weaving of cotton by machinery. The power-loom, although it had been for some time invented in England, was far less used in that country, in proportion to the quantity of cotton spun, than at the present day, and was wholly unknown in the United States. After deliberation, the enterprise was resolved upon. A model of a common loom was procured by Mr. Lowell and his friend—both equally ignorant of the practical details of the mode in which the power-loom was constructed—and their joint attention was bestowed on the re-invention of that machine. The winter of 1812–13 was passed at Waltham, where a water-power had been purchased, in bringing the loom to perfection. On being completed, it was found to answer the purpose so entirely, as to warrant the immediate construction, on the same plan, of all the looms needed for the establishment."— *Page 31 of Memoir, prefixed to the first volume of Lowell Lectures by John Gorham Palfrey.*

These were the first power-looms that were brought into successful operation in this country. They were the invention, as is stated above, of Messrs. Lowell and Jackson, aided by one important mechanical movement, which the genius of Mr. Paul Moody supplied. Power-looms had been invented in this country prior to that of Messrs. Lowell and Jackson's, and no less than twenty-five models had been patented at Washington, at the time they set theirs up. But theirs was the first that wove cloth to any considerable amount. A machine upon which he had spent so much thought and time, was naturally an object of great interest to Mr. Lowell. A friend of his, once finding him almost wholly lost in thought, while intently surveying the model, asked him what he could find in that machine which so absorbed his attention; Mr. Lowell replied, "that he had been reflecting upon the immense results which that piece of mechanism was destined to work out, and he would make the prediction that, within fifty years, cotton cloth would be sold for fourpence a yard." At a time when ten cents was paid per yard, for weaving alone, and the cloth cost thirty-three cents per yard, this prediction was regarded as the effusion of an enthusiast. It is needless to add that the prophecy has been literally fulfilled.

In a speech, made in the Massachusetts House of Representatives, in January, 1828, Mr. Nathan Appleton, while referring to the successful efforts of Mr. Lowell, has the following brief but emphatic sentence: "Seldom had a mind of so much science been turned to this subject, and never was a triumph more complete."

In consequence, however, of the ill success which had attended previous attempts, the public feeling was strong against any further manufacturing efforts. It is stated by Henry Lee, Esq. of Waltham, in one of a series of interesting articles contributed by him to the Boston Daily Advertiser, in 1830, that when Mr. Lowell first made the proposal to engage in the business, "many of his nearest connections used all their influence to dissuade him from the pursuit of what they deemed a visionary and dangerous scheme. These, too, were among those who knew, or thought that they knew, the full strength of his mind, the accuracy of his calculations, his industry, patience, and perseverance, and, withal, his power and influence over others whose aid was essential to his success; they still thought him *mad*, and did not recover from that error till they themselves had *lost their own senses*, of which they evinced symptoms at least, by shortly purchasing into the business of this visionary schemer at thirty, forty, fifty, and even sixty per cent, advance."

From the Memoir by Mr. Everett, we again quote:

"Mr. Francis Cabot Lowell repaired to Washington in the winter of 1816; and, in confidential intercourse with some of the leading members of Congress, he fixed their attention on the importance, the prospects, and the dangers of the cotton manufacture, and the policy of shielding it from foreign competition by legislative protection. Constitutional objections, at that time, were unheard of. The Middle States, under the lead of Pennsylvania, were strong in the manufacturing interest. The West was about equally divided. The New England States, attached, from the settlement of the country, to commercial and navigating pursuits, were less disposed to embark in a new policy, which was thought adverse to some branches of foreign trade, and particularly to the trade with India, from which the supply of coarse cottons was principally derived. The planting States, and eminently South Carolina, then represented by several gentlemen of distinguished ability, held the balance between the rival interests. To the planting interest it was demonstrated by Mr. Lowell, that, by the establishment of the cotton manufacture in the United States, the southern planter would greatly increase his market. He would furnish the raw material for all those American fabrics which should take the place of manufactures imported from India, or partly made in England from India cotton. He would thus, out of his own produce, be enabled to pay for all the supplies which he required from the north. This simple and conclusive view of the subject prevailed, and determined a portion of the south to throw its weight into the scale in favor of a protective tariff. The minimum duty on cotton fabrics, the corner stone of the system, was proposed by Mr. Lowell, and is believed to have been an original conception on his part. It was recommended by Mr. Lowndes; it was advocated by Mr. Calhoun, and was incorporated into the law of 1816. To this provision of law, the fruit of the intelligence and influence of Mr. Lowell, New England owes that branch of industry which has made her amends for the diminution of her foreign trade; which has kept her prosperous under the exhausting drain of her population to the West; which has brought a market for his agricultural produce to the farmer's door; and which, while it has conferred these blessings on this part of the country, has been productive of good, and nothing but good, to every other portion of it. For these public benefits—than which none, not directly connected with the establishment of our liberties, are of a higher order, or of a more comprehensive scope—the people of the United States are indebted to Mr. Francis Cabot Lowell; and in conferring his name upon the NOBLE CITY of the arts in our neighborhood, a monument not less appropriate than honorable has been reared to his memory. What memorial of a great public benefactor so becoming as the bestowal of his name on a prosperous community, which has started, as it were, from the soil at the touch of his wand? Pyramids and mausoleums may crumble to the earth, and brass and marble mingle with the dust they cover, but the pure and well deserved renown, which is thus incorporated with the busy life of an intelligent people, will be remembered, till the long lapse of ages and the vicissitudes of fortune shall reduce all of America to oblivion and decay." *Pages 37-39.*

Mr. Lowell died in 1817, at the age of forty-three.

Waltham, the Parent of Lowell

The war of 1812, as before remarked, gave encouragement to the cotton manufacture in this country. A company of gentlemen, residing principally in Boston, commenced, in 1814, the erection of factories in Waltham. With a capital stock of six hundred thousand dollars, they made purchases of land and mill privileges on Charles River, erected three brick manufactories, and supplied them with machinery, comprising eight thousand and sixty-four spindles, and two hundred and thirty-one looms. Here they employed about four hundred persons, mostly females, working up seven hundred thousand pounds of cotton, and making two million yards of cloth per year.

This undertaking proved highly successful. Here was a demonstration that this kind of business was practicable and gainful; and it attracted the attention of men of enterprise and wealth. Here also was originated and matured that plan of carrying on the manufacturing business, which should properly be called the "Waltham System." This system will hereafter be minutely described. It was transferred to Lowell, which thus had the benefit of the experiments and results of the elder place. Nor is this the extent of the obligations which Lowell owes to Waltham. Her first machinery was made there, and from there also came some of her ablest and most scientific manufacturers, with many skilful and faithful overseers and laborers.

In 1820, Mr. Paul Moody had charge of the Waltham Mills, and a friend of his, Mr. Ezra Worthen, a former partner in business, was connected with the manufacturing establishment at Amesbury. From his childhood Mr. Worthen had been acquainted with the neighborhood of the Pawtucket Falls; and when the profitableness of the manufacturing business led to inquiries for water-power, the immense advantages which this place held out soon struck his eye. While on a visit to Waltham, he expressed a wish to Mr. Patrick T. Jackson, one of the principal Directors of the company there, that they would set up works in some new place, and give him employment in conducting them. Mr. Jackson replied, that they would willingly do this, if he would find a good water power. Immediately Mr. Worthen named the Pawtucket Falls; and with a piece of chalk drew a map of the river and canal on the floor. The rude sketch was sufficient to give Mr. Jackson a favorable impression, who requested Mr. Moody to visit, with Mr. Worthen, the place which the latter gentleman had described. It was not long before they explored this whole neighborhood, tracing the course of the canal, surveying the adjoining land and shores, and satisfying themselves that the place afforded great facilities for building up a large manufacturing town. Soon after the reception of their highly favorable report, the Directors of the Waltham Company resolved to procure this eligible site.

Purchase of the Canal and Farms

Thomas M. Clark, a merchant of Newburyport, and one of the Directors of the canal round Pawtucket Falls, was taken into the confidence of the gentlemen connected with the Waltham Company, and was by them employed to purchase the shares of the Locks and Canals Corporation. These shares, five hundred in number, were bought at prices varying from eighty to one hundred dollars per share. In the autumn of 1821, Mr. Clark came to East Chelmsford to purchase the farms on which the city of Lowell is now built. The first purchase that was made was the farm of Nathan Tyler—a tract of land lying between Merrimack Street on the north, the Pawtucket Canal on the south, the Merrimack Canal on the west, and coming down to the junction of the rivers, where the Massachusetts Mills now stand. Here was a territory of forty acres, for which, including sixty acres of outlands in Tewksbury, the sum of eight thousand dollars was given. The farm of Josiah Fletcher, lying between Merrimack Street and Merrimack River, and next above the farm of Nathan Tyler, was then purchased, containing sixty acres, for which about the same sum was paid. Next above this, and bordering on Merrimack River, was the Cheever farm, the old homestead of which is still standing a short distance above the Lawrence Corporation. This farm contained one hundred and ten acres, nine undivided tenths of which were bought for one thousand eight hundred dollars. The owner of the other one tenth had agreed to convey it for two hundred dollars; but dying suddenly insolvent, it was sold by order of the court, the Locks and Canals Company giving, for seven and a half tenths thereof, upwards of three thousand dollars. The remaining two and a half tenths were bought a year afterwards for nearly five thousand dollars—so rapidly did the value of land rise. In 1822 the farm of the widow of Joseph Warren was purchased, a tract of land of about thirty acres, lying between Central Street and Concord River, with the Pawtucket Canal on the north, and extending up nearly as far as Richmond's Mills on the south. For this the sum of five thousand dollars was paid. Within these boundaries Mr. Thomas Hurd owned two or three acres of land in the near neighborhood of his Woollen Mill, which was situated where the Mechanics' Mills now stand. The farm of Mr. Joseph Fletcher, the homestead of which still stands on the high land in the rear of the upper part of Appleton Street, came down to the Pawtucket Canal on the north, and Central Street on the east, and contained about one hundred acres. This was not purchased until 1824, for which the sum of ten thousand dollars was paid.

Here then was nearly four hundred acres bought at prices averaging not far from one hundred dollars per acre. Thus was possession obtained both of the Pawtucket Canal, and of the territory on which the densely settled part of Lowell now stands, and the cost of the whole was about one hundred thousand dollars.

Commencement of Operations

On the sixth day of February, 1822, the purchasers of the above named property were incorporated as the 'Merrimack Manufacturing Company.' Vigorous measures were adopted in the following spring to enlarge the Pawtucket Canal, a step of primary importance, in order to admit a larger body of water. Five hundred men were constantly employed. The canal was made sixty feet wide, and capable of bearing a current of water eight feet deep. This was not completed until the latter part of the summer of 1823, and the expenditure was nearly one hundred and twenty thousand dollars.

Meanwhile a lateral canal—the Merrimack—was dug from the Pawtucket Canal to the Merrimack River. It was on the banks of this river that the Merrimack Manufacturing Company commenced the erection of mills. Mr. Ezra Worthen was appointed Superintendent of this company's works. He came here in the spring of 1822. The foundation of the first mill was laid in that year, and the first return of cloth was in November, 1823. It was from Mr. Worthen, as before remarked, that the first suggestion came to establish manufactures in this place. He was invited to carry his suggestion into execution. He barely lived long enough to see a great promise in his fruitful idea. He died June 18, 1824. A man of much manufacturing experience, and of great mechanical talent, his loss in the infancy of the enterprize was deeply felt.

Reorganization

It soon became apparent that here were mill privileges enough for several independent manufacturing companies. It was then deemed expedient that one company should have charge of the disposal and sale of the land and water-power, and of the furnishing of machinery, without entering itself into the manufacture of cotton. The old charter of 1792 was sufficient for this arrangement, with an amendment enacted by the legislature in January 1825. By this amendment the Proprietors of the Locks and Canals Company were authorized to purchase and hold all, or any part, of the real estate held by the Merrimack Manufacturing Company; to purchase and hold any other real estate in the towns of Chelmsford, Dracut, and Tewksbury, not exceeding in value one hundred thousand dollars, exclusive of improvements; and were also authorized to sell or lease land and water power.

Under this act the Locks and Canals Company proceeded to effect a reorganization, increasing the number of their shares to twelve hundred, at five hundred dollars per share, and taking into their hands the whole property of the Merrimack Manufacturing Company. It then sold to this company the land and water-power which it now possesses. This latter company, therefore, though at one time the owners of the whole water-power, hold the property they now possess under the same title with the other corporations in this city. By this arrangement the operations of this place were conducted on a better system, and scope was given for the action of as many distinct companies as the Locks and Canals could supply with water-power and land. To the furnishing of this power, and of mills and machinery to make it available, has the sphere of the Locks and Canals Company been ever since confined.

Locks and Canals Company

This sketch of the successive steps in the history of this young city, may be appropriately followed by a statement of the extent of the operations of the chief establishments here, together with a summary of these operations as they exist at the present time.

We begin with the Locks and Canals Company, whose works are carried on, as we have before seen, under the charter of 1792. Their capital stock is six hundred thousand dollars. They supply water-power to the other corporations, manufacture machinery, railroad-cars and engines, and contract for the erection of mills. They have two shops—one of which is the largest in the United States—a smithy and a foundry. They keep, usually, five hundred male laborers employed; but, when building mills, they give work, directly or indirectly, to seven hundred more. They manufacture one thousand two hundred and twenty-five tons of wrought and cast iron per year, and consume annually fifteen thousand bushels of charcoal, two hundred chaldrons of smiths' coal, four hundred tons of hard coal, two hundred cords of wood, and two thousand three hundred gallons of oil. They can furnish machinery complete for a mill of five thousand spindles in four months; and lumber and materials are always at command, with which to build or rebuild a mill within that time, if required. Beside selling a large amount of land, on which the city now stands, at prices varying from one eighth to six eighths of a dollar per square foot, it has had the profits of all the mills and boarding-houses it has built on good contracts for other corporations, the profits likewise of the manufactures of its shops; and, in addition to this, it reserves and receives an annual rent for the water power disposed of for each mill. Within the last few months, this company has disposed of a large portion of its lands and buildings in Lowell, making sales to the amount of four hundred and seventy-five thousand dollars. The stock of this company has been sold at more than three hundred and fifty per cent. advance above par. In the recent sale of their property, the shops and smithy, and the boarding-houses connected with them, were purchased by individuals who were incorporated this year into a company by the name of the 'Machine Shop.' The manufacture of machinery, railroad-cars, and engines, is for the present here carried on in the same manner and to the same extent as heretofore.

Merrimack Manufacturing Company

The act incorporating this company was passed in 1822. Its capital stock is two millions of dollars. It has five cotton mills, extensive print works, and one hundred and fifty-five boarding-houses. It runs forty-one thousand six hundred spindles, and one thousand three hundred looms. It gives employment to one thousand two hundred and fifty females, and to five hundred and fifty males. It manufactures two hundred and fifty thousand yards of cloth per week, working up in that time fifty-six thousand pounds of cotton. It consumes, annually, five thousand tons of anthracite coal, two hundred cords of wood, and thirteen thousand gallons of oil. The stock of this company is at great advance above par, and dividends have recently been made of ten per cent. for six months.

Hamilton Manufacturing Company

Incorporated in 1825. Capital stock one million two hundred thousand dollars. It has three mills, extensive print works, and fifty boarding-houses. It runs twenty-two thousand one hundred and forty-four spindles, and six hundred and eight power looms. It employs six hundred and fifty females, and two hundred and fifty males. It makes one hundred and ten thousand yards of cloth per week, manufacturing in that time forty-two thousand pounds of cotton. It consumes, annually, three thousand tons of anthracite coal, five hundred cords of wood, and six thousand five hundred gallons of oil.

Appleton Manufacturing Company

This Company was incorporated in 1828, and in the same year commenced the erection of their mills. Their capital stock is six hundred thousand dollars. In their two mills they run eleven thousand seven hundred and seventy-six spindles, and four hundred looms. They have thirty boarding-houses, and employ three hundred and forty females, and sixty-five males. They make one hundred thousand yards of cloth per week. They work up thirty-six thousand pounds of cotton per week. Of coal they use three hundred tons per year, and of oil three thousand four hundred and forty gallons.

Lowell Manufacturing Company

The Lowell Company was incorporated in 1828. Their capital stock is six hundred thousand dollars. They have two mills, one for the manufacture of cotton, and one of the manufacture of carpets, and twenty-seven boarding-houses. They run six thousand spindles for cotton, and one hundred and fifty-two looms. Beside these they have fifty power looms for carpet weaving, and forty hand looms, for the same purpose. They manufacture over ninety-five thousand yards of cotton cloth per week, and over seven thousand yards of carpeting. They consume yearly five hundred tons of coal, five hundred cords of wood, four thousand gallons of olive oil, and four thousand gallons of sperm oil. The power looms for carpet weaving are the first and only ones that have ever been successfully employed. They are the invention of a young but highly distinguished machinist, formerly of Lowell, and have been the objects of much admiration.

Middlesex Manufacturing Company

Incorporated in 1830. Capital stock seven hundred and fifty thousand dollars. This Company has two mills, one of which is very large, and two dye-houses. It manufactures broadcloths and cassimeres. It runs seven thousand two hundred spindles, forty-five looms for broadcloth, one hundred and thirty-two for cassimeres. It employs five hundred and fifty females, and two hundred and fifty males. It makes twelve thousand yards of cassimere per week, and two thousand two hundred yards of broadcloth. It works up one million pounds of wool per year, and three million teasles. It consumes annually six hundred tons of coal, one thousand five hundred cords of wood, fifteen thousand gallons of oil for oiling wool, and six thousand gallons of sperm oil.

Suffolk Manufacturing Company

Incorporated in 1830. Capital stock six hundred thousand dollars. It has two mills running eleven thousand eight hundred and seventy-two spindles, and four hundred and four looms. It has thirty boarding-houses, and employs three hundred and forty females, and seventy males. It makes one hundred thousand yards of cloth per week, chiefly drillings, using for this thirty-six thousand pounds of cotton. It consumes annually three hundred tons of coal, fifty cords of wood, and three thousand five hundred gallons of oil.

Notes

1. Albert Gallatin, "Manufactures," April 17, 1810, in *American State Papers, Finance,* 2:127; Peter J. Coleman, *The Transformation of Rhode Island, 1790–1860* (Providence: 1963), pp. viii. 130–131. Ware, *Early New England Cotton Manufacture,* pp. 30, 128, 301–302.

2. Almy and Brown MSS, Moses Brown to T. Rogerson. November 11, 1810.

3. Ware, *Early New England Cotton Manufacture,* pp. 61–62.

4. The Lowell system has been researched well. Among the better books and articles are Ware, *Early New England Cotton Manufacture;* Hannah Josephson, *Golden Threads: New England's Mill Girls and Magnates* (New York, 1949); Nathan Appleton, *Introduction of the Power Loom, and Origins of Lowell* (Lowell, 1858); Dublin, *Women at Work;* Kenneth F. Mailloux, "The Boston Manufacturing Company," *Textile History Review* 5 (January 1964): 3–29; Carl Gersuny, "'A Devil in Petticoats' and Just Cause: Patterns of Punishment in Two New England Textile Factories," *Business History Review* 50 (Summer 1976): 131–152. See also *Niles Weekly Register,* June 3 and September 9, 1826; May 19, 1827; July 5 and July 26, 1828; July 6, 1833; Louis McLane, "Report of the Secretary of the Treasury," 1832, *Documents Relative to the Manufactures in the United States,* 2 vols., 22d Cong., 1st sess., House Executive Document no. 308 (Washington, 1833), 1:340–341 (hereafter referred to as *McLane Report*); "Statistics of Lowell, Massachusetts," *Hunts Merchants Magazine* 1 (July–December 1839): 90.

5. Tench Coxe, "Digest of Manufactures," in *American State Papers, Finance,* 2:666–812.

6. *Niles Weekly Register,* November 16, 1816.

7. Robert B. Zevin, *The Growth of Manufacturing in Early-Nineteenth-Century New England* (New York, 1975), pp. 10-3, 10-4, 10-12.

8. Peter J. Coleman. "Rhode Island Cotton Manufacturing: A Study in Economic

Conservatism," *Rhode Island History* 23 (July 1964): 68; Bagnall, *Textile Industries of the United States*, p. 546; David John Jeremy, *Transatlantic Industrial Revolution: The Diffusion of Textile Technologies between Britain and America, 1790–1830s* (Cambridge, Mass., 1981), p. 98. Thomas R. Smith, *Cotton Textile Industry of Fall River, Massachusetts: A Study in Industrial Localization* (New York, 1944), p. 24; see also an advertisement for the Gilmore loom in *Manufacturers' and Farmers' Journal and Providence and Pawtucket Advertiser*, April 6, 1820; and Slater MSS, Samuel Slater and Sons, vol. 191.

9. Zevin, *Growth of Manufacturing in Early-Nineteenth-Century New England*, p. 8.

10. Arthur H. Cole, *Wholesale Commodity Prices in the United States, 1700–1861: Statistical Supplement: Actual Wholesale Prices of Various Commodities* (Cambridge, Mass., 1938), pp. 184–242.

11. Zevin, *Growth of Manufacturing in Early-Nineteenth-Century New England*, pp. 10-1–10-49; see also Ware, *Early New England Cotton Manufacture*, p. 111.

12. Gilbane, "Social History of Samuel Slater's Pawtucket," pp. 136–138, 146–147. In January 1810 Slater dissolved his partnership with his kinsmen. For an excellent discussion of Slater's various business transactions see N. S. B. Gras and Henrietta M. Larson, *Casebook in American Business History* (New York, 1939), pp. 218–229; La Porte, "Birth of America's Spinning Industry II," pp. 678–679; Orra L. Stone, *History of Massachusetts Industries: Their Inception, Growth, and Success*, 4 vols. (Boston, 1930), 1:38–39; Samuel Batchelder, *Introduction and Early Progress of the Cotton Manufacture in the United States* (Boston, 1863), p. 49.

13. Almy and Brown MSS, Moses Brown to F. Waterman, February 23, 1802, quoted in Conrad, "Evolution of Industrial Capitalism in Rhode Island," p. 157.

14. Almy and Brown MSS, Almy and Brown to Gilbert Everingham, October 2, 1802, quoted in Conrad, "Evolution of Industrial Capitalism in Rhode Island," p. 158.

15. Ibid.

16. White, *Memoir of Samuel Slater*, pp. 215, 259; *McLane Report* 1:970–971; Bagnall, *Textile Industries of the United States*, pp. 397–400; James Montgomery, *Practical Detail of the Cotton Manufacture of the United States of America and the State of the Cotton Manufacture of That Country Contrasted and Compared with That of Great Britain with Comparative Estimates of the Cost of Manufacturing in Both Countries* (Glasgow, 1840), pp. 153, 179; Batchelder, *Introduction and Early Progress of the Cotton Manufacture*, pp. 52–53; Lewton, "Samuel Slater and the Oldest Cotton Machinery in America," p. 507.

17. La Porte, "Birth of America's Spinning Industry, II." p. 679.

18. "Two Hundred Years of Progress: Webster-Dudley, 1739–1939." *Webster Times*, 1939, p. 7; Slater and Sons, *Slater Mills at Webster*, p. 25; *Massachusetts Spy* (Worcester), January 15, 1823; Lewton, "Samuel Slater and the Oldest Cotton Machinery in America," p. 507.

19. "Two Hundred Years of Progress," pp. 8–9; Slater and Sons, *Slater Mills at Webster*, pp. 22, 25; George Robert Means, "The Industrial Development of Webster, Massachusetts." Master's thesis, Clark University, 1932, pp. 53, 68–70; D. Hamilton

Hurd, *History of Worcester County, Massachusetts, with Biographical Sketches of Many of Its Pioneers and Prominent Men*, 2 vols. (Philadelphia, 1889), 1:362: Lewton, "Samuel Slater and the Oldest Cotton Machinery in America," p. 507.

20. *Massachusetts Spy* (Worcester), January 15, 1823; see also Slater and Sons, *Slater Mills at Webster*, p. 25; James Lawson Conrad, Jr., "The Establishment of the Textile Industry in Dudley, Massachusetts, 1812–1920." Master's thesis, Clark University, 1963, p. 56.

21. Bagnall, *Textile Industries of the United States*, pp. 595–596.

22. William Davis, ed., *New England States: Their Constitutional, Judicial, Educational, Commercial, Professional, and Industrial History*, 2 vols. (Boston, 1897), 1:150.

23. Slater MSS, Steam Cotton Manufacturing Company, vol. 11, especially 1827 and October 6, 1834; see also Leander J. Bishop, *History of American Manufactures from 1608 to 1860*, 3 vols. (Philadelphia, 1864), 3:387–388.

24. Coleman, *Transformation of Rhode Island*, p. 109; Alfred D. Chandler, Jr., "Samuel Slater, Francis Cabot Lowell, and the Beginning of the Factory System in the United States" (Harvard Business School, 1977) p. 23 (mimeo).

25. Slater MSS, Slater and Wardwell, vol. 10, Wardwell to Slater, February 10, 1829.

26. Ibid., Samuel Slater and Sons, vol. 216, Tiffany, Anderson Company to Samuel Slater and Sons, October 12, 1833.

27. Ibid., Union Mills, vol. 117, Storrs to George Blackburn and Company, February 13, 1845; Storrs to R. and D. M. Stebbins, February 28, 1845; Samuel Slater and Sons, vol. 210, Underhill and Company to Samuel Slater and Sons, July 3, 1845; see also Slater and Sons, *Slater Mills at Webster*, pp. 33–34.

28. Slater and Sons, *Slater Mills at Webster*, p. 25; "Two Hundred Years of Progress," pp. 8–9; Slater MSS, vol. 235, Samuel Slater to John Slater, April 22, 1831; Steam Cotton Manufacturing Company, vol. 11, February 18, 1831; April 28, and December 15, 1830; February 10, March 28, and May 13, 1831; January 13, 1832; May 6, 1833; see also Bishop, *History of American Manufactures*, 3:387–388.

29. Bishop, *History of American Manufactures*, 3:287–288; Coleman, *Transformation of Rhode Island*, pp. 150, 111.

30. Coleman, "Rhode Island Cotton Manufacturing," p. 68; Bagnall, *Textile Industries of the United States*, p. 546; Batchelder, *Introduction and Early Progress of the Cotton Manufacture*, pp. 70–72; *Manufacturers' and Farmers' Journal and Providence and Pawtucket Advertiser*, April 6, 1820.

31. Slater MSS, Samuel Slater and Sons, vol. 191. July 1829–July 1830; see also Zevin, *Growth of Manufacturing in Early-Nineteenth-Century New England*, pp. 10-41, 10-42.

32. Workers' opposition to the new technology is discussed in [Tucker, *Samuel Slater and the Origins of the American Textile Industry*,] chap. 9.

33. Means, "Industrial Development of Webster," pp. 12, 17, 18, 58.

34. Louis C. Hunter, *A History of Industrial Power in the United States, 1780–1930* (Charlottesville, 1979), vol. 1. *Waterpower in the Century of the Steam Engine*, 519–520.

35. Until the 1850s water power was the primary mode of power throughout the New England textile districts. Manufacturers only reluctantly abandoned water wheels. Severe climatic conditions such as drought encouraged some manufacturers to install steam engines. This was the case in Waltham, where in 1836 the owners of the Boston Manufacturing Company installed a steam engine as an auxiliary source of power to be used during periods of low water. Other manufacturers switched from water to steam power when they expanded operations and found that local streams could not supply adequate power. See Hunter, *History of Industrial Power in the United States*, 1:9–10, 516–521.

36. Coleman, *Transformation of Rhode Island*, p. 109; Chandler, "Samuel Slater, Francis Cabot Lowell, and the Beginning of the Factory System," p. 23; see also Alfred D. Chandler, Jr., "A Reply," *Business History Review*, 53 (Summer 1979): 256.

37. *McLane Report*, 1:576–577.

38. Zachariah Allen to F. C. Lowell, November 30, 1825, Francis Cabot Lowell II, Business Correspondence, 1793–1827, Massachusetts Historical Society, Boston (hereafter referred to as Lowell MSS).

39. Slater and Sons, *Slater Mills at Webster*, p. 25.

40. *McLane Report*, 1:929.

41. Ibid., 1:576–577.

42. Slater MSS, Slater and Tiffany, vol. 124.

43. Ibid., Slater and Tiffany, vol. 80, Hand-Loom Weavers, 1812–1829, especially Timothy Corbin, April–March 1819. See also Chandler, *Visible Hand*, p. 63, Gras and Larson, *Casebook in American Business History*, pp. 226–227.

44. *Massachusetts Spy* (Worcester), January 8, 1823.

45. Coleman, "Rhode Island Cotton Manufacturing," pp. 71–77; Ware, *Early New England Cotton Manufacture*, p. 74; Slater MSS, Union Mills, vol. 169. Wage receipts, Artimas See and Company, June 15, 1827; George Bauen, August 10, 1827; Samuel Slater and Sons, vol. 191, Hand-Loom Weavers.

46. White, *Memoir of Samuel Slater*, pp. 241–242.

47. Slater MSS, Samuel Slater and Sons, vol. 235, Samuel Slater to John Slater, March 30, 1821; see also White, *Memoir of Samuel Slater*, pp. 241–242.

48. Slater MSS, Samuel Slater and Sons, vol. 235, Samuel Slater to John Slater, February 23, March 4, March 27, and May 4, 1826; March 12, March 15, and November 16, 1828.

49. Ibid., Samuel Slater and Sons, vol. 235, Samuel Slater to John Slater, November 16, 1828.

50. Ibid., Samuel Slater and Sons, vol. 235, Samuel Slater to John Slater, April 22, 1831; *McLane Report*, 1:928.

51. *Niles Weekly Register*, June 28, 1828.

52. Gilbane, "Social History of Samuel Slater's Pawtucket," p. 492.

53. Samuel Slater to Moses Brown, Cyrus Butler, Brown & Ives, January 7, 1829, quoted in White, *Memoir of Samuel Slater*, p. 246.

54. Samuel Slater to Moses Brown, Cyrus Butler, Brown & Ives, July 29, 1829, quoted in White, *Memoir of Samuel Slater*, p. 247.

55. Conrad, "Evolution of Industrial Capitalism in Rhode Island." p. 325.

56. White, *Memoir of Samuel Slater*, pp. 244–248; "A Financier of the Old School," *Proceedings of the Worcester Society of Antiquity* 5 (1879): 9–10; see also *Niles Weekly Register*, June 28, 1828, July 4, 1829.

57. White, *Memoir of Samuel Slater*, pp. 244–245.

58. Ibid., p. 245.

59. Slater MSS, Samuel Slater and Sons, vol. 235, Samuel Slater to John Slater II, January 19, 1834, quoted in Conrad, "Evolution of Industrial Capitalism in Rhode Island," p.47.

60. Karl Polanyi, *The Great Transformation* (Boston, 1957 [1944]), p. 68.

61. Ibid., p. 75; see also Bendix, *Work and Authority in Industry*, p. 47.

62. Polanyi, *Great Transformation*, p. 57; see also Christopher Clark, "The Household Economy, Market Exchange, and the Rise of Capitalism in the Connecticut Valley, 1800–1860," *Journal of Social History* 13 (1979): 169–173; Judith McGaw, "The Sources and Impact of Mechanization: The Berkshire County, Massachusetts, Paper Industry, 1801–1885, as a Case Study," Ph.D. dissertation, New York University, 1977, pp. 157–177.

63. Slater MSS, Sutton Manufacturing Company, vol. 1, Company Minutes, 1838; and Webster, Mass., Vital Statistics, Death, 1843.

64. Chandler, "Samuel Slater, Francis Cabot Lowell, and the Beginnings of the Factory System," p. 22; Coleman, "Rhode Island Cotton Manufacturing," p. 66; Bagnall, *Textile Industries of the United States*, p. 399; Ware, *Early New England Cotton Manufacture*, p. 76.

65. *McLane Report*, 1:576–577.

66. See [Tucker, *Samuel Slater and the Origins of the American Textile Industry*,] chap. 8.

67. *Massachusetts Spy* (Worcester), October 30, 1822; *Plebeian and Millbury Workingman's Advocate*, January 25, 1832; *Manufacturers' and Farmers' Journal and Providence and Pawtucket Advertiser*, January 12 and February 20, 1826.

QUESTIONS FOR REVIEW AND DISCUSSION

1. How would you characterize Samuel Slater's management style? Were Slater and Francis Cabot Lowell primarily inventor-entrepreneurs, or were they business managers?

2. Compare the financial organization of Slater's mills with that of the Lowell group. Did the nature of the two kinds of establishments, or the character of the proprietors, result in different styles of management?

3. Why did Slater continue to depend on hand looms until 1829–1830?

4. Did considerations other than profit enter into Slater's business decisions? Is this true of contemporary business decisions?
5. Compare as nearly as possible the organization or "departmentalization" of the Slater mills with that of the Lowell mills.
6. Discuss the role of the Locks and Canals Company in the development of manufacturing in Lowell.
7. Explain how Francis Cabot Lowell exhibited not only technological expertise but political sense as well.
8. What kind of decisions and planning went into the Merrimack Manufacturing Company?
9. Did the manufacturing establishments in Lowell appear to compete with or to complement each other?

4

The Cotton
Factor

Throughout the nineteenth century, cotton accounted for one-third to one-half of the value of all exports from the United States. Between 1800 and 1860, the consumption of raw cotton in the United Kingdom rose from 52 million pounds to over 1 billion pounds. Production of cotton in the United States rose from 152,000 bales to over 4.3 million bales in the same period (see Table 4–1, pages 114–115) and represented two-thirds of the world's total annual supply.

Cotton was the world's primary business before the Civil War, just as petroleum has become the major concern in recent decades. By 1860 American textile manufacturers were consuming one-third of the world's total supply of cotton. Income from cotton, and inescapably from slavery, was shared by southern planters and by northern and southern business-persons who earned profits from the freight, the sales commissions, the insurance premiums, the warehousing, and the manufacturing and distribution of finished cotton goods.

Douglass C. North believes that cotton was the major expansive force in the growth of the antebellum economy:

> It was cotton which was the most important influence in the growth in the market size and the consequent expansion of the economy . . . it was cotton that initiated the concomitant expansion in income, in the size of the social overhead invest-

ment (in the course of its role in the marketing of cotton) in the Northeast which were to facilitate the subsequent rapid growth of manufacture. Cotton also accounted for the accelerated pace of westward migration as well as for the movement of people out of self-sufficiency into the market economy.[1]

Douglass C. North suggests that income received from the marketing of cotton in the South flowed directly to the West and to the Northeast (and then to England and Europe) for the purchase of goods and services. The West provided wheat, corn, pork, and beef. The Northeast provided financial, transportation, marketing, and manufacturing services. Northern textile mills bought raw cotton and marketed finished cloth. The textile industry in turn stimulated expansion of the machine-tools industry and other supportive industries. The major cargo of ships and railways before 1860 was cotton. The expansion of transportation industries in turn stimulated expansion in the iron, steel, and coal industries. The initial marketing of the cotton crop was the business of the cotton factor.

The case studies that follow are derived from Harold D. Woodman's *King Cotton and His Retainers: Financing and Marketing the Cotton Crop of the South, 1800–1925* and from Lewis C. Gray's, *History of Agriculture in the Southern United States to 1860*, describe the nature and character of one of the nation's largest but most decentralized businesses in the nineteenth century. The cotton factor was one of thousands of independent proprietorships or partnerships located primarily in the South, in coastal or inland commercial centers, through whose hands passed, even in 1860, a crop worth about $200 million. The role of the cotton factor was to match the seller with the buyer and to make the necessary financial arrangements and money transfers. This free market in cotton, which had worldwide dimensions, functioned remarkably well and is basic to an understanding of the American economy and of business developments in the nineteenth century.

Although the cotton factor survived the post–Civil War era, its role changed from that of essentially an independent broker to that of an agent for a purchaser. The expansion of the railroads, the telegraph, and the transatlantic cable and development of new interior markets eventually displaced the need for the factor. The sharecropper and crop-lien systems also affected the marketing of cotton and thus the role of the cotton factor after the Civil War.

Note

1. Douglass C. North, *The Economic Growth of the United States, 1790–1860* (New York: Norton 1966; Englewood Cliffs, N.J.), 68.

Harold D. Woodman

SELLING THE CROP

A planter with cotton to sell found buyers as near at hand as the gates of his plantation or as far away as the wharves of Liverpool. To secure the highest net return he had to select the proper buyer in the right market at the most propitious time. This was no easy task and planters with a substantial crop to sell ordinarily entrusted the responsibility to an expert—the cotton factor. Every town had factors or their representatives eager to serve the planters.

Closest at hand for most plantations were the larger interior towns. Situated at river, road, and railroad junctions, these towns became important cotton markets as production spread and increased in volume. By 1860 the most important interior cotton markets were Fayetteville, Columbia, Augusta, Milledgeville, Macon, Atlanta, Montgomery, Nashville, Memphis, and Shreveport.[1]

Sales close to home obviously kept marketing expenses low. Yet, despite the extra costs (higher transportation and insurance bills, extra handling, and the like) most planters found it advantageous to have their crop sold in the coastal cities where buyers in greater numbers produced a more active demand. Charleston, Savannah, Mobile, and New Orleans became the largest cotton markets in the South.[2]

A few shipped their cotton directly to factors in Liverpool. Fanny Kemble, in

Harold D. Woodman, *King Cotton and His Retainers: Financing and Marketing the Cotton Crop of the South, 1800–1925* (Lexington, Kentucky: University of Kentucky Press, 1968), 15–29.

many markets available would offer the most advantageous sale at any given moment. For example, in a single crop year, the Augusta factors, Heard and Simpson, sold cotton not only in Augusta but in Charleston, New York, Baltimore, and Liverpool as well.[20]

The best market of course was one that netted the planter the highest return and it was the factor's responsibility to find it. With prices fluctuating as much as 5 cents per pound—and more—throughout the season in every market,[21] he was expected to be wise enough to make a sale when prices reached their peak. This meant that a successful factor had to be an expert salesman, aware of the needs of the local buyers, and alert to the trends in supply and demand in his own and in other markets of the world.

Once he consigned his crop to a factor, the planter did not lose sight of it. He could and did keep informed. Newspapers published in the market cities brought him estimates of the quantity of cotton produced and the prices being paid in the Southern, Northern, and European markets. Factors, too, regularly sent him reprints of this information,[22] as well as letters and circulars which offered estimates of the probable size of the crop, the prospects for prices, and appraisals of the demand based on their assessment of political and economic conditions in Europe and at home and guesses as to the amount of raw cotton in the hands of the manufacturers.[23]

Advice on the best time to sell often accompanied such information. For example, in the late summer of 1827 a New Orleans factor urged one of his customers to take advantage of an early demand. Stocks of cotton in the hands of Northern manufacturers were very low, he wrote, "from which we infer that they will be forced into this market with their orders at the opening of the Season, and this with the aid of speculators, will probably enable us to obtain better prices than at a later period when the trade falls into its regular channels."[24] Several years later Reynolds, Byrne and Company gave similar advice for different reasons. The prospects for a large crop were very great, they wrote, and therefore "we advise our friends very particularly to ship as early as possible and accept the then market prices in preference to holding on for still higher rates," for prices would soon decline in the face of a heavy crop.[25]

Armed with such information, planters sometimes insisted that they, rather than their factors, make the decision when to sell. A Georgia planter was adamant on this point:

> It has been my custom to sell my cotton when I have been in Augusta & I expect ever to do the same—I have Heard [sic] that you did not want cotton sent you, unless you had to selling of it. Now when I want my cotton sold & I am not in Augusta, then I shall expect my Factor to sell—not otherwise. This being the case, if you would rather not have me send my cotton to you, say so & I will try & Make some other arrangements—

otherwise, I shall be pleased to send my cotton to you. . . . If you conclude to take it, under the circumstances, then I want the cotton Insured . . . & Held for further instructions—as I would rather have it all sold together & besides, I will risque getting more for it.[26]

Perhaps it was the thrill of gambling along with the expectation of greater gains which induced a planter to retain control over the sale of his own crop. Mississippi planter James W. Monette, following the New Orleans market from his plantation, in early December 1846 wrote his New Orleans factors, Buckner and Stanton, that he wanted his cotton held "for better prices" which he hoped would soon be available. Two weeks later he indicated that "if the next steamer from Liverpool brings favorable news, we think the Orleans market must have an upward tendency." His expectations were realized when the market began to advance after the first of the year but Monette wrote that he would hold for at least 12 cents per pound on his best cotton "unless an unexpected decline should overtake the European market." By the end of January prices had improved still further, but the planter had upped his demands to no less than 12.5 cents per pound. Mid-March found him still predicting a further rise, but by the first week of April conditions had changed so radically that he indicated he would settle for a sale at 11 cents.[27]

Planters like Monette who bound their factors so closely were at a distinct disadvantage. News about market conditions was often stale by the time it arrived in the mails. Information about a rise in prices might not reach the planter before a contrary tendency governed the market and the advantage lost. If the cotton was being held until the planter came to town to sell his own crop, peak prices might have come and gone before the planter arrived.

Usually, therefore, planters allowed their factors wide discretion. Typical were the instructions of a South Carolina planter: consider the crop "as committed to your better judgement."[28] "Still you must bear in mind that I leave all to your own judgment which in such matters, is no doubt better than mine," a Mississippian wrote the New York factors who had his cotton.[29]

A factor was expected to have the skill, experience, and sources of information that would make his judgment superior to that of the planter. Superior judgment was expected to lead to profitable results, as Richard J. Dunett's advice—and warning—to his Augusta factor made clear:

I hope, gentlemen, that you will look well to my interest & sell at the proper time, (even at once if you think it safest). I have been strongly solicited to patronise another house, but my invariable reply has been that I never give up an old friend for a new one, without a good reason. I have thought that whilst a market is regularly going up, it may be safe to hold, but I hope you will not allow it to go down with the cotton on hand; but you are in the market with more lights before you than we have so far off, & of course have more facilities to form correct conclusions, & I doubt not, but that you will do what your judgement dictates to be best in the premises.[30]

Few customers were so minatory. The factor was aware of his duties and needed no reminders of it. When the cotton consigned to his care arrived, he would dispatch a letter to the planter acknowledging receipt. Soon the planter would be advised of the quality of his cotton and the prospects for prices. Unless under specific instructions, the factor would sell when he deemed best without waiting for the planter's approval and the planter would usually hear about the sale only after it had already been made.[31]

Often a factor bound by a planter's specific orders would urge him to change his instructions when market conditions seemed to warrant it. Maunsel White wrote a customer that he would hold for better prices as instructed but urged a prompter sale: "The demand is now good, & brisk sales making at 9 to 10 cts. & if very fine a little [hig]her & I doubt much if they will be better in a month hence."[32]

Sometimes explicit instructions were ignored. For example, in May 1823 a New Orleans merchant informed his planter customer that his 50 bales of cotton had been sold at one-half cent below the planter's minimum instructed limit. "This may be improper," the factor admitted, "and you have a right to claim the half cent." But, after close examination of the cotton "we were convinced that more than the 12¢ offered could not be obtained. . . . We hope you will be satisfied that we consulted your interest, if we disobeyed your instructions."[33]

One New Orleans factorage firm made it very clear to its customers that it would use its own discretion if it would be to the advantage of the planter: "As factors, we shall endeavor to act with reference to the *interest* of our Correspondents, even if for the moment, it should be at variance with their wishes, unless we are laid under positive instructions."[34]

A profitable sale involved more than mere timing. The factor also had to decide the best way of selling. A planter's crop often contained several grades, which could be sold separately at varying prices or together at an average price for the lot. Furthermore, the factor usually had the bales of many planters in his possession at one time and could, if he thought it advantageous, sell the crop of several planters in a single transaction. For example, the New Orleans factor Maunsel White informed one of his customers that he had just made a sale of some eleven hundred bales at "the highest offer I could get or expected to get" and that "I have included yours in the number." Proceeds of this sale would vary according to the quality of each planter's cotton and therefore, he explained, "it will take some time to go thro' the entire, so that I cannot send you the a/c [account] Sales for a few days."[35]

A planter might dictate the way his cotton should be sold,[36] but usually this decision was left to the factor. Buyers often required a special grade, variety, and quantity of cotton and these needs had to be recognized in the interests of a good sale. A New Orleans factor described how a buyer entered his office in early February 1851 expecting to purchase about four hundred bales for shipment to Spain, "whereupon, I took down the samples of a number of small crops of Prairie cottons, suitable for the Spanish market, placed them on the table for sale, made a list of them and sold them."[37]

Obviously, a factor could not discharge his responsibility to seek out the best sale without being able to classify, grade, and sample cotton in his possession. Since the value of the staple varied considerably according to quality and grade, an error in classification could be costly. There is some evidence, however, that this danger was lessened through the skilled aid of another group of merchants, the cotton brokers.

The exact role these cotton brokers played is unclear. Directories and newspapers carried advertisements of numerous firms calling themselves cotton brokers. When in 1836 New Orleans brokers organized themselves and appointed a committee "to give a correct report of sales, and to revise the prices each week," the leading commercial newspaper of that city announced that its list of cotton sales would thenceforth be "taken from their register" and its price quotations would be "in conformity to their views."[38] The brokers also seem to have been given certain regulatory powers over the cotton trade. A meeting of "cotton buyers and cotton brokers" was held in October 1859 "for the purpose of devising means to redress certain abuses and grievances existing in connection with the cotton trade of New Orleans." After agreeing on a set of rules, the group set up a committee of fifteen cotton brokers to enforce these regulations and empowered the committee "to adopt such other rules amongst themselves to secure a more uniform and satisfactory method of receiving cotton."[30]

That brokers were in the best position to have a "correct report" of weekly sales and prices and to enforce trading rules indicates that they were participants in cotton sales. Often their participation is noted in the records. A New Orleans factor, describing a sale, wrote that the buyer came to his office "accompanied by A. Desmare, Broker."[40] Many—but not all—accounts of sales rendered by factors to planters listed the name of a broker along with the name of the individual or firm making the purchase.[41]

It is clear that the cotton broker, in addition to other duties, was often an intermediary between buyer and seller, probably helping the two parties to agree on the grade and quality of the cotton under consideration. "We had the cotton valued by one of our best brokers," a New Orleans factor testified during litigation arising over a dispute concerning the price received for a planter's cotton.[42] In another case, testimony showed both buyer and seller hiring brokers "to inspect" the list of cotton offered for sale to determine quality.[43]

Even with the help of brokers, factors had to be experts, alert to price movements, buyers' needs, crop size and quality, and the like. The need for expert knowledge inevitably led to specialization. Although some factors sold more than one commodity,[44] by and large it appears that factors in the larger markets specialized in the selling of one or another of the South's staples. Advertisements in journals, directories, and newspapers usually indicated that the merchant was a factor exclusively for cotton or rice or sugar or tobacco. Rarely was more than one commodity handled by a single house.[45]

Every cotton market had many different kinds of buyers with whom the factor dealt. Some were mainly speculators. "The purchases yesterday were principally on Speculation," wrote a Charleston factor, "Cotton to be restored and resold later."[46] The extent of such speculative activity varied from day to day and from year to year, depending on estimates of crop size, anticipated demand, political conditions, and the vitality of the hundreds of rumors circulating in the market. With the characteristic exaggeration of a foreign visitor, Edward Sullivan described cotton speculation in the New Orleans market:

> During the whole winter the city is thronged with cotton speculators. . . . I had no idea mercantile affairs were so entirely a matter of speculation. People make bets about the probable rise and fall in the price of cotton, and book them in the same way as a man does his bets on the "Derby." It appears that the real amount of the yield of cotton is never exactly known, and all the great speculators have touts, who are despatched into the different cotton districts to send information to their employers. As their accounts differ considerably, so does the spirit of gambling increase, each man considering his information better than his neighbor's, and backing it accordingly. Fortunes are made and lost as quickly as on the Stock Exchange, and numbers of bankruptcies occur every winter.[47]

Such frenzy was not a regular feature of the market. Sometimes a rash of speculation would take hold of the market as it did briefly in 1843 when "many parcels of Cotton changed hands repeatedly."[48] In other seasons it could be reported that "speculation has been comparatively unknown."[49]

Most sales were made to buyers who expected to ship the cotton to another market. Some of these buyers also were primarily speculators, hoping to resell and still realize a profit after transportation costs had been paid. Thus, for example, a buyer would purchase cotton from a Memphis factor and then order it shipped down the Mississippi to a New Orleans factor with instructions to seek out another buyer in the Southern port.[50]

Such buyer-speculators usually operated between Southern markets and those in the North or Europe. William C. Murray of Charleston, for instance, purchased cotton from factors in the South Carolina port and shipped it to merchants abroad to be resold, hoping that the proceeds less transportation, insurance, selling commissions, and other costs, would leave a profit.[51]

A buyer-speculator could utilize the possibilities of several of the world's cotton markets. He might make purchases in one of the Southern ports and then order the cotton sent to New York. If satisfied with prices offered there, he would order a sale. If not, he would have the cotton sent to one of the European markets. Since most of the cotton shipped to New York in this manner was later exported to Europe,[52] speculators in this trade developed a simpler method of shipment. The cotton was sent directly from the Southern ports to Europe, but samples taken from each bale went to New York. This method—called selling "in transit"—gave the speculator the option of selling out in New York (by sample) or of holding for a European sale, and it saved the extra expense of sending the cotton first to New York and then to Europe. First begun in the early 1850's, "in transit" sales by 1858 came to some two hundred thousand bales per year in New York. Buyers in New Orleans and Mobile were the largest users of this method, but merchants in Charleston, Savannah, and other ports also took advantage of it.[53]

Many buyers were not themselves speculators but were buying on orders from others. Northern and European merchants and manufacturers would order a quantity of cotton purchased for them, often stipulating a maximum price and a certain grade. Buyers, working on a commission for their services, would bargain with factors in an attempt to fill the order at the limits set. Available evidence seems to indicate that these buyers sometimes speculated as well; that is, they bought and shipped cotton on their own as well as on other's account. The Savannah firm of Cohen and Fosdick, for example, bought cotton on order for a Boston company, Coffin and Weld. The Northern concern resold the staple in Boston. Sometimes Cohen and Fosdick would merely fill the order as directed; at other times they shared the risk (and, hopefully, the profit) by investing some of their own funds in a shipment sent to the Boston merchants.[54] Godfrey Barnsley carried on a similar business as a buyer for English merchants and cotton spinners. He bought large lots of cotton from local factors, sorted the bales according to the quality ordered, and then shipped the staple to the various British firms as instructed. He also bought cotton on his own account; he never resold it in Savannah but consigned it for sale in England.[55] Advertisements and "Business Cards" in newspapers and directories indicate that large numbers of firms in the South were engaged in this "buying on foreign account."

Through his factor, then, the cotton planter could deal with buyers of every description in an intricate worldwide marketing system. His factor supplied him with information and advice concerning the sale of his crop, or, as was so often the case, took the whole responsibility for selling his cotton. But this was only a part of the factor's responsibilities. The planter usually turned to his factor for aid long before he had any cotton to sell.

Notes

1. Lewis Cecil Gray, *History of Agriculture in the Southern United States to 1860* (Washington, D.C., 1933), II, 711, 714; Ulrich B. Phillips, *Life and Labor in the Old South* (Boston, 1929), 141–42. If he chose, a planter might sell his crop to a storekeeper in the local village or to speculators who came to the plantation.

2. Gray, *History of Agriculture*, II, 711.

3. Frances Anne Kemble, *Journal of a Residence on a Georgia Plantation in 1838–1839*, ed. John A. Scott (New York, 1961), 202.

4. Mack Swearingen, "Thirty Years of a Mississippi Plantation: Charles Whitmore of 'Montpelier,'" *Journal of Southern History*, I (May, 1935), 208.

5. Gray, *History of Agriculture*, II, 711; James H. Lanman, "The American Cotton Trade," *Hunt's Merchants' Magazine*, IV (March 1841), 221; [Joseph Holt Ingraham], *The Southwest. By a Yankee* (New York, 1835), II, 93; Charles S. Davis, *The Cotton Kingdom in Alabama* (Montgomery, 1939), 141; Edward Baines, Jr., *History of the Cotton Manufacture in Great Britain* (London, [1835]), 317, citing evidence of Mr. Gabriel Shaw of Thomas Wilson & Co., London, before Select Committee of the House of Commons on Trade, Manufactures, and Shipping, 1833; Norman Sydney Buck, *The Development of the Organization of Anglo-American Trade, 1800–1850* (New Haven, 1925), 91–93.

6. *Semi-Weekly Appeal* (Memphis), Jan. 24, 1845 in typescript MSS dated April 1962 in envelope marked "Biography: Goodwyn, William Adolphus," Goodwyn Institute Library, Memphis, Tenn.

7. *Tri-Weekly Flag & Advertiser* (Montgomery), Feb. 23, 1847, Nov. 4, 1848.

8. *New Orleans Price Current*, Aug. 13, 1836.

9. *Daily Alabama Journal* (Montgomery), Feb. 27, 1851.

10. *Daily Chronicle & Sentinel* (Augusta), Jan. 2, 1850.

11. *New Orleans Price Current*, Sept. 1, 1860.

12. Jackson, Todd & Co. to Leverich, Philadelphia, April 16, 1840, Charles P. Leverich Papers, Mississippi Department of Archives and History, Jackson, Miss.; Washington Jackson & Co. to Johnson, New Orleans, Jan. 23, 1844, William Johnson Papers, also in Mississippi Department of Archives and History.

13. I. Rae Habersham to Jones, New York, Oct. 19, Nov. 10, 1854, Feb. 16, 1856, Wm. Neyle Habersham to Jones, New York, March 31, 1856, George Noble Jones Papers, Georgia Historical Society, Savannah, Ga.

14. The *New Orleans Price Current*, for example, would regularly carry notices announcing the formation of "co-partnerships" with partners in New Orleans and New York. The same paper would carry advertisements of New Orleans firms offering to forward cotton to their "friends" in New York or Liverpool, or Havre, or London. Firm names of the various companies would often be similar. For example, on Dec. 10, 1859 Hewitt, Norton

& Co. (New Orleans) advertised that it would send cotton to be sold in Liverpool by James Hewitt & Co. or to New York, consigned to Hewitt & Co.

15. Ralph W. Hidy, *The House of Baring in American Trade and Finance* (Cambridge, Mass., 1949), 174–75, 185–86, 359, 363.

16. *William and James Brown and Company* v. *Thomas McGran*, 14 Peters (U.S.) 479 (1840); *Brown Shipley & Co.* v. *P. A. Clayton*, 12 Cobb (Ga.), 564 (1853); John Crosby Brown, *A Hundred Years of Merchant Banking* (New York, 1950), 255, and circular announcing the opening of the New York firm reprinted on 190–91.

17. In 1804 Andrew Jackson and his partner John Hutchings were dissatisfied with the price their New Orleans factors, Boggs, Davidson & Co., were able to get for cotton in the Crescent City and they instructed the Southern firm to send the cotton to Liverpool for sale. The New Orleans firm quickly complied. N. Davidson to Jackson, New Orleans, July 14, 1804, Jackson and Hutchings to Boggs, Davidson & Co., Hunters Hill, Tenn., July 31, 1804, in John Spencer Bassett (ed.), *Correspondence of Andrew Jackson* (Washington, D.C., 1926), I, 96–98, 99–101.

18. In June and July of 1841 many factors in New Orleans were still holding cotton from the previous summer's crop, reluctant to take the prices the local buyers were offering. Rather than reduce their prices, the city's commercial journal reported, the factors "have commenced shipping their stocks to Liverpool and Havre." *New Orleans Price Current*, June 19, June 26, July 10, 1841.

19. "We are ourselves opposed to shipping any produce out of this market," wrote a New Orleans merchant to a planter, "having found it, by experience and an insight into the transactions of others, in nine times out of ten the best spot for the planter." The factor warned that great losses had been sustained by those who did ship to the North or to Europe but hastened to add that if so directed he would send cotton to New York for sale. John Hagan & Co. to Hamilton, New Orleans, May 7, 1829, W. S. Hamilton Papers, Southern Historical Collection, University of North Carolina Library, Chapel Hill, N.C.

20. See letters during the first seven months of 1859 to Heard & Simpson from A. Gardelle in Charleston, J. E. Clemm in Baltimore, and Isaac Low & Co. in Liverpool. Gardelle mentioned shipments to New York but there is no indication as to which firm received the cotton there. Stephen D. Heard Papers, Southern Historical Collection, University of North Carolina Library, Chapel Hill, N.C. In a single year a planter might sell his crop in more than one market. For example, Coffin & Pringle, cotton factors of Charleston, sold part of John Fripp's 1856 crop in Charleston and part the firm shipped on to Liverpool for sale. A/c current. Fripp with Coffin & Pringle, Charleston, June 10, 1857, John Edwin Fripp Papers, Southern Historical Collection, University of North Carolina Library, Chapel Hill, N.C.

21. For figures showing high and low prices paid in various markets for various grades of cotton during the antebellum period see E. J. Donnell, *History of Cotton* (New York, 1872), *passim*. Cf. figures given in James E. Boyle, *Cotton and the New Orleans Cotton Exchange* (Garden City, N.Y., 1934), 155, 176–80. Each issue of the commercial journals carried information on prices and sales since the last issue and each year at the start of the marketing season (Sept. 1) an "Annual Statement" would summarize the trends for the previous year.

22. The *Price Currents* published in the port cities printed abridged editions of their paper, reduced in size and available in bulk orders. They also printed letter sheets, a folded page on one side of which was reprinted information from the latest edition, the other side left blank for the merchant's letter. Almost every collection of planter's papers contains such reprinted or letter sheets.

23. For example of such letters and circulars see Reynolds, Byrne & Co. to Walker, New Orleans, Sept. 20, 1830, Oct. 16, 1830, Sept. 25, 1831, Zachariah Walker Papers, Mississippi Department of Archives and History, Jackson, Miss.; Gribble & Montgomery's "Annual Circular," dated New Orleans, Aug. 16, 1848 in Eli J. Capell and Family Papers, Meritt M. Shilg Memorial Collection, Department of Archives and Manuscripts, Louisiana State University, Baton Rouge, La. Almost every collection of planters' papers contain such letters.

Factors provided information to the planters; they usually did not solicit it. On one occasion, however, the planter did have better information than his factor. Maunsel White wrote to Andrew Jackson (Jan. 29, 1831) that the trend in cotton prices would depend on whether there would be war in Europe. "On this subject however, you Must be better advised than any one else in these states, and if it were not asking too much, or what might be improper for me to ask, I would ask yr opinion on that subject." Bassett, *Correspondence of Andrew Jackson*, IV, 228.

24. John Hagan & Co. to Hamilton, New Orleans, Aug. 24, 1827, W. S. Hamilton Papers.

25. To Johnson, New Orleans, Aug. 19, 1833, William Johnson Papers. As will be shown, factors did not always advise an immediate sale once the cotton was in their hands. Preseason advice that an early sale would be best was common, probably because the factors wanted the planters to hurry the cotton to them.

26. B. W. Heard to Heard & Simpson, Redmont, Ga., Jan. 14, 1859, Stephen D. Heard Papers.

27. Letters dated Washington, Miss., Dec. 3, Dec. 16, 1846, Jan. 8, Jan. 25, March 18, March 31, April 7, 1847, James W. Monette Papers, Mississippi Department of Archives and History, Jackson, Miss.

28. John B. Bull to Stoval & Simmons, Willington, S.C., Jan. 22, 1838, Bull-Morrow Papers, Georgia Historical Society, Savannah, Ga.

29. W. Newton Mercer to Leverich, Laurel Hill [near Natchez, Miss.], June 20 [1840], Charles P. Leverich Papers. Even James Monette, who kept his factors under such close instructions in 1846–1847, gave his factors more leeway in 1848—perhaps because of his own lack of success earlier. He instructed them in mid-September "to make the best disposition" they could. "If you think speedy sales best—select your own time." To Buckner & Stanton, Washington, Miss., Sept. 16, 1848, James W. Monette Papers. See also *ibid.*, Oct. 17, 1848.

30. To Simpson & Heard, Montevideo, Dec. 6, 1858, Stephen D. Heard Papers.

31. Most collections of planters' papers contain such letters. A convenient source illustrating the general procedure are letters from factors who sold cotton from Mrs. James K. Polk's plantation published in John Spencer Bassett, *The Southern Plantation Overseer as*

Revealed in His Letters (Northampton, Mass., 1925). See esp. Pickett, Perkins & Co. to Mrs. Polk, New Orleans, Jan. 3, 1850 (p. 229), Jan. 5, 1852 (pp. 231–32), Pickett, Macmurdo & Co. to Mrs. Polk, New Orleans, March 1, 1854 (pp. 237–38), W. S. Pickett to Mrs. Polk, New Orleans, June 23, 1854 (p. 239).

Price was not the only item determining when a sale would be made. If the planter needed ready cash to pay a debt or to make a purchase, or if the factor was unable to continue carrying a previously incurred debt, it was necessary to make a sale at an early date to meet these needs. . . .

32. To Walker, New Orleans, April 9, 1829, Zachariah Walker Papers.

33. Dicks, Booker & Co. to Hamilton, New Orleans, May 16, 1823, W. S. Hamilton Papers. See also *Ward et al.* v. *Warfield et al.*, 3 Robinson (La.) 468 (1848).

34. Gribble & Montgomery's "Annual Circular," New Orleans, Aug. 16, 1848, Eli J. Capell and Family Papers.

35. To Walker, New Orleans, Jan. 29, 1828, Zachariah Walker Papers.

36. James Monette, directing his factor's actions in 1847 very closely, insisted that his better cotton be sold separately from the inferior grades and dictated the minimum price he would accept for each lot. To Buckner & Stanton, Washington, Miss., Jan. 8, 1847, James W. Monette Papers. Another Mississippi planter, while giving his New York factor free rein to make the best sale nevertheless urged the merchant to sell his cotton in small lots to insure high prices. W. Newton Mercer to Leverich, Laurel Hill, Feb. 7, 1840, Charles P. Leverich Papers.

37. C. Toledano, *Appeal to the Public* ([New Orleans, 1851]), 1.

38. *New Orleans Price Current*, Dec. 10, 1836.

39. *Hunt's Merchants' Magazine*, XLII (1860), 105–106.

40. Toledano, *Appeal to the Public*, 1.

41. For examples of such accounts see Washington, Jackson & Co. to Capell, New Orleans, Dec. 16, 1841, Jenkins & Bonner to Capell, New Orleans, Dec. 31, 1841, Sales by Gribble & Montgomery for Capell, Eli J. Capell and Family Papers.

42. *Ward et al.* v. *Warfield et al.*, 3 Robinson (La.), 468 (1848).

43. Buckner, Stanton & Newman v. Delany, Rice & Co., as reported in *Hunt's Merchants' Magazine*, XLIII (1860), 322.

44. A Charleston factor, for example, sold both cotton and rice for the South Carolina planter James Gregorie in 1858. John Colcock to Gregorie, Charleston, May 21, 1858, Gregorie-Elliott Papers, Southern Historical Collection, University of North Carolina Library, Chapel Hill, N.C. Another Charleston factor sold "ground nuts" for one of his customers. See a/c sales on a/c of Mrs. A. Lovell by A. W. Campbell, Charleston, May 1, 1834, Langdon Cheves Collection, South Carolina Historical Society, Charleston, S. C. This sale of 133½ bushels of nuts (along with the sale of 55 bales of cotton) was probably an accommodation rather than a regular practice. Other accounts with Campbell in this collection, at least, show no other sales than cotton.

45. For material dealing with sugar factorage see J. Carlyle Sitterson, "Financing and Marketing the Sugar Crop of the Old South," *Journal of Southern History*, X (Mary 1944), 188–99; Wendell Holmes Stephenson, *Alexander Porter, Whig Politician of Old*

Louisiana (Baton Rouge, 1934), *passim*. Information on rice factorage may be found in J. H. Easterby, *The South Carolina Rice Plantation* (Chicago, 1945), 357–439 in the same author's "The South Carolina Rice Factor as Revealed in the Papers of Robert F. W. Allston" *Journal of Southern History*, VII (May 1941), 160–72.

46. Gardelle to Heard & Simpson, Charleston, March 25, 1859, Stephen D. Heard Papers.

47. *Rambles and Scrambles in North and South America* (London, 1852), 217–18.

48. *New Orleans Price Current*, Sept. 2, 1844.

49. *Ibid.*, Sept. 1, 1848. The extent of speculation at any given time can be accurately gauged by reading the reports on the state of the cotton market published in each edition of the commercial newspapers in each port city. In their "Annual Statements" the amount of speculation during the year under review as well as when it was most prevalent were carefully reported.

50. *The Farmers and Merchants Bank of Memphis* v. *Franklin et al.*, 1 Robinson (La.), 393 (1846).

51. L. Trapmann to Murray, Charleston, Jan. 21, 1839, April 22, 1839, May 28, 1839, June 1, 1839, Bacot-Huger Collection. Murray sold cotton in Liverpool, Antwerp, and Havre. In some of these transactions—many of them very large, involving hundreds of bales—Murray had partners, once including the captain of the ship on which the cotton was sent.

52. Even as late as the 1850's only about one bale in five grown in the United States was consumed in this country. James L. Watkins, *King Cotton* (New York, 1908), 30.

53. New York Chamber of Commerce, *Annual Report, 1858* (New York, 1859), pp. 13–14; Henry Hentz, "Reminiscences of the Cotton Trade of Old," *New York Times*, Dec. 29, 1890, as reprinted in *Cotton and Finance* (New York), I (Nov. 30, 1912), 396.

54. The course of business between these two firms can be followed in the letters from Cohen & Fosdick to Coffin & Weld during 1844, 1848, 1849, 1850, and 1851, Cohen & Fosdick Papers, Georgia Historical Society, Savannah, Ga.

55. "Barnsley v. MacLellan, Copy Correspondence," Godfrey Barnsley Papers, Emory University Library, Atlanta, Ga. Cotton could replace cash as a means to remit funds abroad. Thus the New York hardware merchants Phelps Dodge & Co. instructed Southern merchants who had been selling their goods to use the proceeds to buy cotton. This cotton was shipped to the Liverpool firm of Phelps James & Co. and sold. The proceeds were then invested in metal products for export to the parent firm. Richard Lewitt, *A Merchant Prince of the Nineteenth Century: William E. Dodge* (New York, 1954), 40–54.

Lewis C. Gray

LOCAL MARKET ORGANIZATION AND METHODS

After the beginning of commercial production the existing marketing organization for the older staples was employed for a time. Rice and indigo factors of the South Carolina coast and tobacco merchants of North Carolina and Virginia purchased the crop outright or consigned it to correspondents in Great Britain.[1] In time the factor became a specialist in the marketing of cotton. He was usually located in one of the great export towns, such as Charleston, Savannah, Mobile, and New Orleans.

By far the greater proportion of Southern cotton moved through those four ports, and they were the centers of greatest activity in the buying and selling of cotton. In 1851 Mobile boasted 42 fireproof brick warehouses, capable of storing 310,000 bales, and 12 compresses, with a capacity of 7,000 bales a day.[2] A little cotton was hauled from the back country of the southeastern States to Virginia and Pennsylvania markets, and some Tennessee cotton went up the Ohio river and through New York and Pennsylvania canals to interior factories, and also to Philadelphia and New York. A good deal of cotton was shipped from Memphis up river to Louisville and Cincinnati. Between 1853 and 1856 cotton received overland by New York, Baltimore, and Philadelphia averaged 10,000 to 14,000 bales a year.[3]

Lewis C. Gray, *History of Agriculture in the Southern United States to 1860* (Washington, D.C.: Carnegie Institute, 1933). Reprint edition, Gloucester, Mass.: Peter Smith, 1958, pp. 711–714.

The greater part of the Southern crop produced on plantations was shipped to the ports on consignment to factors, who sold it for the customary commission of 2.5 per cent. Small farmers had to do business with local merchants who made advances on the crop. The buying function came to be carried on largely by brokers in the port cities, who acted in the interest of foreign dealers and manufacturers. As in the case of the older staples, the cotton factor maintained with respect to the planter the joint relationship of commission merchant and banker, selling his cotton and crediting the proceeds to an account which was frequently overdrawn for the purchase of slaves and other commodities. Nor infrequently the factor served as a purchasing agent in obtaining various kinds of commodities needed by the planter, for which a second commission of 2.5 per cent was charged. A few planters maintained the older custom of consigning the product direct to Liverpool or New York.[4] Factors were sometimes tempted to act in the double role of seller and buyer of cotton. An article published in 1858 complained:[5]

> As it is strongly suspected that many cotton *Factors* are also cotton *Speculators*, having interests directly opposed to the interests of the planters and interior shippers, it behooves the latter to scan with a suspicious eye, the singular and improbable statements and estimates of the supply of cotton, put forth by the former.

. . . in the Cotton Belt the factor became the most important immediate source of credit advances. The colonial practice of the factor importing and dealing in slaves and selling slaves on credit had been largely discontinued, and the internal trade was too disreputable for this highly respectable class to engage in. The factors merely loaned money to planters to purchase from slave dealers. The latter also sold slaves on credit to purchasers, and sometimes advanced money on slaves. The greater part of the goods advanced and money loaned by factors was informally secured by the crops, although the crop lien system was not fully developed until after the Civil War. Planters were allowed to draw bills of exchange on security of their crops, which were sometimes discounted at banks, on acceptance by the factors, usually at a commission of 2.5 per cent besides interest, but often higher.[6] Factors charged interest varying from 8 to 12 per cent, sometimes on the face of the loan, sometimes on money actually received by the planter. Charges were often much higher, particularly in the earlier years of rapid expansion. In 1824 it was stated that Louisiana planters were paying from 10 to 30 per cent for "indulgence." Planters were urging the legislature to provide "cheap money," a measure which the merchants were strongly opposing.[7]

In addition to the formal charges of interest and commissions there was a much larger element of interest charges in the form of credit prices for goods purchased which were higher than cash prices.[8] The exclusive right to sell the planter's crop was made the condition on which the factor furnished credit. The planter's absolute dependence was intensified by the penalty commission clause of the factorage contract, whereby the planter not only agreed to consign his entire crop to the factor, but also guaranteed that the crop would not fall below a certain number of bales under penalty of paying the commission on each bale of the shortage. This bound the planter still more strongly to the one-crop system.

In addition to commissions and interest on advances, there were various charges incident to the shipment and handling of the cotton crop, such as for freight, storage, insurance, drayage, weighing, sampling, and repairing bales. The factor was supposed to charge merely at cost for these services, but in time the various charges became fixed by custom, and factors often made handsome incomes from them.[9]

Naturally this system of marketing was unfavorable to the development of interior concentration markets, and there was not a great deal of progress in that direction until after the Civil War. Even before the coming of the railways, however, cotton produced in areas above the fall line tended to be sold at towns located at the head of navigation, such as Fayetteville, Columbia, Augusta, Milledgeville, Macon, Columbus, Montgomery, Shreveport, and Nashville.[10] Memphis became the most important interior market. For the year ending August 31, 1860, its shipments amounted to 391,918 bales.[11] The building of railways stimulated the growth of the interior cotton business at these and other points. The development of interior banks was having a similar tendency. To some extent they broke the dependence of planters on port factors. Nevertheless some of the business at the interior markets was carried on by factors. Disastrous periods like the panic of 1837 forced interior banks themselves to engage more or less in the cotton business in order to protect themselves. About 1839 banks in interior towns of Alabama and Mississippi had become the principal purchasers or shippers of cotton, displacing the merchants in large measure.[12]

Cotton factors sometimes bought on their own account or as agents for others, but in the later years of the antebellum period it is probable that the bulk of the purchases were made from factors as agents for the planters by resident purchasing agents representing American and British firms, who were sometimes merchants and sometimes manufacturers.[13]

Table 4-1. Acreage, supply and price per pound of cotton, United States, 1820–1879

Year beginning August 1	Acreage	Production	Exports	Price
	1,000 acres	1,000 bales*	1,000 bales*	Cents
1820		335	250	14.9
1821		377	289	14.7
1822		439	347	11.2
1823		387	287	14.7
1824		450	353	17.9
1825		533	409	13.4
1826		732	589	10.2
1827		565	421	10.3
1828		680	530	9.9
1829		764	597	9.7
1830		732	554	10.1
1831		805	644	9.1
1832		816	649	11.4
1833		931	769	13.1
1834		962	775	16.3
1835		1,062	847	16.7
1836		1,129	888	14.4
1837		1,428	1,192	10.0
1838		1,093	827	13.2
1839		1,634	1,488	9.4
1840		1,348	1,060	9.6
1841		1,398	1,169	8.1
1842		2,035	1,585	7.2
1843		1,750	1,327	7.8
1844		2,079	1,746	5.9
1845		1,806	1,095	7.8
1846		1,604	1,054	10.9
1847		2,128	1,629	8.5
1848		2,615	2,053	7.2
1849		1,975	1,271	12.0
1850		2,136	1,854	12.6
1851		2,799	2,186	9.3
1852		3,130	2,223	11.0
1853		2,766	1,976	11.0
1854		2,708	2,017	10.3
1855		3,221	2,703	10.3
1856		2,874	2,097	13.2
1857		3,012	2,237	12.5
1858		3,758	2,773	12.1

Year beginning August 1	Acreage	Production	Exports	Price
	1,000 acres	1,000 bales*	1,000 bales*	Cents
1859		4,310	3,535	11.3
1860		3,841	615	12.3
1861		4,491	10	28.2
1862		1,597	23	65.2
1863		449	24	91.2
1864		299	18	95.4
1865		2,094	1,301	44.3
1866	7,666	2,097	1,402	32.2
1867	7,864	2,520	1,408	24.5
1868	6,973	2,366	2,490	28.6
1869	7,751	3,011	1,980	25.3
1870	9,236	4,352	2,896	17.0
1871	8,285	2,974	1,851	21.9
1872	9,580	3,933	2,437	20.2
1873	10,998	4,168	2,706	17.3
1874	10,753	3,836	2,524	15.7
1875	11,348	4,631	3,003	13.1
1876	11,747	4,474	2,869	11.9
1877	12,606	4,773	3,198	11.8
1878	13,539	5,074	3,265	10.0
1879	14,474	5,756	3,711	12.1

*Bales of 500 pounds gross weight.

Notes

1. Stone, *Influence of the Factorage System on Southern Agriculture (South in the Building of the Nation*, V), 398–404.

2. Watkins, *King Cotton*, 148.

3. Proceedings of the Richmond Commercial Convention of 1851, quoted in *ibid.*, 259; Ellison, *Handbook of the Cotton Trade*, 23.

4. *Hunt's Merchants' Magazine*, IV, 221; *De Bow's Review*, XXV, 713; *Southern Cultivator*, VIII, 24; Du Bose, *William Lowndes Yancey*, 77; Abernethy, *Formative Period in Alabama*, 89.

5. *Farmer and Planter*, IX, 159.

6. Du Bose, *William Lowndes Yancey*, 78; *De Bow's Review*, VII, 412; XVIII, 359; XXIII, 375; XXV, 714; *Hunt's Merchants' Magazine*, IV, 224; Hammond, M. B., *Agricultural Credit and Crop Mortgages (South in the Building of the Nation*, V), 457–461; Stone, "Cotton Factorage System," in *American Historical Review*, XX, 561; Buck, *Anglo-American Trade, 1800–1850*, pp. 66–80.

7. *Louisiana Herald* (Alexandria), Mar. 3, 1824.
8. Moore, A. N., *History of Agricultural Credit*, Chap. II (Unpublished thesis).
9. Stone, "Cotton Factorage System," in *American Historical Review*, XX, 562.
10. Phillips, U. B., *Transportation in the Eastern Cotton Belt*, 6.
11. Donnell, *History of Cotton*, 493.
12. *Farmers' Register*, VI, 61; Buck, *Anglo-American Trade*, 1800–1850, p. 67.
13. Ibid., 80–93.

QUESTIONS FOR REVIEW AND DISCUSSION

1. Imagine that you are a cotton factor in New Orleans in 1848. Review the contacts, negotiations, and arrangements that you would have to make to purchase, acquire, and ship 70 bales of cotton from a planter along the Mississippi River near Baton Rouge to a cotton manufacturer in Boston. Indicate the price to be paid, total contract costs, shipping processes and arrangements, warehousing, consignment arrangements, and arrangements for financing and/or transferring funds.

2. Get together with several members of the class. Have two persons act as factors who are competing to purchase a planter's crop. The other members of the group should act as the planter, shipping agents, warehouse operators, insurance brokers, manufacturers' buyers, and bankers. The factors should complete oral negotiations, which are agreed to in writing, with each of these persons. The class then should evaluate each of these persons' costs and profits, including those of the factors.

3. What were the alternative methods to using a factor by which planters might dispose of their cotton crops? Examine the advantages and disadvantages of each method.

4. What situations seemed to give a resident factor an advantage over planters in the marketing of raw cotton?

5. What were both the advantages and the disadvantages for a New England textile manufacturer's representative purchasing raw cotton directly from a planter?

6. What impact did the Civil War have on the marketing and price of cotton? Explain why the entry of raw cotton into the northern markets in the United States and into international markets was possible during the Civil War?

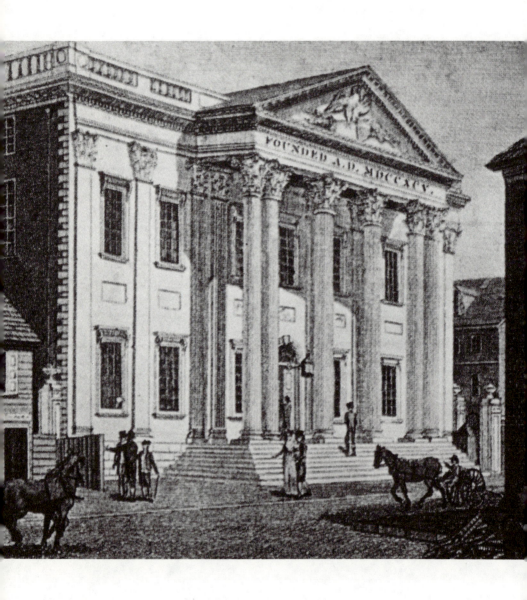

5

Banking

Before the Civil War, central, or national, banking was the function of the First Bank of the United States (1791–1811) and the Second Bank of the United States (1816–1836). During the existence of the First and Second banks, and after those times, banking services were provided by a variety of state-chartered banking institutions and by private individuals. The following case study by Larry Schweikart examines the entrepreneurial aspects of antebellum banking in the South by studying the careers of several southern bankers. Were there common career patterns or characteristics among these southern banking entrepreneurs? What were the incentives, opportunities, and challenges for a banking career in the Old South. It might be useful to read Schwiekart's case study in conjunction with the case studies on cotton marketing in Chapter 4. An understanding of the entrepreneurial aspects of antebellum banking also requires a review of the history of the First and Second banks of the United States.

The First and Second banks contributed significantly to the economic development of the United States during its critical growth period, 1790–1840, by attracting an estimated $300 to $500 million in foreign investments and by providing standards for domestic trade and commerce. After the demise of the Second Bank of the United States economic growth was even more rapid, which suggests that the bank might have been imposing excessive restraints on the monetary supply. State and private banking expanded rapidly after the national bank ceased operation in 1836.

The First Bank of the United States was chartered by Congress in 1791 for 20 years with a capital stock of $10 million—$2 million to be subscribed by the federal government, and the remainder to be held by private investors. The bank was to be the sole depository of federal funds and was authorized to issue bank notes (paper money) equal in face value to the amount of its stock. The notes were legal tender and redeemable in gold. During its existence the First Bank loaned the federal government $13.5 million, maintained a reasonably stable currency, and provided millions of dollars in capital to private interests.

Thomas Jefferson, in "Opinion Against the Constitutionality of a National Bank," argued that the loose construction of the Constitution, advocated by Alexander Hamilton in his defense of a national banking program, would impair the authority of the states, lead to the federal government's accumulation of unbridled power, and eliminate a check on the tyranny of a national majority. In large measure because of Jefferson's opposition to the First Bank, and to other of Hamilton's financial proposals, Jefferson resigned as secretary of state in 1793 to lead the Democratic-Republican party in opposition to Federalist programs. By the time of its expiration in 1811, however, the First Bank had won many supporters, even among Jeffersonians. The lack of a national bank during the critical years of the War of 1812 led to the creation of a Second Bank of the United States in 1816.

The Second Bank of the United States was given a 20-year charter that provided for $35 million in capital stock—$7 million to be subscribed by the federal government. The Second Bank was to be managed by 25 directors—20 were to be elected by the stockholders and 5 were to be appointed by the president of the United States. After some troublesome years in which it overissued paper currency and allowed excessive losses, the Second Bank soon reestablished stable fiscal policies in 1819 under the direction of Langdon Cheves, a respected South Carolina lawyer. Cheve's policies were too conservative for many stockholders and he was forced to resign. He was replaced in 1823 by Nicholas Biddle, a brilliant and strong-willed man.

Under Biddle the Second Bank expanded its (1) note issue from $3.5 million to $19 million, (2) domestic bills of exchange from $9 million to $49 million, and (3) profits to a regular dividend of 7 percent with comfortable surpluses. The Second Bank was at least in part fulfilling the role of supplying capital to an expanding economy. The Second Bank, however, created enmity among powerful interests. State and private banks chafed under the financial controls and sanctions of the national bank. The states protested the immunity of the branches of the Second Bank from state taxation and the impairment of state sovereignty that had been implied by the *McCulloch* v. *Maryland* decision in 1819. Some individuals, including President Andrew Jackson, believed that gold should be the only medium of exchange because bank notes tended to fluctuate in value.

In 1832 Congress approved a measure that would have extended the life of the Second Bank for 20 years, although the original charter did not expire until 1836. Jackson vetoed the measure and charged that the Second Bank was a monopoly that conferred special benefits and privileges on its stockholders. He said that it catered to sectional interests, was subject to foreign control, concentrated power in the hands of a few people in the United States, and abused its power.

Nicholas Biddle responded by drastically reducing credit and currency. Jackson countered by refusing to deposit federal money in the bank. When Biddle failed to frighten the government into approving a charter, he reversed his policies and flooded the country with easy credit and paper money. The ensuing speculative boom was halted when Jackson issued the Specie Circular, which required payment for public land in gold or silver.

The Second Bank was subsequently given a charter by the state of Pennsylvania but was forced into bankruptcy in 1841. National banking ended from that year until 1863, when The National Currency Act reimposed a degree of federal regulation on banking. The number of national banks that were chartered rose from 66 in 1863 to 2,076 by 1880. For the most part, however, until the approval of the Federal Reserve Act in 1913, banking remained the province of state-chartered institutions and of individual proprietors.

Larry Schweikart

ENTREPRENEURIAL ASPECTS OF ANTEBELLUM BANKING

It is often forgotten that bankers, like other businessmen, can be entrepreneurs. Of course, the tellers, clerks, and bookkeepers in a bank are no more entrepreneurs than are the machinists and supervisors in an ironworks (unless they themselves assume the risk of a business). However, the individuals who capitalized their own banks or who established mercantile businesses that eventually evolved into banks before the Civil War clearly captured the entrepreneural spirit.[1]

Most antebellum bankers learned their trade either by moving through the ranks at an established bank or in another business that developed or required skills similar to those found in banking. It is the latter group that is of interest here. These men (I have not identified a single woman engaged in antebellum banking) generally followed one of three approaches: (1) expanding an existing business to include lending and receiving of deposits in order to facilitate their mercantile trade; (2) entering banking in conjunction with another business— usually a railroad or other internal improvement project; or (3) entering a banking partnership as a natural adjunct to their procedures of making personal loans. Once involved in banking, however, these entrepreneurs found it either

The author gratefully acknowledges the Institute for Humane Studies, the Earhart Foundation, the Economic History Association, and the University of California, Santa Barbara, for grants that supported the research for this study.

more profitable or more enjoyable than their other businesses. Many became full-time bankers or, having proved their abilities on their own, accepted leadership positions at established banks.[2]

The American South in the antebellum period provides a unique case study in banking entrepreneurship because the South has often been viewed by historians as economically backward. But in fact the South had its share of bankers and en-trepreneurs. By reviewing the careers, problems, duties, and investment practices of these bankers, the entrepreneurial aspects of banking come into sharper focus and some similarities in the career patterns of these men become evident. While many traits were shared among these bankers, the least visible but most common trait was the "spirit of enterprise" that was identified by George Gilder.[3]

James Rhind of Savannah, Georgia, typified the independent southern banker-businessman. Rhind's records show that he was rejected for military ser-vice because of nearsightedness, that he smoked imported cigars, and that he read the *New York Home Journal*. He was not a man of exceptional means, as seen from his personal purchases at the general store over a nine-month period in 1849: numerous candles, jars of pickles, coffee, tea, pepper, soap, and party items, including "1 bunch cigars" and eight bottles of champagne. Rhind had been a cotton farmer for several years before beginning his banking business with a partner in Augusta under the name of Gardelle and Rhind. No doubt Rhind wanted to escape the fees that cotton factors demanded. Opening in addition his own agency in Savannah under the name of James Rhind & Company, he con-tinued Gardelle and Rhind until he split with Gardelle in 1848. At that point he returned to Augusta and engaged in banking.[4]

In 1853 Rhind made a career move that placed him at the cashiership of the prominent Bank of Augusta. Cashiers were not mere tellers; they usually ran the daily operations of the bank and stood, in authority, below only the president and directors. Nevertheless, a cashier had more direct responsibility for the bank's condition than did the president or the directors. Accordingly, with Rhind's ap-pointment came a warning from Arthur Rose, a friend and president of the Bank of Charleston, who implored, "Never let the sweetness of your disposition be ruf-fled by the thousand and one petty annoyances incidental to business."[5]

Traditionally, when one took a position as an officer of a bank, bonds or securi-ties were posted as a way for the bank to insure against criminal activity. Rose posted $5,000 worth of Rhind's bond—the limit to which "certain confidential en-gagements" would permit him to go. Besides the important friendship of Rose, Rhind had New York contacts who introduced him to Charles Forget, the nephew of "Mr. Melly of the highly respectable Melly Romilly & C of Liverpool[,] who visits our country with a view to extend the connexions [sic] of said firm."[6]

However exotic some of Rhind's acquaintances may have been, his professional activities remained those of all bankers—exchanging drafts, evaluating notes, and extending loans, all fairly boring business. When boredom was broken, it was not always a welcome change for it usually meant that a customer was upset. To refuse a draft risked implicating the "good name" of an individual who may have been prone to violence. Rhind once refused the drafts of John McFallows who then visited the banker demanding an explanation. The bank had refused McFallows's drafts because of "money due nearly 1 year ago, [and] upon the ground that you don't wish to cause undo [sic] engagements to pay money." McFallows challenged this reasoning as "an excuse . . . unworthy of you as a businessman, and one I am not disposed to allow." Admitting to having been "myself much embarrassed at times," McFallows claimed he never "afixed [sic] my signature to notes & debts when I owed money, especially when time was given." Rhind refused to relent, and McFallows withdrew "all propositions."[7]

Other farmers and planters also made the transition to banking. Nathan C. Munroe of Macon, Georgia, had also dabbled in factorage and had been involved in the Bank for Savings in Macon as early as 1835. In 1843 G. B. Earhart, the cashier of the Mechanics Bank of Augusta, asked Munroe to manage an agency that the bank planned to establish in Macon. Munroe accepted, after carefully limiting his liabilities, and was appointed to a six-month term as cashier. Several reappointments followed, continuing until 1850. In addition to his $150-a-month gross salary (from which he had to pay his assistant), he requested and received regular vacations. Munroe immediately set about establishing his office, instructing the Mechanics Bank to buy "books, stationery, fuel & [such]." He arranged for a temporary office with the Commercial Bank, a competitor in town.[8]

Although Rhind and Munroe followed career patterns that resembled those of many southern bankers, they were entrepreneurs for only part of their careers. Both Rhind and Munroe shifted to what might better be termed management at a certain point. As Rondo Cameron suggested, insofar as banks "are enterprises, bankers are entrepreneurs." Moreover, he argued, if "the entrepreneur is defined as the individual or individuals vested with decision-making authority . . . bankers are clearly entrepreneurs." Certainly Rhind and Munroe fit this definition, but for purists who prefer the definition of entrepreneur as one who takes the risk and, in essence, as one who owns the business, other bankers come to mind.[9]

Among those who began and ended their careers as true entrepreneurs, George Walton Williams and Edmond Jean Forstall represent two of the most famous and well chronicled. Williams established Williams and Company of Augusta, Georgia, which was a mercantile business with "some banking interests attached to [its] workings." Before long, Williams took a partner, New Yorker David Hand, and opened a second store, Hand and Williams Company, in

Charleston. Because the northerner Hand longed to return to New York, the partnership was dissolved in 1855, and Williams fell back on Williams and Company. According to his biographer, Williams had "a record as a financial genius and [was] a strong advocate for economy in city government." Charleston's leaders put him on the ways and means committee to make use of his abilities.[10]

When war erupted, Williams headed a special committee to oversee fee schedules on foreign vessels that entered Charleston harbor. A loyal Confederate, Williams was too old for the first Conscription Act and was exempted from the second because of his position in city government. His business continued to exist throughout the war, although it did not function after 1863—much of his labor force had gone into military service. During 1861, his company was ravaged by fire but recovered to do a healthy trade in 1862. From 1863 until the occupation of Charleston by Union forces, his business lay dormant. However, he had taken great pains to maintain his ties with northern commercial houses and those ties permitted him to build up credit in banks in Liverpool and in London. This credit, which provided the basis for Williams' postwar banking, reopened on June 1, 1865, as a separate division of the company.[11]

Meanwhile, Williams was already searching for opportunities under the new banking laws, especially the National Bank Act of 1864. He went to Washington to make the necessary arrangements, then to New York to obtain financing for a national bank in Charleston. Although he wished to be president of the new bank in Charleston, his friends convinced him to reopen George W. Williams and Company instead. Nevertheless, Williams was a driving force in establishing the First National Bank of Charleston and served as a director for many years.[12]

Even more famous than Williams was Edmond Jean Forstall who epitomized the southern merchant-banker-entrepreneur. Forstall, who grew up in a mercantile family, began associating with Gordon, Grant & Company, a New Orleans company that frequently advanced money to planters, and became a partner in the firm in 1823. After the Lizardi brothers, merchant-bankers from Paris, took over the company, Forstall remained the managing partner. In 1818 he became a director of the Louisiana State Bank, thus formalizing his already adequate training in banking still further.

Ironically, for all his acclaim as a banker, Forstall never devoted himself full time to banking. Instead, his other operations gave him blocks of free time in which he could concentrate on financial matters. Forstall was appointed and served a short time as comptroller of the Consolidated Association of the Planters of Louisiana, the first Louisiana property bank. He relied on his contacts with the famous Baring Brothers of London and persuaded that firm to purchase a large number of the Louisiana property bank's bonds. By 1830, however, his association with the Barings turned into a liability when forces within the property bank demanded his resignation on the grounds that he was an agent of foreign interests.[13]

Forstall immediately promoted a second property bank, the Union Bank of Louisiana, and prepared its charter based on that of the Consolidated Association of Planters. Within two years he had become involved in yet a third property bank, the Citizens Bank of Louisiana. That bank soon placed him on the board of directors and assigned him the task of negotiating the sale of bonds. He promptly persuaded the state to pledge its "faith and credit" to support the bonds and by 1836 was the bank's president.[14]

As president, Forstall kept tight reign on lending policies. This, combined with the fact that Forstall "routed the bank's foreign business, including further sales of bonds, . . . through his mercantile house," led a majority of the directors to oppose him. They soon forced him to resign, but Forstall returned to direct the liquidation of the bank's affairs in 1842. He then became an agent for both Hope and Company of Amsterdam and Baring Brothers of London, in which capacity he served until his death in 1873.[15]

The career pattern of Williams and Forstall was repeated by numerous bankers in the South. Thomas Branch of Richmond also entered banking through mercantile businesses—Thomas Branch and Brother; Thomas Branch and Sons; Branch, Sons, and Company; and others. Thomas Branch and Sons, which had been identified as a banking firm by 1853, had little difficulty during the Panic of 1857. Branch had a reputation for conservatism and stability that was enhanced by his honesty and willingness to send clients to other representatives. He advised one customer that "you could do better in New York than here." Throughout the 1850s, banking and brokerage took a back seat to Branch's mercantile business, which featured the "new fertilizing manure 'Pozzuolana' " and "genuine Peruvian Government Guano." Of course, Branch also stocked wheat, oats, cotton, bags, salt, mackerel, and other goods.[16]

Branch's sons made the major transition to banking after the Civil War. At that time, Thomas Branch and Sons's investments included real estate, securities, salt mining, public baths, and more than a dozen other subsidiaries. Formal banking procedures characterized the firm in 1871 when Thomas Branch founded the Merchants National Bank in Richmond.

A similar career pattern was followed by David N. Kennedy, who opened a dry goods store upon his arrival in Clarksville, Tennessee, in 1842. Two years later he was elected a director of the branch of the Bank of Tennessee located in Clarksville. Within a year, he parlayed the directorship into the presidency and in 1851 took the position of cashier for three years. Kennedy then left the state banking system to organize the Northern Bank of Tennessee. This bank survived the

Civil War thanks to Kennedy's daring action of loading the bank's gold into saddlebags and riding out of town as Federal troops occupied Clarksville. After arriving in New Orleans on a steamer, he sent the bank's assets to England. At the end of the war, he returned and reopened the bank. Kennedy, like Forstall, had a hand in improving antebellum banking practices. He overturned the endorser system, a system that discriminated against people who were good credit risks but lacked social contacts by granting a loan on the basis of an endorsement by a well-known individual. Kennedy made the sole requirement for obtaining a loan the ability to repay it.[17]

As Williams, Forstall, and Kennedy learned, merchant-bankers could encounter many kinds of troubles, from hostile borrowers to jealous directors to political enemies. In Tennessee, there may have existed legal barriers to merchants acting as bank directors. Henry Ewing, cashier of the main branch of the Bank of Tennessee, wrote to J. Currin of the Columbia branch that five of its recently elected directors were merchants, which, in the opinion of the state's attorney general, "is a legal disqualification and renders their appointment a nullity." Not all merchant-bankers succeeded to the degree that Kennedy, Williams, and Forstall did. Samuel McCorkle of Paris, Tennessee, worked as a surveyor and bill collector and, on the side, dealt in real estate. With the Chickasaw session in 1832, he jumped into land speculation with both feet. This activity led him to become involved in several land companies, which acted as banks for mortgages. Among these companies were the Pontotoc Land Company, the Hernando Railroad and Banking Company, and the Holly Springs Real Estate Banking Company. McCorkle became president of the latter company, as well as a partner in the New York and Mississippi Land Company.[18]

McCorkle's Holly Springs Real Estate Banking Company, an unchartered bank, issued notes based on the declared value of the land that was pledged as collateral, rather than on the purchase price or market value of the land. When the full impact of the Panic of 1837 was felt, McCorkle's real estate bank collapsed. Suits were undertaken against the officers, and McCorkle settled, apparently out of court, by paying from his private funds to cover bank debts. As president, McCorkle's responsibilities and liabilities were plainly understood.

Other entrepreneur-bankers understood their role less clearly. For example, George Gibbs opened and operated the Jacksonville, Florida, agency of the Planters Bank of Fairfield, South Carolina. As one of his duties, Gibbs had to keep and prepare the agency's books for inspection by the parent institution. Told that he was being held responsible for bad debts at the agency, Gibbs welcomed the president of the bank, J. R. Aitken, and "the lawyers you propose bringing with you." It should be mentioned that Nathan C. Munroe, at the Mechanics Bank, had carefully limited his liabilities apparently so as not to include bad debts,

admitting responsibility only for "such errors as may occur in the telling or counting or paying out the funds of the Agency." Gibbs offered to personally go to New
York to take possession of the stock put up for the debt, warning Aitken, "Unless
you take the stock offered, you will probably lose the debt." He also demanded
that Aitken pay for Gibbs to employ "*a reliable man* to keep my office open in my
absence, [and] supply him with funds to *continue the agency*."[19]

The case of George Gibbs represented the murky middle ground between entrepreneur and employee; surely, no Florida cashier would be expected on his
own to track down bank debts in New York. Another entrepreneur-banker who
encountered problems was W. E. Johnson. Was Johnson, a businessman and
planter from Camden, South Carolina, a banker or not? He extended substantial
personal loans to interior borrowers, using his accounts with the Charleston banking house of Conner and Company. Eventually, Johnson formally assumed a
banking role as the president of the Camden Bank, which thrust him into the position of making the major decisions on investment and credit. The bank had
invested in the Southern Rail Road Company of Vicksburg, Mississippi; but the
railroad's president, William Smedes, had also taken personal loans from
Johnson, owing him almost $8,000 by the outset of the Civil War. Smedes con-
stantly petitioned Johnson for more time—it was "absolutely impractical to raise
money here at any rate or upon any securities." Smedes reported the "strongest
mercantile houses have gone down," including those of his own factors. Johnson
rescheduled the payments at an interest rate of 10 percent a year, and Smedes
vowed "to pay every cent I owe in the world as soon as property once more has
value."[20]

The debtor soon forgot his obligations, at which point Johnson pressed Smedes,
accusing him of a "financial scheme" which he had "neither the time nor strength
to pursue." Smedes responded with an irrational discussion of the Confederate
constitution and of the inflationary crisis, on which he counted to raise the value of
slaves, whereby he could sell slaves and repay the debt. As if to draw a final ounce of
sympathy from Johnson, Smedes made reference to his poor health and to his eight
children. Such appeals were common. Another debtor lamented having "been
compelled to deny myself the common necessities of life for a long time." One
should not exaggerate the power of credit, not to mention the problems it fostered.
Joseph Baldwin, a contemporary observer, noted that during "flush times" credit
was a thing in abundance and "to refuse it . . . were an insult for which a bowie-
knife were not too summary or exemplary a means of redress."[21]

Panic conditions, conversely, placed a somewhat different strain on bankers.
Regaled in the legislatures, harassed in the newspapers, occasionally accosted on
the streets, and continually pressed to resume paying full-value specie (gold and

silver) for the banknotes they generated, the financiers did not enjoy their best moments during depressions. Land values plummeted, and with them went many entrepreneurs' collateral. Reports of financial disaster causing insanity may have been exaggerated, but it is likely that business failures contributed to the suicides of the Andrews brothers, one of whom was a banker in Mobile. Generally, however, the response to panic conditions by bankers was simply to ride them out, and, when possible, reorganize along more efficient lines.[22]

Because of the personal nature of lending, brokers, factors, and bankers operated somewhat interchangeably. Once formally involved in a bank, however, the entrepreneur devoted his attention to managerial aspects that separated the banker from the factor or broker. For example, the letters of the Springs family of South Carolina, which was associated with the Merchants Bank, reveal the concerns of those who bore the risk of the bank. In response to a request that he move to the branch in Charleston, Mr. H. Hutchinson agreed, "provided M. Blackwood would stay . . . here and be a little more exacting of the attention of those in the bank." On another occasion John Springs was apprised that "many stockholders . . . think it would be to [the best] interest of the Bank to ease out Mr. Blue and put in someone else." More than a few bankers failed to oversee their charges properly. The directors of the Union Bank of Florida permitted one of their number, John Shepard, to receive a loan to purchase land costing $54,000 with no down payment and 23 years to repay. Other evidence of incompetence or plain bad luck exists in abundance. But the worst embarrassment was reserved for the directors of the Fayetteville branch of the State Bank of Arkansas, who adopted a resolution of thanks to Onisemus Evans for his "fidelity and ability in the discharge of his duty as clerk" of the bank. Two weeks later at a meeting of the board of directors, the records showed a completely different appraisal of Evans—he "has failed in the discharge of his duties. . . . [I]n neglecting to write the books up in a correct and mercantile manner and whereas the said neglect [was] the cause of an increase of heavy expense to this bank. . . . "[23]

Actually, the personal contacts of the entrepreneurs cut both ways. Bankers held a place of moderate esteem in southern society, and certainly counting the local banker as a friend (or even counting on him to be a soft touch, as in the case of William Smedes) produced a number of visible, as well as intangible, benefits. However, bankers also made enemies, not all of which were associated with rejected loan applications. In that respect, Arkansas had more than its share of violence. On one occasion, John Wilson, president of the Real Estate Bank of Arkansas and speaker of the Arkansas house of representatives, provoked by an insult by antibank leader Joseph Anthony during a session of the house, charged down from his speaker's chair and, pulling a bowie knife, slashed to death his unfortunate critic. In another incident, a sale of collateral property at Helena by the State Bank precipitated an armed possession of the courthouse by a mob. Backed by a force of 50 deputies, the sheriff threatened to storm the building. A bloody situation was averted when the judge who was scheduled to auction the property withdrew. A similar episode developed in Tennessee, where banker Jeptha Fowlkes, surrounded in controversy, had taken possession of the Farmers' and Merchants' Bank of Memphis, along with other directors. The bank was floundering in legal troubles and debt. More than a few of the creditors disliked Fowlkes, and they persuaded a former director, General Levin Coe, to "rescue" the bank. Tempers grew heated as probank and antibank groups exchanged public threats. Some of Fowlkes's supporters ran into Coe and his friends outside the courtroom and a gun battle ensued. Bullets flew as Coe, who had fired three pistols already, could not unsnag the fourth one from his jacket, was hit, and died with a pistol ball in his spine.[24]

Fortunately for most bankers, daily activities proved far less violent or exciting than the escapades just described. After capitalizing a bank, the banker faced an endless series of decisions, such as the quality of paper, the availability of specie, and the wisdom of making a particular loan. Although usually the cashier oversaw the books and directed the internal procedures of the bank, frequently the president and/or directors became involved in decisions on notes. Cashiers frequently worked into the evening (John Ehringhaus, cashier of the Elizabeth City branch of the Bank of North Carolina, reported working until nine o'clock many evenings) and occasionally on Sunday.

Henry Ewing of the Bank of Tennessee system introduced a set of tight standards to be followed by all cashiers within the Bank of Tennessee system. He did not hesitate to reprimand a sloppy bookkeeper or cashier whose ledger-keeping habits diverged from his own. Satisfied that "any error [was] from mere inadvertence," Ewing carefully refrained from excessive criticism, assuring one cashier who made bookkeeping errors that Ewing himself was "as liable as others."

While most cashiers maintained efficient books and performed their duties honestly, more than a few ravaged the institutions for which they worked. Again, Arkansas seemed to have more than its share. William Ball, the cashier, had embezzled more that $46,000 from the State Bank of Arkansas before disappearing in Texas. The new board of directors so strongly suspected Ball of theft that it resolved to "employ such additional counsel as may be necessary to prosecute or bring suit on the Bond of the late cashier, Mr. Ball, in order to compel him to account for the several deficits that appear in his several reports."[25]

Still, even fairly reliable cashiers could become the target of personal or political attacks. Datum Orin Davis, of the Salisbury branch of the Bank of North Carolina, learned that his president and directors received several letters urging his removal. According to one critic, Davis was involved in "other pursuits,—namely, Note-shaving and loan dealing, buying, selling, and swapping horses—and, —*that these horse trades have been carried on mostly with a certain description of dealing in the bank.*" [Italics added.] The correspondent warned against "converting a banking house into a shaving shop," and "in making a Shylock and a 'horse jockey' of the cashier." These criticisms seem to be based more on the fact that Davis declined a loan than on actual facts: Davis remained the bank's cashier for some time.[26]

Wartime burdens only compounded the normal difficulties involved in banking. The letters of Theodore Honour provide a fascinating record of a banker during the latter stages of the Civil War. From March 1 to April 30, 1864, Honour's bank (the Bank of Charleston, Columbia branch) requested and received from the Confederate army a 60-day release from service for the cashier to return to Columbia and prepare the bank for a possible Federal invasion. During the war, both while in the service and while at the bank, Honour's salary was sufficient to meet the needs of his family, but he earned it, working late at night and dealing with constant boredom and ever-dwindling numbers of workers. Finding the burden heavy, Honour nevertheless reminded himself not to "grumble as I am under great obligations to the bank." When Honour was away, John Cheesborough, a cashier, efficiently filled in. Honour rejected Cheesborough's suggestion to relocate the bank out of Columbia and expressed resignation that "when my 60 days are out I shall have to go back to camp." During the Federal occupation of Charleston, Cheesborough effectively ran the bank. Indeed, the Honour and Cheesborough papers present a rare look at antebellum bankers in two distinctly different states of their careers: Honour, the established administrator, and Cheesborough, the ambitious cashier.[27]

If indeed a bank had an efficient, reliable cashier, the bank's directors would delegate the routine business to him, so they could concentrate on lending activities. The letterbooks of the Mobile branch of the Bank of Alabama, the Bank of Tennessee, and the Fayetteville branch of the Arkansas State Bank all reveal the inner workings of directors' meetings. Even though those banks were state institutions, the decision-making process was much the same in private banks. When making daily business decisions, bankers flew their entrepreneurial colors noticeably. A host of projects—in the South often dominated by agriculture—demanded bankers' attention and funds.

William Wright, of the Merchants Bank of South Carolina, in reporting the condition of his bank to John Springs, a friend and a director of the bank, noted, "We have not made any debt which we look upon as bad or doubtful." Springs also received regular reports from the cashier at the Bank of Hamburg. One recurring point of discussion, that of officers' salaries, marks one of the few recorded instances of directors voicing concern about the pay given employees. Different correspondents suggested to Springs that the officers accept a cut in pay to keep the bank solvent. One correspondent argued that salaries were "too high for so small a concern & . . . should be reduced." The officers could afford a reduction in pay, it was reasoned, because of the "cheapness of living." One employee tried to suggest he earned every cent by noting, "I have avoided the streets and confined myself to *Banks*."[28]

As entrepreneurs, bankers invested in a variety of projects and companies, including a number of railroad companies, that profited by the steady flow of funds produced by association with a bank. The Georgia Railroad and Banking Company, the Southwestern Railroad Bank of South Carolina, and others established just such a relationship. Some banks provided direct loans, such as the Decatur branch of the Bank of Alabama, which loaned more than $500,000 to the Tuscumbia, Cortland, and Decatur Railroad Company. However, railroad projects were scrutinized as closely as any other investment. Charles Mills, cashier of the Marine Bank of Georgia, received a loan request in 1855 from W. E. Danell of the Atchafalaya Rail Road Company in Louisiana. Mills explained that the bank was not "desirous of doing local business, particularly at long term." Still, banks financed more than a few railroads—the Bank of Pensacola supported the Alabama, Georgia, and Florida Railroad Company, and three railroad banks sprang up in Mississippi. Six Louisiana banks channeled almost $900,000 into railroad banks or into companies that serviced railroads and canals but lacked banking privileges. James Robb, and influential New Orleans banker, constantly campaigned for more investments in railroads.[29]

In addition to investing in railroads, bankers channeled money into a variety of improvement banks, including canal banks, gas company banks, and even a hotel bank. John Caldwell, for example, launched a promising enterprise, the New Orleans Gas Light and Banking Company, that nevertheless fell on hard times when the state placed a series of demands on its capital. A number of industrial and manufacturing companies also received credit, but industrial investments proved quite risky. For example, the Nesbitt Manufacturing Company of South Carolina became involved in a scandal, and a South Carolina commission house lost $9,000 in an ironworks that failed. In some cases, state laws required state-chartered banks to support certain projects such as schools.

Agriculture, however, remained the major recipient of credit from southern bankers. Most southern bankers did not evolve into large-scale finance capitalists as northern bankers did because the Civil War imposed huge losses on the South and the role of agriculture remained important in southern society. While some estimates of southern industry suggest that it may have been extremely profitable, some of these profits doubtless reflected the monopolistic conditions that arose from the relative isolation of markets in the South. What also affected these high profits without a corresponding flood of investment capital was the social accept-ability of financing slave-based plantation agriculture, an effect that is difficult to measure but that nonetheless existed.[30]

Southern bankers came from all walks of life and entered banking for a variety of reasons. Few inherited banking from their families. One exception was Theodore Honour, whose banking reputation probably was exceeded only by that of his father, John Henry Honour. Many bankers who began with mercantile businesses needed the flexibility of credit that banking provided. Planters, often tired of working with factors or other credit agents, found refuge by starting their own banks. Local citizens from a variety of professions found themselves on bank boards and then developed an interest in banking. Railroad builders and internal-improvement companies quickly came to appreciate the benefits of a steady cash flow that banks could provide. Coming from such diverse backgrounds, with such disparate interests, southern entrepreneur-bankers resist generalizations. Cer-tainly, they do not fall into a "class" in the traditional economic or social meaning of the term. Instead, these bankers adopted attitudes towards a commercialized and capitalistic economy that separated them from the "planter mentality" that was identified by Eugene Genovese. One specialized state study, that of Alabama by J. Mills Thornton III, identified increasing tensions between planters and bankers over the nature of the economy. Thornton noted that the planters re-coiled from the capitalistic commercial world that threatened to engulf their own agrarian culture and that, if anything, bankers constituted one segment of the new alien society. Rather than, as Genovese maintained, bankers being controlled by planters, the planters saw themselves falling under the control of a national com-mercial economy in which bankers represented a highly visible group.[31]

Southern bankers often passed through several changes in their careers—from laborer, to manager, to owner. Occasionally, as in the case of Nathan Munroe, a man might be both a bank manager and an entrepreneur in his own agricultural business. Banking permitted extensive flexibility between occupations, as well as upward mobility within the banking profession itself. This extensive mobility gradually began to diminish as the Civil War approached and as bank owners rec-ognized the need for professional, trained management. But such management was an efficiency required only of large, established banks; entrepreneurs still could and did have an impact on the economy. New banks filled a demand for credit. While perhaps greater efficiencies could have been wrung out of the oper-ations, demand usually proved sufficient to encourage the establishment of more banks. In states such as Arkansas, where the law prohibited state-chartered bank-ing after the collapse of the Real Estate Bank, a number of private unchartered bankers conducted business until after the Civil War. Indeed, in Texas, Arkansas, Florida, Mississippi, and to an extent in Missouri, private unincorporated bankers became the major source of local capital. This development was paralleled in northern states such as Wisconsin.[32]

Whenever a businessman had a mercantile business, it usually constituted the capital backing for a newly formed bank until the legislature granted a charter and a formal stock sale took place. In cases where planters capitalized a bank, occasionally they could use the property bank structure—that is, pledging their mortgages for the bank's capital. More typically, planters such as William Johnson, William Godfrey of South Carolina, and James Rhind began private lending and then moved into established banking, or at least into more formalized financial procedures. Yet it is clear from the evidence that these individuals differed considerably from factors. Often the two groups were antagonistic. Quite naturally, when the State Bank of Alabama embarked on a course of cotton factorage after the Panic of 1837, the Alabama factors voiced the greatest opposition.[33]

Movement by entrepreneurs *from* banking into other business operations occurred, but with less frequency than movement by entrepreneurs *into* banking. Bankers became railroaders, manufacturers, and industrialists whenever the combined social and economic climate permitted. Only in this respect did southern bankers differ from their northern counterparts. Whereas the latter sailed smoothly downriver with capitalistic currents, the former had to paddle upstream against the current of the planter mentality. Overcoming this obstacle to some extent, southern bankers performed vital services in a region that frequently distrusted banks and often struggled to balance the antinomic ends of sound money and easy credit. By 1860 in seven of the ten southern states (Texas is excluded), solid and healthy banking systems existed as evidence that the region's entrepreneurs had achieved some degree of success.[34]

Bankers in the South had traveled different paths to arrive at the level of commercial and capitalistic development that had long been a part of the North's economy. Had they survived for another generation without the disruption of the Civil War, the antebellum entrepreneur-bankers might have had as great an impact on southern politics as they had on the southern economy. On the eve of the Civil War, the entrepreneurial spirit was clearly at work in finance and banking in the South, as well as in the North. Contrary to popular belief, however, southern legislative tendencies often impeded laissez-faire and prohibited even greater entrepreneurial activity. The South, which had seen the Jacksonians dominate many of its states' governments, inherited a distrust of banks and corporations. In this perspective, the accomplishment of bringing the South's financial houses onto a plane where they were growing annually as rapidly as those of the North suggests that southern antebellum bankers deserve to be ranked with America's best.[35]

Notes

1. The best discussion of "the entrepreneural spirit" appears in George Gilder, *The Spirit of Enterprise* (New York: Simon and Schuster, 1984).

2. Some of this material appears in Larry Schweikart, "Banking in the American South, 1836–65" (Ph.D. dissertation, University of California, Santa Barbara, 1983).

3. The North also had an abundance of banker-entrepreneurs. For a case study, see Alice Smith, *George Smith's Money: A Scottish Investor in America* (Madison: State Historical Society of Wisconsin, 1966); for a broader picture, consult Fritz Redlich, *The Molding of American Banking: Men and Ideas*, 2 vols. (New York: Johnson Reprint Corp., 1966 [1947–1951]).

4. List of items purchased from G. T. and Ben Dooley, April–December, 1849, Rhind-Stokes Collection, MS 1305, box 1, folder 9, University of Georgia Library [UG]. Rhind's biographical information also appears in the collection.

5. Arthur G. Rose to James Rhind, May 30, 1854, MS 1305, box 1, folder 6, and James Rhind to Arthur Rose, June 6, 1853, MS 1305, box 1, folder 5, all in UG.

6. Arthur G. Rose to James Rhind, May 30, 1854, MS 1305, box 1, folder 6, and James Rhind to Arthur Rose, June 6, 1853, MS 1305, box 1, folder 5, all in UG. For laws regarding the bonding of officers, see John Loomis to William Wright, December 11, 1841, Adelaide Mears Collection, Duke University [DU].

7. John McFallows to James Rhind, April 11, 1853, MS 1305, box 1, folder 5, UG.

8. Nathan C. Munroe to G. B. Earhart, Oct. 17, 1843, memorandum and letter of appointment, Oct. 25, 1843, and memorandum, July 10, 1844, all in Macon, Ga., Banking, MS 1450, UG.

9. Rondo Cameron, "The Banker as Entrepreneur," *Explorations in Economic History*, Fall 1963, 50–55.

10. Merton Coulter, *George Walton Williams* (Athens, Ga.: Hibriten Press, 1976), 23, 31, 34, 39, 43, 46, 163.

11. Ibid., 64–65, 68, 71, 163–65.

12. Ibid.,164–65.

13. Irene Neu, "Edmond Jean Forstall and Louisiana Banking," *Explorations in Economic History*, Summer 1970, 383–398.

14. Ibid., 386–387. Also see Irene Neu, "J. B. Moussier and the Property Banks of Louisiana," *Business History Review* 35 (1961): 550–57.

15. Neu, "Edmond Jean Forstall," 389.

16. James Branch Cabell, *Branchiana, Being a Partial Account of the Branch Family in Virginia* (Richmond: Whittet & Shepperson, 1907), 51–68; Thomas Branch to L. L. Masters, to Thomas Bass, both Nov. 30, 1850, in Branch Letterbook, 1850, Thomas Branch Collection, Virginia Historical Society [VHS].

17. *The Northern Bank of Tennessee*, 1954, pamphlet in Tennessee Library & Archives [TLA].

18. Henry Ewing to J. Currin, June 14, 1839, Bank of Tennessee Letterbook, 1839–

41, record Group 47, series 5, vols. 15 and 16, TLA; Biographical Sketch, Samuel McCorkle Papers, Mississippi Department of Archives and History [MDAH].

19. For the problems of the Holly Springs Real Estate Banking Company, see *Edward Boisgerard and John Delafield* v. *Samuel Neill*, case #2650, 1842, and *Edward Boisgerard and John Delafield* v. *Abram McWillie*, case #2654, 1844, both in Drawer 50, MDAH; material on Gibbs appears in George Gibbs to J. R. Aitken, March 19, 1855, University of Florida Library; Nathan C. Munroe to G. B. Earhart, Oct. 17, 1843, MS 1450, UG.

20. William C. Smedes to W. E. Johnson, Dec. 15, 1860, Feb. 20 and Oct. 5, 1861, Johnson Papers, South Caroliniana Library [SC].

21. William C. Smedes to W. E. Johnson, Dec. 15, 1860, Feb. 20, Oct. 5, 1861, Johnson Papers, SC; Joseph Baldwin, *Flush Times of Alabama and Mississippi: A Series of Sketches* (New York: D. Appleton Co., 1957 [1853]), 83.

22. For panics, see Schweikart, "Banking in the American South," pp. 43–67, 435–37, 588–98; John Bettersworth, *Confederate Mississippi* (Baton Rouge: Louisiana State University Press, 1943), pp. 85–92; Bertram Korn, *The Jews of Mobile, Alabama, 1763–1841* (Cincinnati: Hebrew Union College Press, 1970), 37, 49; Morton Rothstein, "Sugar and Secession: A New York Firm in Ante-bellum Louisiana," *Explorations in Economic History*, Winter 1968, 115–31. Also see Larry Schweikart, "Secession and Southern Banks," *Civil War History*, June 1985, for the impact of the secession-related panic on southern banks.

23. H. Hutchinson to John Springs, Oct. 20, 1846, J. Wright to John Springs, April 13, 1847, in Springs Family Papers, Southern Historical Collection [SHC], University of North Carolina [UNC]. For material on Florida banks' lending practices, see Julia Smith, *Slavery and Plantation Growth in Antebellum Florida, 1821–1860* (Gainesville: University of Florida Press, 1914), 132–33. Material on Arkansas appears in entries dated Oct. 1, 15, 1841, in the Letterbook of the Fayetteville branch of the State Bank of Arkansas, 1840–46, Arkansas History Commission [AHC].

24. The stories of the bloody episodes in Arkansas appear in Ted Worley, "The Control of the Real Estate Bank of the State of Arkansas," *Mississippi Valley Historical Review*, December 1950, pp. 403–26, and W. D. Blocher, *History of Arkansas Finances* (Little Rock, Ark.: Evening Star Office, 1876), p. 30. Material on the Fowlkes-Coe feud is found in James Roper, ed., *Chronicles of the Farmers' and Merchants' Bank of Memphis (1832–1847)*, by Jessie, the "Scribe" (Memphis: Burrow Library Monograph, Number 4, 1960), introduction.

25. John Ehringhous to Duncan Cameron, Feb. 2, Mar. 9, 1837, Letterbook, Elizabeth City branch of the Bank of North Carolina, in William Griffen, *Ante-Bellum Elizabeth City: The History of a Canal Town* (Elizabeth City, N.C.: Roanoke Press, 1970), 75–76; Henry Ewing to S. D. Mitchell, Aug. 10, 1839, Bank of Tennessee Letterbook, record group 47, series #5, vols. 15 and 16, TLA; Letterbook of the Fayetteville branch of the Bank of Arkansas, July 2 [?], 1841, April 2, July 15, Dec. 12, 1842, all in AHC.

26. Charles Fisher to Thomas Wright, Mar. 9, 1848, in Orin Davis Papers, SHC,

UNC. Material on Ewing appears in Larry Schweikart, "Tennessee's Antebellum Banks: Part 1," *Tennessee Historical Quarterly*, June 1986, and "Part 2," ibid, Sept. 1986.

27. Material on Honour appears in Katherine Honour, "Theodore A. Honour: His Life and Letters of the Civil War Period" (M.A. thesis, East Tennessee State University, 1979), 9–16, 35–38, 62–63; "John Henry Honour, D.D.," in "In Memory of Rev. John H. Honour, D.D.," *City Year Book, 1885* (Charleston: News and Courier Book Presses, 1885); Theodore Honour to Beckie Honour, Feb. 4, 22, Mar. 3, 17, 22, 29, Apr. 5, 14, and n.d., 1864, all in Theodore Honour Papers, SC. Also see the letters of John Cheesborough to Lou Cheesborough, Aug. 7, 14, 27, 1861, June 20, 25, Aug. 22, 24, 1862, July 15, 27, 1863, John Cheesborough Papers, SHC, UNC.

28. William Wright to John Springs, Jan. 1, 1845, G. Shannon to John Springs, May 10, 1845, Alex Sparks to John Springs, Sept. 25, 1845, H. Hutchinson to John Springs, Jan. 20, 1846, all in Springs Family Papers, SHC, UNC.

29. Lending policies are discussed in Schweikart, "Banking in the American South," chapter 6. The activities of the Decatur branch of the Bank of Alabama appear in Larry Schweikart, "Alabama's Antebellum Banks," *Alabama Review*, June 1985. For Mills's comment, see Charles Mills to W. E. Daviell, 1855, Charles Mills Letterbooks, University of North Carolina.

30. A thorough discussion of lending in Louisiana may be found in George Green, *Finance and Economic Development in the Old South, Louisiana, 1804–1861* (Stanford: Stanford University Press, 1972). Also see Bray Hammond, *Banks and Politics in America from the Revolution to the Civil War* (Princeton, N.J.: Princeton University Press, 1957); Harold Woodman, *King Cotton and His Retainers; Financing and Marketing the Cotton Crop of the South, 1800–1825* (Lexington: University of Kentucky Press, 1968); W. B. Worthen, *Early Banking in Arkansas* (Little Rock: Democrat Printing and Litho Co., 1906); J. E. Dovell, *History of Banking in Florida 1828–1954*, 3 vols., (Orlando: Florida Bankers Association, 1955, 1964, 1977); Robert Weems, "The Bank of the Mississippi: A Pioneer Bank of the Old Southwest, 1809–1844" (Ph.D. dissertation, Columbia University, 1952); Brantson Holder, "The Three Banks of the State of North Carolina, 1810–1872" (Ph. D. dissertation, University of North Carolina, 1937); and Thomas Govan, "The Banking and Credit System in Georgia" (Ph.D. dissertation, Vanderbilt University, 1936). Profits in southern manufacturing are estimated by Fred Bateman and Thomas Weiss, "Manufacturing in the Antebellum South," *Research in Economic History*, ed. Paul Uselding (Greenwich: JAI Press, 1976), 1:1–45.

31. Larry Schweikart, "Antebellum Southern Bankers: Origins and Mobility," *Business and Economic History*, ed. Jeremy Atack (Urbana, Ill: University of Illinois Bureau of Business Research, 1985); Thornton, *Politics and Power*, effectively refutes theories that place bankers in an economic "class," as suggested by Eugene Genovese, *The Political Economy of Slavery* (New York: Random House, 1961), and Susan Feiner, "The Financial Structures and Banking Institutions of the Antebellum South: 1811 to 1832" (Ph.D. dissertation, University of Massachusetts, 1981).

32. A more detailed discussion of private capital, including sources as unlikely as the

Harmony Society, appears in Larry Schweikart, "Private Bankers in the Antebellum South," *Southern Studies*, Summer 1986. While almost all students of southern banking admit that private banks existed in great numbers and that all attempts to adequately count them have failed, any estimates on their exact number have been slow in arriving. Therefore, using two separate states in which a minimum number of private bankers are known, I have produced the following estimates:

Estimates of Private Bankers

State	1830	1840	1850	1860

Model A: Florida (1850) = 1 bank to 14,000 population (Numbers in parentheses indicate upperbound estimates.)

State	1830	1840	1850	1860
Florida	2	3 (5)	6 (9)	10 (14)
Louisiana	15 (22)	25 (35)	37 (52)	50 (71)
Virginia	67 (104)	73 (102)	79 (112)	87 (122)
North Carolina	45 (74)	53 (75)	62 (87)	70 (99)
Tennessee	48 (68)	59 (8)	71 (10)	79 (111)
Georgia	36 (52)	49 (69)	64 (91)	75 (106)
South Carolina	35 (50)	42 (50)	47 (67)	50 (70)
Mississippi	9 (14)	26 (30)	27 (60)	56 (79)
Alabama	22 (31)	42 (59)	55 (77)	68 (96)
Arkansas		7 (9)	15 (21)	31 (43)

Model B: Arkansas (1860) = 1 bank to 52,000 population

State	1830	1840	1850	1860
Florida		1	1	3
Louisiana	4	7	10	14
Virginia	20	20	21	23
North Carolina	14	14	17	19
Tennessee	13	16	19	21
Georgia	10	13	17	20
South Carolina	11	11	13	13
Mississippi	3	7	12	15
Alabama	4	11	15	18
Arkansas		2	4	8

Model C: Average of Arkansas + Florida = 1 bank to 33,000 population

State	1830	1840	1850	1860
Florida	1	1	2	3
Louisiana	6	11	15	21
Virginia	31	31	34	37
North Carolina	22	23	26	30
Tennessee	20	25	30	33
Georgia	16	21	27	32
South Carolina	17	18	20	21
Mississippi	4	11	18	24
Alabama	9	18	23	29

Source: Census data from *Historical Statistics of the United States: Colonial Times to 1870*, Bicentennial Ed. (Washington, D.C.: U.S. Bureau of the Census, 1975), 2 parts, 1:4, 26, 28, 30, 32, 34–35; Florida banking numbers from J. E. Dovell, *History of Banking in Florida*, 3 vols.

(Orlando: Florida Bankers Association, 1955, 1964, 1977), 1:42. Dovell referred to four private bankers operating in Franklin in his 1847 statistics. Franklin itself was not included in 1850 numbers. If an adjustment is made for these banks, then the ratio becomes one bank per 10,000 people. These estimates are given in parentheses in Model A. Arkansas data from W. B. Worthen, *Early Banking in Arkansas* (Little Rock, Ark.: Democrat Printing and Litho Co., 1906), 114–23. The discussion of Arkansas bankers after the Civil War appears in Worthen, *Early Banking in Arkansas*, 114–123.

33. Willam Brantley, *Banking in Alabama, 1816–1860*, 2 vols. (Birmingham, Ala.: William Brantley, 1961, and Oxmoor Press, 1967), 2:40–47, 64–69, 134.

34. Estimates of the growth of southern banking are found in Schweikart, "Banking in the American South," see tables 6.1–6.39. A comparison with northern growth is made in Larry Schweikart, "Southern Banks and Economic Growth: A Reassessment," *Journal of Southern History*, February 1987.

35. Discussions of southern regulatory policy as it related to banks appears in Schweikart, "Banking in the American South," chaps. 2–3, and Larry Schweikart, "How the Jacksonians Opposed Industrialization," *Reason Papers*, Fall 1986.

QUESTIONS FOR REVIEW AND DISCUSSION

1. Describe the career paths of three bankers mentioned in this case study. Did they share any common entrepreneurial characteristics?
2. What were some of the occupations in which entrepreneurs could engage and still perform a variety of banking functions before the Civil War?
3. Discuss some of the duties, responsibilities, and problems of antebellum bankers, both as employees and as officers of a bank.
4. Why did cashiers and other officers of some southern banks come under personal attack? What was the social position of antebellum bankers?
5. Explain the tendency of southern bankers to invest in agriculture. Why did these bankers not direct more investment toward industry?
6. How does the new evidence about southern bankers change previously accepted notions of the southern economy? How do the biographies of these bankers challenge concepts of a banking "class"?

6

The Supreme Court and the Corporation

Relationships between the federal government and business are ill-defined in the Constitution. Section 8 of Article I gave Congress the power to lay and collect "taxes, duties, imposts and excises, to pay the debts and provide for the common defense and general welfare of the United States. . . ." Congress was also authorized to regulate commerce with foreign nations and among the several states, to establish uniform laws relating to bankruptcies, to coin money and fix standards of weights and measures, to establish post offices and roads, and to give patents and copyrights to inventors and authors. The Tenth Amendment to the Constitution reserved those powers not delegated to the federal government to the states. The Supreme Court and Congress have, over the succeeding two hundred years, respectively made rulings or passed laws on questions affecting commerce and industry's impact on the public welfare.

Congress and the states proceeded to grant charters, patents, monopolies, and privileges to various business enterprises much as they had done during the period of the Articles of Confederation, and as the colonies had done before independence was declared. For example, Congress chartered the First Bank of the United States for 20 years in 1791 and the Second Bank again for 20 years in 1816 (see Chapter 5). States chartered or incorporated a variety of banks, canal companies, manufacturing enterprises, and railroads.

Inevitably the question arose as to which licensing authority, that of one state or another, or that of one state or the federal government, had primacy in the granting of certain rights to private businesses. These issues or questions sometimes appeared for a final decision in front of the Supreme Court of the United States.

Chief justices John Marshall and Roger B. Taney presided over the Supreme Court from 1801 to 1836 and from 1836 to 1864 respectively. Each had a major role in defining both judicial policy and the powers of the federal government as they related to the states and to business. In the 1803 landmark decision, *Marbury* v. *Madison*, John Marshall established the precedent of judicial review of acts of Congress, thus establishing the precedent of the Supreme Court's right to interpret the Constitution. Considering the great amount of business and commercial activity during the years from 1800 to 1877, few issues were brought before the Supreme Court for settlement. The decisions that were made, however, were very important, for there was no other governmental authority, or regulatory agency, that was organized or disposed to intervene directly in conflicts of interest between public authority and private rights. The Supreme Court and its decisions, in other words, antedate the emergence of federal regulatory agencies.

As late as 1900, there were only six federal regulatory agencies—the largest ones being the Interstate Commerce Commission, established by Congress in 1887, and the Patent and Trademark Office, established by Congress in 1789. Although for all practical purposes the authority over and the regulation of business enterprises throughout the period from 1789 to 1877 rested with the state governments, it had become increasingly clear that businesses often attained national, not just regional or local, dimensions and that the states could not and should not have sole authority over their activities. The Supreme Court reaffirmed the states' preeminence over commerce *within the state* in the famous case of *Munn* v. *Illinois* (1877), but in 1886 the Supreme Court severely limited the authority of the state to regulate *interstate* commerce. In the Interstate Commerce Act of 1887, Congress defined the authority of the federal government over interstate commerce, thus marking the beginning of the "regulatory age."

By 1930 there were fourteen federal regulatory agencies. To the Interstate Commerce Commission and the Patent Office had been added the Federal Reserve System, the Federal Trade Commission, and ten other agencies. Between 1930 and 1940 ten more agencies were established, including the Federal Communications Commission, the Civil Aeronautics Board, and the Securities and Exchange Commission. Twenty-eight more were added between 1940 and 1960, including the Atomic Energy Commission and the Small Business Administration. In the next 20 years, 1960–1980, the number of federal regulatory agencies doubled and included agencies with authority over broad sectors of the private economy such as the Environmental Protection Agency.

The Supreme Court cases, which make up the case studies for this chapter, are the antecedents for the regulatory policy that evolved over a period of almost 200 years in the United States. Perhaps in that context these cases are less important for their rulings on the law, or for their results on legal actions, than they are for establishing a rationale for reviewing the authority of the various levels of government over contracts, corporations, and commerce.

The case of *McCulloch v. Maryland* (1819) discusses the authority of the state to tax a branch of the Second Bank of the United States that was incorporated by Congress. The cases *Dartmouth College v. Woodward* (1819) and *Charles River Bridge v. Warren Bridge* (1837) relate to contracts and grants of authority to private businesses by the states. *Gibbons v. Ogden* (1824) concerns the conflicting grant of exclusive rights to competing business enterprises by a state and by Congress. Again, the decision in these cases is less important than is the perception of governmental authority in relation to the rights of corporations and of the states.

Necessarily, the following Supreme Court cases offer a very abbreviated treatment of the questions relating to contracts, commerce, and governmental authority. A case book in American constitutional law would help in understanding and reviewing this important body of information. For a study of the legislative dimensions of governmental regulations refer to Bernard Schwartz's five-volume work, *Economic Regulation of Business and Industry: A Legislative History of U.S. Regulatory Agencies* (1973).

SUPREME COURT CASES

McCulloch *v.* Maryland
4 Wheat. 316, 4 L.Ed. 579 (1819).

The critical issue in *McCulloch* v. *Maryland* (1819) is which government has authority over property rights, the federal government or the state governments. The Maryland legislature had approved a bill that required the banks operating within the state to pay a tax on the bank notes they issued, or to pay an annual operating fee of $15,000 to the state. A branch of the Second Bank of the United States, a private corporation chartered by Congress, operated within the state of Maryland. James W. McCulloch, a cashier of the Baltimore branch of the Second Bank of the United States, failed to comply with the state law. The questions raised by Chief Justice Marshall were: Did Congress have the authority to charter a bank? Did the state of Maryland have the authority to tax the branch of a federally chartered bank that was operating within the state?

Chief Justice Marshall delivered the opinion of the Court: In the case now to be determined, the defendant, a sovereign state, denies the obligation of a law enacted by the legislature of the Union, and the plaintiff, on his part, contests the validity of an act which has been passed by the legislature of that state. The constitution of our country, in its most interesting and vital parts, is to be considered; the conflicting powers of the government of the Union and of its members, as marked in that constitution, are to be discussed; and an opinion given, which may essentially influence the great operations of the government. No tribunal can approach such a question without a deep sense of its importance, and of the awful responsibility involved in its decision. But it must be decided peacefully, or remain a source of hostile legislation, perhaps of hostility of a still more serious nature; and if it is to be so decided, by this tribunal alone can the decision be made. On the Supreme Court of the United States has the constitution of our country devolved this important duty.

The first question made in the cause is, has Congress power to incorporate a bank? . . .

The power now contested was exercised by the first Congress elected under the present constitution. The bill for incorporating the bank of the United States did not steal upon an unsuspecting legislature, and pass unobserved. Its principle was completely understood, and was opposed with equal zeal and ability. After being resisted, first in the fair and open field of debate, and afterwards in the executive cabinet, with as much persevering talent as any measure has ever experienced, and being supported by arguments which convinced minds as pure and as intelligent as this country can boast, it became a law. The original act was permitted to expire; but a short experience of the embarrassments to which the refusal to revive it exposed the government, convinced those who were most prejudiced against the measure of its necessity and induced the passage of the present law. It would require no ordinary share of intrepidity to assert that a measure adopted under these circumstances was a bold and plain usurpation, to which the constitution gave no countenance.

These observations belong to the cause; but they are not made under the impression that, were the question entirely new, the law would be found irreconcilable with the constitution.

In discussing this question, the counsel for the state of Maryland have deemed it of some importance, in the construction of the constitution, to consider that instrument not as emanating from the people, but as the act of sovereign and independent states. The powers of the general government, it has been said, are delegated by the states, who alone are truly sovereign; and must be exercised in subordination to the states who alone possess supreme dominion. . . .

The government of the Union, . . . (whatever may be the influence of this fact on the case), is, emphatically, and truly, a government of the people. In form and in substance it emanates from them. Its powers are granted by them, and are to be exercised directly on them, and for their benefit.

This government is acknowledged by all to be one of enumerated powers. The principle, that it can exercise only the powers granted to it, would seem too apparent to have required to be enforced by all those arguments which its enlightened friends, while it was depending before the people, found it necessary to urge. That principle is now universally admitted. But the question respecting the extent of the powers actually granted, is perpetually arising, and will probably continue to arise, as long as our system shall exist.

In discussing these questions, the conflicting powers of the general and state governments must be brought into view, and the supremacy of their respective laws, when they are in opposition, must be settled.

If any one proposition could command the universal assent of mankind, we might expect it would be this—that the government of the Union, though limited in its powers, is supreme within its sphere of action. This would seem to result necessarily from its nature. It is the government of all; its powers are delegated by all; it represents all, and acts for all. Though any one state may be willing to control its operations, no state is willing to allow others to control them. The nation, on those subjects on which it can act, must necessarily bind its component parts. But this question is not left to mere reason; the people have, in express terms, decided it by saying, "this constitution, and the laws of the United States, which shall be made in pursuance thereof," "shall be the supreme law of the land," and by requiring that the members of the state legislatures, and the officers of the executive and judicial departments of the states shall take the oath of fidelity to it.

The government of the United States, then, though limited in its powers, is supreme; and its laws, when made in pursuance of the constitution, form the supreme law of the land, "anything in the constitution or laws of any state to the contrary notwithstanding."

Among the enumerated powers, we do not find that of establishing a bank or creating a corporation. But there is no phrase in the instrument which, like the articles of confederation, excludes incidental or implied powers; and which requires that everything granted shall be expressly and minutely described. Even the 10th amendment, which was framed for the purpose of quieting the excessive jealousies which had been excited, omits the word "expressly," and declares only that the powers "not delegated to the United States, nor prohibited to the states, are reserved to the states or to the people;" thus leaving the question, whether the particular power which may become the subject of contest has been delegated to the one government, or prohibited to the other, to depend on a fair construction of the whole instrument. The men who drew and adopted this amendment had experienced the embarrassments resulting from the insertion of this word in the articles of confederation, and probably omitted it to avoid those embarrassments. A constitution, to contain an accurate detail of all the subdivisions of which its great powers will admit, and of all the means by which they may be carried into execution, would partake of a prolixity of a legal code, and could scarcely be embraced by the human mind. It would probably never be understood by the public. Its nature, therefore, requires, that only its great outlines should be marked, its important objects designated, and the minor ingredients which compose those objects be deduced from the nature of the objects themselves. That this idea was entertained by the framers of the American constitution, is not only to be inferred from the nature of the instrument but from the language. Why else were some of the limitations, found in the ninth section of the 1st article, introduced? It is also, in some degree, warranted by their having omitted to use any restrictive term which might prevent its receiving a fair and just interpretation. In considering this question, then, we must never forget that it is a constitution we are expounding.

Although, among the enumerated powers of government, we do not find the word "bank" or "incorporation," we find the great powers to lay and collect taxes; to borrow money; to regulate commerce; to declare and conduct a war; and to raise and support armies and navies. The sword and the purse, all the external relations, and no inconsiderable portion of the industry of the nation, are entrusted to its government. It can never be pretended that these vast powers draw after them others of inferior importance, merely because they are inferior. Such an idea can never be advanced. But it may with great reason be contended, that a government, entrusted with such ample powers, on the due execution of which the happiness and prosperity of the nation so vitally depends, must also be entrusted with ample means for their execution. The power being given, it is the interest of the nation to facilitate its execution. It can never be their interest, and cannot be presumed to have been their intention, to clog and embarrass its execution by withholding the most appropriate means. Throughout this vast republic, from the St. Croix to the Gulf of Mexico, from the Atlantic to the Pacific, revenue is to be collected and expended, armies are to be marched and supported. The exigencies of the nation may require that the treasure raised in the north should be transported to the south, that raised in the east conveyed to the west, or that this order should be reversed. Is that construction of the constitution to be preferred which would render these operations difficult, hazardous, and expensive? Can we adopt that construction (unless the words imperiously require it) which would impute to the framers of that instrument, when granting these powers for the public good, the intention of impeding their exercise by withholding a choice of means? If, indeed, such be the mandate of the constitution, we have only to obey; but that instrument does not profess to enumerate the means by which the powers it confers may be executed; nor does it prohibit the creation of a corporation, if the existence of such a being be essential to the beneficial exercise of those powers. It is, then, the subject of fair inquiry, how far such means may be employed. . . .

But the constitution of the United States has not left the right of Congress to employ the necessary means for the execution of the powers conferred on the government to general reasoning. To its enumeration of powers is added that of making "all laws which shall be necessary and proper, for carrying into execution the foregoing powers, and all other powers vested by this constitution, in the government of the United States, or in any department thereof."

The counsel for the state of Maryland have urged various arguments, to prove that this clause, though in terms a grant of power, is not so in effect; but is really restrictive of the general right, which might otherwise be implied, of selecting means for executing the enumerated powers. . . .

But the argument on which most reliance is placed, is drawn from the peculiar language of this clause. Congress is not empowered by it to make all laws, which may have relation to the powers conferred on the government, but such only as may be "necessary and proper" for carrying them into execution. The word "necessary" is considered as controlling the whole sentence, and as limiting the right to pass laws for the execution of the granted powers, to such as are indispensable, and without which the power would be nugatory. That it excludes the choice of means, and leaves to Congress, in each case, that only which is most direct and simple.

Is it true that this is the sense in which the word "necessary" is always used? Does it always import an absolute physical necessity, so strong that one thing, to which another may be termed necessary, cannot exist without that other? We think it does not. If reference be had to its use, in the common affairs of the world, or in approved authors, we find that it frequently imports no more than that one thing is convenient, or useful, or essential to another. To employ the means necessary to an end, is generally understood as employing any means calculated to produce the end, and not as being confined to those single means, without which the end would be entirely unattainable. Such is the character of human language, that no word conveys to the mind, in all situations, one single definite idea; and nothing is more common than to use words in a figurative sense. Almost all compositions contain words, which, taken in their rigorous sense, would convey a meaning different from that which is obviously intended. It is essential to just construction, that many words which import something excessive should be understood in a more mitigated sense—in that sense which common usage justifies. The word "necessary" is of this description. It has not a fixed character peculiar to itself. It admits of all degrees of comparison; and is often connected with other words, which increase or diminish the impression the mind receives of the urgency it imports. A thing may be necessary, very necessary, absolutely or indispensably necessary. To no mind would the same idea be conveyed by these several phrases. This comment on the word is well illustrated by the passage cited at the bar, from the 10th section of the 1st article of the constitution. It is, we think, impossible to compare the sentence which prohibits a state from laying "imposts or duties on imports or exports, except what may be absolutely necessary for executing its inspection laws," with that which authorizes Congress "to make all laws which shall be necessary and proper for carrying into execution" the powers of the general government, without feeling a conviction that the convention understood itself to change materially the meaning of the word "necessary," by prefixing the word "absolutely." This word, then, like others, is used in various senses; and, in its construction, the subject, the context, the intention of the person using them, are all to be taken into view.

Let this be done in the case under consideration. The subject is the execution of those great powers on which the welfare of a nation essentially depends. It must have been the intention of those who gave these powers, to insure, as far as human prudence could insure, their beneficial execution. This could not be done by confiding the choice of means to such narrow limits as not to leave it in the power of Congress to adopt any which might be appropriate, and which were conducive to the end. This provision is made in a constitution intended to endure for ages to come, and, consequently, to be adapted to the various crises of human affairs. To have prescribed the means by which government should, in all future time, execute its powers, would have been to change, entirely, the character of the instrument, and give it the properties of a legal code. . . .

Take, for example, the power, "to establish post-offices and post-roads." This power is executed by the single act of making the establishment. But, from this has been inferred the power and duty of carrying the mail along the post-road, from one post-office to another. And, from this implied power, has again been inferred the right to punish those who steal letters from the post-office, or rob the mail. It may be said, with some plausibility, that the right to carry the mail, and to punish those who rob it, is not indispensably necessary to the establishment of a post-office and post-road. This right is indeed essential to the beneficial exercise of the power, but not indispensably necessary to its existence. So, of the punishment of the crimes of stealing or falsifying a record or process of a court of the United States, or of perjury in such court. To punish these offenses is certainly conducive to the due administration of justice. But courts may exist, and may decide the causes brought before them, though such crimes escape punishment. . . .

. . . This clause, as construed by the state of Maryland, would abridge, and almost annihilate this useful and necessary right of the legislature to select its means. That this could not be intended, is, we should think, had it not been already controverted, too apparent for controversy. . . .

The result of the most careful and attentive consideration bestowed upon this clause is, that if it does not enlarge, it cannot be construed to restrain the powers of Congress, or to impair the right of the legislature to exercise its best judgment in the selection of measures to carry into execution the constitutional powers of the government. If no other motive for its insertion can be suggested, a sufficient one is found in the desire to remove all doubts respecting the right to legislate on that vast mass of incidental powers which must be involved in the constitution, if that instrument be not a splendid bauble.

We admit, as all must admit, that the powers of the government are limited, and that its limits are not to be transcended. But we think the sound construction of the constitution must allow to the national legislature that discretion, with respect to the means by which the powers it confers are to be carried into execution, which will enable that body to perform the high duties assigned to it, in the manner most beneficial to the people. Let the end be legitimate, let it be within the scope of the constitution, and all means which are appropriate, which are plainly adapted to that end, which are not prohibited, but consist with the letter and spirit of the constitution, are constitutional. . . .

If a corporation may be employed indiscriminately with other means to carry into execution the powers of the government, no particular reason can be assigned for excluding the use of a bank, if required for its fiscal operations. . . .

But, were its necessity less apparent, none can deny its being an appropriate measure; and if it is, the degree of its necessity, as has been very justly observed, is to be discussed in another place. Should Congress, in the execution of its powers, adopt measures which are prohibited by the constitution; or should Congress, under the pretext of executing its powers, pass laws for the accomplishment of objects not entrusted to the government, it would become the painful duty of this tribunal, should a case requiring such a decision come before it, to say that such an act was not the law of the land. But where the law is not prohibited, and is really calculated to effect any of the objects entrusted to the government, to undertake here to inquire into the degree of its necessity, would be to pass the line which circumscribes the judicial department, and to tread on legislative ground. This court disclaims all pretensions to such a power. . . .

After the most deliberate consideration, it is the unanimous and decided opinion of this court that the act to incorporate the bank of the United States is a law made in pursuance of the constitution, and is a part of the supreme law of the land. . . .

It being the opinion of the court that the act incorporating the bank is constitutional, and that the power of establishing a branch in the state of Maryland might be properly exercised by the bank itself, we proceed to inquire:

2. Whether the state of Maryland may, without violating the constitution, tax that branch?

That the power of taxation is one of vital importance; that it is retained by the states; that it is not abridged by the grant of a similar power to the government of the Union; that it is to be concurrently exercised by the two governments: are truths which have never been denied. But, such is the paramount character of the constitution that its capacity to withdraw any subject from the action of even this power, is admitted. The states are expressly forbidden to lay any duties on imports or exports, except what may be absolutely necessary for executing their inspection laws. If the obligation of this prohibition must be conceded—if it may restrain a state from the exercise of its taxing power on imports and exports—the same paramount character would seem to restrain, as it certainly may restrain, a state from such other exercise of this power, as is in its nature incompatible with, and repugnant to, the constitutional laws of the Union. A law, absolutely repugnant to another, as entirely repeals that other as if express terms of repeal were used.

On this ground the counsel for the bank place its claim to be exempted from the power of a state to tax its operations. There is no express provision for the case, but the claim has been sustained on a principle which so entirely pervades the constitution, is so intermixed with the materials which compose it, so interwoven with its web, so blended with its texture, as to be incapable of being separated from it without rending it into shreds.

This great principle is, that the constitution and the laws made in pursuance thereof are supreme; that they control the constitution and laws of the respective states, and cannot be controlled by them. . . .

. . . All subjects over which the sovereign power of a state extends, are objects of taxation; but those over which it does not extend, are, upon the soundest principles, exempt from taxation. This proposition may almost be pronounced self-evident.

The sovereignty of a state extends to everything which exists by its own authority, or is introduced by its permission; but does it extend to those means which are employed by Congress to carry into execution—powers conferred on that body by the people of the United States? We think it demonstrable that it does not. Those powers are not given by the people of a single state. They are given by the people of the United States, to a government whose laws, made in pursuance of the constitution, are declared to be supreme. Consequently, the people of a single state cannot confer a sovereignty which will extend over them. . . .

We find, then, on just theory, a total failure of this original right to tax the means employed by the government of the Union, for the execution of its powers. The right never existed, and the question whether it has been surrendered, cannot arise.

But, waiving this theory for the present, let us resume the inquiry, whether this power can be exercised by the respective states, consistently with a fair construction of the constitution.

That the power to tax involves the power to destroy; that the power to destroy may defeat and render useless the power to create; that there is a plain repugnance, in conferring on one government a power to control the constitutional measures of another, which other, with respect to those very measures, is declared to be supreme over that which exerts the control, are propositions not to be denied. But all inconsistencies are to be reconciled by the magic of the word CONFIDENCE. Taxation, it is said, does not necessarily and unavoidably destroy. To carry it to the excess of destruction would be an abuse, to presume which, would banish that confidence which is essential to all government.

But is this a case of confidence? Would the people of any one state trust those of another with a power to control the most insignificant operations of their state government? We know they would not. Why, then, should we suppose that the people of any one state should be willing to trust those of another with a power to control the operations of a government to which they have confided the most important and most valuable interests? In the legislature of the Union alone, are all represented. The legislature of the Union alone, therefore, can be trusted by the people with the power of controlling measures which concern all, in the confidence that it will not be abused. This, then, is not a case of confidence, and we must consider it as it really is. . . .

If the states may tax one instrument, employed by the government in the execution of its powers, they may tax any and every other instrument. They may tax the mail; they may tax the mint; they may tax patent-rights; they may tax the papers of the custom-house; they may tax judicial process; they may tax all the means employed by the government, to an excess which would defeat all the ends of government. This was not intended by the American people. They did not design to make their government dependent on the states. . . .

It has also been insisted, that, as the power of taxation in the general and state governments is acknowledged to be concurrent, every argument which would sustain the right of the general government to tax banks chartered by the states, will equally sustain the right of the states to tax banks chartered by the general government.

But the two cases are not on the same reason. The people of all the states have created the general government, and have conferred upon it the general power of taxation. The people of all the states, and the states themselves, are represented in Congress, and, by their representatives, exercise this power. When they tax the chartered institutions of the states, they tax their constituents; and these taxes must be uniform. But, when a state taxes the operations of the government of the

United States, it acts upon institutions created, not by their own constituents, but by people over whom they claim no control. It acts upon the measures of a government created by others as well as themselves, for the benefit of others in common with themselves. The difference is that which always exists, and always must exist, between the action of the whole on a part, and the action of a part on the whole—between the laws of a government declared to be supreme, and those of a government which, when in opposition to those laws, is not supreme.

But if the full application of this argument could be admitted, it might bring into question the right of Congress to tax the state banks, and could not prove the right of the states to tax the bank of the United States.

The court has bestowed on this subject its most deliberate consideration. The result is a conviction that the states have no power, by taxation or otherwise, to retard, impede, burden, or in any manner control the operations of the constitutional laws enacted by Congress to carry into execution the powers vested in the general government. This is, we think, the unavoidable consequence of that supremacy which the constitution has declared.

We are unanimously of opinion that the law passed by the legislature of Maryland, imposing a tax on the bank of the United States, is unconstitutional and void.

This opinion does not deprive the states of any resources which they originally possessed. It does not extend to a tax paid by the real property of the bank, in common with the other real property within the state, nor to a tax imposed on the interest which the citizens of Maryland may hold in this institution, in common with other property of the same description throughout the state. But this is a tax on the operations of the bank, and is, consequently, a tax on the operation of an instrument employed by the government of the Union to carry its powers into execution. Such a tax must be unconstitutional.

. . . It is, therefore, adjudged and ordered, that the said judgment of the said Court of Appeals of the state of Maryland in this case, be, and the same hereby is, reversed and annulled. And this court, proceeding to render such judgment as the said Court of Appeals should have rendered; it is further adjudged and ordered, that the judgment of the said Baltimore County Court be reversed and annulled, and that judgment be entered in the said Baltimore County Court for the said James W. McCulloch.

Dartmouth College *v.* Woodward
4 Wheaton 518 (1819)

In the first half of the nineteenth century, the Supreme Court generally followed William Blackstone's old world rule that "so great is the regard of the law for private property" that the Court would accept no violation of those rights, "even for the general good of the whole community." That rule formed the basis for the Supreme Court's decision in *Dartmouth College* v. *Woodward*. Dartmouth College was established as a private institution by royal charter in 1769. In 1816 the state of New Hampshire approved legislation that converted the college into a public institution. The trustees of Dartmouth brought suit. The defendant, William Woodward, was the secretary of the board that the state legislature created to oversee the actions of Dartmouth's trustees.

Chief Justice Marshall delivered the opinion of the Court: The title of the plaintiffs originates in a charter, dated the 13th day of December, in the year 1769, incorporating twelve persons therein mentioned, by the name of "The Trustees of Dartmouth College," granting to them and their successors the usual corporate privileges and powers, and authorizing the trustees, who are to govern the college, to fill up all vacancies which may be created in their own body.

The defendant claims under three acts of the legislature of New Hampshire, the most material of which was passed on the 27th of June, 1816, and is entitled, "An act to amend the charter, and enlarge and improve the corporation of Dartmouth College. . . . "

It can require no argument to prove, that the circumstances of this case constitute a contract. An application is made to the crown for a charter to incorporate a religious and literary institution. In the application it is stated, that large contributions have been made for the object, which will be conferred on the corporation, as soon as it shall be created. The charter is granted, and on its faith the property is conveyed. Surely, in this transaction, every ingredient of a complete and legitimate contract is to be found.

The points for consideration are,

1. Is this contract protected by the constitution of the United States?
2. Is it impaired by the acts under which the defendant holds? . . .

That the framers of the constitution did not intend to restrain the States in the regulation of their civil institutions, adopted for internal government, and that the instrument they have given us is not to be so construed, may be admitted. The provision of the constitution never has been understood to embrace other contracts than those which respect property, or some object of value, and confer rights which may be asserted in a court of justice. It never has been understood to restrict the general right of the legislature to legislate on the subject of divorces. Those acts enable some tribunal, not to impair a marriage contract, but to liberate one of the parties because it has been broken by the other. When any State legislature shall pass an act annulling all marriage contracts, or allowing either party to annul it without the consent of the other, it will be time enough to inquire whether such an act be constitutional.

The parties in this case differ less on general principles, less on the true construction of the constitution in the abstract, than on the application of those principles to this case, and on the true construction of the charter of 1769. This is the point on which the cause essentially depends. If the act of incorporation be a grant of political power, if it create a civil institution to be employed in the administration of the government, or if the funds of the college be public property, or if the State of New Hampshire, as a government, be alone interested in its transactions, the subject is one in which the legislature of the State may act according to its own judgment, unrestrained by any limitation of its power imposed by the constitution of the United States.

But if this be a private eleemosynary institution, endowed with a capacity to take property for objects unconnected with government, whose funds are bestowed by individuals on the faith of the charter; if the donors have stipulated for the future disposition and management of those funds in the manner prescribed by themselves; there may be more difficulty in the case, although neither the persons who have made these stipulations, nor those for whose benefit they were made, should be parties to the cause. . . .

Dartmouth College is really endowed by private individuals, who have bestowed their funds for the propagation of the Christian religion among the Indians, and for the promotion of piety and learning generally. From these funds the salaries of the tutors are drawn; and these salaries lessen the expense of education to the students. It is then an eleemosynary . . . and, as far as respects its funds, a private corporation.

Do its objects stamp on it a different character? Are the trustees and professors public officers, invested with any portion of political power, partaking in any degree in the administration of civil government, and performing duties which flow from the sovereign authority?

That education is an object of national concern, and a proper subject of legislation, all admit. That there may be an institution founded by government, and placed entirely under its immediate control, the officers of which would be public officers, amenable exclusively to government, none will deny. But is Dartmouth College such an institution? Is education altogether in the hands of government? Does every teacher of youth become a public officer, and do donations for the purpose of education necessarily become public property, so far that the will of the legislature, not the will of the donor, becomes the law of the donation? These questions are of serious moment to society, and deserve to be well considered.

Doctor Wheelock, as the keeper of his charity school, instructing the Indians in the art of reading, and in our holy religion; sustaining them at his own expense, and on the voluntary contributions of the charitable, could scarcely be considered as a public officer, exercising any portion of those duties which belong to government; nor could the legislature have supposed, that his private funds, or those given by others, were subject to legislative management, because they were applied to the purposes of education. When afterwards, his school was enlarged, and the liberal contributions made in England and in America, enabled him to extend his cares to the education of the youth of his own country, no change was wrought in his own character, or in the nature of his duties. Had he employed assistant tutors with the funds contributed by others, or had the trustees in England established a school, with Dr. Wheelock at its head, and paid salaries to him and his assistants, they would still have been private tutors; and the fact that they were employed in the education of youth, could not have converted them into public officers, concerned in the administration of public duties, or have given the legislature a right to interfere in the management of the fund. The trustees, in whose care that fund was placed by the contributors, would have been permitted to execute their trust, uncontrolled by legislative authority.

Whence, then, can be derived the idea, that Dartmouth College has become a public institution, and its trustees public officers, exercising powers conferred by the public, for public objects? Not from the source whence its funds were drawn; for its foundation is purely private and eleemosynary. Not from the application of those funds; for money may be given for education, and the persons receiving it do not, by being employed in the education of youth, become members of the civil government. Is it from the act of incorporation? Let this subject be considered.

A corporation is an artificial being, invisible, intangible, and existing only in contemplation of law. Being the mere creature of law, it possesses only those properties which the charter of its creation confers upon it, either expressly, or as incidental to its very existence. These are such as are supposed best calculated to effect the object for which it was created. Among the most important are immortality, and, if the expression may be allowed, individuality; properties by which a perpetual succession of many persons are considered as the same, and may act as a single individual. They enable a corporation to manage its own affairs, and to hold property without the perplexing intricacies, the hazardous and endless necessity of perpetual conveyances, for the purpose of transmitting it from hand to hand. It is chiefly for the purpose of clothing bodies of men, in succession, with these qualities and capacities, that corporations were invented, and are in use. By these means a perpetual succession of individuals are capable of acting for the promotion of the particular object, like one immortal being. But this being does not share in the civil government of the country, unless that be the purpose for which it was created. Its immortality no more confers on it political power, or a political character, than immortality would confer such power or character on a natural person. It is no more a State instrument, than a natural person exercising the same powers would be. If, then, a natural person, employed by individuals in the education of youth, or for the government of a seminary in which youth is educated, would not become a public officer, or be considered as a member of the civil government, how is it that this artificial being, created by law, for the purpose of being employed by the same individuals for the same purposes, should become a part of the civil government of the country? Is it because its existence, its capacities, its powers, are given by law? Because the government has given it the power to take and to hold property in a particular form, and for particular purposes, has the government a consequent right substantially to change that form, or to vary the purposes to which the property is to be applied? This principle has never been asserted or recognized, and is supported by no authority. Can it derive aid from reason?

The objects for which a corporation is created are universally such as the government wishes to promote. They are deemed beneficial to the country; and this benefit constitutes the consideration, and, in most cases, the sole consideration, of the grant. In most eleemosynary institutions, the object would be difficult, perhaps unattainable, without the aid of a charter of incorporation. Charitable, or public spirited individuals, desirous of making permanent appropriations for charitable or other useful purposes, find it impossible to effect their design, securely and certainly, without an incorporating act. They apply to the government, state their beneficent object, and offer to advance the money necessary for its accomplishment, provided the government will confer on the instrument, which is to execute their designs, the capacity to execute them. The proposition is considered and approved. The benefit to the public is considered as an ample compensation for the faculty it confers, and the corporation is created. If the advantages to the public constitute a full compensation for the faculty it gives, there can be no reason for exacting a further compensation, by claiming a right to exercise over this artificial being a power which changes its nature, and touches the fund, for the security and application of which it was created. There can be no reason for implying in a charter, given for a valuable consideration, a power which is not only not expressed, but is in direct contradiction to its express stipulations.

From the fact, then, that a charter of incorporation has been granted, nothing can be inferred which changes the character of the institution, or transfers to the government any new power over it. The character of civil institutions does not grow out of their incorporation, but out of the manner in which they are formed, and the objects for which they are created. The right to change them is not founded on their being incorporated, but on their being the instruments of government, created for its purposes. The same institutions, created for the same objects, though not incorporated, would be public institutions, and, of course, be controllable by the legislature. The incorporating act neither gives nor prevents this control. Neither, in reason, can the incorporating act change the character of a private eleemosynary institution. . . .

[I]t appears, that Dartmouth College is an eleemosynary institution, incorporated for the purpose of perpetuating the application of the bounty of the donors, to the specified objects of that bounty; that its trustees or governors were originally named by the founder, and invested with the power of perpetuating themselves; that they are not public officers, nor is it a civil institution, participating in the administration of government; but a charity school, or a seminary of education, incorporated for the preservation of its property, and the perpetual application of that property to the objects of its creation. . . .

This is plainly a contract to which the donors, the trustees, and the crown (to whose rights and obligations New Hampshire succeeds) were the original parties. It is a contract made on a valuable consideration. It is a contract for the security and disposition of property. It is a contract, on the faith of which, real and personal estate has been conveyed to the corporation. It is then a contract within the letter of the constitution, and within its spirit also, unless the fact that the property is invested by the donors in trustees, for the promotion of religion and education, for the benefit of persons who are perpetually changing, though the objects remain the same, shall create a particular exception, taking this case out of the prohibition contained in the constitution.

It is more than possible that the preservation of rights of this description was not particularly in the view of the framers of the constitution, when the clause under consideration was introduced into that instrument. It is probable that interferences of more frequent recurrence, to which the temptation was stronger, and of which the mischief was more extensive, constituted the great motive for imposing this restriction on the State legislatures. But although a particular and a rare case may not, in itself, be of sufficient magnitude to induce a rule, yet it must be governed by the rule, when established, unless some plain and strong reason for excluding it can be given. It is not enough to say, that this particular case was not in the mind of the convention, when the article was framed, nor of the American people, when it was adopted. It is necessary to go further, and to say that, had this particular case been suggested, the language would have been so varied as to exclude it, or it would have been made a special exception. The case being within the words of the rule, must be within its operation likewise, unless there be something in the literal construction so obviously absurd or mischievous, or repugnant to the general spirit of the instrument, as to justify those who expound the constitution in making it an exception. . . .

The opinion of the court, after mature deliberation, is, that this is a contract, the obligation of which cannot be impaired, without violating the constitution of the United States. This opinion appears to us to be equally supported by reason, and by the former decisions of this court.

We next proceed to the inquiry, whether its obligation has been impaired by those acts of the legislature of New Hampshire, to which the special verdict refers.

From the review of this charter, which has been taken, it appears that the whole power of governing the college, of appointing and removing tutors, of fixing their salaries, of directing the course of study to be pursued by the students, and of filling up vacancies created in their own body, was vested in the trustees. On the part of the crown, it was expressly stipulated that this corporation, thus constituted, should continue forever; and that the number of trustees should forever consist of twelve, and no more. By this contract, the crown was bound, and could have made no violent alteration in its essential terms, without impairing its obligation.

By the Revolution, the duties as well as the powers of government devolved on the people of New Hampshire. It is admitted, that among the latter was comprehended the transcendent power of parliament, as well as that of the executive department. It is too clear to require the support of argument, that all contracts and rights, respecting property, remained unchanged by the Revolution. The obligations, then, which were created by the charter to Dartmouth College, were the same in the new that they had been in the old government. The power of the government was also the same. A repeal of this charter at any time prior to the adoption of the present constitution of the United States, would have been an extraordinary and unprecedented act of power, but one which could have been contested only by the restrictions upon the legislature, to be found in the constitution of the State. But the constitution of the United States has imposed this additional limitation, that the legislature of a State shall pass no act "impairing the obligation of contracts."

It has been already stated, that the act "to amend the charter, and enlarge and improve the corporation of Dartmouth College," increases the number of trustees to twenty-one, gives the appointment of the additional members to the executive of the State, and creates a board of overseers, to consist of twenty-five persons, of whom twenty-one are also appointed by the executive of New Hampshire, who have power to inspect and control the most important acts of the trustees.

On the effect of this law, two opinions cannot be entertained. Between acting directly, and acting through the agency of trustees and overseers, no essential difference is perceived. The whole power of governing the college is transferred from trustees, appointed according to the will of the founder, expressed in the charter, to the executive of New Hampshire. The management and application of the funds of this eleemosynary institution, which are placed by the donors in the hands of trustees named in the charter, and empowered to perpetuate themselves, are placed by this act under the control of the government of the State. The will of the State is substituted for the will of the donors, in every essential operation of the college. This is not an immaterial change. The founders of the college contracted, not merely for the perpetual application of the funds which they gave, to the objects for which those funds were given; they contracted also, to secure that application by the constitution of the corporation. They contracted for a system, which should, as far as human foresight can provide, retain forever the government of the literary institution they had formed, in the hands of persons approved by themselves. This system is totally changed. The charter of 1769 exists no longer. It is reorganized; and reorganized in such a manner, as to convert a literary institution, moulded according to the will of its founders, and placed under the control of private literary men, into a machine entirely subservient to the will of government. This may be for the advantage of this college in particular, and may be for the advantage of literature in general; but it is not according to the will of the donors, and is subversive of that contract on the faith of which their property was given. . . .

It results from this opinion, that the acts of the legislature of New Hampshire, which are stated in the special verdict found in this cause, are repugnant to the constitution of the United States, and that the judgment on this special verdict ought to have been for the plaintiffs. The judgment of the state court must, therefore, be reversed. . . .

Charles River Bridge *v.* Warren Bridge
11 Pet. 420, 9 L.Ed. 773 (1837)

Acting under a charter issued by the state of Massachusetts in 1785, the Charles River Bridge Company erected a toll bridge across the Charles River. The company agreed to compensate Harvard College for impairing an exclusive franchise, which had been granted to Harvard in 1650, to operate a ferry across the Charles River. In 1828, the Massachusetts legislature authorized the construction of a second (and badly needed) toll bridge near the site of the first bridge. The Charles River Bridge Company brought suit, arguing that the legislature had unconstitutionally set aside its contractual rights. The case went to the Supreme Court of the United States on a writ of error from the Massachusetts Supreme Court.

Mr. Chief Justice Taney delivered the opinion of the Court: Upon what ground can the plaintiffs in error contend that the ferry rights of the college have been transferred to the proprietors of the bridge? If they have been thus transferred, it must be by some mode of transfer known to the law; and the evidence relied on to prove it, can be pointed out in the record. How was it transferred? It is not suggested that there ever was, in point of fact, a deed of conveyance executed by the college to the bridge company. Is there any evidence in the record from which such a conveyance may, upon legal principle, be presumed? The testimony before the court, so far from laying the foundation for such a presumption, repels it in the most positive terms. The petition to the legislature, in 1785, on which the charter was granted, does not suggest an assignment, nor any agreement or consent on the part of the college; and the petitioners do not appear to have regarded the wishes of that institution, as by any means necessary to ensure their success. They place their application entirely on considerations of public interest and public convenience, and the superior advantages of a communication across Charles River by a bridge, instead of a ferry. . . .

This brings us to the act of the legislature of Massachusetts, of 1785, by which the plaintiffs were incorporated by the name of "The Proprietors of the Charles River Bridge"; and it is here, and in the law of 1792, prolonging their charter, that we must look for the extent and nature of the franchise conferred upon the plaintiffs.

Much has been said in the argument of the principles of construction by which this law is to be expounded, and what undertakings, on the part of the state, may be implied. The court thinks there can be no serious difficulty on that head. It is the grant of certain franchises by the public to a private corporation, and in a matter where the public interest is concerned. The rule of construction in such cases is well settled, both in England and by the decisions of our own tribunals. In 2 Barn. & Adol., 793, in the case of the *Proprietors of the Stourbridge Canal* v. *Wheeley and others*, the courts says, "The canal having been made under an act of parliament, the rights of the plaintiffs are derived entirely from that act. This, like many other cases, is a bargain between a company of adventurers and the public, the terms of which are expressed in the statute; and the rule of construction, in all such cases, is now fully established to be this; that any ambiguity in the terms of the contract must operate against the adventurers, and in favor of the public, and the plaintiffs can claim nothing that is not clearly given them by the act." And the doctrine thus laid down is abundantly sustained by the authorities referred to in this decision.

. . . The argument in favour of the proprietors of the Charles River bridge, is . . . that the power claimed by the state, if it exists, may be so used as to destroy the value of the franchise they have granted to the corporation. . . . The existence of the power does not, and cannot depend upon the circumstance of its having been exercised or not. . . .

. . . The object and end of all government is to promote the happiness and prosperity of the community by which it is established, and it can never be assumed, that the government intended to diminish its powers of accomplishing the end for which it was created. And in a country like ours, free, active, and enterprising, continually advancing in numbers and wealth, new channels of communication are daily found necessary, both for travel and trade; and are essential to the comfort, convenience, and prosperity of the people. A state ought never to be presumed to surrender this power, because, like the taxing power, the whole community has an interest in preserving it undiminished. And when a corporation alleges, that a state has surrendered, for seventy years, its power of improvement and public accommodation, in a great and important line of travel, along which a vast number of its citizens must daily pass, the community has a right to insist, in the language of this court above quoted, "that its abandonment ought not to be presumed in a case in which the deliberate purpose of the state to abandon it does not appear." The continued existence of a government would be of no great value, if by implications and presumptions it was disarmed of the powers necessary to accomplish the ends of its creation; and the functions it was designed to perform, transferred to the hands of privileged corporations. The rule of construction announced by the court was not confined to the taxing power; nor is it so limited in the opinion delivered. On the contrary, it was distinctly placed on the ground that the interests of the community were concerned in preserving, undiminished, the power then in question; and whenever any power of the state is said to be surrendered and diminished, whether it be the taxing power or any other affecting the public interest, the same principle applies, and the rule of construction must be the same. No one will question that the interests of the great body of the people of the state would, in this instance, be affected by the surrender of this great line of travel to a single corporation, with the right to exact toll, and exclude competition for seventy years. While the rights of private property are sacredly guarded, we must not forget that the community also has rights, and that the happiness and well-being of every citizen depends on their faithful preservation.

Adopting the rule of construction above stated as the settled one, we proceed to apply it to the charter of 1785, to the proprietors of the Charles River bridge. This act of incorporation is in the usual form, and the privileges such as are commonly given to corporations of that kind. It confers on them the ordinary faculties of a corporation, for the purpose of building the bridge; and establishes certain rates of toll, which the company is authorized to take: this is the whole grant. There is no exclusive privilege given to them over the water of Charles River, above or below their bridge; no right to erect another bridge themselves, nor to prevent other persons from erecting one, no engagement from the state, that another shall not be erected; and no undertaking not to sanction competition, nor to make improvements that may diminish the amount of its income. Upon all these subjects, the charter is silent; and nothing is said in it about a line of travel, so much insisted on in the argument, in which they are to have exclusive privileges. . . .

. . . In short, all the franchises and rights of property, enumerated in the charter, and there mentioned to have been granted to it, remain unimpaired. But its income is destroyed by the Warren bridge; which, being free, draws off the passengers and property which would have gone over it, and renders their franchise of no value. This is the gist of the complaint. For it is not pretended, that the erection of the Warren bridge would have done them any injury, or in any degree affected their right of property, if it had not diminished the amount of their tolls. In order, then, to entitle themselves to relief, it is necessary to show, that the legislature contracted not to do the act of which they complain; and that they impaired, or in other words, violated, that contract by the erection of the Warren bridge.

The inquiry, then, is, does the charter contain such a contract on the part of the state? Is there any such stipulation to be found in that instrument? It must be admitted on all hands, that there is none; no words that even relate to another bridge, or to the diminution of their tolls, or to the line of travel. If a contract on that subject can be gathered from the charter, it must be by implication: and cannot be found in the words used. Can such an agreement be implied? The rule of construction before stated is an answer to the question; in charters of this description, no rights are taken from the public, or given to the corporation, beyond those which the words of the charter, by their natural and proper construction, purport to convey. There are no words which import such a contract as the plaintiffs in error contend for, and none can be implied. . . .

Indeed, the practice and usage of almost every state in the Union, old enough to have commenced the work of internal improvement, is opposed to the doctrine contended for on the part of the plaintiffs in error. Turnpike roads have been made in succession, on the same line of travel; the later ones interfering materially with the profits of the first. These corporations have, in some instances, been utterly ruined by the introduction of newer and better modes of transportation and traveling. In some cases, railroads have rendered the turnpike roads on the same line of travel so entirely useless, that the franchise of the turnpike corporation is not worth preserving. Yet in none of these cases have the corporations supposed that their privileges were invaded, or any contract violated on the part of the state. Amid the multitude of cases which have occurred, and have been daily occurring for the last forty or fifty years, this is the first instance in which such an implied contract has been contended for, and this court called upon to infer it, from an ordinary act of incorporation, containing nothing more than the usual stipulations and provisions to be found in every such law. The absence of any such controversy, when there must have been so many occasions to give rise to it, proves that neither states, nor individuals, nor corporations, ever imagined that such a contract could be implied from such charters. It shows, that the men who voted for these laws never imagined that they were forming such a contract; and if we maintain that they have made it, we must create it by a legal fiction, in opposition to the truth of the fact, and the obvious intention of the party. We cannot deal thus with the rights reserved to the states; and by legal intendments and mere technical reasoning, take away from them any portion of that power over their own internal police and improvement, which is so necessary to their well-being and prosperity.

And what would be the fruits of this doctrine of implied contracts, on the part of the states, and of property in a line of travel by a corporation, if it should now be sanctioned by this court? To what results would it lead us? If it is to be found in the charter to this bridge, the same process of reasoning must discover it, in the various acts which have been passed, within the last forty years, for turnpike companies. And what is to be the extent of the privileges of exclusion on the different sides of the road? The counsel who have so ably argued this case, have not attempted to define it by any certain boundaries. How far must the new improvement be distant from the old one? How near may you approach, without invading its rights in the privileged line? If this court should establish the principles now contended for, what is to become of the numerous railroads established on the same line of travel with turnpike companies; and which have rendered the franchise of the turnpike corporations of no value? Let it once be understood, that such charters carry with them these implied contracts, and give this unknown and undefined property in a line of travelling; and you will soon find the old turnpike corporations awakening from their sleep and calling upon this court to put down the improvements which have taken their place. The millions of property which have been invested in railroads and canals, upon lines of travel which had been before occupied by turnpike corporations, will be put in jeopardy. We shall be thrown back to the improvements of the last century, and obliged to stand still, until the claims of the old turnpike corporations shall be satisfied; and they shall consent to permit these states to avail themselves of the lights of modern science, and to partake of the benefit of those improvements which are now adding to the wealth and prosperity, and the convenience and comfort, of every other part of the civilized world. Nor is this all. This court will find itself compelled to fix, by some arbitrary rule, the width of this new kind of property in a line of travel; for if such a right of property exists, we have no lights to guide us in marking out its extent, unless, indeed, we resort to the old feudal grants, and to the exclusive rights of ferries, by prescription, between towns; and are prepared to decide that when a turnpike road from one town to another, had been made, no railroad or canal, between these two points, could afterwards be established. This court is not prepared to sanction principles which must lead to such results. . . .

The judgment of the supreme judicial court of the commonwealth of Massachusetts, dismissing the plaintiffs' bill, must therefore, be affirmed with costs.

[Justice McLean delivered an opinion in which he urged that the bill be dismissed for want of jurisdiction, although he thought that the plaintiffs' claim had merit.]

Justice Story, dissenting. . . .

The present . . . is not the case of a royal grant, but of a legislative grant, by a public statute. The rules of the common law in relation to royal grants have, therefore, in reality, nothing to do with the case. We are to give this act of incorporation a rational and fair construction; according to the general rules which govern in all cases of the exposition of public statutes. We are to ascertain the legislative intent; and that once ascertained, it is our duty to give it a full and liberal operation. . . .

I admit, that where the terms of a grant are to impose burdens upon the public, or to create a restraint injurious to the public interests, there is sound reason for interpreting the terms, if ambiguous, in favour of the public. But at the same time, I insist, that there is not the slightest reason for saying, even in such a case, that the grant is not to be construed favourably to the grantee, so as to secure him in the enjoyment of what is actually granted. . . .

. . . Our legislatures neither have, nor affect to have any royal prerogatives. There is no provision in the constitution authorizing their grants to be construed differently from the grants of private persons, in regard to the like subject matter. The policy of the common law, which gave the crown so many exclusive privileges, and extraordinary claims, different from those of the subject, was founded in a good measure, if not altogether, upon the divine right of kings, or at least upon a sense of their exalted dignity and preeminence over all subjects, and upon the notion, that they are entitled to peculiar favour, for the protection of their kingly privileges. They were always construed according to common sense and common reason, upon their language and their intent. What reason is there, that our legislative acts should not receive a similar interpretation? Is it not at least as important in our free governments, that a citizen should have as much security for his rights and estate derived from the grants of the legislature, as he would have in England? What solid ground is there to say, that the words of a grant in the mouth of a citizen, shall mean one thing, and in the mouth of the legislature shall mean another thing? That in regard to the grant of a citizen, every word shall in case of any question of interpretation or implication be construed against him, and in regard to the grant of the government, every word shall be construed in its favour? That language shall be construed, not according to its natural import and implications from its own proper sense, and the objects of the instrument; but shall change its meaning, as it is spoken by the whole people, or by one of them? There may be very solid grounds to say, that neither grants nor charters ought to be extended beyond the fair reach of their words; and that no implications ought to be made, which are not clearly deducible from the language, and the nature and objects of the grant. . . .

But it has been argued, and the argument has been pressed in every form which ingenuity could suggest, that if grants of this nature are to be construed liberally, as conferring any exclusive rights on the grantees, it will interpose an effectual barrier against all general improvements of the country. . . . For my own part, I can conceive of no surer plan to arrest all public improvements, founded on private capital and enterprise, than to make the outlay of that capital uncertain, and questionable both as to security, and as to productiveness. No man will hazard his capital in any enterprise, in which, if there be a loss, it must be borne exclusively by himself; and if there be success, he has not the slightest security of enjoying the rewards of that success for a single moment. . . .

Upon the whole, my judgment is that the act of the legislature of Massachusetts granting the charter of Warren bridge, is an act impairing the obligation of the prior contract and grant to the proprietors of Charles River bridge; and, by the Constitution of the United States, it is, therefore, utterly void. I am for reversing the decree of the state court (dismissing the bill), and for remanding the cause to the state court for further proceedings. . . .

Justice Thompson concurred in this opinion. . . .

Gibbons v. Ogden
9 Wheat. 1, 6 L.Ed. 23 (1824)

The state of New York in 1808 granted to Robert Fulton and Robert Livingston an exclusive license to operate steamboats on the Hudson River for 30 years. Aaron Ogden operated a steamboat on the river under the Fulton and Livingston franchise. Thomas Gibbons began operation on the Hudson River under a coasting license obtained from the federal government in apparent violation of the state of New York's license. Ogden's exclusive rights were upheld by the New York Supreme Court and Gibbons appealed to the Supreme Court of the United States.

Chief Justice Marshall delivered the opinion of the Court: As preliminary to the very able discussions of the constitution, which we have heard from the bar, and as having some influence on its construction, reference has been made to the political situation of these states, anterior to its formation. It has been said, that they were sovereign, were completely independent, and were connected with each other only by a league. This is true. But when these allied sovereigns converted their league into a government, when they converted their congress of ambassadors, deputed to deliberate on their common concerns, and to recommend measures of general utility, into a legislature, empowered to enact laws on the most interesting subjects, the whole character in which the states appear, underwent a change, the extent of which must be determined by a fair consideration of the instrument by which that change was effected.

This instrument contains an enumeration of powers expressly granted by the people to their government. It has been said, that these powers ought to be construed strictly. But why ought they to be so construed? Is there one sentence in the constitution which gives countenance to this rule? In the last of the enumerated powers, that which grants, expressly, the means for carrying all others into execution, congress is authorized "to make all laws which shall be necessary and proper" for the purpose. But this limitation on the means which may be used, is not extended to the powers which are conferred; nor is there one sentence in the constitution, which has been pointed out by the gentlemen of the bar, or which we have been able to discern, that prescribes this rule. We do not, therefore, think ourselves justified in adopting it. What do gentlemen mean, by a strict construction? If they contend only against that enlarged construction, which would extend words beyond their natural and obvious import, we might question the application of the term, but should not controvert the principle. If they contend for that narrow construction which, in support of some theory not to be found in the constitution, would deny to the government those powers which the words of the grant, as usually understood, import, and which are consistent with the general views and objects of the instrument—for that narrow construction, which would cripple the government, and render it unequal to the objects for which it is declared to be instituted, and to which the powers given, as fairly understood, render it competent—then we cannot perceive the propriety of this strict construction, nor adopt it as the rule by which the constitution is to be expounded. As men whose intentions require no concealment, generally employ the words which most directly and aptly express the ideas they intend to convey, the enlightened patriots who framed our constitution, and the people who adopted it, must be understood to have employed words in their natural sense, and to have intended what they have said. If, from the imperfection of human language, there should be serious doubts respecting the extent of any given power, it is a well settled rule, that the objects for which it was given, especially, when those objects are expressed in the instrument itself, should have great influence in the construction. . . . We know of no rule for construing the extent of such powers, other than is given by the language of the instrument which confers them, taken in connection with the purposes for which they were conferred.

The words are: "Congress shall have power to regulate commerce with foreign nations, and among the several states, and with the Indian tribes." The subject to be regulated is commerce; and our constitution being, as was aptly said at the bar, one of enumeration, and not of definition, to ascertain the extent of the power, it becomes necessary to settle the meaning of the word. The counsel for the appellee would limit it to traffic, to buying and selling, or the interchange of commodities, and do not admit that it comprehends navigation. This would restrict a general term, applicable to many objects, to one of its significations. Commerce, undoubtedly, is traffic, but it is something more—it is intercourse. It describes the commercial intercourse between nations, and parts of nations, in all its branches, and is regulated by prescribing rules for carrying on that intercourse. The mind can scarcely conceive a system for regulating commerce between nations which shall exclude all laws concerning navigation, which shall be silent on the admission of the vessels of the one nation into the ports of the other, and confined to prescribing rules for the conduct of individuals, in the actual employment of buying and selling or of barter. If commerce does not include navigation, the government of the Union has no direct power over that subject, and can make no law prescribing what shall constitute American vessels, or requiring that they shall be navigated by American seamen. Yet this power has been exercised from the commencement of the government, has been exercised with the consent of all, and has been understood by all to be a commercial regulation. All America understands, and has uniformly understood, the word "commerce," to comprehend navigation. It was so understood, and must have been so understood, when the constitution was framed. The power over commerce, including navigation, was one of the primary objects for which the people of America adopted their government, and must have been contemplated in forming it. The convention must have used the word in that sense, because all have understood it in that sense; and the attempt to restrict it comes too late. If the opinion that "commerce," as the word is used in the constitution, comprehends navigation also, requires any additional confirmation, that additional confirmation is, we think, furnished by the words of the instrument itself. It is a rule of construction, acknowledged by all, that the exceptions from a power mark its extent: for it would be absurd, as well as useless, to except from a granted power, that which was not granted—that which the words of the grant could not comprehend. If, then, there are in the constitution plain exceptions from the power over navigation, plain inhibitions to the exercise of that power in a particular way, it is a proof that those who made these exceptions, and prescribed these inhibitions, understood the power to which they applied as being granted. The 9th section of the last article declares, that "no preference shall be given, by any regulation of commerce or revenue, to the ports of one state over those of another." This clause cannot be understood as applicable to those laws only which are passed for the purposes of revenue, because it is expressly applied to commercial regulations; and the most obvious preference which can be given to one port over another, in regulating commerce, relates to navigation. But the subsequent part of the sentence is still more explicit. It is, "nor shall vessels bound to or from one state, be obliged to enter, clear or pay duties in another." These words have a direct reference to navigation. . . .

The word used in the constitution, then, comprehends, and has been always understood to comprehend, navigation within its meaning; and a power to regulate navigation, is as expressly granted, as if that term had been added to the word "commerce." To what commerce does this power extend? The constitution informs us, to commerce "with foreign nations, and among the several states, and with the Indian tribes." It has, we believe, been universally admitted, that these words comprehend every species of commercial intercourse between the United States and foreign nations. No sort of trade can be carried on between this country and any other, to which this power does not extend. It has been truly said, that commerce, as the word is used in the constitution, is a unit, every part of which is indicated by the term.

If this be the admitted meaning of the word, in its application to foreign nations, it must carry the same meaning throughout the sentence, and remain a unit, unless there be some plain intelligible cause which alters it. The subject to which the power is next applied, is to commerce, "among the several states." The word "among" means intermingled with. A thing which is among others, is intermingled with them. Commerce among the states, cannot stop at the external boundary line of each state, but may be introduced into the interior. It is not intended to say, that these words comprehend that commerce, which is completely internal, which is carried on between man and man in a state, or between different parts of the same state, and which does not extend to or affect other states. Such a power would be inconvenient, and is certainly unnecessary. Comprehensive as the word "among" is, it may very properly be restricted to that commerce which concerns more states than one. The phrase is not one which would probably have been selected to indicate the completely interior traffic of a state, because it is not an apt phrase for that purpose; and the enumeration of the particular classes of commerce to which the power was to be extended, would not have been made, had the intention been to extend the power to every description. The enumeration presupposes something not enumerated; and that something, if we regard the language or the subject of the sentence, must be the exclusively internal commerce of a state. The genius and character of the whole government seem to be, that its action is to be applied to all the external concerns of the nation, and to those internal concerns which affect the states generally; but not to those which are completely within a particular state, which do not affect other states, and with which it is not necessary to interfere, for the purpose of executing some of the general powers of the government. The completely internal commerce of a state, then, may be considered as reserved for the state itself.

But, in regulating commerce with foreign nations, the power of congress does not stop at the jurisdictional lines of the several states. It would be a very useless power, if it could not pass those lines. The commerce of the United States with foreign nations is that of the whole United States; every district has a right to participate in it. The deep streams which penetrate our country in every direction pass through the interior of almost every state in the Union, and furnish the means of exercising this right. If congress has the power to regulate it, that power must be exercised whenever the subject exists. If it exists within the states, if a foreign voyage may commence or terminate at a port within a state, then the power of congress may be exercised within a state.

This principle is, if possible, still more clear, when applied to commerce "among the several states." They either join each other, in which case they are separated by a mathematical line, or they are remote from each other, in which case other states lie between them. What is commerce "among" them; and how is it to be conducted? Can a trading expedition between two adjoining states, commence and terminate outside of each? And if the trading intercourse be between two states remote from each other, must it not commence in one, terminate in the other, and probably pass through a third? Commerce among the states must of necessity, be commerce with the states. In the regulation of trade with the Indian tribes, the action of the law, especially, when the constitution was made, was chiefly within a state. The power of congress, then, whatever it may be, must be exercised within the territorial jurisdiction of the several states. The sense of the nation on this subject, is unequivocally manifested by the provisions made in the laws for transporting goods, by land, between Baltimore and Providence, between New York and Philadelphia, and between Philadelphia and Baltimore.

We are now arrived at the inquiry—what is this power? It is the power to regulate; that is, to prescribe the rule by which commerce is to be governed. This power, like all others vested in congress, is complete in itself, may be exercised to its utmost extent, and acknowledges no limitations, other than are prescribed in the constitution. These are expressed in plain terms, and do not affect the questions which arise in this case, or which have been discussed at the bar. If, as has always been understood, the sovereignty of congress, though limited to specified objects, is plenary as to those objects, the power over commerce with foreign nations, and among the several states, is vested in congress as absolutely as it would be in a single government, having in its constitution the same restrictions on the exercise of the power as are found in the constitution of the United States. The wisdom and the discretion of congress, their identity with the people, and the influence which their constituents possess at elections, are, in this, as in many other instances, as that, for example, of declaring war, the sole restraints on which they have relied, to secure them from its abuse. They are the restraints on which the people must often rely solely, in all representative governments. . . .

But it has been urged, with great earnestness, that although the power of congress to regulate commerce with foreign nations, and among the several states, be co-extensive with the subject itself, and have no other limits than are prescribed in the constitution, yet the states may severally exercise the same power within their respective jurisdictions. In support of this argument, it is said that they possessed it as an inseparable attribute of sovereignty before the formation of the constitution, and still retain it, except so far as they have surrendered it by that instrument; that this principle results from the nature of the government, and is secured by the tenth amendment; that an affirmative grant of power is not exclusive, unless in its own nature it be such that the continued exercise of it by the former possessor is inconsistent with the grant, and that this is not of that description. The appellant conceding these postulates, except the last, contends that full power to regulate a particular subject implies the whole power, and leaves no residuum; that a grant of the whole is incompatible with the existence of a right in another to any part of it. Both parties have appealed to the constitution, to legislative acts, and judicial decisions; and have drawn arguments from all these sources to support and illustrate the propositions they respectively maintain.

The grant of the power to lay and collect taxes is, like the power to regulate commerce, made in general terms, and has never been understood to interfere with the exercise of the same power by the states; and hence has been drawn an argument which has been applied to the question under consideration. But the two grants are not, it is conceived, similar in their terms or their nature. Although many of the powers formerly exercised by the states are transferred to the government of the Union, yet the state governments remain, and constitute a most important part of our system. The power of taxation is indispensable to their existence, and is a power which, in its own nature, is capable of residing in, and being exercised by, different authorities at the same time. We are accustomed to see it placed, for different purposes, in different hands. Taxation is the simple operation of taking small portions from a perpetually accumulating mass, susceptible of almost infinite division; and a power in one to take what is necessary for certain purposes, is not in its nature incompatible with a power in another to take what is necessary for other purposes. Congress is authorized to lay and collect taxes, etc., to pay the debts, and provide for the common defense and general welfare of the United States. This does not interfere with the power of the states to tax for the support of their own governments; nor is the exercise of that power by the states an exercise of any portion of the power that is granted to the United States. In imposing taxes for state purposes, they are not doing what congress is empowered to do. Congress is not empowered to tax for those purposes which are within the exclusive province of the states. When, then, each government exercises the power of taxation, neither is exercising the power of the other. But when a state proceeds to regulate commerce with foreign nations, or among the several states, it is exercising the very power that is granted to congress, and is doing the very thing which congress is authorized to do. There is no analogy then, between the power of taxation and the power of regulating commerce.

In discussing the question whether this power is still in the states, in the case under consideration, we may dismiss from it the inquiry, whether it is surrendered by the mere grant to congress, or is retained until congress shall exercise the power. We may dismiss that inquiry because it has been exercised, and the regulations which congress deemed it proper to make are now in full operation. The sole question is, can a state regulate commerce with foreign nations and among the states while congress is regulating it? . . .

The idea that the same measure might, according to circumstances be arranged with different classes of power, was no novelty to the framers of our constitution. Those illustrious statesmen and patriots had been, many of them, deeply engaged in the discussion which preceded the war of our revolution, and all of them were well read in those discussions. The right to regulate commerce, even by the imposition of duties, was not controverted; but the right to impose a duty for the purpose of revenue, produced a war as important, perhaps, in its consequences to the human race, as any the world has ever witnessed.

These restrictions [those in Art. I, Sec. 10, barring states from laying duties on imports or exports] . . . are on the taxing power, not on that to regulate commerce; and presuppose the existence of that which they restrain, not of that which they do not purport to restrain.

But the inspection laws are said to be regulations of commerce, and are certainly recognized in the constitution as being passed in the exercise of a power remaining with the states.

That inspection laws may have a remote and considerable influence on commerce, will not be denied; but that a power to regulate commerce is the source from which the right to pass them is derived, cannot be admitted. The object of inspection laws, is to improve the quality of articles produced by the labor of a country; to fit them for exportation; or it may be, for domestic use. They act upon the subject, before it becomes an article of foreign commerce, or of commerce among the states, and prepare it for that purpose. They form a portion of that immense mass of legislation, which embraces everything within the territory of a state, not surrendered to a general government; all of which can be most advantageously exercised by the states themselves. Inspection laws, quarantine laws, health laws of every description, as well as laws for regulating the internal commerce of a state, and those which respect turnpike roads, ferries, etc., are component parts of this mass.

No direct general power over these objects is granted to congress, and, consequently, they remain subject to state legislation. If the legislative power of the Union can reach them, it must be, where the power is expressly given for a special purpose, or is clearly incidental to some power which is expressly given. It is obvious, that the government of the Union, in the exercise of its express powers, that, for example, of regulating commerce with foreign nations and among the states, may use means that may also be employed by a state, in the exercise of its acknowledged powers; that, for example, of regulating commerce within the state. If congress licenses vessels to sail from one port to another, in the same state, the act is supposed to be, necessarily, incidental to the power expressly granted to congress, and implies no claim of a direct power to regulate the purely internal commerce of a state, or to act directly on its system of police. So, if a state, in passing laws on subjects acknowledged to be within its control, and with a view to those subjects, shall adopt a measure of the same character with one which congress may adopt, it does not derive its authority from the particular power which has been granted, but from some other which remains with the state. All experience shows that the same measures, or measures scarcely distinguishable from each other, may flow from distinct powers; but this does not prove that the powers themselves are identical. Although the means used in their execution may sometimes approach each other so nearly as to be confounded, there are other situations in which they are sufficiently distinct to establish their individuality.

In our complex system, presenting the rare and difficult scheme of one general government whose action extends over the whole, but which possesses only certain enumerated powers; and of numerous state governments, which retain and exercise all powers not delegated to the Union, contests respecting power must arise. Were it even otherwise, the measures taken by the respective governments to execute their acknowledged powers would often be of the same description, and might sometimes interfere. This, however, does not prove that the one is exercising, or has a right to exercise, the powers of the other.

It has been said that the act of August 7, 1789, acknowledges a concurrent power in the states to regulate the conduct of pilots, and hence is inferred an admission of their concurrent right with congress to regulate commerce with foreign nations, and amongst the states. But this inference is not, we think, justified by the fact. Although congress cannot enable a state to legislate, congress may adopt the provisions of a state on any subject. When the government of the Union was brought into existence, it found a system for the regulation of its pilots in full force in every state. The act which has been mentioned, adopts this system, and gives it the same validity as if its provisions had been specially made by congress. But the act, it may be said, is prospective also, and the adoption of laws to be made in future, presupposes the right in the maker to legislate on the subject. The act unquestionably manifests an intention to leave this subject entirely to the states, until congress should think proper to interpose; but the very enactment of such a law indicates an opinion that it was necessary; that the existing system would not be applicable to the new state of things, unless expressly applied to it by congress. . . . The acknowledged power of a state to regulate its police, its domestic trade and to govern its own citizens, may enable it to legislate on this subject to a considerable extent; and the adoption of its system by congress, and the application of it to the whole subject of commerce, does not seem to the court to imply a right in the states so to apply it of their own authority . . . the adoption of the state system being temporary, being only "until further legislative provision shall be made by congress," shows, conclusively, an opinion, that congress could control the whole subject, and might adopt the system of the states, or provide one of its own. . . .

Since, however, in exercising the power of regulating their own purely internal affairs, whether of trading or police, the states may sometimes enact laws, the validity of which depends on their [not] interfering with, and being contrary to, an act of congress passed in pursuance of the constitution, the court will enter upon the inquiry whether the laws of New York, as expounded by the highest tribunal of that state, have, in their application to this case, come into collision with an act of congress, and deprived a citizen of a right to which that act entitles him. Should this collision exist, it will be immaterial whether those laws were passed in virtue of a concurrent power "to regulate commerce with foreign nations and among the several states," or, in virtue of a power to regulate their domestic trade and police. In one case and the other, the acts of New York must yield to the law of congress, and the decision sustaining the privilege they confer, against a right given by a law of the Union, must be erroneous. This opinion has been frequently expressed in this court, and is founded, as well on the nature of the government, as on the words of the constitution. In argument, however, it has been contended, that if a law passed by a state, in the exercise of its acknowledged sovereignty comes into conflict with a law passed by congress in pursuance of the constitution, they affect the subject, and each other, like equal opposing powers. But the framers of our constitution foresaw this state of things, and provided for it, by declaring the supremacy not only of itself, but of the laws made in pursuance of it.

The nullity of any act, inconsistent with the constitution, is produced by the declaration, that the constitution is the supreme law. The appropriate application of that part of the clause which confers the same supremacy on laws and treaties, is to such acts of the state legislatures as do not transcend their powers, but though enacted in the execution of acknowledged state powers, interfere with, or are contrary to, the laws of congress, made in pursuance of the constitution, or some treaty made under the authority of the United States. In every such case, the act of congress, or the treaty, is supreme; and the law of the state, though enacted in the exercise of powers not controverted, must yield to it. . . .

Justice Johnston: The history of the times will . . . sustain the opinion, that the grant of power over commerce, if intended to be commensurate with the evils existing, and the purpose of remedying those evils, could be only commensurate with the power of the states over the subject. . . .

The "power to regulate commerce," here meant to be granted, was that power to regulate commerce which previously existed in the states. But what was that power? The states were unquestionably, supreme; and each possessed that power over commerce, which is acknowledged to reside in every sovereign state. The definition and limits of that power are to be sought among the features of international law; and, as it was not only admitted, but insisted on by both parties, in argument, that, "unaffected by a state of war, by treaties, or by municipal regulations, all commerce among independent states was legitimate," there is no necessity to appeal to the oracles of the *jus commune* for the correctness of that doctrine. The law of nations, regarding man as a social animal, pronounces all commerce legitimate, in a state of peace, until prohibited by positive law. The power of a sovereign state over commerce, therefore, amounts to nothing more than a power to limit and restrain it at pleasure. And since the power to prescribe the limits to its freedom, necessarily implies the power to determine what shall remain unrestrained it follows, that the power must be exclusive; it can reside but in one potentate; and hence, the grant of this power carries with it the whole subject, leaving nothing for the state to act upon. . . .

. . . Power to regulate foreign commerce, is given in the same words, and in the same breath, as it were, with that over the commerce of the states and with the Indian tribes. But the power to regulate foreign commerce is necessarily exclusive. The states are unknown to foreign nations: their sovereignty exists only with relation to each other and the general government. Whatever regulations foreign commerce should be subjected to in the ports of the Union, the general government would be held responsible for them; and all other regulations, but those which congress had imposed, would be regarded by foreign nations as trespasses and violations of national faith and comity.

But the language which grants the power as to one description of commerce, grants it as to all; and, in fact, if ever the exercise of a right, or acquiescence in a construction, could be inferred from contemporaneous and continued assent, it is that of the exclusive effect of this grant.

A right over the subject has never been pretended to, in any instance, except as incidental to exercise of some other unquestionable power. . . .

When speaking of the power of congress over navigation, I do not regard it as a power incidental to that of regulating commerce; I consider it as the thing itself; inseparable from it as vital motion is from vital existence.

Commerce, in its simplest signification, means an exchange of goods: but in the advancement of society, labor, transportation, intelligence, care, and various mediums of exchange, become commodities, and enter into commerce; the subject, the vehicle, the agent, and their various operations, become the objects of commercial regulation. Shipbuilding, the carrying trade, and propagation of seamen, are such vital agents of commercial prosperity, that the nation which could not legislate over these subjects, would not possess power to regulate commerce. . . .

It is impossible, with the views which I entertain of the principle on which the commercial privileges of the people of the United States among themselves, rests [sic], to concur in the view which this court takes of the effect of the coasting license in this cause. I do not regard it as the foundation of the right set up in behalf of the appellant. If there was any one object riding over every other in the adoption of the constitution, it was to keep the commercial intercourse among the states free from all invidious and partial restraints. And I cannot overcome the conviction, that if the licensing act was repealed tomorrow, the rights of the appellant to a reversal of the decision complained of, would be as strong as it is under this license. . . .

. . . This court doth further direct, order and decree, that the bill of the said Aaron Ogden be dismissed, and the same is hereby dismissed accordingly.

QUESTIONS FOR REVIEW AND DISCUSSION

1. What key constitutional issue was decided in each of the following cases: *McCulloch* v. *Maryland, Dartmouth College* v. *Woodward, Charles River Bridge* v. *Warren Bridge*, and *Gibbons* v. *Ogden?* Are there secondary or related constitutional questions that the Court decided, or dismissed as not pertinent?
2. As shown in these cases, what was the Supreme Court's view of a corporation? (*See* particularly *Dartmouth College* v. *Woodward*.)
3. According to those Supreme Court decisions, what seem to be the requirements for having a binding contract?
4. According to those Supreme Court decisions, are there times or conditions when public interests might prevail over private rights? What modern examples could be used for elaboration or discussion of this issue?
5. In issues relating to federal authority versus state authority over commerce, how did the Supreme Court usually decide? Why? Are there inconsistencies?
6. How did Chief Justice Marshall justify the power of the federal government to create corporations? According to Marshall, did the states have equal au-

thority? Are states prohibited from incorporating businesses insofar as the opinions of the justices would suggest?

7. Why is the power to tax, a critical issue in the relationship between the federal government and the states?

8. Could the inference be made from *Gibbons* v. *Ogden* that the power of the federal government over navigation includes authority over air traffic, radio and television transmissions, and space traffic?

9. In what areas today might state authority and federal authority, as they relate to regulating business activity, be in conflict?

7

The Coming of
the Railroads

Industrialization in the United States would not
have developed as rapidly as it did without the nearly simultaneous spread of
an extensive railroad network. Beginning in the 1820s with the first
construction of such early lines as the Baltimore and Ohio, the Charleston
and Hamburg, and the Boston and Lowell, railroads by the time of the Civil
War linked the Mississippi Valley with the Atlantic seaboard. During the
Civil War the rail systems of both the North and the South played key
strategic roles as troops and supplies were continually shuttled between the
various combat theaters. Just four years after the end of the fighting, an
event of historic significance took place when the Union Pacific and the
Central Pacific met near Ogden, Utah, in 1869, completing the nation's
first transcontinental line. By 1900 five transcontinentals tied the Pacific
Coast to the Mississippi Valley, and overall track mileage in the United
States had grown from 35,000 miles in 1865 to almost 200,000. (See Table
2-3, p. 50.)

But the railroads did more than just provide vital transportation services.
They also represented the cutting edge of big business in nineteenth century
America. Railroad officials were pioneers in modern management techniques
out of necessity. Because of the size and geographic spread of their
enterprises, they were required to cope with and master unprecedented

problems in corporate finance, business administration, and labor, competitor, and government relations. In the early 1870s, for example, the Pennsylvania Railroad, one of the East's main trunk lines, already represented a capital investment of $400 million. By way of comparison, even the largest textile mills of the time required an investment of only some $500,000.

The case that follows centers on the railroad's part in the adoption of the legal instrument of the corporation as a device for the organization of large-scale business enterprises. The case also probes the railroad experience in governmental relations. The complicated subject of public assistance to private corporations, as first exemplified by the railroad land-grant issue, remains controversial among economists and economic historians to this day. Where does the public interest lie? An analysis of the early record of American railroads can provide some important evidence on which to base an answer to that question.

David M. Potter
E. David Cronon
Howard R. Lamar

THE RAILROAD AND
THE EMERGENCE OF
THE CORPORATION

One basic phase of the nineteenth-century economic transformation was the development of the modern corporation as the characteristic unit of American business organization. Corporations have existed since ancient times, but the modern corporation is quite distinct, economically if not legally, from these earlier forms.

A corporation may be defined as an organization recognized by law as having an identity separate from the identity of the individuals who own it or compose it. If it is a business corporation, ownership is usually represented by shares of stock which are transferable and which thus make it possible for title to change without corresponding change in the identity of the corporation itself.

Since these shares may be distributed among many owners, the corporate form enables any number of individuals to act through a single management and under a common name in operating a business enterprise or enterprises, in holding and managing property, and in distributing the profits or beneficial interests from such enterprise or property among the shareholders. The structure of the corporation is fixed and sanctioned by a grant from the government, either by special legislative act (as in the case of the Bank of the United States), charter, or certifi-

David M. Potter, E. David Cronon, and Howard R. Lamar, eds., *Select Problems in Historical Interpretation: The Railroads* (New York: Holt, Rinehart and Winston, Inc., 1960), 1–23.

cate. The system of shareholding makes possible certain distinctive features: among these are the transferability of ownership; the independent existence of the corporation, apart from the life of the individual owners; and the immunity of shareholders from liability for the corporation's debts.

All these features are conducive to broad distribution of ownership among a large number of people, and it is because of this that the corporation has become an indispensable feature of modern business. At an earlier time in our history almost all businesses were conducted on a small scale, with a limited capital, and were operated by their owners. The small grocery, the bakery, the haberdashery, the cobbler's shop, and the like represented this type of owner-operation, and many of the great mercantile and banking houses of the seventeenth and eighteenth centuries were likewise based upon the capital and the managerial skill that a single family could bring into their enterprise. As a variation upon exclusive ownership by an individual, the partnership existed to permit joint ownership by more than one person. But no partnership could embrace any very large number of owners, for the death of a single partner would terminate the arrangement, and each partner was liable for the full indebtedness of the partnership. Thus no one could safely invest unless he knew and trusted all the other partners and unless he personally kept fully informed as to the affairs of the business.

Until the third decade of the nineteenth century, business enterprise was conducted almost entirely by private owners and by partnerships. During this earlier time corporations were rare and existed only by the special and explicit permission of the government.

Usually the purpose of creating a corporation was to enable it to exercise powers that partook of sovereignty—for example, in the case of a turnpike company, the power of eminent domain, the forcing of private owners to sell the land which might be needed for a right of way; or, in the case of a shipping corporation, the power of occupying shore land for wharves. Also, as a usual thing, the corporation enjoyed certain monopoly rights—the right to issue banknotes, the exclusive right to the marketing of a specific commodity. The East India Company, for instance, one of the greatest corporations of all times, enjoyed monopoly privileges (at least so far as British subjects were concerned) of trading throughout India, and for 200 years it possessed extraordinary governmental powers.

In Colonial America a number of the colonies were founded by corporations. Virginia and Massachusetts were both settled by incorporated companies; Connecticut and Rhode Island possessed corporate charters which they used as constitutions, continuing them in force even after the American Revolution. Despite these instances, however, the corporation was not popular in Colonial times in America, where governmental power and special monopoly were both objects of suspicion and hatred. At the time when Washington became President there were less than two dozen corporations in America, and none of these was of great magnitude. Most of them were canal or turnpike or bank companies which had sought incorporation because they needed special governmental rights and which had been set up by special acts of the legislatures in the states where they operated.

Early in the nineteenth century a new reason for incorporation came into play—a reason far more pressing than the desire to exercise government functions or to enjoy monopoly privileges. This was the desire to find a means of financing large-scale economic projects which were too great to be handled by individual men of wealth. The building of a railroad required a huge investment—$15,000,000 in the case of the Baltimore and Ohio, $25,000,000 for the Erie, $30,000,000 for the New York Central—and that at a time (1845) when only three American families, the Astors, the Stuyvesants, and the Vanderbilts, held fortunes of substantially more than $1,000,000. The only way in which the necessary funds could be raised was by the cooperative action of a large number of investors. Such investors could not personally participate in the management of the enterprise, as earlier types of owners had done, and they could not use the partnership as a device for their association, because the death of an individual would disrupt the whole arrangement and the debts of the enterprise as a whole would hang like an impending doom over the head of each member. But incorporation would insure an existence for the business, independent of the lives of the investors, and its principle of *limited liability* (hence the British term "Ltd.") would protect the personal estate of the investor, and he would hazard only the loss of what he had invested.

The rapid increase in the United States of projects in which large capitalization and therefore multiple ownership and therefore limited liability were required led to a growing volume of requests for incorporation. As the requests multiplied, the state governments found it increasingly unsatisfactory to pass a special law in connection with each, and they also found that special consideration of each separate request paved the way for corruption of the legislators. Consequently, beginning with New York in 1811, and extending to all the other states in due time, laws were adopted under which enterprisers could qualify and could then automatically receive charters of incorporation. By 1850, such general incorporation laws were common. Under these laws rigid requirements were laid down to protect creditors. Usually it was required that a certain proportion of the projected capital should be paid in before business operations began, that the shares should have a par value and should not be issued except upon payment of such par value, that capital should not be paid out as dividends to the disadvantage of the creditors, and that in cases where subscribers received stock without paying the full par value, they were liable to the creditors to the extent to which they had underpaid. The issuance of securities was rigidly controlled.

As a result both of the need for large-scale capitalization in railroads and other industries and of the readiness with which incorporation could be secured, the number of corporations began to increase rapidly at an early date, and the diffusion of ownership became pronounced. Between 1800 and 1823, no less than 557 manufacturing establishments were incorporated in New England, New York, and Pennsylvania. As early as 1838, the Western Railroad of Massachusetts was owned by 2331 stockholders, which means of course that its capital was drawn from 2331 separate investors. In 1853 the New York Central had 2445 stockholders and the Pennsylvania Railroad had 2600 at about the same time.

From that time to the present the place of corporations in American business has grown steadily, and corporations of incredible vastness characterize the economy today. By 1919, for instance, 31 percent of all the manufacturing organizations in the United States were corporations, and these corporations employed 86 percent of the workers and produced 87 percent of the products turned out in the manufacturing field. By 1929 it was estimated that 200 corporations controlled 22 percent of the wealth of the nation, and there were at least fourteen American corporations whose assets amounted to $1,000,000,000 each. In point of stockholder participation, American Telephone and Telegraph boasted 600,000 stockholders; General Motors had a stockholder list of 350,000 names, and the Pennsylvania Railroad of 233,000.

As the problems of bigness and of monopoly came to the fore after the Civil War, there was a strong tendency to condemn the large corporations, sometimes without distinguishing between the abuses of corporate entity and the mere existence of corporations. Also, some corporations became monopolies, and this led to denunciation of corporate monopoly, sometimes as if corporation and monopoly were the same. In view of these loose generalizations, it is well to remember that the corporation is the characteristic form of little business as well as big business. By 1919 there were 91,000 corporations engaged in manufacturing. Most of these, of course, were companies of modest size with no pretensions to monopolistic status and with few of the qualities that have been objected to in a monopoly. In other words, the corporate form has become a basic unit in the American economy, and while its use has been criticized, at times rightly, the attack is not directed against the corporate form itself but only against some of the ways in which that form has been employed.

If the railroads' need of great capital funds had contributed to the development of the corporation as a new type of business organization, their need of certain governmental powers and favors tended to bring about new relationships between government and business. At a time when the traditional American view insisted upon the separation of business and the state and upon the maintenance of *laissez faire*, the railroads invariably needed to invoke the governmental power of eminent domain in order to secure their rights of way, and they usually appealed for governmental aid in the costly projects that they undertook. These appeals were based upon the premise that the completed roads would perform a public service and would be of value to society as a whole.

If such aid were sought today, it would probably take the form of a money grant, but in a period when government was poor in funds and rich in undeveloped and undistributed acreage, it took the form of land grants. Many of the states, such as Illinois and Texas, made grants of land to the railroads, and in the areas where the federal government retained title to the public domain, it also made grants.

The most extensive government land grants were made to the transcontinental railroad companies, such as the Union Pacific, Central Pacific, Southern Pacific, Northern Pacific, and Santa Fe, which were built in the 60's, 70's, and 80's. For a number of reasons the government was disposed to be especially generous in its support of these projects. It was recognized, to begin with, that the investment would be extremely heavy, and further, that the returns were certain to be poor for many years, since the roads ran for hundreds of miles through unsettled country where no traffic would appear until the region had been developed. Also, these roads were regarded as serving a very important national purpose, for they would tend to strengthen the ties of union between the eastern and the Pacific Coast states. The secession of the South had made everyone sensitive to the need for all possible bonds of union.

The first of the transcontinental lines received its charter from Congress in 1862 (amended in 1864). Under the terms of this charter two railroad companies were authorized: one, the Union Pacific to build westward from Council Bluffs; the other, the Central Pacific, to build eastward from Sacramento until the two should meet.

If such a project were undertaken today, public attention would focus upon the question to what extent the government had borne the expense, and whether government ought to exercise most of the control (as it has subsequently done with the water power of the Tennessee Valley and with the potentialities of atomic energy). Emphasis would be placed upon the argument that where public powers were invoked and public assets were contributed, the public welfare ought to be closely safeguarded by governmental supervision of the finances and by participation in the affairs of the railroad. At that time, however, the philosophy of *laissez faire* stood in the way of such considerations, and the public, fascinated by the picturesque and heroic aspects of the construction, neglected to note the cost of the methods used or to question whether the government had provided safeguards to assure that the nation would gain the services of a railroad worth as much as the loans and land grants made by the government. Yet it was evident even then that the government was providing assets much more valuable than those invested by private projectors, and it was possible to regard the builders either as enterprising capitalists whose object was to build and operate a transcontinental railroad and who received government assets to aid them in this important public work, or as shrewd manipulators whose object was to gain possession of public assets and who used the construction of a railroad as a pretext for their demands on the government. The following selections will throw some light on the questions of how much aid the government gave, how members of Congress felt at the time about such extensive aid, how much the land-grant aid contributed to build the railroads or to enrich the builders, and how public aid was abused by the manipulation of funds.

The Charter of the Union Pacific

The first act of aid to railroad building on a vast scale was the charter granted by Congress to the Union Pacific Railroad on July 1, 1862.

An Act to Aid in Construction of a Railroad and Telegraph Line from the Missouri River to the Pacific Ocean and to Secure to the Government the Use of the Same for Postal, Military, and other Purposes.

Be it enacted . . . That Walter S. Burgess . . . [and 157 other persons named in the act] together with five commissioners to be appointed by the Secretary of the Interior, and all persons who shall or may be associated with them, and their successors, are hereby created and erected into a body corporate . . . by the name . . . of "The Union Pacific Railroad Company" . . . [The capital stock is fixed at 100,000 shares of $1000 each ($100,000,000), and it is specified that 2000 shares must be sold before the company can begin operations. At one point it is required that 10 percent must be paid in on such sales (2000 shares at $100 = $200,000), but the next sentence provides that when 2000 shares are subscribed and $10 a share is paid in ($20,000), there shall be a meeting of stockholders and thirteen directors shall be chosen, and thereafter the stockholders shall constitute the company] . . . and the said corporation is hereby authorized . . . to lay out, . . . construct, furnish, maintain, and enjoy a continuous railroad and telegraph . . . from a point on the one hundredth meridian of longitude west from Greenwich, between the south margin of the valley of the Republican River and the north margin of the valley of the Platte River . . . to the western boundary of Nevada Territory. . . .

SEC. 2. *And be it further enacted,* That the right of way through the public lands be, and the same is hereby, granted to said company for the construction of said railroad and telegraph line; and the right, power, and authority is hereby given to said company to take from the public lands adjacent to the line of said road, earth, stone, timber, and other materials for the construction thereof; said right of way is granted to said railroad to the extent of two hundred feet in width on each side of said railroad where it may pass over the public lands, including all necessary grounds for stations, buildings, workshops, and depots, machine shops, switches, side tracks, turntables, and water stations. The United States shall extinguish as rapidly as may be the Indian titles to all lands falling under the operation of this act and required for the said right of way and grants hereinafter made.

SEC. 3. *And be it further enacted*, That there be, and is hereby, granted to the said company, for the purpose of aiding in the construction of said railroad and telegraph line, and to secure the safe and speedy transportation of the mails, troops, munitions of war, and public stores thereon, every alternate section of public land, designated by odd numbers, to the amount of five alternate sections per mile on each side of said railroad, on the line thereof, and within the limits of ten miles on each side of said road, not sold, reserved, or otherwise disposed of by the United States . . . *Provided*, That all mineral lands shall be excepted from the operation of this act; but where the same shall contain timber, the timber thereon is hereby granted to said company. And all such lands, so granted by this section, which shall not be sold or disposed of by said company within three years after the entire road shall have been completed, shall be subject to settlement and preemption, like other lands, at a price not exceeding one dollar and twenty-five cents per acre, to be paid to said company.

SEC. 4. *And be it further enacted*, That whenever said company shall have completed forty consecutive miles of any portion of said railroad and telegraph line . . . patents shall issue conveying the right and title to said lands to said company, on each side of the road as far as the same is completed, to the amount aforesaid; and patents shall in like manner issue as each forty miles of said railroad and telegraph line are completed upon certificate of said commissioners.

SEC. 5. *And be it further enacted*, That for the purposes herein mentioned the Secretary of the Treasury shall, upon . . . the completion and equipment of forty consecutive miles of said railroad and telegraph . . . issue to said company bonds of the United States of one thousand dollars each . . . bearing 6 per centum per annum interest . . . to the amount of sixteen of said bonds per mile for such section of forty miles; and to secure the repayment to the United States . . . of the amount of said bonds . . . the issue of said bonds and delivery to the company shall ipso facto constitute a first mortgage on the whole line of the railroad and telegraph, together with the rolling stock, fixtures, and property of every kind. . . .

SEC. 6. *And be it further enacted*, That the grants aforesaid are made upon condition that said company shall pay said bonds at maturity, and shall keep said

railroad and telegraph line in repair and use, and shall at all times transmit dis-
patches over said telegraph line, and transport mails, troops, and munitions of
war, supplies, and public stores upon said railroad for the government, whenever
required to do so by any department thereof, and that the government shall at all
times have the preference in the use of the same for all the purposes aforesaid (at
fair and reasonable rates of compensation, not to exceed the amounts paid by private parties for the same kind of service); and all compensation for services
rendered for the government shall be applied to the payment of said bonds and interest until the whole amount is fully paid. . . .

SEC. 11. *And be it further enacted,* That for three hundred miles of said road
most mountainous and difficult of construction, to wit: one hundred and fifty
miles westwardly from the eastern base of the Rocky Mountains, and one hundred and fifty miles eastwardly from the western base of the Sierra Nevada, said
points to be fixed by the President of the United States, the bonds to be issued to
aid in the construction thereof shall be treble the number per mile herein-before
provided . . . and between the sections last named of one hundred and fifty miles
each, the bonds to be issued to aid in the construction thereof shall be double the
number per mile first mentioned. . . .

SEC. 18. *And be it further enacted,* That whenever it appears that the net earnings of the entire road and telegraph, including the amount allowed for services
rendered for the United States, after deducting all expenditures, including re-
pairs, and the furnishing, running, and managing of said road, shall exceed ten
per centum upon its cost, exclusive of the five per centum to be paid to the United
States, Congress may reduce the rates of fare thereon, if unreasonable in amount,
and may fix and establish the same by law. And the better to accomplish the objects of this act, namely, to promote the public interest and welfare by the
construction of said railroad and telegraph line, and keeping the same in working
order, and to secure to the government at all times (but particularly in time of
war) the use and benefits of the same for postal, military and other purposes, Congress may, at any time, having due regard for the rights of said companies name
herein, add to, alter, amend, or repeal this act.

Debates on Increasing the Grants

In spite of the inducements offered by the act of incorporation of the Union Pacific, the promoters hesitated to proceed, and as a consequence, members of
Congress proposed to liberalize the terms by amending the charter. Specifically,
the proposed changes were (1) the width of the right of way should be reduced
to 200 feet; (2) the land grant should amount to ten sections of land on each side
of the track for each mile of track, the land selected to lie within twenty miles of

the track; (3) the exemption of mineral land should not apply to coal and iron; (4) the charges for the hauling of government supplies should be paid one half in cash instead of being credited in toto against the company's indebtedness to the government; (5) the bonds and land grants should become available after each twenty miles of construction had been completed; (6) the United States would permit the company to issue its own bonds, secured by a first mortgage upon the property, and accordingly the security for the government's loan of bonds should become a second mortgage rather than a first mortgage; (7) the number of elected directors should be increased to fifteen and the number of government-appointed directors to five. All these proposals were adopted in 1864, but only after debates which pointed up some of the implications of these sweeping changes. Representatives John V. L. Pruyn of New York, Elihu B. Washburne of Illinois, and Thaddeus Stevens of Pennsylvania engaged in the following discussion on June 21, 1864.

MR. PRUYN: There is one cardinal question at the outset which the House is called upon to determine, and that is by what agency this road shall be built. The company chartered in 1862 was authorized to commence operations whenever $2,000,000 should have been subscribed and 10 percent or $200,000 paid in on that amount.

The grant by the Government in aid of the work is divisible into two parts; in the first place, the right of way over the whole territory of the United States, wherever the Government still holds land, and a large land grant to the company in addition; and secondly, and which is the most important present aid, a large issue of Government bonds, which the company are to receive and sell for the purpose of enabling them to build the road. I do not recollect what these bonds would amount to, but I think it is entirely safe to estimate them at $100,000,000.

MR. WASHBURNE: Ninety-five million and eighty-eight thousand dollars.

MR. STEVENS: The sum is to be $16,000 a mile to the foot of the Rocky Mountains, then $48,000 a mile for one hundred and fifty miles, then $32,000 a mile to the base of the Nevada mountains, then $48,000 a mile for one hundred and fifty miles, then $15,000 a mile until they reach San Francisco; not exceeding in all $100,000,000.

MR. PRUYN: Substantially then the state of the case is this: that in consideration of $2,000,000 subscribed by individuals, of which 10 percent has been paid, the Government of the United States gives the right of way and makes a large land grant in aid of this road, and then gives it $100,000,000 in addition. Now, it will be observed in order to secure the faithful application of this fund as far as these individuals are concerned, looking at it in that point of view and without reference to who the individuals are, and taking it for granted, if you please, that the fund will all be rightly and fairly appropriated, they contribute 2 percent only of the money, and no part, of course, of the real estate. If we consider the whole as an investment of $150,000,000, it would be a contribution of 1.5 percent, or at $200,000,000 but 1 percent on the part of the company which undertakes to build this road, toward its construction.

In other words, the Government in fact builds the road, and ought to control or own it, and then no land grant could be called for. The Government is the party to be responsible for this outlay when once commenced; and when you begin it you must go through with it, cost what it may, or otherwise lose what you put in. No company can be expected to operate it at a loss. . . .

In the shape in which it now stands it is virtually admitted by the company—and I have no doubt it is true—that the company cannot go on and construct this road with the grant in bonds made by the act of 1862. Now, how shall we proceed? Shall we hand this over to gentlemen who contribute one or two percent of the amount, with whose appointment we have nothing to do, over whom we have no control except in a very indirect way; shall we hand over this great public work with the large grant attached to it to such a body of men—I care not how wealthy or respectable or influential they may be—or shall we at once in some plain, direct, and efficient manner take charge of it ourselves?

I believe I hazard very little in saying, from conversations with some of the leading men of the country who have taken an interest in this matter, that a board might be organized by the Government, consisting of five, seven, or nine individuals of experience, character, and position, who would, in view of the great public benefits to be conferred by that work, undertake to supervise its construction without any pay. If such a board can be procured, it will work more efficiently, more thoroughly, and more actively than any other organization, at any rate more satisfactorily than any corporate organization such as that which now exists. . . .

MR. WASHBURNE: . . . I come now to the tenth section of the bill, and I confess to a sort of admiration of the sublime audacity which parties must have to come here and ask Congress to enact such a provision into a law. I have called attention to other provisions of an extraordinary nature, but this proposed enactment throws all others far into the shade, and stands out in bold relief as an indication of the "base uses" that this company have conceived that Congress may be put to in their behalf. I carefully read the section that every gentleman may know its exact meaning and purport:

"SEC. 10. *And be it further enacted,* That section five of said act be so modified and amended that the Union Pacific Railroad Company, the Central Pacific Railroad Company, and any other company authorized to participate in the construction of said road, may issue their first mortgage bonds on their respective railroads and telegraph lines to an amount not exceeding the amount of the bonds of the United States authorized to be issued to said railroad companies respectively. *And the lien of the United States bonds shall be subordinate to that of the bonds of any or either of said companies hereby authorized to be issued on their respective roads, property, and equipments.* And said section is further amended by striking out the word 'forty' and inserting in lieu thereof the words 'on each and every section of not less than twenty.' . . . "

The bonds of the United States are to be issued to the company, and the Government is to have no *prior lien* for its security; but by this provision the company representing as it may but 1 percent or a little over of the amount that the Government is liable for, is to subordinate that Government to its own interests, raise money on the security of the means that the Government has furnished, give a first mortgage for the security of that money, and leave the United States as a *second mortgagee*, obliged to pay off the first mortgage before it can be in a position to take advantage of any security there might by possibility be as a second mortgagee. But who is wild enough to believe that should the provisions of this section become a law the remaining security of the Government will be worth a straw? It is worse than idle to contend that we shall have any security left for all our liability if this bill shall pass. And further, by the fifth section of the law bonds cannot be issued till *forty* consecutive miles of the road are fully completed and equipped. It is now proposed by this tenth section to strike out forty and make it twenty. This company, not content with snatching from the Government the security it now holds for the bonds it issues, cannot even wait to finish the forty miles of road at present required before grabbing what is proposed to put into their hands, but they must cut it down so that they can go in on twenty miles. Sir, on my responsibility as a Representative, I pronounce this as the most monstrous and flagrant attempt to overreach the Government and the people that can be found in all the legislative annals of the country. . . .

MR. STEVENS [*speaking for the committee which had reported the bill*]: Your committee came at once to the determination not to burden the nation at this time with any further liabilities or obligation. They said to the company, "Take what land you choose; it is worth nothing to the Government; it is not held out for sale; it is worth nothing except as it becomes populated, and as you populate it you do us a benefit; do not ask us for more bonds; we will take off some of the restrictions and make the conditions lighter, so as to enable you to go on with the work. . . . "

We agreed, also, to double the amount of lands. What lands? Why, the sections on each side of the road! The gentleman lives in the West, and knows all about this matter. He knows that after we get beyond the one hundredth degree of longitude the land is hardly worth holding. From there, for some five hundred miles to the Rocky Mountains, the concession of land, except upon some small streams, is merely of nominal value. In the Rocky Mountains it is solid land, and yet it is not very valuable. When you get to the other side of the Rocky Mountains, to what is called the plains, you find a barren valley that bears nothing but sage of the bitterest kind, and that never can be made fertile for any use whatever. Then you come upon the Sierra Nevada, and when you pass over that range of mountains you find no land worth anything until you get into California, and there the lands have all been taken up long ago.

It is also charged, Mr. Speaker, that we allow this company to issue its own bonds and give a first mortgage. That is true; but that does not take a dollar from the Government now. It does not weaken the Administration in carrying on this war and defraying its expenses. The only doubt is whether this road will bear the two mortgages. It is very clear that unless the second mortgage is to be got in this way the road will never be finished and will never earn a dollar. I doubt not that when this road is finished and the vast travel between the two oceans sets in over it, when the business not only of this country but the commerce of the far East shall be brought across this continent to the population on this side of the Rocky Mountains and on its way to Europe, as it will be the only short thoroughfare, the road will be so productive as not only to pay all its liabilities but to make its stock very valuable.

Suppose the road does cost $200,000,000. The amount of the interest will be $12,000,000 a year. The Central road of Pennsylvania receives more than half that in tolls. Last year and the year before the railroad between Pittsburgh and Philadelphia received $7,000,000. The Erie Canal of New York I believe receives some $6,000,000 of tolls annually, and I believe the New York Central railroad receives more.

A MEMBER: Ten million dollars a year.

MR. STEVENS: Ten million dollars I am told. If these lines, on such short distances, have such receipts, I imagine we can hardly figure up the amount that will be received on this great work. . . . Ten, sir, I say that both these mortgages will be fairly paid, in time; and although the bonds of the Government may be postponed to the others, the Government will receive vast advantages from the very fact that the road is finished and pours the wealth of California into its coffers, besides keeping together the Union as it now is.

How Federal Aid was Used—Credit Mobilier

When Congress was debating the amendment of the Union Pacific charter, Representative Pruyn had questioned the wisdom of handing over immense public assets "to gentlemen who contribute one or two percent of the amount." His objections, however, were overruled and, in the five years following, the construction of the

Union Pacific went forward at a pace which seemed to vindicate the terms of the charter. The building of the road was pushed with great energy. The resourcefulness of the engineers in getting over the Sierra Nevada, and the staunchness of the workers who labored under every obstacle of cold, heat, landslide, and Indian menace made possible the completion of the epic undertaking within five years. In 1869, the Union and Central Pacific lines met at Promontory Point in Utah, and the first transcontinental line was thus completed.

The pride of America in this physical achievement was soon marred by revelations of the misuse of government aid. It was discovered that a construction company, the Credit Mobilier of America, had contrived to divert most of the assets to itself and that, while doing so, it had attempted to avoid Congressional scrutiny by bribing Congressmen with shares of stock in the enterprise. This factor of political corruption was the first major revelation, but it was soon followed by an investigation which showed the way in which promoters had enriched themselves by the manipulation of federal aid without incurring any economic risk of their own fortunes. The manner in which this was done was reported in 1873 by the Congressional Committee which investigated the affair.

This act was not passed to further the personal interests of the corporators, nor for the advancement of commercial interests, nor for the convenience of the general public alone; but in addition to these the interests, present and future, of the Government, as such, were to be subserved. A great highway was to be created, the use of which for postal, military, and other purposes was to be secured to the Government "at all times," but particularly in time of war. Your committee deem it important to call especial attention to this declared object of this act, to accomplish which object the munificent grant of lands and loan of the Government credit was made. . . .

Congress relied for the performance of these great trusts by the corporators upon their sense of public duty; upon the fact that they were to deal with and protect a large capital of their own which they were to pay in in money; upon the presence of five directors appointed by the President especially to represent the public interests, who were to own no stock; one of whom should be a member of every committee, standing or special; upon commissioners to be appointed by the President, who should examine and report upon the work as it progressed; in certain cases upon the certificate of the chief engineer, to be made upon his professional honor; and lastly, upon the reserved power to add to, alter, amend, or repeal the act.

Your committee find themselves constrained to report that the moneys borrowed by the corporation, under a power given them, only to meet the necessities of the construction and endowment of the road, have been distributed in dividends among the corporators; that the stock was issued, not to men who paid for it at par in money, but who paid for it at not more that 30 cents on the dollar in road making; that of the Government directors some of them have neglected their duties and others have been interested in the transactions by which the provisions of the organic law have been evaded; that at least one of the commissioners appointed by the President has been directly bribed to betray his trust by the gift of $25,000; that the chief engineer of the road was largely interested in the contracts for its construction; and that there has been an attempt to prevent the exercise of the reserved power in Congress by inducing influential members of Congress to become interested in the profits of the transaction. So that of the safeguards above enumerated none seems to be left but the sense of public duty of the corporators.

Your committee, therefore, proceed to report the facts as they have been able to gather them from the evidence, relative to the manner in which the parties in whom these trusts were reposed have discharged them, and the consequences which have followed.

By reference to the first section of the act of 1862, it will be seen that a subscription of $2,000,000, two thousand shares of $1000 each, and the payment of 10 percent thereon, was a condition-precedent to organization.

The sum of about $2,180,000 was subscribed, and 10 percent (about $218,000) paid in, and thereupon, in October, 1863, the company was organized by the election of a board of directors, &c.

The first contract for the construction of the road was made with one H. M. Hoxie, who seems to have been a person of little pecuniary responsibility. His proposal to build and equip one hundred miles of the railroad and telegraph is dated New York, August 8, 1864, signed H. M. Hoxie, by H. C. Crane, attorney. It was accepted by the company September 23, 1864. On the 30th of September, 1864, Hoxie agreed to assign this contract Thomas C. Durant, who was then vice-president and director of the Union Pacific Railroad Company, or such parties as he might designate. On the 4th of October, 1864, this contract was extended to the one hundredth meridian, an additional one hundred and forty-six and forty-five hundredths miles, the agreement for extension being signed by Crane as attorney of Hoxie. Hoxie was an employee of the company at the time, and Mr. Crane, who signed as Hoxie's attorney, was Durant's "confidential man," as Durant himself expresses it.

By this contract and its extension Hoxie agreed to build two hundred and forty-six and forty-five hundredths miles of road, to furnish money on the securities of the company, to subscribe $1,000,000 to the capital stock, and he was to receive $50,000 per mile for the work.

On the 11th day of October, 1864, an agreement was entered into by Durant, Bushnell, Lambard, McComb, all directors of the Union Pacific Railroad Company, and Gray, a stockholder, to take from Hoxie the assignment of his contract (which assignment he had previously bound himself to make to such persons as Durant should designate,) and to contribute $1,600,000 for the purpose of carrying the contract out.

This Hoxie contract and its assignment were a device by which the persons who were the active managers and controllers of the Union Pacific Railroad Company caused said corporation to make a contract with themselves for the construction of a portion of its road, by which also they got possession of all the resources which it would be entitled to by the completion of said portion, and by which they evaded, or sought to evade, the requirement that the capital stock should be fully paid in in money, by substituting for such payment a fictitious or nominal payment in road building and equipment, each share being treated as being worth much less than its par value. . . .

The parties above named having procured the assignment to themselves of this contract, were liable individually as partners for all debts incurred in the joint undertaking. They therefore took steps to procure corporate powers as a shield against such risk, and secured for that purpose the control of a corporation afterward known as the Credit Mobilier of America. . . .

[The report shows that in 1859, the Pennsylvania legislature had granted a corporation charter for a company to be known as the Pennsylvania Fiscal Agency. The terms of this charter were extremely loose, leaving the company wide latitude in the functions which it could exercise and in the localities where it could exercise them, so that although the annual meeting of the company had to be held in Pennsylvania, its officers and operations might be almost anywhere.]

On the 3d day of March, 1864, Thomas C. Durant, vice-president of the Union Pacific Railroad Company, purchased this charter for the purpose of using the corporation for the construction of the Union Pacific Railroad.

On the 26th day of March, 1864, by an act of the legislature of the State of Pennsylvania, the name was changed to "The Credit Mobilier of America."

By the terms of purchase of the charter, an agency was to be established in the city of New York, and when the subscription was made, it was upon the condition that the full powers of the board of directors should be delegated to the New York agency, and that a railway bureau should be established at said agency, of five managers, three to be directors of the company (afterward changed to seven managers,) who should have the management of railway contracts, subject to the approval of the president. By these means this Pennsylvania corporation, so far as the management of its affairs was concerned, substantially expatriated itself, and, clothed with the extraordinary powers acquired from the State of Pennsylvania, it proceeded to take upon itself the control of the Union Pacific Railroad Company in the manner following:

It purchased the outstanding stock of that corporation, amounting to about $2,180,000, on which about $218,000 had been paid to the railroad company, the Credit Mobilier paying for this stock the amount already paid. At the time of this purchase the shares of Union Pacific stock were $1,000 each. After the act of 1864 was passed these shares were canceled, and a re-issue was made in shares of $100 each. The re-issue was made to the stockholders of the Credit Mobilier, and by this process the stockholders of the two corporations were made identical. By this means the persons who under the guise of a corporation that was to take the contract to build the road held complete control of the corporation for which the road was to be built.

These things accomplished, they took charge of construction under the Hoxie contract, and the portion of the road lying between Omaha and the one hundredth meridian was constructed under it.

This contract cost the Union Pacific Railroad Company $12,974,416 24
It cost the Credit Mobilier 7,806,183 33
Profit 5,168,232 91

This profit is a profit in stock and bonds estimated at par. Their actual value will appear hereafter.

The next event in this history is as follows, and it is stated here to show the animus of those who were managing this great trust:

The Hoxie contract had been completed, finishing the road to the one hundredth meridian, a distance of two hundred and forty-six and forty-five hundredths miles. An agreement was then made (November 10, 1866), by Thomas C. Durant, vice-president of the Union Pacific Railroad Company, with a Mr. Boomer for the construction of one hundred and fifty-three and thirty-five hundredths miles west from the one hundredth meridian. By the terms of this agreement Boomer was to be paid $19,500 per mile for that portion between the one hundredth meridian and the east bank of the North Platte, and for that portion lying west of the North Platte within the limits of the agreement $20,000 per mile; the bridge over the North Platte, and station-buildings equipment, &c., to be an additional charge.

This contract was never ratified by the company, but under it the work progressed, and fifty-eight miles of road had been completed and accepted by the Government. The books of the company fail to show what this fifty-eight miles had cost the company; but from the best evidence that could be procured your committee believe that the cost had not been to exceed $27,500 per mile for construction and equipment, the excess over the contract price being for station-houses, equipment, &c. Inasmuch as the charter required that the station-houses, equipment, &c., should be built and furnished before acceptance by the Government, and inasmuch as the records of the Department show that the fifty-eight miles had been accepted, your committee feel warranted in finding that this had been done and that the cost of the whole was not to exceed $27,500 per mile. But notwithstanding this, on the 5th day of January, 1867, the board of directors by a resolution extended the Hoxie contract over this fifty-eight miles of then completed road, thereby proposing to pay to the Credit Mobilier the sum of $22,500 per mile for this fifty-eight miles, amounting to the sum of $1,345,000, without any consideration whatever.

The following is the resolution of date January 5, 1867:

Resolved, That the Union Pacific Railroad Company will, and do hereby, consider the Hoxie contract extended to the point already completed, namely, three hundred and five miles west from Omaha, and that the officers of this company are hereby authorized to settle with the Credit Mobilier at $50,000 per mile for the additional fifty-eight miles.

That it was proposed to give the Credit Mobilier this profit, if that is the proper word to be used in such a connection, is verified by the fact that subsequently the sum of $1,104,000 was paid to the Credit Mobilier on account of this fifty-eight miles, for the construction of which it never had even the semblance of a contract. . . .

Your committee present the following summary of cost of this road to the railroad company and to the contractors, as appears by the books:

Cost to Railroad Company

Hoxie contract	$12,974,416 24
Ames contract	57,140,102 94
Davis contract	23,431,768 10
Total	93,546,287 28

Cost to Contractors

Hoxie contract	$ 7,806,183 33	
Ames contract	27,285,141 99	
Davis contract	15,629,633 62	
		50,720,958 94
		42,825,328 34

To this should be added amount paid Credit Mobilier on account of fifty-eight miles 1,104,000 00

Total profit on construction 43,929,328 34

[The preceding selections have shown that the Credit Mobilier received $93,000,000 at the expense of the Union Pacific Railroad Company. The questions naturally arise: In what form did Union Pacific make such a payment, and in what way were funds raised to pay for the construction? As to the form of payment, the answer is that only a minor fraction of the payment was made in cash; most of it was in securities of the railroad. That is, the railroad company possessed a great power to borrow: the Government, by issuing Government bonds at the rate of from $16,000 to $48,000 per mile of construction, became a guarantor for borrowing in these amounts; the actual railroad, when constructed, would serve as security for additional loans in the form of bonds, the bondholders being protected by a first mortgage on the road; similarly, funds could be borrowed on the land grants held by the road. The railroad company, therefore, instead of paying cash, turned over such bonds, as well as some stocks, to the construction company (which thus became, in a sense, also a finance company) and the construction company raised funds by selling these securities. In so far as the construction company raised more funds than were needed for building the road, plus a reasonable profit, they were enriching themselves at the expense of the creditors who were left holding a mortgage on property which was not worth what they had paid for it. The investigating committee tried to determine the amount of this diversion of assets by the following summary.]

... The committee calls attention to the following facts:

First-mortgage bonds issued	$27,213,000	00
Sold at a discount of	3,494,991	23
Net proceeds	23,718,008	77
Government bonds issued	$27,236,512	00
Sold at a discount of	91,348	72
	27,145,163	28
Aggregate net proceeds of both classes	$50,863,172	05
Cost of whole road to the contractors	50,720,958	94
	142,213	11

... It appears, then, speaking in round numbers, that the cost of the road was $50,000,000, which cost was wholly re-imbursed from the proceeds of the Government bonds and first-mortgage bonds; and that from the stock, the income bonds, and land-grant bonds, the builders received in cash value at least $23,000,000 as profit, being a percentage of about 48 percent on the entire cost. ...

The claim that these gentlemen had aided the enterprise with their own personal credit at first seemed a forcible one, but it disappears when carefully examined.

Let us see exactly what risk was assumed at the beginning of the execution of the Oakes Ames contract. If the contract on the whole appeared at any time during the progress of the work likely to be unprofitable, the clause giving the trustees an irrevocable proxy to vote on six-tenths of every man's stock enabled them to obtain the consent of both the nominal parties to its abandonment.

They were to have their bonds of both classes for each twenty miles when that twenty miles was completed, and, on the certificate of the chief engineer and commissioners, a proportionate share for uncompleted work. They were entitled by their contract to about $3,000,000 profits on the portion of the road which had been completed under a previous contract, but was included at a higher price in theirs. All they put at risk, therefore, was what they had to advance to build each twenty miles of the road, and this risk only lasted until that sum was re-imbursed on the completion of such section of twenty miles. This, at the rate fixed for the first hundred miles under the Oakes Ames contract, would amount to $840,000 for twenty miles, supposing there were no profits, and at the rate for the last hundred miles, to $1,920,000. But they divided among themselves on the 12th of December, 1867, less than two months after they got the contract, as before shown, a large amount in first-mortgage bonds and a like amount in stock par value, and from time to time made the other dividends hereinbefore set forth. Thus it appears that they divided, December 12, 1867, among themselves as profits at that date, a larger sum than they ever put at risk in the whole transaction. . . .

It is also said that it is unjust to look at this question in the light of the present; that we should go back to the condition of things before the road was built, when the whole scheme seemed, to the prudent capitalists of the country, visionary and perilous. This is true; and if these gentlemen assumed great risks from which others shrank, and thereby great benefits inured to the public, they should have all due credit. But we think they differed from other capitalists, not in taking a risk, but in having discovered that the road could be built at vast profit without risk, the resources furnished by the Government being more than ample for the purpose.

The Land Grant Question

In the case of the Union and Central Pacific railroads, the most valuable form of federal aid was the loan of government bonds to a total amount of about $60,000,000. The land grants were in this case secondary. But after the national desire for a transcontinental railroad had been fulfilled and the misappropriations of Credit Mobilier had been exposed, no more money subsidies were offered, and the later transcontinental railroads either received no aid of any kind, as in the case of the Great Northern, or they received land grants as in the case of the Northern Pacific, the Santa Fe, and the Southern Pacific. These later land grants tended to be even more extensive than those of the Union Pacific. The statistics of these grants are impressive, and their magnitude has been discussed in almost all the textbooks of American history, usually with an emphasis upon the great extent and value of the properties involved. Hence the grants are condemned as a squandering of public resources in acts of favoritism toward special interests.

The traditional adverse view of the land grants may be challenged, however, as was shown by an article, "The Railroad Land Grant Legend in American History Texts," published in 1945. The author of this article, Robert S. Henry, is both a railroad man and a historian. His railroad affiliations may lead one to question whether he is entirely objective in his approach, but his facts have not been challenged, and his critics have complained primarily that he did not include state grants and that he does not show how settlers were sometimes excluded for long periods from zones in which the railroads were entitled to locate their claims. His justification for confining his discussion to federal grants is that these have been the traditional target of criticism. He also discusses the later action of the Central Pacific and Union Pacific on their obligation to repay the government loan, since this is part of the question how much aid the railroads received in gift form.

In 1850, the United States government had a public domain of approximately 1,400,000,000 acres, vacant, unoccupied, and for lack of transportation, largely unusable and unsalable. Between that year and the end of 1871, the government undertook to use a portion of this land to encourage and assist the building of railroads in vacant or sparsely settled sections, in the same way in which previously it had aided the building of wagon roads and canals. The resulting series of transactions came to be known as the Federal railroad land grants, a subject frequently mentioned in high school and college texts which are the first, last, and only works on the history of their country read by many, if not most, Americans. This paper is the result of an examination of the treatment of the Federal land-grant transactions in thirty-seven representative texts.

Since the treatment of a subject of this sort in such works must be brief, and even, in a sense, incidental, accuracy both as to the essential facts themselves and as to their place and proportion in the whole setting becomes all the more important. This inquiry is directed, therefore, to these facts and the manner of their treatment. . . .

A balanced story of the Federal land grant transactions requires reasonably correct answers to these questions, at the very least:

How much land was granted to railroads, and what proportion was this of the whole public domain?

What proportion of the railroad mileage of the country received land grants from the government?

What was this land worth?

What were the terms and conditions of the grants? Were they gifts, or did the government get as well as give?

How Much Land?

The first of these questions, purely a matter of recorded fact, deals with the amount of land granted to railroads by the United States government. In the standard general work on the subject, Donaldson's *Public Domain*, published by the government in 1884, the total amount of land that would be necessary to fulfill all the acts granting lands to railroads was estimated at 155,504,994 acres. The amount of land actually patented to railroads, however, fell substantially short of this acreage, for a variety of reasons—noncompletion of the lines or other failure to comply with the conditions of the grants, or lack of sufficient acreage within the designated limits to fulfill the terms of the grants. The acreage to which the railroads actually received title appears in the annual reports of the Commissioner of the General Land Office, the latest such report showing a total of 131,350,534 acres.

How Much Railroad Was Built with the Aid of Land Grants?

The second, and equally simple, question deals with the extent of railroad mileage, the construction of which was aided by the government's land grants. Such grants were made in aid of a total of 18,738 miles of railroad line—less than 8 percent of the total mileage of railroads built in the United States. The fact that more than 92 percent of all the railroad mileage in the United States was built without the aid of an acre of Federal land grants is nowhere brought out in the texts examined. . . .

The same tendency to exaggerate the government's financial part in railroad building appears in the treatment of the bond aid extended to six of the companies chartered to build the pioneer "Pacific" railroads. The government made a loan of its bonds to these railroads, in the total amount of $64,623,512. The roads were to pay 6 percent interest on the bonds and to pay them off. During the long period of development and light traffic they were not always able to meet these charges, but in the final settlement in 1898 and 1899 the government collected $63,023,512 of principal plus $104,722,978 in interest—a total repayment of $167,746,490 on an initial loan of $64,623,512. Professor Hugo R. Meyer of

Harvard was well justified in saying that "for the government the whole outcome has been financially not less than brilliant"—but none of this appears in the treatment of the transaction in the texts. Thirty-four of the thirty-seven texts examined mention the bond aid to these Pacific roads. In one-third of the works, it is not made clear whether the financial assistance referred to was a loan or a gift. Three describe the aid definitely as gifts—which they were not. Twenty-one refer to the transactions as loans, but only four mention the fact that the loans were repaid, while three make the positively erroneous statement that the loans were never repaid.

WHAT WERE THE LAND GRANTS WORTH?

One measure of the value of the lands granted—though no one would contend that it is the correct one—would be the cost to the government of acquiring them, which, according to Donaldson, was an average of 23.3 cents an acre. On that basis, the 131,351,000 acres which the railroads received could be said to be worth less than $31,000,000.

Another possible measure is the standard "minimum" price at which the government offered the public domain for sale in the land grant period. This price was $1.25 an acre, though the government was never able to realize even this figure as an average selling price. But if the new railroad companies had bought from the government the 131,350,534 acres actually received, and had paid the full established price, the lands would have cost them $164,188,167. . . .

A more correct measure of value is the one applied in all ordinary transfers between buyer and seller—the worth of the land granted and received at the time of sale. During the period in which the land grants were being made to the railroads, the average sale price of government lands in the land grant states was less than $1 an acre. Applying that price to the lands granted to the railroads gives a value as of the time of the grants, of less than $130,000,000.

It is sometimes contended that the measure of value in this case should be the amount finally realized by the railroads on their lands, after the roads had been built and after years of colonizing, advertising, sales effort, and development costs had been put upon them. There is no more basis for setting up such a measure of value than there would be for putting it at the 23 cents an acre which it cost the government to acquire the lands in the first place, but because the point is raised in some of the works examined, it may be noted that the average realizations of the railroads from their Federal land grants, plus the estimated value of the lands remaining unsold, was put at $3.38 an acre according to one government study, while in another report, including both state and Federal grants, the average is $2.81 an acre. . . .

The real contribution of the Federal land grants to the spread of the rails in the

West and the newer South was not the cash realized upon them, but the fact that they furnished a basis of credit which got the job started and made it possible to get it done. The land-grant acreage could be certified, patented, and sold only as the railroad itself was completed, in sections, and then could be sold mostly on long-time credit. The selling price had to be low to get it sold at all, and the expense of sale was necessarily high. The net realization from the sales, particularly during the period of construction, were but a tiny fraction of the cost of building the railroads. Thus, the Auditor of Railroad Accounts of the Department of the Interior reported that up to 1880 the several companies going to make up the five pioneer "Pacific" routes had sold only $36,383,795 worth of land. "The lands have been sold in small tracts, some for cash, but most of them on time," the Auditor wrote in describing the sales of one of the several companies concerned. The cost up to that time of building the several Pacific routes is shown in the same report as having been $465,584,029. This, the Auditor thought and so reported, was excessive, or a least much more than similar roads could have been built for when the report was made. Even the lesser figure of $168,045,000, which he estimated as enough to reproduce the roads, however, was considerably more than four times the realizations from land sales up to that date. Looking to the future, the Auditor estimated that the value of the railroad lands unsold in 1880 was $78,889,940, making a total estimated value for all lands sold and to be sold of $115,273,735, as against a total estimated cost of the several "Pacific" railroads, to completion, of $634,165,613. The Auditor thought that similar railroads could be built for $286,819,300, but even this figure is more than double the estimated total realizations from the lands granted to the "Pacifics. . . . "

THE NATURE OF THE LAND GRANT TRANSACTION

The questions dealt with so far—that is, the amount of land granted and its relationship to the whole, the extent of the railroads thus aided and their relationship to the whole, and the value of the aid so extended—are, after all, matters of detail. . . . The main question is, what was the nature of that transaction? Were the Federal land grants gifts? Or were they trades by which the government got, as well as gave, direct consideration? . . .

Almost without exception, the works examined treat the transactions as "gifts," or "donations," or, as some put it, "free" or "outright" gifts, without in any way referring to the fact that the railroads which received these "gifts" or "donations" were required to haul mail and government freight and passengers at less than their regular charges.

While the conditions of the several grants vary, in the overwhelming majority of cases the Acts of Congress making grants to railroads adopted the phraseology of the earlier canal and wagon road grants in requiring that the railroad to be built should "be and remain a public highway for the use of the government of the United States, free from toll or other charge upon the transportation of any property or troops of the United States." The effect of this clause, as finally determined by the Supreme Court, was that the government was entitled to the use of the roadbed without toll, by analogy to the free right of passage for its vehicles or boats over grant-aided wagon roads and canals, but that this did not extend so far as to require the railroad company to provide and operate without charge the engines, cars, and other equipment needed for transportation over the railroads.

Under a formula subsequently worked out by the United States Court of Claims, the deduction from ordinary charges on account of this provision of the land grant acts was established at 50 percent. Still later, by a series of Acts of Congress, the same percentage of deduction from commercial rates was made applicable to the limited number of land-grant roads whose grants did not contain the "toll-free" provision in this form, while even railroads which received no land grant whatever from the government have long since entered into "equalization agreements" by which they also undertake to handle government traffic at the same rates applying by law on the land grant lines. Compensation for handling mail on land-grant lines was fixed by Act of Congress in 1876 at 80 percent of the rates applying on other railroads.

In the Transportation Act of 1940, the Congress eliminated these provisions insofar as they applied to mail pay and to rates on the government's civilian passenger and freight traffic. Deductions of 50 percent were continued, however, on the charges for transportation of military and naval personnel and property moving for military and naval and not for civil uses.

The resulting situation is thus described by a Committee of the House of Representatives in the most recent statement on the subject:

"Certain of our railroads, because of lands granted by the Government many years ago to aid in the construction of lines of road now owned by them, are under statutory obligation to transport certain specified classes of Government traffic over such land-grant lines at 50 percent of their established tariff charges for such transportation. While that statutory requirement applies to only 14,411 miles of railroad, the reduced charges for which it provides have been extended to many times that mileage as the result of so-called equalization agreements entered into with the Government by other railroads to enable them to handle Government traffic."

Thus it is that although less than 10 percent of railroad mileage received grants of land, either Federal or state, the whole railroad system of the nation has paid for them a direct monetary return far exceeding the value of the lands granted.

"It is probable," said the Congressional Committee report already referred to, "that the railroads have contributed over $900,000,000 in payment of the lands which were transferred to them under the Land Grant Acts. This is double the amount received for the lands sold by the railroads plus the estimated value of such lands still under railroad ownership. Former Commissioner Eastman estimated that the total value of the lands at the time they were granted . . . was not more than $126,000,000."

Almost without exception, however, the history textbooks have failed to develop this major and essential fact that, whatever may have been its shortcomings, the land-grant policy touched off national and individual energies which in a few short years accomplished the greatest engineering, construction, and colonization project ever undertaken up to that time, a project which transformed the West from a wilderness to a civilized community and welded the nation into one.

QUESTIONS FOR REVIEW AND DISCUSSION

1. What are the economic advantages and disadvantages of incorporation, compared with other forms of business organization?
2. Discuss the public subsidies for railroad construction that were provided in the nineteenth century. What was the justification for granting those subsidies? Are there comparable public subsidies for private enterprise today?
3. What specific benefits, or subsidies, were offered to the incorporators of the Union Pacific Railroad? Were those benefits ultimately beneficial or injurious? To whom might they have been beneficial or harmful?
4. Should private industries that receive public aid be publicly regulated or controlled? Why or why not?
5. Why did general laws for incorporation replace specific charters for incorporation?
6. Should incorporation be primarily a function of the states or of the federal government?
7. What were the conclusions reached by the congressional investigators into the construction of the Union Pacific by the Credit Mobilier? Would a similar investigation today reach similar conclusions? How has the perception of the relationship between corporations and government changed since the nineteenth century?
8. How does Robert S. Henry's study interpret the issue of the effects of government subsidies to the railroads on corporate expansion?

8

The Early
Antitrust
Movement

Few issues in American domestic affairs have been more persistently debated than that of the impact of large-scale business enterprises upon the life of the nation. Essentially, the debate has focused upon the question whether the classic American economic values of free competition and equal opportunity for all are compatible with the existence of big business in the United States. The problem, according to one historian, has been whether "the corporation had to be made to conform to American institutions and principles or those institutions and principles had to be changed to accommodate the corporation."[1]

The Industrial Revolution reached the United States long before the Civil War, but the factories of the antebellum years were essentially small or medium-sized firms that employed limited numbers of workers and represented relatively modest capital investments. Corporations of substantial size did not appear until the mid-nineteenth century with the growth of the railroads. Huge industrial corporations finally emerged after 1870 when John D. Rockefeller founded the Standard Oil Company. From 1870 to 1911, John D. Rockefeller's organization became, in the minds of a great many Americans, the epitome of what was threatening and disruptive in the new phenomenon of big business.

Corporate power in the form of monopolies and trusts wrought massive changes in American society. Many people came forward to criticize big business and the effect it was having on life in America. Among those critics were the numerous small businesspeople who were hard-pressed to compete with the new forces being unleashed in the economy. In the preface to his masterful biography of John D. Rockefeller, historian Allan Nevins wrote: "Great business aggregations are not built without frustrating, crushing, or absorbing multitudinous small enterprises. To many caught in the midst of the transformation, its destructive and exploitive aspects seem paramount."[2] Nevins went on to argue that the constructive aspects of the transformation were ultimately of more importance to the nation than the destructive aspects were. Nevins' judgment, however, would not have been shared by the many small entrepreneurs who were submerged by the tidal wave of, for example, the Standard Oil Company's rise to supremacy in the petroleum industry.

George Rice of Marietta, Ohio, certainly would not have shared Nevins' view. Rice was probably the best-known and most widely publicized small businessman of his time. To his generation of Americans, Rice was the intrepid entrepreneur who, for 20 years, fought the Standard Oil octopus in the court of public opinion and before virtually every governmental regulatory or investigative body in the land. His pamphlets, newspaper and magazine articles, and speeches played a significant part in generating the antitrust movement in the United States.

The case study that follows, *Trust and Antitrust: George Rice and the War Against Standard Oil*, does two things. First, it traces the preindustrial origins of the antimonopoly tradition in the United States. Second, it focuses on George Rice and John D. Rockefeller, opponents in the struggle that followed the emergence of big business in America. Their lives thus serve as a mirror of the debate over what their contemporaries termed the "trust problem." Rice's life further illustrates the characteristic American response to the "trust problem," which was the antitrust movement.

Notes

1. John Tipple, "Big Businessmen and a New Economy," *The Gilded Age*, ed. by H. Wayne Morgan (Syracuse, N.Y.: Syracuse University Press, 1970), 25.

2. Allan Nevins, *Study in Power: John D. Rockefeller* (New York: Charles Scribner's Sons, 1953), vol. 1, viii.

C. Joseph Pusateri

TRUST AND ANTITRUST: GEORGE RICE AND THE WAR AGAINST STANDARD OIL

Competition and Monopoly in the American Mind

Traditionally, the functioning of the American economy has centered upon the contributions of individuals following their own interests and seeking their own goals. Producers and consumers have reacted to each other's tastes and aspirations and thereby allocated the available resources of the nation. The economy thus became the sum product of the acts of individuals, past and present. In the last century, however, the most successful of these individuals gained prominence and exercised their influence collectively rather than singly, by working through the legal and artificial person of the modern corporation. This development, whatever its benefits in efficiency of output and costs, was not congenial to many Americans, who saw the new developments as closing too many doors to material achievement formerly open to enterprising men and women acting on their own initiative, and not aligned with larger organizations.

The ideal of an equal opportunity for each citizen to acquire and to operate his or her own business died hard. Dating back to the colonial period, ease of entry into small business had been a most important difference between the Old World of Europe and the New World in America. Skilled workmen had readily gone into business for themselves in a colonial Massachusetts, unhampered by difficulties in securing official permission or guild acceptances. But all that appeared to be changing by the late nineteenth century, and to many Americans it seemed perfectly obvious that democracy could not survive when a society was dominated by what they regarded as "anonymous economic units." For them "the anonymous man of modern industrialism" was really no man at all.[1]

To a certain extent, the responses to the rise of big business in America were reflective of attitudes and values which are usually associated with pre-industrial society. In that sense they testified to the continuing strength of the agrarian spirit in America. While manufacturing was hardly an unknown activity in our colonial experience, market and transportation limitations dictated that factories had to be widely dispersed rather than geographically concentrated and the strength of their influence was not great. Meanwhile, the advocates of agrarian values spoke with considerable authority.

No stronger advocate of the latter spirit could be found than Thomas Jefferson. In his *Notes on Virginia* he preached the gospel of agrarianism. Writing before the Declaration of Independence, Jefferson argued that Americans should confine their activities to cultivating the soil and let Europe involve itself in manufacturing: "While we have land to labor then, let us never wish to see our citizens occupied at a work bench. . . . "[2]

But the agrarian Jefferson was not to remain so all his life. Changing economic conditions altered his views on manufacturing, so much so that he could write Benjamin Austin in 1816: "You tell me I am quoted by those who wish to continue our dependence on England for manufactures. There was a time when I might have been so quoted with more candor, but within the thirty years which have since elapsed, how are circumstances changed!" He could by 1816 write: "We must now place the manufacturer by the side of the agriculturist," and he could add: "Experience has taught me that manufactures are now as necessary to our independence as to our comfort; and if those who quote me as of a different opinion, will keep pace with me in purchasing nothing foreign where an equivalent of domestic fabric can be obtained without regard to difference of price, it will not be our fault if we do not soon have a supply at home equal to our demand, and wrest that weapon of distress from the hand which has wielded it."[3]

The views that Jefferson came to express were, of course, those held much earlier by his former antagonist, Alexander Hamilton. The *Report on Manufactures*, submitted by Hamilton as Secretary of the Treasury to Congress in December 1791, was a classic statement in defense of industrialism and of government assistance for nascent industries. Manufactures promote the public good, argued the aggressive Treasury head, because they harness the artificial force of mechanization to aid man, because a division of labor is created which results in heightened efficiency, because new employment is provided furnishing "greater scope for the diversity of talents," and because the agricultural sector of the economy benefits from new markets for its produce and for the natural resources of the nation. Hamilton had concluded "that a manufacturing interest would not only be socially useful but would form an indispensable part of America's harmonic economic development."[4]

Interestingly, some critics of Hamilton's *Report* were manufacturers themselves. Small artisans and shopkeepers approved of the general applause for manufacturing but feared that Hamilton's relish for a government-business alliance and its promotion would result only in creating a steamroller against which they themselves would not be able to contend—the large scale, incorporated, heavily capitalized manufacturing enterprise. Such organizations, in the words of one critic, would "inevitably destroy the infant manufactures of our country, and consign the useful and respectable citizens personally engaged in them to contempt and ruin."[5] Nevertheless, Hamilton built better than he knew, for his Jeffersonian opponents would one day occupy his ideological position. "His philosophy remained a basic ingredient in American tradition, though the idiom was to change from time to time."[6]

It was not, however, so much the heritage of America's early agrarian spirit that brought Americans to protest against the emergence of corporate combinations after the Civil War. It was instead a long tradition of commitment to the principle of free competition as the perfect economic regulator and vigorous opposition to the destroyer of that competition—monopoly power. For Americans, indeed for anyone claiming an Anglo-Saxon heritage, the word "monopoly" carried more than simply economic connotations. There were social, political, even emotional attachments to the word.

The United States has given more sustained attention to the issues of competition and monopoly than any other nation. Problems involving freedom in the marketplace have influenced our public policies since the founding of the Republic. To most Americans, little trained in economics, the definitions of "competition" and "monopoly" seem clear enough. Competition implies many buyers and sellers in a market with no single firm or individual able to control price, demand, or supply. On the other hand, the monopolist is the only seller of a particular commodity for which there is no close substitute and the market is his to command.[7]

Obviously, this clear distinction does not describe a real market situation where neither pure competition nor pure monopoly exists. Each market situation is a complex compound of varied forces. Nevertheless, Americans ascribe value to the concept of competition as the ruling force, believing "that producers and sellers put forth their best efforts when threatened by effective rivals; that the economic desires of society are fulfilled when no individuals or groups within the marketplace possess the power to exploit; in short, that competition as a market force compels the best possible economic results."[8]

Anti-monopoly (or, as Americans came to refer to it, antitrust) sentiment dated from sixteenth-century English origins. The word "monopoly" itself was first used by Thomas More in 1516, and the first recorded common law case involving the monopoly issue was decided in 1599. The case, *Davenant* v. *Hurdis* (also referred to as *The Merchant Tailors'* case), involved a rule passed by the London tailors' guild in 1571. It required each merchant belonging to the guild and having cloth finished by outside labor to have at least half the work done by guild members. But Davenant, a merchant member, refused to obey the rule and later refused to pay the fine imposed by the guild. When the guild ordered Hurdis to take from Davenant goods equal in value to the fine, Davenant charged him with trespass. Davenant's attorney, the great Sir Edward Coke, argued that the guild rule was illegal since it tended towards the creation of a monopoly. The court accepted Coke's reasoning, holding that "a rule of such nature as to bring all trade or traffic into the hands of one company, or one person, and to exclude all others, is illegal."[9]

A quarter of a century later came what has been termed "the high watermark of English anti-monopoly policy." The Statute of Monopolies passed by Parliament in 1624 and the first major legislation on the subject of monopoly put an end to the granting of private monopolies by the Crown. It "reflected the general aversion of the law to monopoly based on special privilege."[10] Such sentiments would not be long in making the transatlantic crossing to North America.

Monopolies were opposed with as great a vigor in the English colonies as they had been in the mother country. This was so because a principal reason for colonists leaving England had been their aversion to unjustified privilege, and because monopoly power was the antithesis of the individualistic spirit characteristic of life in the new land. To a substantial extent this spirit was the product of the favorable economic condition prevailing in colonial America, and it soon became "part and parcel of the nation's democratic faith." Both religion and philosophy buttressed the belief. Evangelical Christianity placed its emphasis on personal regeneration; and transcendentalism, with its identification of the individual soul with God, served the same purpose.[11]

The word "individualism" itself was, appropriately, first coined in the English translation of Alexis de Tocqueville's *Democracy in America*. Of the Americans he observed, Tocqueville remarked: "They owe nothing to any man, they expect nothing from any man, they acquire the habit of always considering themselves as standing alone, and they are apt to imagine that their whole destiny is in their own hands." But while Tocqueville regarded such an attitude as a social danger,

Americans celebrated it as the ideal.[12] Ironically, the unintended result of the cult of the unrestrained individual would be to accelerate the forces of organization that would bring its era to an end. Such a possibility was not anticipated prior to the Civil War, however, as most businesses were forced by the period's economic restraints to operate as local enterprises. But with the rise of larger opportunities following the War, the new corporate manager found himself "in the favored position of operating in an economy dedicated to the idea of freely competing individuals, yet left unhampered by the ordinary restrictions. Under such auspicious circumstances, he soon outdistanced unorganized rivals in the race for wealth."[13]

It was not difficult for a John D. Rockefeller to announce, shortly after the beginning of the twentieth century, that "the day of individual competition in large affairs is past and gone" and that large-scale enterprise "has come to stay—that is a thing that may be depended upon."[14] He had had a good deal to do with the one age closing and the next beginning.

In colonial times American hostility to monopoly was not lessened by the fact that some of the most objectionable exercises of England's power on this continent were the practices and privileges of chartered royal trading companies. In a sense it could be argued that the depositing of the British East India Company tea in Boston harbor in 1773 was simply a more romantic than usual form for an antitrust action. It was also the legislature of colonial Massachusetts that decreed "there shall be no monopolies granted or allowed among us but of such new inventions as are profitable to the country, and that for a short time." Boston had also been the 1639 site of merchant Robert Keayne's legal chastisement on the grounds of charging extortionate prices. For demanding what was regarded as beyond a reasonable price for a bag of nails and various other items, Keayne was not only fined heavily but was very nearly excommunicated from the church as well.[15]

A number of states expressed the desire to see an anti-monopoly provision in the Constitution, and certainly the monopoly issue was raised when Hamilton proposed the chartering of the First Bank of the United States. It fell to the Jacksonians, however, to raise the monopoly issue most vigorously during the course of their war against the Second Bank of the United States. In the message accompanying his veto of the bill rechartering the Bank, Jackson warned: "In the full enjoyment of the gifts of Heaven and the fruits of superior industry, economy, and virtue, every man is equally entitled to protection by law; but when the laws undertake to add to these natural and just advantages artificial distinction . . . to make the rich richer and the potent more powerful, the humble members of society—the farmers, mechanics, and laborers—who have neither the time nor the means of securing like favors to themselves, have a right to complain of the injustice of their

Government."[16] The veto message, more demagogic than economic, was an unsubtle attempt at the employment of long-standing American views on monopoly in a political campaign being carried on by Jackson against partisan enemies. The Bank was not a monopoly and it is questionable whether many astute followers of the President ever honestly thought it so.

There were other institutions besides central banks against which the cry of monopoly was also raised in ante-bellum America. One of the most unpopular of these was the exclusive right to operate steamboats on the waters of New York State and in the West won by the partnership of Robert Livingston and Robert Fulton. In March, 1824, Chief Justice John Marshall, speaking for a unanimous Supreme Court of the United States, struck down the steamboat monopoly in his *Gibbons* v. *Ogden* opinion. Unlike most Marshall decisions, this one met with great popular approval as newspapers all across the country praised it as "profound, masterful, and farsighted." It had freed American commerce from the grip of special privilege.[17]

Somewhat the same fears were being expressed regarding corporations in general as were being voiced against the Livingston-Fulton steamboat monopoly. The view that corporations were somehow evil in themselves stemmed from our English and colonial heritages. Corporations and their predecessors, the joint stock companies, came into existence only by special actions of political bodies including the King himself. The special consideration involved in granting corporate privileges to private individuals formed together as an artificial entity smacked of public favoritism and seemed to violate our tradition of equality of opportunity.

When corporation charters, following the Revolutionary War, continued to be awarded by special acts of state legislatures, suspicion also continued unabated. Between 1783 and 1801 alone almost 350 business corporations were created within the United States to participate in the surge of the new nation's economy.[18] Complicating the issue was the fact that, overwhelmingly, the corporations receiving charters in these years and those shortly afterwards could be classified in the public service or utility category. They provided what economists term "social overhead capital," turnpikes, bridges, canals, and water systems; and because they operated within the public sphere and supplied necessary services, it was not uncommon for them to receive monopoly privileges of one type or another as part of their franchise.

The generous state authorities were also not unmindful of the political influence of many of the individuals involved in the fledgling enterprises when these same liberties were bestowed. Nevertheless, influence or not, many would-be corporations were forced to invest considerable time and money in convincing state legislators that their charter requests should be granted. The promoters of the Delaware and Raritan Canal Company, for example, saw two years of work and some $3,000 lavished on the New Jersey legislature before a charter was finally secured.[19]

Given such circumstances, it was not surprising that many Americans regarded the corporation as a new threat to democracy. Only a handful of citizens could afford the investment required to take advantage of the corporate form. The issue thus became one of deciding upon a public policy towards the corporations. Some, particularly those radical Jacksonians known as the Locofocos, urged the destruction of all such devices. They claimed that all specially chartered enterprises were "monopolies, inasmuch as they are calculated to enhance the power of wealth, produce inequalities among the people, and to subvert liberty." In the same vein it was contended: "To have the land scattered over with incorporated companies, is to have a class of privileged, if not titled, nobility."[20]

The corporation was not, of course, without its vigorous defenders. From the judicial bench John Marshall played that role in decisions such as the one rendered in the Dartmouth College case. Daniel Webster, who had in fact appeared as attorney for Dartmouth College in that litigation, likewise proved a champion of corporate ventures. Recognizing that the corporation usually represented significantly larger accumulations of capital than either proprietorships or partnerships, he argued against the popular fears of its greater size. Webster contended that there were no ideas more unfounded and disreputable "than those which would represent capital, collected, necessarily, in large sums, in order to carry on useful processes in which science is applied to art, in the production of articles useful to all, as being hostile to the common good, or having an interest separate from that of the majority of the community. All such representations, if not springing from sinister design, must be the result of great ignorance, or great prejudice."[21]

The compromise finally arrived at was the enactment by the states of general incorporation laws. Under these laws state officials were authorized to issue charters to any qualified applicants without acts of the legislature being required. In effect, the process had been democratized and some of the old complaints about the corrupt methods used to secure privileged franchises—monopolies—could no longer be sustained. The first statutes of this type were passed in Massachusetts in 1809 and in New York in 1811, but it was not until after the Panic of 1837 and the long depression following that crisis that a substantial number of states followed suit. Not until 1875, however, did the number of states featuring general incorporation laws exceed those still chartering by special legislative acts.[22]

Given this heritage of opposition to monopoly and centralized power, it was inevitable that Americans adversely affected by the sweeping economic transformation taking place following the Civil War would react angrily. As historian

John Tipple has pointed out, the large industrial corporation was out of place in a society whose "institutions had been built around the social and political concept of the free individual." It quickly became clear that "as an artificial person created by charter and comprising many individuals and their wealth, the corporation was infinitely greater in size and power than the isolated individual about whom American society had been conceived." As a result an immediate question was posed. "What was to be done with such a monster? Either the corporation had to be made to conform to American institutions and principles or those institutions and principles had to be changed to accommodate the corporation."[23]

George Rice versus Rockefeller's Standard Oil

On the afternoon of October 12, 1898, two men faced each other in the New Amsterdam Hotel in New York City. They had not seen each other in some years and now they found themselves, as they had so often in the past, on opposite sides in a legal proceeding. The slighter in stature and somewhat younger of the two men approached the other with hand extended in a gesture of friendship.

"How are you, George? We are getting to be gray-haired men now, aren't we? Don't you wish you had taken my advice years ago?"

The older of the two, pointedly ignoring the proffered hand, replied bitterly: "Perhaps it would have been better for me if I had. You have certainly ruined my business, as you said you would."

Surprised at the vehemence of the reply to his greeting, the younger man drew back, denying the charge. The attacker persisted, however: "But I say it is so. You know well that by the power of your great wealth you have ruined my business, and you cannot deny it!"

Seeing no point in continuing what he considered to be a hopeless conversation, the first man turned away, commenting to the small crowd of onlookers as he left the room that there was not one word of truth in the accusations.

The incident was closed only for the moment. Four days later—Sunday, October 16—a description of the encounter was printed, amid a full page article detailing the older man's charge, in one of the nation's most widely read newspapers, *The New York World. The World* headlined its account with the banner: "How I Was Ruined by Rockefeller." The author of the story, the angry attacker during the New Amsterdam incident a few days before, was George Rice of Marietta, Ohio. His antagonist was one of the most powerful and feared men in the United States, John Davison Rockefeller, creator of and dominant force in the globe-straddling Standard Oil empire.[24]

The twin stories of Rice and Rockefeller reveal much of the developing history of a key industry in the American economy, an industry that has been marked by controversy from its inception in 1859 until our present-day headlines of Arab oil embargoes and rising energy costs. Yet Rice and Rockefeller also symbolize much more. In many ways they stand as personal embodiments of two converging forces in the evolution of the nation—the concern and the passion to maintain equality of economic opportunity for all Americans on the one hand, and the desire and drive to amass the most stupendous material achievements possible in the most efficient manner available on the other. Opportunity and achievement—two goals between which a choice was often forced because frequently one could not be sought without sacrificing a measure of the other.

For many Americans, freedom itself has come to be defined in primarily economic terms. One contemporary scholar has written that in large part freedom today is "the right to earn a living in the way of one's own choosing, to launch an enterprise, to save and invest, to own property, and, above all, to share in the income and wealth that a progressive economy generates."[25]

For the individual who takes utmost advantage of his or her granted opportunity, there has always been a special kind of popular approval. Fellow citizens have looked upon such persons with particular admiration. They have become legendary heroes—the self-made woman or man. As Irvin G. Wyllie has stated, the self-made man "represents our most cherished conceptions of success, and particularly our belief that any man can achieve fortune through the practice of industry, frugality, and sobriety."[26]

Such a figure was George Rice. He was born in Swanton Falls, Vermont, just four miles below the Canadian-American border, in 1835. He had entered the infant oil business at a relatively early age, first operating as a producer, owning oil well properties in the Pennsylvania fields of the 1860s. Then in the 1870s he switched the base of his operations to Ohio and took on the additional task of refining the crude oil secured from his wells into kerosene, the principal petroleum product of that era. In 1875, he and Charles Leonard established the Ohio Oil Works on the banks of the Ohio River at Marietta. Two years later, Rice bought Leonard out and operated thereafter as a sole proprietor until he shut the plant down permanently in 1896.

His operations in the refining field were always relatively small scale. He once noted to a Congressional investigating committee that "The executive part of the business is done altogether by my family. One daughter keeps the books, another daughter does nine-tenths of the correspondence, and my son-in-law is the general manager." Rice himself claimed to tend to outside matters, meaning the marketing of his illuminating oil output.[27]

The world of George Rice was not to be a happy one, however. He sought his markets first in the Great Lakes region and later in the Southern states, but in each instance he found himself confronted by a truly formidable enemy—the overmastering competition posed by the operations of Rockefeller's burgeoning Standard Oil organization. Thus the long war between the two men began.

Standard Oil can be regarded as representing the second of the two influences in American economic life mentioned earlier—material achievement. In the two decades after its emergence on the petroleum scene, it transformed an industry marked by chronic excess capacity, instability, and general aimlessness into one of the cutting edges of an enormous American economic expansion. During the Rockefeller years the United States displaced Great Britain as the leading producer of manufactured goods in the world, a position that this country was never again to relinquish.

But one means to reach the end of material achievement lay in combination, the merging and consolidating of ever more and ever larger units of capital, labor, technology, and managerial expertise. Observers simplistically but accurately called the resulting combinations "big business," and a new age was ushered in. While there was little doubting the effectiveness of combination, there was also little doubting that the price that had to be paid lay in the sacrifice of a measure of the equality of opportunity held dear by the Founding Fathers. Gordon S. Wood has noted that the generation of the Declaration of Independence "who hoped for so much from equality assumed that republican America would be a community where none would be too rich or too poor, and yet at the same time believed that men would readily accede to such distinctions as emerged as long as they were fairly earned." It was said by some early writers that what was required was a "fundamental law, favoring an equal or rather a general distribution of property." The very author of the Declaration itself, Thomas Jefferson, had written that an equal division of all inheritance would be the ideal corrective to "overgrown wealth," thereby, in the words of another Founding Father, "giving every citizen an equal chance of being rich and respectable."[28]

But combination implied inequality; it signalled that some would be rich and some would be poor whereas the Revolutionary generation had assumed "that equality of opportunity would necessarily result in a rough equality of station."[29] Nevertheless, and here is where a quandary of policy emerged, combination was also desirable because it allowed firms to attain greater efficiencies, taking advantage of economies of scale available only to the larger enterprises. If the savings were then passed on to customers in the form of lower prices, individual real incomes were thereby increased.[30] Of course, combinations might not pass on those savings to consumers; they might, indeed, find advantage in using their real power to fix prices artificially.

For John Rockefeller, however, the choice was not a difficult one as he unhesitatingly chose the path of combination and defended his choice vigorously all the days of his long life. As he readily admitted: "I have been frank to say that I believe in the spirit of combination and cooperation when properly and fairly conducted in the world of commercial affairs, on the principle that it helps to reduce waste; and waste is a dissipation of power."[31]

Rockefeller's willingness to adopt the strategy of combination, or cooperation as he often preferred to call it, was deeply tied to his own ingrained passion for order. An insight into his motivations can be gained by a brief look at his early life. He was born in western New York state in 1839. His father engaged in a variety of occupations including that of an itinerant patent medicine salesman. Even after his son had become enormously wealthy and a dominant force in a major industry, the father continued traveling a circuit of western towns, billing himself as "Dr. William Rockefeller, the Celebrated Cancer Cure Specialist." He was a flamboyant figure, powerful of physique, jovial in manner, aggressive in style, characteristics which, with the exception of the last, were not to be shared by his eldest son. The mother of the family, on the other hand, was a startling contrast. Infected with a deep puritan piety, she was frugal in her habits, strait-laced in her behavior, and a firm believer in stern discipline. The personality of the son closely resembled that of his mother though the vision and business shrewdness of his father were obviously not lost upon him.

Significantly, the uncertainties of John Rockefeller's early home life, frequent changes of residence and long paternal absences while "Doctor" Rockefeller rode the circuit, created in the young man a distaste for uncertainty, a relishing of order and security, and a zeal for structuring each situation he might encounter. Most of all, he abhorred waste. His mother's favorite maxim, "willful waste makes woeful want," repeated endlessly it seemed, was not without its effect on her children.[32]

The Rockefeller family moved to Ohio in 1853, and it was in Cleveland two years later that John secured his first full-time employment, as an assistant book-keeper for a local commission merchant. He threw himself into the new-found world of business with unbridled enthusiasm. He found his work place "delightful to me—all the method and system of the office."[33]

Four years later—the same year that saw the birth of the petroleum industry with Edwin Drake's successful well in Titusville, Pennsylvania—Rockefeller went into business for himself, forming a partnership to operate as a commission merchant in agricultural products and other miscellaneous goods. The firm, Clark and Rockefeller, was successful from the start and generated sufficient profits to allow the partners to look for other areas of potential investment. Petroleum offered such a possibility.

Eschewing the wildly speculative drilling and production phase of the petroleum industry, Rockefeller chose to invest in a refinery transforming the Pennsylvania crude oil into kerosene for illumination and a then small number of by-products. Refining required only a moderate amount of capital in order to begin operations, the demand for kerosene was expanding, and Cleveland, by virtue of its location on several rail lines and Lake Erie, was well suited to tap most western and many eastern markets. By 1863, when Cleveland boasted twenty refineries and was fast becoming the center of the rapidly developing industry, Rockefeller and Clark accepted the proposition of Samuel Andrews, an experienced and talented refiner, that together they build a plant. The first two men were to provide the necessary capital and Andrews the technical ability. By 1867, Rockefeller had dissolved the commission business and was concentrating completely on refining in a new partnership styled Rockefeller, Andrews, and Flagler, the immediate predecessor of the Standard Oil Company.

The history of Standard Oil in its Rockefeller years fell into three general, overlapping phases. The first of these, that of "combination," lasted from the inception of the corporation in 1870 until the end of the decade. The impetus for this phase stemmed from the then current conditions in the refining industry. With little capital required for entry into the petroleum industry, unrestrained competition was the rule. Prices fluctuated wildly; failures among producers and refiners alarmingly increased during the 1860s, and waste was everywhere. "Lack of balance between functions was chronic: first production would outrun the throughput by refiners; then manufacturing capacity would exceed both current production of raw materials and the rate of consumption of finished products. Oilmen knew from bitter experience that their business was wasteful, risky, hazardous, and unstable."[34]

The response of the Standard Oil Company management, headed by Rockefeller, was in accord with the maternal dictum: willful waste makes woeful want. Following what its chief executive officer called "our plan," Standard Oil's policy was to eliminate the "wasteful" competition by "convincing" other manufacturers to either cease operations or to join the Rockefeller group in a loose alliance. Standard Oil possessed two substantial advantages in working its will on its competitors. It was the most efficient producer, and it had developed close ties with the railroads it utilized for its freight shipments. In order to reduce unit costs, the firm had begun to engage in a variety of auxiliary enterprises including the provision of its own chemicals, barrels, and transportation equipment. Further, the railroads proved quite willing to grant discounts or "rebates" on freight charges to an expanding operation like Standard Oil's, and such advantages could prove decisive in a competitive struggle.

Critics of the Rockefeller organization castigated it severely for its use of the rebate weapon. George Rice himself railed continually against "the combined hosts of the Standard Oil Company and its co-conspirators, the railroads," who refused to allow him "the same rates, advantages, and facilities, in all respects, that the most favored or larger shipper has, in order that we may be able to compete in the general markets." But what was called "the utterly unscrupulous manipulation of railroad rates by the Rockefellers and their associates in order to destroy competition" was seen in a quite different light by Standard Oil executives.[35]

Rockefeller denied the charges of unfair competition. He claimed: "The profits of the Standard Oil Company did not come from advantages given by railroads. The railroads, rather, were the ones who profited by the traffic of the Standard Oil Company, and whatever advantage it received in its constant efforts to reduce rates of freight was only one of the many elements of lessening cost to the consumer which enabled us to increase our volume of business the world over because we could reduce the selling price."[36]

By 1879, Standard's combination effort had proved so successful that its alliance of companies controlled 90 percent of the refined petroleum sold in the United States. As important, "they showed a profound faith in the permanence of the industry, a belief not generally held in years when the petroleum business was characterized by instability, rapid exhaustion of producing fields, and doubts about the appearance of new ones."[37]

In the second phase of its history, that of "consolidation," Standard Oil welded its loose alliance of companies into a tight amalgam, centrally controlled and rationally organized and administered. The device utilized to bring about the consolidation was the "trust," a system whereby Standard stock as well as that of other allied companies was placed in the hands of nine trustees who thus wielded a control over the combine which was complete and unquestionable. And with the control of the Standard Oil Trust, as the new structure was called, came control over the industry as a whole. Never before had Americans witnessed such an enormity of power centralized in so few hands.

Consolidation was completed with the perfection of the trust agreement in 1882. But even prior to that date, Rockefeller and his associates had begun a third phase of the organization's development—"vertical integration." In actual fact, Standard Oil had been emphasizing vertical integration since before its chartering as a corporation in 1870. As early as 1864, at Rockefeller's urging, it had begun making its own barrels and even purchasing its own tracts of land to provide the timber. In 1866 Rockefeller had recruited his younger brother William into the organization to set up a New York office specializing in the marketing of petroleum products for the export trade. In the years after the establishment of the Trust, Standard Oil faced a series of challenges from both foreign and domestic sources, challenges which led it to speed the process of integration. The bulk of Standard's market lay overseas, and the development of Russian oil competition prompted the creation of tanker fleets and foreign subsidiaries to meet the

Russian threat in Europe and in Asia. In the United States the continual discovery of new crude oil fields and the appearance of independent refiners led Standard Oil, for the first time, into crude production on a massive scale and to control over a network of trunk pipelines linking the fields to the refineries. By the close of the 1890s, Standard Oil had completed the fashioning of a vast, vertically integrated structure involved in every aspect of its industry.[38]

The achievements of the petroleum industry in its Rockefeller years were indeed impressive. From a production of only a few barrels in 1859, output had soared to nearly sixty million barrels yearly by the turn of the century. The bulk of this crude oil production was refined into kerosene, the world's first inexpensive illuminant. As one historian of the industry has noted: "Few products associated with America have had so extensive an influence as kerosene on the daily living habits of so large a proportion of the world's population." But illumination was not the sole application for petroleum. By 1900 some two hundred by-products accounted for at least half of the industry's sales, and numbered among them were the lubricating oils essential to the development of industrialization. Moreover, this expansion of output was being achieved while prices to consumers were being reduced. The wholesale price of kerosene, for example, declined from 45¢ a gallon in 1863 to about 6¢ by 1895, a decline faster than any other drop in the general wholesale price level of commodities.[39]

Petroleum men had every right to feel proud of themselves; theirs was a truly impressive material accomplishment. Yet, they found the public reaction to their record contained as much wrath as it did admiration. Many Americans argued strongly that the social cost of economic progress had been too great; that this progress had required the rise of big business as embodied in the giant corporation, and that that instrumentality was destroying America's traditional role as a land of opportunity. Very often the persons who joined the fight against big business were those whose jobs or businesses had been directly and adversely affected by the economic transformation.

A small manufacturer such as George Rice, determined to maintain his independence in the face of a galloping combination movement, would speak out against the phenomenon in cataclysmic tones. Of Standard Oil he wrote: "History proves that there is no crime in the calendar—save possibly murder—of which it is not guilty or capable. It is the blue-ribbon enemy of everything moral and religious, although it includes within its corporation canting hypocrites who occupy front seats beneath the altar in churches that are desecrated by their presence." And harkening back to the example of the American colonists and their revolt against George III, he warned: "The last resort is for the people to retake into their own hands the power that has been delegated and abused. Vigilance Committees have more than once had a purifying influence. There may be conditions which will again render them a necessity. There is a limit to human forbearance. Has that limit yet been reached?"[40]

After 1880 more and more of the attention of concerned Americans focused upon the industrial corporations, especially those that had by the process of combination come to dominate a key industry. In March 1881 a young Chicago journalist, Henry Demarest Lloyd, fired what might be regarded as the starting gun in the race by the public and its representatives to check the accelerating power of industrial enterprise. In that month Lloyd published in the *Atlantic Monthly* an article titled, "The Story of a Great Monopoly," dealing with the success of the Standard Oil Company. The article, so popular that the issue had to be reprinted six times, brought to the attention of most Americans for the first time the fact that the petroleum industry had come to be dominated by a single organization. From that point on, the glare of the spotlight was never shifted from the oil giant and its officials. Pamphlets, speeches, articles, books, state and federal investigations remained dramatically focused upon the operations of Standard Oil. It came for most Americans to particularly typify their new and uncertain industrialized society, and when in 1890 in response to a tidal wave of public pressure, Congress placed upon the statute books the Sherman Antitrust Act, it could be said with only slight exaggeration that the law had been passed with Standard Oil primarily in mind.

But enacting an antitrust law, it soon became clear, was not the same as solving the problem of monopoly power in the United States. During the decade of the 1890s, a combination of lukewarm presidential interest in antitrust prosecutions, inadequate financing by the Congress of a miniscule Justice Department, and unfavorable judicial interpretations of key sections of the act resulted in little progress in the campaign against the trusts. The Standard Oil Company had itself apparently made government action against it more uncertain by abandoning the old trust framework and adopting instead, in the late 1890s, a holding company structure.

The Standard Oil Company (New Jersey) now became the parent corporation for the family of firms that formerly operated within the trust umbrella. Thus despite the passage of the Sherman Act specifically outlawing the trust device as a means of controlling an industry, the oil trust continued in existence under the guise of a new legal form. No wonder that George Rice could write his friend, Henry Demarest Lloyd, in 1897 that "surely the devil is at the helm to guide the Standard Oil Trust in all its devilish work, and there seems to be no overruling providence to demur or stop them, and laws are of no account, and our national emblem becomes a fraud and a farce."[41]

The 1890s had been busy years for Rice. He continually besieged the Justice Department with requests for antitrust action against Standard Oil. The Department did not respond favorably to his call, however, and during the McKinley years it even informed Rice that the "alleged combination against which you complained," was "not of an interstate character."[42]

More sympathetic to Rice's aims was Frank Monnett, an ambitious and energetic Ohio Attorney-General. Acting upon evidence and even funds supplied by Rice, Monnett instituted a suit against the Standard Oil Company of Ohio in 1898 seeking a forfeiture of its corporate charter. Despite a considerable body of sensational testimony and even the face-to-face New Amsterdam Hotel confrontation between Rice and Rockefeller described earlier, the Supreme Court of Ohio dismissed the suit in December, 1900. For Frank Monnett the decision had become academic as his Republican party had denied him renomination as Attorney-General in 1899 in punishment for his aggressive activities in the antitrust field. Rice thus lost an influential ally.[43]

Three years later, in 1902, Rice was supplying a fresh ally, Ida Tarbell, with the facts of his oil industry experiences, details which would shortly appear in her *History of the Standard Oil Company* series for *McClure's Magazine*. Rice was portrayed in that work as a dogged and embattled defender of American free enterprise against the onslaughts of concentrated economic power.[44]

At the same time, not entirely through with the judicial process, Rice had returned to the courts. In between testifying in antitrust actions in states ranging from Nebraska to Texas, he also filed suit in the United States Court of Appeals in Trenton, New Jersey, charging the Standard Oil combination with violation of the Sherman Act and asking for triple damages totalling three million dollars. It was his contention that Standard Oil had destroyed his Marietta business. The suit was still pending at the time of his death on February 28, 1905, and was later dismissed by the Court on technical grounds.[45]

In his obituary, the *New York Times* stated that Rice's life "had been spent in his fight for what he considered the right, and he often declared that he would rather be right than rich." *The Petroleum Gazette* added: "It is within the facts to say that no other single individual has been so instrumental as Mr. Rice was in forcing revelations of the inner workings of the Standard Oil Company."[46] The comments of other reform journals echoed a similar tone.

Rice was to receive a posthumous vindication of sorts as Standard Oil soon faced what appeared to be a final collision with the federal government. A 1905 Congressional resolution mandated an investigation of the petroleum situation by the recently established Bureau of Corporations. Unfortunately for Standard Oil, the commissioner of the Bureau, James R. Garfield, had lately been taken to task by the press for a report on the meat industry that the public regarded as insufficiently critical, given the current popularity of Upton Sinclair's graphic novel, *The Jungle*. Garfield, therefore, apparently resolved that the Bureau's oil report would not suffer the same fate. Its release in May 1906 was a body blow to the officials of Standard Oil, who had cooperated fully with the investigating agency.

Garfield supported many of the allegations leveled at Rockefeller's organization over the years and thereby set in motion further actions by Washington. On November 15, of the same year, the Justice Department, with the encouragement of an increasingly progressive Theodore Roosevelt, filed suit in the U.S. Circuit Court for the Eastern District of Missouri against the Standard Oil Company (New Jersey) and the other corporations of the combination. It was the government's contention that Standard Oil, by its past conduct and present stance in the petroleum industry, stood in violation of the Sherman Antitrust Act. Hearings on the suit began in the fall of 1907 and continued for fifteen months.

Despite a vigorous defense, a four-judge circuit court rendered a unanimous decision unfavorable to the Standard Companies. On November 20, 1909, that court found Jersey Standard and most of its subsidiary corporations to be in violation of the Sherman Act as an illegal monopoly. Not surprisingly, the ruling was quickly appealed to the U.S. Supreme Court. There arguments and briefs were again presented by both sides with a final decision not rendered until May 15, 1911.

When it was announced, it merited banner headlines in every newspaper in the land. The Supreme Court, upholding the verdict of the lower circuit court, ordered the oil giant dismembered. Thirty-three companies were to be severed from the parentage of Jersey Standard, including 16 of its 20 largest affiliates.[47]

Ironically, the Court's holding that Standard Oil did constitute a monopoly was reached at the very moment that the organization was losing rather than retaining control over its industry. With Rockefeller himself in retirement from the active management for over ten years, Standard's share of the market in 1911 was the smallest it had been for decades. The opening of new crude fields even faster than it could expand operations to keep pace; the rise of aggressive, integrated competitors such as Pure Oil, Gulf, Texaco; a reduced demand for kerosene, Standard's staple, and a new demand for fuel oil, gasoline, and other products; and a top management in the Jersey structure marked by increasing age and conservatism, all contributed to reducing its share of the nation's refining capacity to just over 60 percent by 1911.[48]

But it would not have been to George Rice's pleasure to have known that the Standard organization, or at least the stockholders of its various companies, seemed to have actually benefited from the Court-ordered separation. All Jersey Standard shareholders received their ratable proportion of stock in the subsidiaries of which the holding company was forced to divest itself. They found themselves in many instances sharing, figuratively, in multiple gold mines rather than a single lode. Dividends of the individual companies generally increased in the following year, and stock prices in a number of instances more than doubled after the dissolution. The investing public, through the information disseminated during the lengthy legal struggle, gauged for the first time the enormous real worth of the various Standard entities and began to bid for the stock accordingly. The principals holding the greatest interests in those companies, and most notably John Rockefeller, found that the Supreme Court of the United States had made them even wealthier than they had been before![49]

Document: The Sherman Act

John Sherman of Ohio was a U.S. Senator for over 25 years. Brother of the general of Civil War fame, he was a former Secretary of the Treasury, a future Secretary of State, and a recognized authority on financial questions. He was also a man considerably disturbed over the diminishing of competition in American industry, and he showed his concern by introducing in Congress, in 1888, 1889, and again in 1890, bills designed to destroy the combinations of capital that were unbalancing the nation's economy.

His 1890 version was referred to the Judiciary Committee of the Senate from which, considerably altered and not to Sherman's taste, it finally emerged. The Senate passed the Committee's product in April with only a single dissenting vote, the House unanimously, and President Benjamin Harrison added his signature on July 2, 1890. The act, which would forever bear John Sherman's name though he seriously considered voting against the final bill, was a momentous piece of legislation.

Blending the traditions of English common law and the American experience, the Sherman Antitrust Act was to serve as the cornerstone of public policy toward big business from that day to the present. As one scholar has phrased it, the act "declares the rules of the game for the American economy, and endows the government with broad authority to control private economic power."[50] Its extreme brevity, however, ensured the necessity in the years to come of judicial interpretation and congressional amendment, both shaped by evolving political debate. Nevertheless, its overall thrust remains clear to this day—competition, not monopoly, is the preferable economic situation, and the door to competition must never be allowed to be permanently closed. To Americans in 1890, at least, the act seemed to speak for itself, plainly and directly. The text of the act follows.

AN ACT TO PROTECT TRADE AND COMMERCE AGAINST UNLAWFUL RESTRAINTS AND MONOPOLIES

Be it enacted by the Senate and the House of Representatives of the United States of America in Congress assembled,

Section 1. Every contract, combination in the form of trust or otherwise, or conspiracy, in restraint of trade or commerce among the several States, or with foreign nations, is hereby declared to be illegal. Every person who shall make any such contract or engage in any such combination or conspiracy shall be punished by fine not exceeding five thousand dollars, or by imprisonment not exceeding one year, or by both said punishments, in the discretion of the court.

Section 2. Every person who shall monopolize, or attempt to monopolize, or combine or conspire with any other person or persons, to monopolize any part of the trade or commerce among the several States, or with foreign nations, shall be deemed guilty of a misdemeanor, and, on conviction thereof, shall be punished by fine not exceeding five thousand dollars, or by imprisonment not exceeding one year, or by both said punishments, in the discretion of the court.

Section 3. Every contract, combination in the form of trust or otherwise, or conspiracy, in restraint of trade or commerce in any Territory of the United States or of the District of Columbia, or in restraint of trade or commerce between any such Territory and another, and between any such Territory or Territories and any State or States or the District of Columbia, or with foreign nations, or between the District of Columbia and any State or States or foreign nations, is hereby declared illegal. Every person who shall make any such contract or engage in any such combination or conspiracy shall be deemed guilty of a misdemeanor, and, on conviction thereof, shall be punished by fine not exceeding five thousand dollars, or by imprisonment not exceeding one year, or by both said punishments, in the discretion of the court.

Section 4. The several circuit courts of the United States are hereby invested with jurisdiction to prevent and restrain violations of this Act; and it shall be the duty of the several district attorneys of the United States, in their respective districts, under the direction of the Attorney General, to institute proceedings in equity to prevent and restrain such violations. Such proceedings may be by way of petition setting forth the case and praying that such violation shall be enjoined or otherwise prohibited. When the parties complained of shall have been duly notified of such petition the court shall proceed, as soon as may be, to the hearing and determination of the case; and pending such petition and before final decree, the court may at any time make such temporary restraining order or prohibition as shall be deemed just in the premises.

Section 5. Whenever it shall appear to the court before which any proceeding under section four of this Act may be pending that the ends of justice require that other parties should be brought before the court, the court may cause them to be summoned, whether they reside in the district in which the court is held or not; and subpoenas to that end may be served in any district by the marshal thereof.

Section 6. Any property owned under any contract or by any combination, or pursuant to any conspiracy (and being the subject thereof) mentioned in section one of this Act, and being in the course of transportation from one State to another, or to a foreign country, shall be forfeited to the United States, and may be seized and condemned by like proceedings as those provided by law for the forfeiture, seizure, and condemnation of property imported into the United States contrary to law.

Section 7. Any person who shall be injured in his business or property by any other person or corporation, by reason of anything forbidden or declared to be unlawful by this Act, may sue therefor in any circuit court of the United States in the district in which the defendant resides or is found, without respect to the amount in controversy, and shall recover threefold the damages by him sustained, and the costs of suit, including a reasonable attorney's fee.

Section 8. That the word "person," or "persons," wherever used in this Act, shall be deemed to include corporations and associations existing under or authorized by the law of either the United States, the laws of any of the Territories, the laws of any State, or the law of any foreign country.

Notes

1. John H. Bunzel, *The American Small Businessman* (New York: Alfred A. Knopf, 1962), p. 114.

2. Carter Goodrich, ed., *The Government and the Economy: 1783–1861* (Indianapolis: The Bobbs-Merrill Company, Inc., 1967), pp. 183–184.

3. *Ibid.*, pp. 184–186.

4. E. A. J. Johnson, *The Foundations of American Economic Freedom: Government and Enterprise in the Age of Washington* (Minneapolis: University of Minnesota Press, 1973), p. 88.

5. *Ibid.*, pp. 89–90.

6. Joseph Dorfman, *The Economic Mind in American Civilization* (New York: The Viking Press, 1946), p. 417.

7. Peter Asch, *Economic Theory and the Antitrust Dilemma* (New York: John Wiley & Sons, Inc., 1970), p. 14.

8. *Ibid.*, p. 2.

9. William Letwin, *Law and Economic Policy in America* (New York: Random House, Inc., 1965), pp. 22–26.

10. Hans B. Thorelli, *The Federal Antitrust Policy: Origination of an American Tradition* (Baltimore: The Johns Hopkins Press, 1955), p. 26.

11. Sidney Fine, *Laissez Faire and the General Welfare State* (Ann Arbor: The University of Michigan Press, 1956), p. 5.

12. John William Ward, "The Ideal of Individualism and the Reality of Organization," in *The Business Establishment*, ed., Earl F. Cheit (New York: John Wiley & Sons, Inc., 1964), pp. 42–45.

13. John Tipple, "Big Businessmen and a New Economy," in *The Gilded Age*, ed., H. Wayne Morgan (Syracuse, N.Y.: Syracuse University Press, 1970), p. 19.

14. John D. Rockefeller, *Random Reminiscences of Men and Events* (New York: Doubleday, Page & Company, 1909), p. 65.

15. Letwin, *Law and Economic Policy*, p. 59; Bernard Bailyn, *The New England Merchants in the Seventeenth Century* (Cambridge, Mass.: Harvard University Press, 1955), pp. 41–42.

16. Arthur M. Schlesinger, Jr., *The Age of Jackson* (Boston: Little, Brown and Company, 1945), p. 90.

17. Maurice G. Baxter, *The Steamboat Monopoly: Gibbons v. Ogden, 1824* (New York: Alfred A. Knopf, 1972), p. 70.

18. Oscar Handlin and Mary F. Handlin, "Origins of the American Business Corporation," *The Journal of Economic History*, V (May, 1945), 4.

19. Thomas C. Cochran, *Business in American Life: A History* (New York: McGraw-Hill Book Company, 1972), p. 77.

20. Letwin, *Law and Economic Policy*, p. 65.

21. Goodrich, *The Government and the Economy*, pp. 392–393.

22. Cochran, *Business in American Life*, p. 78; Letwin, *Law and Economic Policy*, p. 66.

23. Tipple, "Big Businessmen and a New Economy," pp. 17–18.

24. *The New York World*, October 16, 1898.

25. Johnson, *The Foundations of American Economic Freedom*, p. vii.

26. Irvin G. Wyllie, *The Self-Made Man in America* (New York: The Free Press, 1966), p. 6.

27. Testimony of George Rice, U.S. Industrial Commission, *Preliminary Report on Trusts and Industrial Combinations*, U.S. Congress, 1st Sess., 1900, I, 704.

28. Gordon S. Wood, *The Creation of the American Republic, 1776–1787* (Chapel Hill: The University of North Carolina Press, 1969), p. 73; Johnson, *The Foundations of American Economic Freedom*, p. 185.

29. Wood, *The Creation of the American Republic*, p. 72.

30. Letwin, *Law and Economic Policy*, p. 10.

31. Rockefeller, *Random Reminiscences*, p. 155.

32. Allan Nevins, *Study in Power: John D. Rockefeller, Industrialist and Philanthropist* (New York: Charles Scribner's Sons, 1953), I, p. 7.

33. *Ibid.*, I, p. 11.

34. Ralph W. Hidy and Muriel E. Hidy, *Pioneering in Big Business, 1882–1911: History of the Standard Oil Company (New Jersey)* (New York: Harper & Brothers, 1955), p. 9.

35. George Rice, *My Experience* (Washington, D.C.: by the author, 1888), p. 1; William Z. Ripley, *Railway Problems* (Boston: Ginn and Company, 1913), p. xi.

36. Rockefeller, *Random Reminiscences*, p. 112.

37. Hidy and Hidy, *Pioneering in Big Business*, p. 35.

38. Glenn Porter, *The Rise of Big Business, 1860–1910* (Arlington Heights, Ill.: Harlan Davidson, Inc., 1973), p. 66.

39. Harold F. Williamson and Arnold R. Daum, *The American Petroleum Industry: The Age of Illumination, 1859–1899* (Evanston, Ill.: Northwestern University Press, 1959), pp. 725–728.

40. *Oil, Paint and Drug Reporter*, January 25, 1882; George Rice, *Standard Oil Company* (Marietta, Ohio: by the author, 1892), p. 230.

41. Letter of George Rice to Henry Demarest Lloyd, December 8, 1897, Henry Demarest Lloyd Papers, State Historical Society of Wisconsin, Madison, Wisconsin.

42. Thorelli, *The Federal Antitrust Policy*, pp. 408–409.

43. *New York Times*, December 12, 1900; Hoyt L. Warner, *Progressivism in Ohio, 1897–1917* (Columbus: Ohio State University Press, 1964), p. 7.

44. Letter, Rice to Lloyd, January 26, 1902, Lloyd Papers; Ida M. Tarbell, *The History of the Standard Oil Company* (New York: Macmillan Company, 1904), II, p. 46 ff.

45. *New York Times*, August 20, 1904; Thorelli, *The Federal Antitrust Policy*, p. 409.

46. *New York Times*, March 1, 1905; *The Petroleum Gazette*, March, 1905.

47. Hidy and Hidy, *Pioneering in Big Business*, pp. 676–709.

48. Harold F. Williamson, et al., *The American Petroleum Industry: The Age of Energy, 1899–1959* (Evanston, Ill.: Northwestern University Press, 1963), pp. 5–7.

49. Allan Nevins, *John D. Rockefeller: The Heroic Age of American Enterprise* (New York: Charles Scribner's Sons, 1940), II, pp. 607–608.

50. William Letwin, *Law and Economic Policy in America* (New York: Random House, 1965), p. 3.

QUESTIONS FOR REVIEW AND DISCUSSION

1. Should our thinking about the problems of monopolies in the modern world be guided by the philosophy of Thomas Jefferson, by the philosophy of Alexander Hamilton, or by our Anglo-Saxon tradition?
2. Has American history always contained an antimonopoly tradition? In what instances have Americans been willing to accept monopolies as being in the public interest?
3. If you had been John D. Rockefeller, what answer would you have given to George Rice's charges against Standard Oil?
4. What similarities and what differences were there between the individual characters of George Rice and John D. Rockefeller?
5. To what degree did the federal government win its antitrust suit, concluded in 1911, against Standard Oil?
6. If Rice had lived, would he have been satisfied with the Supreme Court's 1911 decision in the case against Standard Oil?

9

American Business Overseas

In 1914 the overseas investment of American business firms in foreign branches, subsidiaries, and similar units already totalled some $2.5 billion. That sum indicates that by the beginning of World War I, American companies had acquired a significant international or, as it would later be called, a multinational character.

There is general agreement that Singer Sewing Machine was America's first multinational corporation. It established branch sales offices and, later, factories in Great Britain and in other European countries during the 1860s. Soon after that Singer was selling over half its machines abroad rather than in the United States. Other large firms, including Standard Oil, International Harvester, Eastman Kodak, American Tobacco, and Westinghouse Electric, quickly followed the Singer example. Furthermore, U.S. policies, whether called Dollar Diplomacy or the Open Door Policy or some other descriptive name, were usually designed to encourage and support the activities of the nation's businesses in their ventures in Europe, in Asia, and in various countries in the Western Hemisphere.

Among the earliest American multinational corporations was the United Fruit Company which was responsible for popularizing, in the United States, an exotic tropical product—the banana. United Fruit dominated the trade in that item for decades. In the process, United Fruit established a controversial record in Latin American countries that caused it to be permanently linked in the minds of Latin Americans with the term "Yankee Imperialism." The size and the scope of United Fruit's operations in several Latin American countries simply overwhelmed those nations and made United Fruit the dominant economic and political force there. United Fruit's overseas record reflects a tangled mixture of constructive accomplishments along with heavy-handed, sometimes ruthless, domination. Where the balance lies is still the subject of intense debate.

The following case study concentrates on the story of United Fruit in one particular country, Colombia. *The United Fruit Company in Colombia*, written by Maurice P. Brungardt, a scholar of Colombian history, emphasizes the Colombian point of view. Business students in the United States should understand the viewpoints of other countries in order to more effectively address the difficult questions that continue to arise about today's multinational corporations and their roles in the world economy.

Maurice P. Brungardt

THE UNITED FRUIT COMPANY IN COLOMBIA

"There must have been three thousand of them," he murmured.

"What?"

"The dead," he clarified. "It must have been all of the people who were at the station."

The woman measured him with a pitying look. "There haven't been any dead here," she said. "Since the time of your uncle, the colonel, nothing has happened in Macondo. . . . "

. . . "You must have been dreaming," the officers insisted. "Nothing has happened in Macondo, nothing has ever happened, and nothing ever will happen. This is a happy town." In that way they were finally able to wipe out the union leaders.

Gabriel García Márquez,
One Hundred Years of Solitude

Introduction

Before 1870 most people in the United States had never heard of, much less eaten, a banana. By 1930, however, not only was the reticent Calvin Coolidge being quoted on the marvels of bananas, but the popular song "Yes, We Have No Bananas" had made its creators rich and famous. That song and a host of banana jokes reflected the reality of U.S. dominance in several Latin American countries.[1]

The United Fruit Company was no joke, however. More than any other entity, United Fruit was responsible for the banana revolution in the eating habits and popular culture of Americans. With $242 million in operating capital in 1930 and a net profit of $9.2 million in 1933,[2] (when many companies were going broke) United Fruit orchestrated the production, transportation, and distribution of billions of bananas. United Fruit controlled 63.6 percent of the bananas exported from nine Latin American countries in 1932 (see Table 9-1). It also directed a complex network of companies and subsidiaries that in turn controlled shipping, railroads, commerce, labor, communications, and, on occasion, law and order in the banana-producing zones of Latin America. To say the least, United Fruit significantly affected the lives of millions of people abroad.

United Fruit made some positive contributions in those countries. Uninhabited jungles were transformed into productive centers of human activity. Many diseases were eliminated by building hospitals and water and sanitation facilities. Railroads, ports, and schools were also built. Millions of dollars in tax revenues and workers' salaries were generated by United Fruit in those host countries.[3]

On the other hand, there was also a dark side to United Fruit's presence. It throttled competition, overthrew governments,[4] bribed presidents,[5] blocked railroads, ruined planters, bankrupted cooperatives, opposed organized labor, dominated workers, and exploited consumers. Such influence by a U.S. corporation in the comparatively weaker nations of Latin America left a legacy of distrust and bitter hatred that the U.S. government and other U.S. companies still have trouble overcoming. It was not without reason that United Fruit was known as *El Pulpo* (the Octopus) and that it provided grist for the literary mills of two Nobel Prize-winning Latin American novelists, Miguel Angel Asturias and Gabriel García Márquez.[6] United Fruit's influence in and impact on Latin America are undisputed by both its critics and its supporters, although in every Latin Ameri-

Table 9-1. Exports of Banana Stems from Major Latin American Producers in 1932

Country	Total Stems	United Fruit Company	Standard Fruit Company
Colombia	7,363,000	6,900,000	
Costa Rica	4,313,000	4,100,000	
Cuba	4,651,000		2,210,929
Guatemala	5,300,000	5,248,000	
Honduras	27,896,000	20,200,000	5,076,920
Jamaica	20,360,600	10,500,000	3,582,866
Mexico	4,205,600	500,000	2,521,563
Nicaragua	3,378,000	1,100,000	1,621,340
Panama	3,600,000	3,000,000	546,269
Total	81,067,200	51,548,000 (63.6%)	15,559,887 (19.2%)

Source: Reconstructed from Charles David Kepner, Jr., *Social Aspects of the Banana Industry*, Studies in History, Economics and Public Law, no. 414 (New York: Columbia University, 1936), 67.

can country that United Fruit touched the particulars are clouded in polemic and myth. Even today United Fruit's role and power, while much reduced from its former dominant position in the banana trade, has been obscured by changes of its name through mergers with other companies.

The history of the United Fruit Company is more than the saga of the rise and fall of a U.S. multinational in Latin America. The story is part of the larger drama of the off-and-on confrontation between the United States and Latin America. The superpower from the North has never really understood Latin America and its problems, much less known how to effectively advance its own long-term interests in the region. Like ships passing in the night, these two great cultures have not comprehended each other. In the case of the United States the ship is an aircraft carrier, without running lights nor known direction, plowing full-steam ahead oblivious to all in its way. In the case of Latin America, there is a flotilla of small craft whose fortune and misfortune is to be swept along by the carrier's wake which swamps, sinks, or seriously damages many of them.

The United Fruit Company's activities in Latin America involved the countries of Colombia, Costa Rica, Cuba, the Dominican Republic, Ecuador, Guatemala, Haiti, Honduras, Jamaica, Mexico, Nicaragua, and Panama. Although the main thrust of this study deals with the Colombian experience, an equally fascinating account could be written about the company in most of those other countries as well.

Early Developments in Colombia's Banana-Producing Zone

In Colombia bananas that are produced for export traditionally have been grown in a small corridor of land in the Department (State) of Magdalena south of the port of Santa Marta, running from the town of Ciénaga (11°01' north latitude) south to Río Fundación (10°22' north latitude). The east-west dimensions of this banana-producing zone are the Great Swamp of Santa Marta (longitude 74°24' west) and the spurs of the Sierra Nevada de Santa Maria (longitude 74°07' west), a single snow-capped mountain, geologically unrelated to the Andes, that rises from sea level to over 18,000 feet.[7] Historically, the development of banana production in the zone went hand-in-hand with railroad construction, with both moving further inland south of Santa Marta. After the railroad was completed between Santa Marta and Ciénaga in 1887, banana fields sprang up to the south. The railroad was extended to Riofrío in 1892, to Sevilla in 1894, and to Aracataca and Fundación in 1906—a total distance from Santa Marta of 59 miles. The United Fruit Company added another 50 miles of spurs off the main track, into the banana plantations.[8]

The first banana trees that were planted specifically for the export market were of the Gros Michael variety and had been brought from Bocas del Toro, Panama in 1887 by José Manuel González Bermúdez, a Colombian planter and resident of Santa Marta. In 1889 the steamer *Simón Dumoi* was loaded with 4,950 stems of González Bermúdez' bananas, but on arriving in New York City some of the bananas were overripe and others were rotten. Thus, the Board of Health ordered that all of them be dumped into the sea.[9] The important note here is that it was a Colombian, not an American, who first ventured to exploit the possibility of shipping bananas from Colombia to *Gringolandia*.

The problem for Colombians was one common to most people in developing countries—a lack of starting capital. In the banana trade, this capital was essential for weathering losses such as those caused by a delay in shipping. In testing the U.S. market, González Bermúdez lost over $20,000 in gold pesos before he folded and sold out to Sanders and Company of New Orleans, who in turn suffered the same fate and gave way to the Colombia Land Company in 1892.[10] Colombian planters did not have the resources to wait out the cycle from production to consumption; and, in general, if they did not lose their land to foreigners, they had to sell their bananas to foreign shippers. From the beginning, Colombians were excluded from the process of shipping and of selling bananas. Not until 1946 with the creation of the Colombian-Ecuadorian-Venezuelan backed shipping line, La Flota Mercante Gran Colombiana, did Colombians have the potential to control the overseas' shipping of their own bananas, which they began to do in 1955.[11]

Although 30,000 stems of bananas were being exported monthly from the banana zone south of Santa Marta by 1899, other commodities such as tobacco, sugar, and coffee were still more important.[12] The town of Ciénaga, for example, was the third largest producer of tobacco in Colombia at that time. Foreign capital had been present in the zone since the 1870s but it did not yet predominate. At the turn of the century, however, this changed as circumstances converged to concentrate potential banana-producing lands and the appropriate transportation infrastructure in the hands of the United Fruit Company. Once United Fruit had control over both the land and the transportation system, its domination of the region was uninterrupted until the Great Banana Strike and Massacre of 1928. How did the United Fruit Company gain so much power in Colombia?

Although Latin American entrepreneurs, as well as state and national governments in Latin America, undertook various railroad building schemes in the nineteenth century, none had the capital or international contacts to successfully bring off those ventures and still maintain control over the most important railroads. The Latin American governments invariably had to call in foreigners to put together the necessary package of venture capital and technological expertise. In the process, Latin American governments provided a series of incentives— land grants, duty-free imports, and subsidies—to get foreign participation. Under such an umbrella United Fruit was able to put together part of its series of inter-locking advantages that eventually gave it undisputed leverage in the banana industry.[13] The development of the railroad in the Colombian banana zone ac-counts for much of United Fruit's later control over the Colombian banana industry.

The first railroad concession in the banana zone was given by the Province (later to be called Department) of Magdalena in 1846. The concession eventually ended up in the hands of Roberto Joy, one of the original shareholders, and an-other Colombian, Julián de Mier. In 1886 the Department of Magdalena approved the transfer of the Mier-Joy concession to a London-based company, which incorporated as the Santa Marta Railway Company. The concession per-mitted the duty-free importation of construction materials, a 100,000 hectare tax-free land grant, and an annual subsidy of $60,000. A year later the national government in Bogotá approved the Department of Magdalena's concession with the restriction that 10 percent of the annual railroad profits go to the govern-ment after the company first covered its costs and a 5 percent interest charge. Showing the federal-local division of interest common to many Latin American countries in the nineteenth century, a division which foreigners often exploited, the national and the department governments bickered over who would spend the 10 percent share of the profits. In 1915 United Fruit settled the problem by closing the books and cavalierly declaring that the railroad was losing money.[14]

When United Fruit gained control of the Santa Marta railroad in 1899, it max-imized the possibilities inherent in the concession clauses by importing any number of items duty free—many of them not related to the railroad business—and by supplying its string of commissaries with articles for profit.[15] What, if any, banana lands that United Fruit acquired through the original land grant is un-clear. On the government's side was the stipulation, dating all the way back to the 1846 concession, that the railroad be extended to the Magdalena River. That was not done until 1955 and then not by United Fruit. The original rationale for the railroad was not to export bananas but to connect Santa Marta and the coast with the interior. Theoretically, United Fruit's ownership of the railroad could have been abrogated, since the terms of the original concession had not been satisfied. In fact, the Colombian government tied United Fruit up in court from 1925 to 1932 until the company finally agreed to lease the railroad from the government for 30 years in exchange for payments of 10 percent of the gross revenues.[16]

Minor Cooper Keith and the Origins of United Fruit

One of the most important factors in United Fruit's eventual domination of the banana zone was its acquisitions of land. The key individual in this drama was the legendary Minor Cooper Keith, described as the "uncrowned king of Central America." Keith, who was born in Brooklyn, New York, in 1848, was the son of a prosperous lumber merchant. His business career really began in 1871 when he joined an older brother who was already managing a railroad in Costa Rica. Keith's career was furthered even more when he married the daughter of that country's president a few years later. Keith reorganized the Costa Rican and Salvadoran national debt by negotiating multimillion pound loans from English bankers, and engineered the building of railroads throughout much of Central America. His International Railways of Central America brought much-needed economic integration to Central America by linking the Atlantic and Pacific oceans and by linking Mexico and El Salvador. This was not achieved, however, without human cost. The first 25 miles of rail out of Limón, Costa Rica, was laid at the cost of 5,000 lives—including Keith's uncle and three brothers.[17]

Keith entered the banana business because his railroads were not carrying enough freight and passengers to pay for the investment for which he was heavily in debt. As a result, in the early 1870s he began growing bananas along his Costa Rican railroad. These bananas were exported to New Orleans, thus giving Keith the cash flow necessary to satisfy his creditors. Keith also experimented with other tropical products, such as sugar, and obviously saw that the opening of new lands and the exporting of tropical commodities was the key to paying for his railroad empire.

Keith was a visionary who usually had many projects in various stages of planning. In addition to his land in Costa Rica, he amassed properties all over Latin America, including holdings near Bocas del Toro, Panama, and Santa Marta, Colombia. These holdings became the basis for his importance in the banana trade.

When Keith first acquired his land in Colombia is not clear, but the vehicle for the acquisition appears to have been the Colombia Land Company. In 1875 that company held 12,500 acres around Riofrío, an important center of banana production by 1894.[18] While Keith was in England in 1883 to renegotiate the defaulted Costan Rican foreign debt, he obviously had acquired this land company, since he issued stock certificates for the British incorporated Colombia Land Company.[19]

When, and to what extent, Keith gained control of the Santa Marta Railway Company is also not clear, although he probably bought enough of the stock after the transfer of the Mier-Joy concession to the London-based company in 1886 to imitate his Costan Rican success story. At any rate, Keith arrived in Santa Marta in 1890 as head of the Colombia Land Company. In that same year, the 1886-transfer of the Mier-Joy railway concession was notarized in Santa Marta as the Santa Marta Railway Company.[20] When Keith again embarked for Costa Rica, he left the Englishman W. C. Copperthwaite as the legal representative both of the Colombia Land Company and of the Santa Marta Railway Company. At that time rights to land and to rails were probably united in Colombia as they had been in Costa Rica. The union of the production and the transportation of bananas, in the hands of Keith, while not complete since much of the banana lands were still under the control of others, was close to fulfillment by the early 1890s. Copperthwaite proceeded to buy 3,333⅓ hectares of potential banana land from José Manuel Gonzalez in the area of Sevilla in 1893—one year later the railroad arrived.[21] As Table 9–2 shows, banana exports increased 500 percent between 1892 and 1905 despite the civil wars that periodically affected the region from 1895 to 1903.[22] By 1894 foreign investment of capital in banana lands had surpassed Colombian investment. In retrospect it appears that foreigners had already won control over Colombia's agrarian sector.[23]

Table 9–2. Exports of Banana Stems from Colombia

Year	Magdalena	Chocó + Nariño	Total
1891	74,915		
1892	171,891		
1893	201,875		
1894	298,766		
1895	155,845		
1896	335,834		
1897	472,454		
1898	420,966		
1899	485,385		
1900	269,877		
1901	253,193		
1902	314,006		
1903	478,448		
1904	787,244		
1905	863,750 (50,000 to England)		
1906	1,397,388		
1907	1,938,711		
1908	2,028,850		
1909	3,222,152		
1910	3,844,519		
1911	4,901,894		
1912	4,005,927		
1913	5,594,151		
1914	5,017,164		
1915	4,094,231		
1916	3,216,361		

continued

Table 9–2. Continued

Year	Magdalena	Chocó + Nariño	Total
1917	4,987,315		
1918	5,292,304		
1919	5,022,069		
1920	6,294,754		
1921	7,404,314		
1922	7,098,852		
1923	7,472,783		
1924	9,177,063		
1925	9,918,815		
1926	10,893,065		
1927	8,625,329		
1928	10,220,042		
1929	10,332,113		
1930	11,034,936		
1931	5,403,743		
1932	6,930,796		
1933	7,311,922		
1934	7,620,619		
1935	7,963,467	61,486	8,024,953
1936	7,964,714	362,164	8,308,878
1937	6,393,697	191,495	6,585,192
1938	7,209,432	283,419	7,492,851
1939	7,273,043	302,027	7,575,070
1940	4,613,435	389,657	5,003,158
1941	2,372,412	293,025	2,672,437
1942	221,529	3,704	225,233
1943	500		500
1944	441,394	18,563	459,957
1945	1,377,965	4,893	1,382,858
1946	2,104,842	5,572	2,110,414
1947	3,245,288	93,364	3,338,652
1948	4,530,532	184,979	4,715,511
1949	6,039,692	239,916	6,279,608
1950	6,272,489	165,345	6,437,834
1951	6,229,694	117,996	6,347,690
1952	6,240,020	214,173	6,454,193
1953	7,579,457	79,853	7,657,310
1954	7,828,907	96,006	7,924,913
1960	8,572,655		
1970	630,000		

Source: Manuel J. Díaz Granados Cotes, "La economía bananera en Colombia," *Economía colombiana*, año II, vol. 7, no. 20, 511–519. Years 1892, 1902, 1903, 1960, and 1970 are from White, *Historia de una ignominia*, 123.

It is important to note that Colombians actively cooperated with the foreign interests and did not present a common front against foreign penetration. As early as 1886, several important Colombian landowning families—the Fergusson Nogueras, the Miers, and the Durans—lent money or acquired stock in the recently incorporated Santa Marta Railway Company. In 1894 another Colombian banana producer, Campo Serrano, the governor of Magdalena, strongly resisted efforts by the national government to take over the railroad, in essence protecting Keith's probable control.[24] There were, therefore, important Colombian landowners who preferred to link up and take their chances with foreign investors rather than with a Colombian business combination.

Another link in the chain that impeded Colombian national interests was forged when the same individual who exercised diplomatic functions also represented company interests. One of the first managers of the Santa Marta Railway Company was the Englishman Mansel F. Carr who arrived in Santa Marta in 1882 and married the sister of Roberto Joy. In 1908 Carr became Great Britain's vice-consul in Santa Marta and was also manager of United Fruit. Julián de Mier, who along with Joy had sold the railway concession to the English in 1886, became consul for both the United States and France in Santa Marta. Following Carr as Britain's vice-consul in 1910 was Phillip Marshall, who was also manager of the Santa Marta Railway Company, and then in 1927 Thomas Bradshaw, who was the manager of United Fruit in Santa Marta.[25] Obviously, it was useful to Keith and later to United Fruit to have the active support of some of the most important Colombian landowners as well as to have diplomatic functions in the hands of the company's managers in Santa Marta.

By the turn of the century, Colombians had lost control over the railroad and were at a growing disadvantage in representing their interests as landowners. At that juncture the Boston Fruit Company emerged as the inheritor of the extraordinary, competitive advantages that Keith had put together in the Colombian banana zone—probable railroad ownership, control of key blocks of land, loyalty of a limited but crucial group of Colombian landowners, and U.S. and British diplomatic leverage.

Keith was a truly remarkable man—arriving in Costa Rica with very little, marrying a president's daughter, building a major railroad through disease-infected jungle, refinancing the Costa Rican foreign debt, and amassing key banana properties in Costa Rica, Panama, and Colombia. He was, however, a wheeler-dealer who in pushing ahead always tended to face a cash-flow problem if anything went wrong. The year 1898 was a bad one for Keith. A New York banking house went under and left Keith with the option of paying off $1.5 million in 90 days or of going bankrupt. Costa Rica's leading families and even the government offered

Keith the credit he needed to survive. His Costa Rican holdings were then hit by fires, plagues, floods, and storms. Finally, in October 1898 the New Orleans firm that distributed his bananas, Hoadley and Company, failed—$1 million of Keith's money was gone. Worse still, Keith was a partner in the firm.[26] Keith needed capital fast or everything he, as well as much of the Costan Rican elite, had worked for would be wiped out. At that point, Keith turned to the Boston Fruit Company.

Boston Fruit was the result of the efforts of Lorenzo Dow Baker, a ship captain, and Andrew W. Preston, a produce salesman and broker. Over time Baker had put together an efficient shipping operation and supplied much of the East Coast of the United States with bananas from Jamaica. Preston was the marketing expert and through the Fruit Dispatch Company had masterminded the distribution of bananas better than anyone else. By investing in more modern and faster ships and by developing a steady and efficient distribution network, Boston Fruit had succeeded where many others had failed.

Boston Fruit's Achilles heel, however, was that most of its banana lands were concentrated in Jamaica. Its investments in the Dominican Republic never worked out, and operations in Cuba were subject to cold spells. All of Boston Fruit's Jamaican banana lands could be wiped out by one hurricane. Both Preston and Baker worried constantly about such a possible catastrophe. As a result, they sought other sources of supply and frequently marketed the bananas of other producers, including those of Minor Cooper Keith. In December 1894, the latter had signed a marketing agreement with Boston Fruit to sell all bananas grown and exported from his Colombian and Panamanian holdings on the East Coast north of Cape Hatteras.[27] As long as this marketing arrangement was in force, Boston Fruit's recurring nightmare of a Jamaican hurricane was less intense—since Keith had more bananas than anyone else. The agreement also allowed Boston Fruit to greatly expand its U.S. distribution network.

When Keith, pressed for cash, walked through the doors of Boston Fruit in late 1898, he fulfilled the firm's wildest dreams. Preston saw the opportunity not only of solving Boston Fruit's supply problem permanently but also of establishing a banana company so big that it could dominate the entire industry. On March 20, 1899, Keith's extensive holdings and Boston Fruit, along with its subsidiaries were merged into the United Fruit Company with an authorized capital stock of $20 million. Keith received $3,964,000 in United Fruit stock, on which he could negotiate to borrow and thus pay off his debts. He also became first vice-president and a director, but most of the positions on the board of directors went to the original partners in Boston Fruit.[28] Clearly, the Boston Fruit Company had picked the fruit that Keith had cultivated so earnestly for 28 years. In the space of two months, United Fruit absorbed twelve banana firms with properties in Boston,

New York City, Philadelphia, Baltimore, New Orleans, Cuba, Jamaica, the Dominican Republic, Costa Rica, Panama, Colombia, and Nicaragua.

United Fruit in Colombia

As the twentieth century opened, Colombians faced a far more formidable company in United Fruit than they had in Keith's operation. United Fruit had access to a wider range of possibilities than any other banana company had. When United Fruit published its first annual report in 1900, paying an initial dividend of $2.50 a share, it (1) owned or leased 250,000 acres in Colombia, Costa Rica, Cuba, the Dominican Republic, Honduras, and Nicaragua; (2) employed 15,000 workers abroad; (3) owned 11 steamers, with 30 other ships under contract; and (4) held title to 117 miles of railroad, with almost 300 boxcars and flatcars and 17 locomotives.[29] What Colombia faced was a company so large that even if the country tried to stand up to this giant, it risked the possibility that United Fruit would close down its Colombian operation and block the entry of Colombian fruit to U.S. and British markets. There was no international antitrust legislation to stop such a scenario from unfolding. United Fruit did not need Colombian bananas, since it now had extensive banana-producing lands in other parts of Latin America as well as vast reserve areas that could be brought into production if needed.

Once these resources were in hand, it was only a matter of time before United Fruit consolidated its hold over Colombian production. The increasing importance of the Colombian banana zone as well as United Fruit's control of it can be judged by the following information. By the end of 1906 there were 15,000 banana workers in the zone. The entire group of 147 Colombian planters and 10 foreign planters had 2,282 hectares in banana production; United Fruit held 799 hectares or 35 percent of the total.[30] By 1915 total hectares in banana production had grown to 14,350. Individual planters had 5,850 (40.7 percent); the French company, Inmobilière et Agricole de Colombie, 2,485 (17.3 percent); and United Fruit, 6,050 (42.0 percent).[31] United Fruit's control was far greater than even these figures suggest, since it also had most of the private planters under contract by 1915. A 1913 report by the French legation in Colombia on the possibility of further French investment in the banana zone indicated that United Fruit already controlled 90 percent of the land that was appropriate for banana cultivation.[32]

When competitors appeared in the Colombian banana zone, United Fruit drove them out of business by refusing to ship their fruit on its railroad or in its ships. If the bananas actually arrived in the United States or Great Britain, United

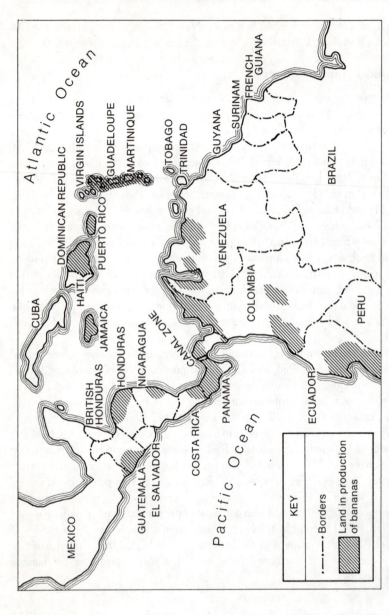

Banana Regions (Adapted from Stacy May and Galo Plaza, *The United Fruit Company in Latin America.* National Planning Association, Washington, 1958.)

KEY

– · – · – Borders

Land in production of bananas

Fruit usually had the fruit embargoed, effectively ruining it because of the inevitable delays inherent in judicial proceedings. The company alleged that the bananas had been produced by growers under contract to United Fruit, a device that United Fruit also used effectively in Colombian courts in Santa Marta.[33] Colombian competitors foolhardy enough to challenge United Fruit either went bankrupt or very quickly accommodated themselves to United Fruit's interests. Potential American competitors had a whole range of weapons that the Colombians did not have, yet the few Americans who fought United Fruit in the marketplace found the going rough. When Keith tried to reestablish his Colombian connections and compete with United Fruit in 1919, United Fruit immediately signed up 200 independent Colombian growers by threatening to shut off their water supply. Since United Fruit controlled the vast irrigation works that had been built over the years in the banana zone, it could and did use water as a weapon to force compliance with its demands.[34] In 1920 United Fruit shut down the Colombian operations of the Atlantic Fruit Company, run by the American Joseph di Giorgio, by having the court in Santa Marta embargo Atlantic's fruit. In 1921 the French Inmobilière et Agricole de Colombie recognized the inevitable and sold its 20,000 hectare holdings to United Fruit for 770,000 gold dollars.[35]

Not only did United Fruit try to eliminate and exclude all other banana companies, foreign and domestic, from the Colombian banana zone, but it also attempted to exercise total control over the land that produced the bananas. United Fruit used Colombians to buy up land in the name of supposedly independent Colombian banana companies, such as the Santa Marta Fruit Company, for eventual resale to United Fruit. In 1910 near Aracataca, home of the novelist Gabriel García Márquez, various Colombians put together a package of 8,000 hectares for Santa Marta Fruit which resold it to United Fruit in 1917.[36]

The economic boom and expansion of the banana zone from 1900 to 1929 attracted workers, usually of *campesino* stock, from Magdalena and from other regions of Colombia—the population of the banana zone grew rapidly. The influx of workers set up its own dynamics which produced significant pressure and competition for land. Not all immigrants to the zone found adequate employment, and many sought survival by cultivating virgin land in subsistence fashion. Before 1875 most of the land in the banana zone was public domain. As the boom developed in the 1890s, and especially after 1900, more and more virgin land was opened up and planted in bananas. United Fruit was determined to regulate banana production by monopolizing land resources and by enforcing highly restrictive contracts with independent growers to limit what could be grown and to whom it could be sold. United Fruit also kept large amounts of land out of banana production, and, in fact, in some areas it did not want the land used at all. United Fruit's rationale for keeping *some* land out of banana production made sense in terms of maintaining a reserve from which it could convert to banana production if the demands of the international market would make that profitable. The logic of not allowing production on *other* land is not immediately evident, but it may have been a way to have a hungry labor force available and disposed to work if there were a need to plant virgin land in bananas.[37]

United Fruit staked out that virgin land as company land. Some of the land had belonged to the government as public domain while other parcels had been claimed by individuals. In the latter case, few persons ever had clear title to the land. Even in cases where colonial documents gave particular individuals a strong claim, the exact dimensions of the plats were unclear and usually extremely vague, since it had never been worth the expense to have them properly surveyed. Many individuals sold fraudulent or very weak titles to United Fruit, but the company employed good Colombian lawyers who extracted maximum benefit from the ambiguous status of those lands. The power and resources that United Fruit wielded in the early twentieth century usually influenced the courts to make the decision in its favor. Undoubtedly some of the land claimed by United Fruit was still public domain and had never been properly alienated either by private or corporate interests.[38] Certainly, Colombian popular opinion regarded all virgin land as public domain that could be occupied and, thereby, claimed by whomever had the will to cultivate it. On many occasions United Fruit faced an invasion of squatters on their uncultivated lands. Squatters were told that the land was private property and that if they did not leave peacefully, they would be expelled. If the *campesinos* forcefully resisted, United Fruit had the local authorities burn them out, incarcerate them, or destroy their crops.[39] Between 1920 and 1929, there were more than 35 cases of these types of expulsions whose lengthy documentation can be found in the Archivo Histórico Nacional de Bogotá.[40] Many more Colombian *campesinos* never had the resources to fight United Fruit and to seek a legal remedy. As a result, their cases are lost to posterity.

By 1930 United Fruit owned about 59,500 hectares in the banana zone of which no more than 20 percent, or 12,000 hectares, were cultivated in any crop. In other words, 80 percent lay fallow and unused. In 1955 United Fruit's holdings were 100,000 acres of which only 7,000 or 7 percent were in bananas.[41] United Fruit regulated banana production in the zone according to the demands of the international market without regard for the pressing social problems related to land use in the region.

United Fruit occupied the largest amount of choice land and forced growers to produce only where, when, and what United Fruit dictated. Some of the richest land for the production of bananas was near Riofrío, but as early as 1908 one writer was complaining:

The arbitrator of the [banana] business in Santa Marta is Mr. Mansel F. Carr, Manager of United Fruit. Without consulting beforehand with him, no one can begin to plant bananas. It is necessary to have a contract in order to assure the sale [of the bananas] . . . and, or course, Mr. Carr makes the contract, [and he] begins to decide if one can or cannot cultivate in such and such land according to the company's interests. This is the reason why the lands . . . of Riofrío, some of the best for bananas, remain uncultivated: United Fruit has indicated it will not give a contract for fruit produced there.[42]

Some contracts were decided beforehand in Boston, showing that Colombia was subject to rules established far away in *Gringolandia*. Even when United Fruit bought land, for which it frequently paid good prices, it held the seller to a very restrictive contract. In such cases the sellers continued producing bananas with the requirement that they "keep and conserve without decline or deterioration said land" and that they "deal only with the company for the buying and selling of all bananas for exportation."[43] On other land that was also appropriate for producing bananas, United Fruit wrote restrictions into its contracts against the planting of fruit. Such contracts with renters prohibited the growing of bananas. If bananas were planted, the rental agreement automatically ended, the cultivator had to turn the land back to United Fruit immediately, and the cultivator had to pay the company a fine of "$2,000 American gold pesos for every 100 hectares."[44]

Even when United Fruit had contracts with important Colombian planters, it tended to bend the rules of the game according to the demands of the international marketplace. The Liberal politician, General Benjamín Herrera, who had a banana plantation in Aracataca and contracts with United Fruit, complained:

> The telegraph keys were precise: When it was communicated from the United States, "SCARCE," ALL [bananas] were received. When . . . "ABUNDANT," the acceptance was submitted to a rigorous classification . . .
>
> In exceptional cases the right of "appeal" was allowed, but this was a joke: when the decision arrived on Thursday, the bananas were already sunburnt and dried out.
>
> Of every three or four stems, one was rejected: for being thin, fat, bruised, wasp-stung, porque sí, porque no. . . .

The General argued:
"This is ruinous!"
"This is wicked!"
"This is criminal!"

The unruffled checkers keep right on:
"Thin."
"Wide."
"Skin-damaged."
"Wasp-bitten."

"Sunburnt."
"Splotches."
"Bruised."
"Porque sí."
"Porque no."[45]

When General Herrera sued United Fruit for excessive rejections and low prices, the manager of United Fruit surreptitiously sequestered pertinent documents from the court. The manager was subsequently sent to jail in October 1916.[46] If General Herrera, who was Colombia's Liberal presidential candidate in 1922, was treated in this fashion, United Fruit certainly did not feel the need to treat the local *campesinos* any better.

Campesinos who tried to acquire land in the banana zone frequently faced the power and influence of United Fruit. Those who gave up their dream of hacking a plot of their own out of the jungle joined the ranks of the rural proletariat who hired out as day laborers to United Fruit or to Colombian growers. *Campesinos* on occasion found themselves pressured to sell their small plots, even when they had clear title. United Fruit controlled the irrigation system and sometimes chose not to supply water to those whose land was downstream. Thus, growers had no recourse but to sell. Other *campesinos* claimed that United Fruit deliberately flooded them out to get their land.[47] Whether United Fruit's monopolization of available land was a device to force subsistence farmers into the marketplace as day laborers is an unanswerable question at this stage in the historical research of that period. However, some *campesinos* who were forced to sell their land complained to the minister of agriculture in 1919: "They do it out of anger that we are not mercenary day laborers of the company."[48] Whatever the case, when the Great Banana Strike and Massacre of 1928 unfolded, United Fruit had a serious labor problem.

The 1928 Strike

Over the years United Fruit had avoided dealing directly with the workers by making use of labor contractors to do the hiring and firing. In that way, United Fruit avoided the responsibility of following the existing labor legislation and, as a result, did not have to meet housing standards nor pay for collective insurance. The striking workers in 1928 demanded that United Fruit follow the spirit of the labor legislation—collective insurance, job-related disability payments, Sunday's as a nonwork day, and adequate housing and hospital facilities. Other demands were increases in wage, collective contracts, abolition of wages paid in script for use in the company stores, and an end to the company commissaries. United Fruit refused to bargain on the grounds that since it did not contract workers directly it was not the employer and was absolved from obeying the existing labor law requirements.[49]

The strike, which resulted, escalated into a tragic confrontation between the Colombian army and strikers both in Ciénaga and in Sevilla on December 6, 1928, in which 68 to 80 people died.[50] Most writers put that figure at several hundred. Popular belief, however, is that over a thousand perished. García Márquez, Colombia's Nobel Prize winner in literature, mentions 3,000 dead in *One Hundred Years of Solitude*.[51] When Colombians speak of the strike, they blame United Fruit and the Conservative government that was in power at the time.

The reality was far more complex. While United Fruit was responsible for unfair labor practices—especially working through labor contractors to avoid existing labor legislation—Colombian growers did the same. Perhaps a more "progressive" U.S. multinational might have set a better example. However, Colombian growers did not want a settlement with the strikers and were terrified that an accommodation would ruin them. They clamored just as much as United Fruit did for government protection and troops. When 5,000 workers paraded before the governor of Magdalena on November 11 and struck on November 12, 1928, both department and company authorities requested national troops. A battalion of 300 soldiers under General Carlos Cortés Vargas arrived in Magdalena on November 13.

Ironically, both the governor and the management of United Fruit wanted a settlement with the workers, but the company's advisors and the Colombian growers were opposed to a settlement. Another complicating factor was the outmoded anarchist-syndicalistic belief of some strikers and their leaders that spontaneous confrontation would solve their problems by collapsing the structures of oppression. For some strikers, any agreement would be a sell out; these strikers undermined the efforts of the leaders to reach a settlement.

Small shopkeepers and grocers at first supported the strikers with food and supplies, hoping to eventually supplant United Fruit's commissaries. But as the days dragged on and expenses mounted, the support of these grocers lessened and the strikers began to run out of food. Tensions intensified. Banana shipments and other property were vandalized. People were intimidated. Strikers tried to convince soldiers to side with them, not believing that in a showdown Colombian soldiers would fire on them. As resources dwindled, strikers appropriated cattle and supplies from local ranchers and shopkeepers. On December 1, the department government decreed that all who did not work were vagrants and subject to arrest. As the ante was increased and strikers found themselves in increasingly straitened circumstances, they scheduled a giant march on the governor of Santa Marta for December 6.

Ignacio Rengifo, minister of war, in Bogotá had received an avalanche of telegrams and letters from Colombian landowners, from United Fruit, and from others complaining about the explosive situation in the banana zone. He answered that he was determined "to oppose tendencies and demonstrations of a subversive character" that were the "fruit of the active and constant propagandistic action of communist agitators."[52] In addition to his concern for public order, he was worried about U.S. intervention and a possible separatist movement. This rumored dismemberment of Colombia was supposedly to be instigated by multinational petroleum companies in Colombia and Venezuela and would establish the minirepublic of Zulia.[53] In view of repeated intervention by the United States in Latin America and its involvement in the breakaway of Panama from Colombia in 1903, which gave Theodore Roosevelt the Panama Canal, such beliefs were not as farfetched then as they may seem today.

Rengifo declared a state of siege in the banana zone on December 5; the order reached General Vargas by 8:00 P.M. in Ciénaga where about 1,500 people were camped in the plaza, waiting for other groups to arrive for the march on Santa Marta the following day. General Vargas issued two proclamations that were consistent with martial law inherent in a state of siege: The first proclamation established "peremptorily the immediate breakup of all groupings greater than three persons"; the second ordered gunfire "on the group if that were the case."

Because he commanded only 300 soldiers and with reports that armed strikers were advancing on Ciénaga from Riofrío, General Vargas decided to resolve the issue before various other groups could join together with those already in the plaza. He deployed his troops to the square and had them and three machine guns in place by 1:30 A.M. on December 6. The state of siege decree and the two martial law proclamations were read through a megaphone to the multitude of 1,500. They were given five minutes to disband. The people did not believe the soldiers would fire and yelled, "Long live the soldier—friend of the people!" "Soldier, join the strike!" "Soldier, we are your brothers!" A short bugle blast announced the end of five minutes. A Captain Garavito warned, "One minute more and we will open fire!" A few people yelled, "Long live the strike!" and "Down with United!" A whistle ended the minute. General Vargas grabbed a megaphone and shouted, "We're going to fire!" One of the strikers replied, "We make you a present of the remaining minute!" There was another short bugle blast, and General Vargas ordered, "Fire!"

At eight o'clock the next morning, the official count listed thirteen dead and nineteen wounded. Two of the wounded succumbed later in the hospital. A stray bullet pierced a house and killed a government worker. Later in the day 400 armed strikers besieged the United Fruit Company's offices in Sevilla and killed a lieutenant. When the soldiers arrived with their machine guns, 29 strikers perished. Another three fell in Aracataca. Between December 7 and 14, thirteen more strikers were buried. It was reported but never confirmed that five to fifteen wounded workers died in hiding from a lack of medical attention. Material damages totaled $1,250,000—U.S. dollars—of which United Fruit suffered $800,000; the railroad, $150,000; and Colombian growers, $300,000.

The strike and its tragic consequences marked a watershed in Colombia's history and foreshadowed the decline of United Fruit's power and influence in the region. For Colombia, the strike discredited the Conservative administration of Miguel Abadía Méndez, president from 1926 to 1930; forced the resignation of Ignacio Rengifo, the minister of war; and led to the election of Enrique Olaya Herrera, president from 1930 to 1934—Colombia's first Liberal president since the 1880s. Colombian governments since then have been more nationalistic, interventionist, and conscious of their role in modernizing Colombia. As a result, they supported the development of Colombian banana cooperatives in competition with United Fruit and the building of a national shipping line to export coffee and bananas.

In 1928, however, the strike suggested government incompetence and collusion with United Fruit. That issue was seized upon by Jorge Eliécer Gaitán, the young leftist Liberal, whose opportunistic and electrifying dissection of the events of the strike before the Colombian Congress in 1929 helped to bring down the Conservatives while it advanced his own career. Gaitán's melodramatic display of a disinterred child's skull before a full Congress and his flashy oratory caused a sensation and led to a Congressional investigation of the strike and of United Fruit's role in the region.[53] Future politicians found that a close association with United Fruit could be a political liability. Colombian politicians of all persuasions found it politically convenient to assail United Fruit. If Gaitán on the far Left got good political mileage out of United Fruit, so did Conservatives on the far Right like Laureano Gómez.[54]

Today most Colombians still believe that, if not thousands, then hundreds were massacred in the Great Banana Strike and Massacre of 1928. United Fruit still has an unrivaled reputation with many Colombians as a force of evil and exploitation. After the strike in 1928, it was a foregone conclusion that United Fruit's role in Colombia would decrease significantly. Although it was many years before United Fruit left Colombia, United Fruit burned its archives and finally closed its operations in Santa Marta in 1966.[55]

Notes

1. For the impact of bananas on U.S. popular culture, see Charles Morrow Wilson, *Empire in Green and Gold: The Story of the American Banana Trade* (New York: Holt, 1947), 168–186; for United Fruit advertisements that passed the censors of several leading

ladies' magazines, see Thomas P. McCann, *An American Company: The Tragedy of United Fruit* (New York: Crown, 1976), 86–87, 180–181, plate 4.

2. Charles David Kepner, Jr. and Jay Henry Soothill, *The Banana Empire: A Case Study of Economic Imperialism* (New York: Vanguard, 1935), 36, 347.

3. The best in-house history of United Fruit is Stacy May and Galo Plaza, *The United Fruit Company in Latin America*, United States Business Performance Abroad Series, no. 7 (Washington, D.C.: National Planning Association, 1958).

4. In 1910 Samuel Zemurray bought the *Hornet*, a surplus navy ship, a case of rifles, a machine gun, and 3,000 rounds of ammunition for Manuel Bonilla, ex-president of Honduras, and squired the latter, Lee Christmas, and Machine Gun Malony out of New Orleans past U.S. government agents and landed them in Honduras where they overthrew President Miguel Dávila. Sam "the Banana Man" got the concession for his Cuyamel Fruit Company which he merged with United Fruit in 1929 for $31.5 million. For the overthrow of Dávila, see Kepner and Soothill, *Banana Empire*, 107–108. The most famous *coup d'état* was United Fruit's work with the Central Intelligence Agency, CIA, in overthrowing Guatemalan President Jacobo Arbenz in 1954 after the government nationalized some of United Fruit's unused land. For the most stimulating account, see Stephen Schlesinger and Stephen Kinzer, *Bitter Fruit: The Untold Story of the American Coup in Guatemala* (New York: Anchor, 1983); for the most scholarly account, see Richard H. Immerman, *The CIA in Guatemala: The Foreign Policy of Intervention* (Austin, Texas: University of Texas, 1982).

5. In 1974 United Fruit paid a bribe of $1.25 million to Honduras's minister of economy, Abraham Bennaton Ramos, and to the chief of state, General Oswaldo Lopez Arellano. The tax on a box of bananas promptly dropped from 50 cents to 25 cents saving United Fruit $6 to $7 million a year. See McCann, *An American Company*, 232–234.

6. Asturias wrote a trilogy of novels on United Fruit: *Viento fuerte* (Strong wind), 1950, *El Papa verde* (Green pope), 1954, and *Los ojos de los enterrados* (The eyes of the buried), 1960. García Márquez' classic, *Cien años de soledad* (One hundred years of solitude), 1967, treats the banana company only tangentially.

7. The contours of the banana zone are stepped off in Roberto Herrera Soto and Rafael Romero Castañeda, *La zona bananera del Magdalena: Historia y léxico* (Bogotá: Caro y Cuervo, 1979), 3.

8. The best material on the railroad is found in Fernando Botero and Alvaro Guzmán Barney, "El enclave agrícola en la zona bananera de Santa Marta," *Cuadernos colombianos* (Medellín), no. 11 (1977), 309–389.

9. Herrera Soto, *La zona bananera*, 6.

10. Botero and Guzmán Barney, "El enclave," 326.

11. July 19, 1985, interview with Ignacio Restrepo, representative of La Flota Mercante Gran Colombiana in New Orleans.

12. Judith White, *Historia de una ignominia: La United Fruit Co. en Colombia* (Bogotá: Presencia, 1978), 18–19.

13. See Kepner and Soothill, *Banana Empire*, 28, 34, 44–51, 80, 102–106, 112–113, 123–128, 136, 141–146, 148, 281–282, 294, 301–302, 380–381.

14. White, *Historia de una ignominia*, 20; a hectare is equal to 2.471 acres.

15. For customs' abuses, see letter to editor of *El Tiempo* (Bogotá), January 1, 1915, reproduced in Jorge Villegas and José Yunis, *Sucesos colombianos: 1900–1924* (Medellín: Universidad de Antioquia, 1976), 203–208.

16. Stephen J. Randall, *The Diplomacy of Modernization: Colombian-American Relations, 1920–1940* (Toronto: University of Toronto, 1977), 140.

17. Keith's colorful career is told in Wilson, *Empire in Green and Gold*, 36–68, 98–116.

18. White, *Historia de una ignominia*, 19.

19. Wilson, *Empire in Green and Gold*, 67.

20. Botero and Guzmán Barney, "El enclave," 323, 326.

21. Ibid., 383.

22. During the War of the Thousand Days (1899–1902) 100,000 perished. Colombia's 1905 census showed a population of 4,143,632. See Departamento de Contraloría, Dirección General de Estadística, *Censo de población de la república de Colombia* (Bogotá: Imprenta Nacional, 1924), 441.

23. Herrera Soto, *La zona bananera*, 6.

24. White, *Historia de una ignominia*, 20–21.

25. Ibid., 19–21.

26. Wilson, *Empire in Green and Gold*, 104–110.

27. Ibid., 69–97.

28. Ibid., 106–109.

29. Ibid., 110.

30. Herrera Soto, *La zona bananera*, 17.

31. Figures reconstructed from those given in Botero and Guzmán Barney, "El enclave," 347–348.

32. Herrera Soto, *La zona bananera*, 17–18.

33. Ibid., 8, 17, for examples.

34. Ibid.

35. Ibid.

36. Botero and Guzmán Barney, "El enclave," 346–348.

37. For a discussion of this, see Catherine LeGrand, "Campesinos y asalariados en la zona bananera de Santa Marta, 1900–1935," *Anuario colombiano de historia social y de la cultura* (Bogotá), no. 11 (1983), 240.

38. Botero and Guzmán Barney, "El enclave," 338–340.

39. LeGrand, "Campesinos," 239.

40. Ibid., 240. See footnote 12 for specific documentation in Archivo Nacional.

41. Botero and Guzmán Barney, "El enclave," 348–349

42. Ibid., 345–346.

43. Ibid., 350–351.

44. Ibid.

45. Quoted in Alberto Luna Cárdenas, *Un año y otros días con el general Benjamín Herrera en las bananeras de Aracataca* (Medellín: Bedout, 1960), 135–136.

46. Herrera Soto, *La zona bananera*, 17.

47. LeGrand, "Campesinos," 240.

48. Ibid.

49. Workers' petition and list of demands are reproduced in Herrera Soto, *La zona bananera*, 28–30.

50. My account follows Herrera Soto, *La zona bananera*, 38–70. Readers should be aware that the 1928 strike is a passionate subject for Colombians and that all works dealing with it should be treated with circumspection. Herrera Soto's account is the most heavily documented, the best presented, and the most logically argued case of what happened. His presentation of who was killed and wounded, where, and when as well as the claims of other authors is particularly incisive.

51. Gabriel García Márquez, *One Hundred Years of Solitude* (New York: Avon, 1971), 285; the strike is covered on pages 280–287.

52. Ibid., 41.

53. Ibid., 23, 32, footnote 6.

54. James D. Henderson, *Las ideas de Laureano Gómez* (Bogotá: Tercer Mundo, 1985), 238–242.

55. White, *La historia de una ignominia*, 120. United Fruit did begin to relocate to the Gulf of Urabá near the Colombian-Panamanian border in the early 1960s. As of 1978, United Fruit had only 32 percent of the banana exports. Standard Fruit had 19 percent, and UNIBAN (Unión de Bananeros), a group of Colombian landowners assisted by the Colombian government, had 49 percent. See Fernando Botero Herrera and Diego Sierra Botero, *El mercado de fuerza de trabajo en la zona bananera de Urabá* (Medellín: CIE, 1981), 48–49.

QUESTIONS FOR REVIEW AND DISCUSSION

1. Should there be international antitrust legislation? Why or why not?

2. What social and economic responsibilities should a U.S. multinational have in a foreign country?

3. What should a U.S. multinational's relationship abroad be with the U.S. government?

4. Should it be overlooked if officers of U.S. companies engage in bribery, intimidation, and corruption—if those practices are somewhat common in a host country? Why or why not?

5. Can monopolistic control of a host country's railroads, land resources, port facilities, and shipping by one foreign-based company ever be justified? Explain.

10

Regulating an Industry: State versus Federal Authority

The regulation of the insurance industry presents an anomaly in the area of governmental regulation. Much of the federal government's authority to regulate business activity has been established by congressional legislation, or by Supreme Court decisions that have interpreted the commerce clause of the Constitution. Few areas of enterprise today are excluded from federal regulation. As early as the case of *Gibbons* v. *Ogden* in 1824 (see Chapter 6), the federal government's authority over commerce has generally been considered to be paramount in relation to the authority of the states. Nevertheless, in areas where the federal government has not acted, supervision or regulatory authority was assumed to be reserved to the states. The American insurance industry was one of those industries that entered the twentieth century with no federal regulations. In this way, the insurance industry was something of an anomaly. By the advent of World War II, the regulation of the insurance industry was still in the hands of the states.

In 1944, the U.S. Supreme Court threatened to change those conditions. The Supreme Court observed that "no modern commercial enterprise directly affects so many persons in all walks of life as does the insurance business. Insurance touches the home, the family, and the occupation or the business of almost every person in the United States." The Supreme Court held that insurance was a business within the definition of the commerce clause of the Constitution and was subject to regulation by Congress under the terms of the Interstate Commerce Act. Congress, however, specifically declined the responsibility for regulating the insurance industry.

The McCarran-Ferguson Act of 1945 specified that "the business of insurance, and every person engaged therein, shall be subject to the laws of the several states which relate to the regulation or taxation of such business." The Supreme Court observed that no phase of economic or business activity "has had a more atypical history than regulation of the business of insurance."

The case study that follows is comprised of five parts: (1) an overview of insurance from its earliest times; (2) an act by the Texas legislature that virtually excluded insurance companies that were based in other states from doing business in Texas by imposing severe controls and constraints (taxes) on such companies; (3) the ruling by the Supreme Court in 1944 that placed the insurance industry under federal authority; (4) the Supreme Court decision in 1946 that interpreted the meaning of the McCarran-Ferguson Act of 1945 and concluded that Congress's unequivocal intention was to leave the insurance industry in the care of the state governments; and (5) the Supreme Court ruling in 1969 that interpreted the Securities and Exchange Commissions' relationship to the insurance industry.

These case study materials, which follow, raise some truly provocative questions that test the presence of government regulation in other areas of commerce. Why has the insurance industry been excepted from federal regulation? Can the states regulate certain areas of commerce better than the federal government? Who are the proponents and benefactors both of governmental regulation and of deregulation? Does the insurance industry seem to favor state regulation or federal regulation, if either? These case study materials provide not only a history of the development of the insurance industry, but also a study of the development of the relationship between the U.S. government and American business.

Henry C. Dethloff

INSURANCE
IS EVERYBODY'S
BUSINESS

Insurance is everybody's business. Insurance requires
the contribution of small sums of money by many individuals to form a pool. The
contributors agree to reimburse members of the pool for certain losses. When
losses occur, as from fire, theft, or accident, sums are withdrawn from the pool
and paid to the policyholder as stated by the agreement or policy adopted by the
contributors. The pool is administered by a business firm called an insurance
company.

It would be difficult to imagine our modern world without insurance, so essential a role does it play today in the conduct of government, business, and
individual affairs. Insurance, along with the creation of the corporation, are
among the primary causes for the growth in prosperity enjoyed by much of the
world in the last two centuries. Incorporating provides limited liability and a
means to raise capital. Insurance provides a means to transfer or spread risk, thus
helping to assure economic survival despite chance, accident, or natural disaster.

Each person who pays an insurance premium takes a "share" in guaranteeing
other members of the group against loss. Insurance seeks to remove or reduce the

Douglas Caddy, *Understanding Texas Insurance*, introduction by Henry C. Dethloff (College Station, Texas: Texas A&M University Press, 1984); in condensed form, *Insurance Is Everybody's
Business*, Series on Public Issues No. 15 (College Station, Texas: Center for Education and Research
in Free Enterprise, 1985).

impact of chance and accidents on economic decisions. Insurance comes in a multitude of forms and packages. It is difficult for the average individual to know what kinds of insurance exist and what insurance is best for him or her. Some insurance is required by the federal government, such as social security, Medicare, and Medicaid. State law often requires some form of insurance, such as automobile liability insurance. Lenders generally require insurance on the life of the person borrowing money or on the loan itself. Most insurance is elective, that is, it is bought by the individual to serve a specific purpose or function. Life insurance, automobile insurance, and health or medical insurance are the most popular and common types of insurance coverage. Yet there are numerous insurance companies and kinds of policies and coverages available in each of these areas. Moreover, each state has different laws and regulations affecting insurance and insurance companies. Despite the fact that insurance is one of the most prevalent facts of everyday life, it is a subject about which most people are very ignorant.

Insurance is a very old business, dating back at least to the time of Hammurabi (2067–2025 B.C.). Until the modern era, insurance was associated almost exclusively with trade and commerce, most often with maritime cargoes. The Phoenicians, the Athenians, and Rome used forms of insurance in their sea commerce. The Dutch and British, who were the major commercial carriers of the world in the seventeenth and eighteenth centuries, became the primary insurers of the modern world. Until the seventeenth century, insurance was "underwritten," that is, agreed to by individuals or associations of individuals, much as is done now by Lloyd's of London.

The great fire of London in 1666 seems to have stimulated the establishment of the first organized stock insurance company. Nicholas Barbon organized the Fire Office, which sold insurance on brick buildings at 2.5 percent of their annual rental value or 5 percent on the annual rental value of wood structures. Although the City of London organized its own insurance program, the courts soon forced its abandonment, and insurance in England remained a private business.

Many new private companies, such as the Friendly Society and, in 1696, the Hand-in-Hand, the first mutual company, were organized in England before 1700. The Hand-in-Hand, which was absorbed by the Commercial Union Assurance Company of London in 1905, became the model for America's first insurance company, the Philadelphia Contributorship for the Insurance of Houses from Loss by Fire, organized by Benjamin Franklin in 1752. In 1763 company directors specified that only the interest on deposits (premiums collected) could be used as operating money, thereby establishing the first insurance company reserve accounts.

No life insurance companies were organized in North America during the colonial or confederation periods, although two British companies organized in

1719 did business in the colonies after 1741. A Presbyterian minister's relief fund was the prototype of a life insurance company, but the relief fund was not a true insurance company in that it depended upon "outside" or charitable contributions. Life insurance did not become popular in the United States until the mid-eighteenth century.

The tontine movement of the seventeenth and eighteenth centuries somewhat discouraged investment in life insurance because of the speculative, gambling nature of the tontine. The tontine was essentially a bet-your-life scheme, whereby survivors divided the pool among themselves after a specified number of years or when a certain number of contributors remained. Also, inadequate and inaccurate mortality tables and vital statistics made premium setting hazardous. But it was more likely changing social values, which accepted the "scientific" notion that life insurance was a form of economic immortality, that triggered its widespread acceptance following the 1850s. The American life insurance industry thereafter began to prosper.

By 1890 life insurance coverage in effect reached an astounding $5 billion. Property and casualty coverage also expanded greatly. This was a result, in part, of the widespread concern for insurance that the great Chicago fire of 1871 generated. Moreover, insurance, both life and casualty, grew apace with urban growth. Insurance was largely an urban phenomenon, and the expansion of coverage was more than proportional to the increase in urban populations. According to R. Carlyle Buley in his history of the American Life Convention, "the details and scope of modern life insurance was largely of American origin,"[1] and, one might add, of relatively recent origin. A number of important occurrences in the late nineteenth and early twentieth centuries affected the development of both life and casualty insurance.

The Actuarial Society of America, organized in 1889, established a professional body dedicated to the preparation and maintenance of accurate data relating to mortality rates and risks. The National Association of Life Underwriters, organized in 1890, was an association of insurance agents, the agent having become the vital marketing device in the insurance industry. By 1890 there were fifty legal reserve life insurance companies organized in the United States, and in 1892 approximately one-half of the world's total life insurance force covered American policyholders. Over the next fifteen years the number of companies and premium income more than doubled.

Although the insurance industry expanded rapidly in the late nineteenth century, phenomenal changes occurred in the first decades of the twentieth century. Population growth, particularly urban growth, contributed to the change. American manufacturing and foreign trade, as well as domestic sales, expanded enormously between 1900 and 1920. U.S. population increased by 40 percent in these two decades. By 1920, for the first time in U.S. history, more Americans lived in the city than in the country. But in addition to these vital statistics, a number of unique factors contributed to the proliferation of life, property, and casualty coverage. The previously mentioned organization of the American Life Convention was a factor. The San Francisco fire and earthquake of 1906 (as had the Chicago fire of 1871 and the Boston fire of 1872) generated enthusiasm for insurance, especially when the industry generally honored the substantive losses incurred. Texans were singularly alerted to the desirability, if not the necessity, of property and casualty insurance by the natural disaster inflicted upon Galveston in the storm of 1900.

Man-made things also stimulated insurance sales. The advent of the automobile and the successful marketing of automobile insurance by such industry leaders as James S. Kemper, who founded Lumbermen's Mutual Casualty Company in 1912, and George Jacob Mecherle, who organized State Farm Mutual in 1922, invigorated the insurance industry. Automobile insurance premiums rose from none in 1900 to $1.25 billion in 1946 to $14.6 billion in 1970. Relatively few Americans are untouched by auto insurance coverage. In a very real sense, it was not just the automobile but the general expansion of commercial activity, population growth, personal wealth, and personal mobility that contributed to the rapidly rising volume of property and casualty insurance. Rapid expansion contributed to problems developing within the industry and to public and private efforts to deal with those problems.

In New York a feud within the management and stockholders of Equitable Insurance Company led to public charges of improper accounting and questionable investment policies. Subsequently the New York insurance commissioner conducted an investigation and charged Equitable with irregular, if not illegal, activities. The governor next called a special session of the legislature that created an investigating committee headed by State Senator William W. Armstrong. For four months in 1905 the committee conducted widely publicized examinations of insurance and business executives. The disclosures were often embarrassing and shocking, even to the industry. The result was the adoption of a report making specific recommendations for insurance reforms, including standardized policy forms, a limit on commissions to agents, a prohibition on prizes and bonuses, legal liability for misrepresenting the terms of an insurance contract, uniform accounting procedures, and a prohibition on investments by insurance companies in common stocks. Most of the Armstrong recommendations were soon enacted into law in New York and other states.

In addition, the organization at Chicago in 1905 of the American Life Convention, comprising largely western and southern life insurance representatives, brought new pressures to bear on legislative reform. The conference favored uniform state laws for the protection of policyholders and opposed federal supervision and controls. The conference and the backwash of the Armstrong investigation influenced legislation in Texas and other states such as Wisconsin. Wisconsin adopted a package of insurance legislation in 1907, which included a requirement that companies selling insurance in the state must deposit securities with the state's secretary of state equal to the value of the policies in force in Wisconsin. Out-of-state insurance companies threatened to withdraw if Wisconsin Governor Robert M. La Follette signed the bills. He signed, and at least fifteen insurance companies discontinued their Wisconsin operations. The state felt obliged to repeal the policy in 1915.

In Texas, under the administration of Governor Thomas M. Campbell, the legislature adopted comprehensive regulations for life, health, accident, home, and fire insurance. And somewhat like the Wisconsin act, the Texas legislature approved the Robertson Insurance Law of 1907, which required life insurance companies to invest 75 percent of life insurance reserves in Texas securities. Also in 1907, Texas separated the duties of the commissioner of insurance from agriculture and joined them with banking responsibilities to create the office of commissioner of insurance and banking (1907–13). A battle erupted in the legislature, but the bill was approved. Twenty-one insurance companies soon discontinued operations in Texas, arguing that the Robertson Law was unfair and unreasonable. Unlike in Wisconsin, Texans refused to repeal the law despite a concerted effort in the legislature in 1915, and the Robertson Law remained effective until 1963. That act had much to do with the growth and development of a nationally significant Texas-based insurance industry, which has been ranked by some as Texas' second biggest business, after oil.

Insurance is the only interstate industry that is regulated primarily by the states instead of the federal government. In most industries government has increasingly exercised influence or control over economic decisions through large-scale public spending, taxation, and regulatory legislation. There are presently about fifty-six major federal regulatory agencies that employ over ninety-thousand persons and operate on budgets in excess of $6 billion. Before 1900 the only two major regulatory agencies were the U.S. Patent Office and the Interstate Commerce Commission. Regulation was greatly extended during the Progressive Era under the leadership of presidents Theodore Roosevelt and Woodrow Wilson. Banking, for example, which had been under direct federal authority in the early 1800s, became essentially state controlled until 1913, when Congress enacted the Federal Reserve Act. World War I, the Great Depression and New Deal programs, and World War II brought greatly extended federal authority over most business activities—if not directly, then indirectly through federal labor, banking, interstate commerce rulings, court decisions, and tax policies.

Federal control over insurance appeared imminent when the Supreme Court, in 1944, held insurance to be a commercial enterprise within the meaning of the Commerce Clause of the Constitution and thereby subject to regulation by the federal government. After strong lobbying efforts by the insurance industry, particularly the National Association of Insurance Commissioners, however, Congress effectively blocked federal assumption of authority in this area by interposing a unique piece of legislation, the McCarran-Ferguson Act of 1945.

The legislative and regulatory history of the insurance industry can be briefly summarized by a series of Supreme Court cases that began in 1868.

In 1868 the U.S. Supreme Court in *Paul* v. *Virginia*, 8 Wall, 168, recognized the right of state governments to regulate the insurance business. This ruling prevailed until 1944, when the Supreme Court reversed itself in *United States* v. *South-Eastern Underwriters Association*, 322 U.S. 533, saying that the business of insurance was interstate commerce and, therefore, was subject to federal regulation. It declared, "No commercial enterprise of any kind which conducts its activities across state lines has been held to be wholly beyond the power of Congress under the Commerce Clause. We cannot make an exception of the business of insurance."

Congress immediately responded to the Court's decision by passing the McCarran-Ferguson Act in 1945, which served to warn the states that bad business practices by the insurance industry had better be cured through state regulation or else federal law would be imposed.

Although insurance regulation continues to be an active area for federal inquiry, it remains under the authority of the state rather than the federal government. This may change as financial intermediaries, that is, banks, insurance companies, and savings and loan institutions, join under the umbrella of corporate conglomerates or begin to duplicate financial services. Insurance companies, for example, as managers of annuity and retirement accounts are increasingly involved in banking and brokerage activities and thus are subject to federal regulation through banking and securities and exchange policies.

Nevertheless, today the sale and terms of an insurance contract are determined by state law. Thus, it is important as a consumer and a citizen of a state to be aware of the general nature of state laws affecting insurance.

Table 10-1. Property-Liability Insurance Companies by State, 1981

State	Home Offices	State	Home Offices
Alabama	21	Missouri	79
Alaska	9	Montana	4
Arizona	16	Nebraska	35
Arkansas	28	Nevada	2
California	134	New Hampshire	30
Colorado	47	New Jersey	40
Connecticut	38	New Mexico	25
Delaware	92	New York	213
District of Columbia	14	North Carolina	55
Florida	44	North Dakota	39
Georgia	31	Ohio	151
Hawaii	11	Oklahoma	56
Idaho	5	Oregon	12
Illinois	286	Pennsylvania	203
Indiana	103	Rhode Island	17
Iowa	48	South Carolina	24
Kansas	34	South Dakota	57
Kentucky	34	Tennessee	48
Louisiana	20	Texas	209
Maine	20	Utah	8
Maryland	30	Vermont	14
Massachusetts	45	Virginia	42
Michigan	49	Washington	23
Minnesota	175	West Virginia	19
Mississippi	6	Wisconsin	201
		Wyoming	3

Source: State insurance departments.

Table 10-2. Number of U.S. Life Insurance Companies by State, Mid-Year 1982

State	Number	State	Number
Alabama	33	Georgia	29
Alaska	1	Hawaii	8
Arizona	534	Idaho	6
Arkansas	25	Illinois	91
California	52	Indiana	57
Colorado	23	Iowa	35
Connecticut	22	Kansas	20
Delaware	55	Kentucky	15
District of Columbia	10	Louisiana	103
Florida	42	Maine	5

continued

Table 10–2. Continued

State	Number	State	Number
Maryland	13	Oregon	7
Massachusetts	17	Pennsylvania	58
Michigan	27	Rhode Island	8
Minnesota	21	South Carolina	26
Mississippi	26	South Dakota	9
Missouri	44	Tennessee	23
Montana	2	Texas	226
Nebraska	30	Utah	14
Nevada	3	Vermont	4
New Hampshire	4	Virginia	12
New Jersey	14	Washington	22
New Mexico	7	West Virginia	2
New York	70	Wisconsin	30
North Carolina	24	Wyoming	2
North Dakota	9	Total U.S.	2,035
Ohio	44		
Oklahoma	71		

Note: Data are based on reports from individual state insurance departments. These companies are considered legal reserve life insurance companies by their respective state insurance departments but may not meet the requirements for this classification as set by other states.

Source: American Council of Life Insurance.

INSURANCE—
REQUIRING
INVESTMENT IN
TEXAS OF PORTION
OF RESERVE FUNDS

H. B. No. 112.   Chapter CLXX

An act to require all incorporated stock or mutual companies doing a life insurance business within the State of Texas, to invest a part of the reserve set apart on account and for the final payment of policies of insurance written on the lives of citizens of Texas, in Texas and other securities and Texas property, or in the bonds of the United States or any State of the United States, and to define Texas securities and the property in which such investments may be made, and to require that a part of the securities in which such reserve is invested be kept on deposit in the vaults of the Treasury of this State, or in National Banks or State Banks or Trust Companies in Texas, designated as depositories for the security of policy holders, and declaring an emergency.

Be it enacted by the Legislature of the State of Texas:
    SECTION 1.   That all stock or mutual companies incorporated under the laws of this State, or any other State of the United States or any foreign country, for the purpose of doing a life insurance business and engaged in doing a life insurance business in the State of Texas, shall, as a condition of their right to do business in

General Laws of Texas (Thirtieth Legislature, 1907), 316–320.

this State, invest and keep invested in Texas securities and in Texas real estate, as hereinafter provided, a sum of money equal to at least seventy-five per cent of the aggregate amount of the legal reserve set apart and apportioned to policies of life insurance written on the lives of citizens of this State; provided, that any such company upon making it to appear to the satisfaction of the Commissioner of Insurance of this State that it cannot safely invest said part of the said reserve or any part thereof in Texas securities or Texas property as provided by this act, may upon being authorized so to do by said Commissioner, invest so much of the same as cannot be so invested in the bonds of the United States or of any State of the United States.

SEC. 2. The phrase "Texas securities" as used in Section 1 of this act, shall be held to include the bonds of the State of Texas; or of any county, city, town or school district in this State; mortgages upon unincumbered real estate situated in this State to an amount not to exceed the amount now permitted by the law of this State, to be loaned thereon by companies incorporated under the laws of this State; the stock of any solvent National bank doing business in this State; the stock of any State bank organized under the laws of this State and doing business in this State; provided, that not more than forty per cent of the stock of any such bank shall be owned by insurance companies; the first mortgage bonds of any solvent dividend-paying corporation incorporated under the laws of this State and doing business in this State, which has never defaulted in the payment of interest thereon; and loans made to policy holders against the reserve value of their policies; said companies may respectively invest the said funds representing the said reserve in the purchase of not more than one building site and in the erection thereon of not more than one office building in any city of this State having a population of more than twenty-five thousand inhabitants, and in case of investment in such real estate, the amount so invested may be treated as a part of the reserve required to be invested in Texas securities and property. Provided, that the Insurance Commissioner of the State shall be empowered to waive the requirements of this act, or any part thereof, upon a sufficient showing by any company affected by the provisions hereof, that it cannot obtain the securities named in Sections 1, 2 and 3 of this act without a sacrifice of the interest of its policy holders, and the Insurance Commissioner shall have the authority to judge of the sufficiency of such showing.

SEC. 3. That all bonds, stocks, mortgages and securities (except policies upon which loans may be made) in which the seventy-five per cent of the insurance reserve belonging or apportioned to policies upon the lives of citizens of Texas, shall be invested as above provided, shall be by the company so investing deposited in the vaults of the Treasury of the State of Texas or with any National bank in this State designated and appointed by the Comptroller of the Currency as a depository for moneys and funds belonging to the United States, or with any State bank or trust company or National bank in this State authorized and appointed by law as a depository for State moneys and funds, and the president of any depository in which any such securities are deposited shall forward to the State Treasurer of this State quarterly, or whenever demanded by him, a statement of the character and amount of the securities so deposited and such securities shall at all times be subject to the payment of any money that may become due on any of such policies of insurance; provided, that no securities when deposited under the provisions of this act, shall be withdrawn without authority, in writing, from the State Treasurer.

SEC. 4. That insurance companies which have loaned, or which may hereafter loan, to Texas policy holders on the sole security of their policies more than twenty-five per cent of the entire reserve, shall only be required to invest in Texas securities the remainder of the said seventy-five per cent of the reserve.

SEC. 5. That the investment and the deposit provided for in this act shall be made of the reserve, on account of current business at least every six months, that is to say, each company shall on or before the thirtieth day of June and the thirty-first day of December of each year invest and deposit the amount of reserve required by this act, on account of the accumulated reserve for the preceding six months. And as to the part of the accumulated reserve upon policies heretofore written upon the lives of citizens of this State and required by this act to be invested and deposited in this State, each company shall have until the first day of January, 1908, in which to invest and deposit twenty-five per cent of the whole amount of such accumulated reserve required by this act to be so invested and deposited, and thereafter each company shall invest and deposit twenty-five per cent of such part of the said accumulated reserve every six months until the whole amount of the reserve required by this act has been so invested and deposited.

SEC. 6. That insurance companies organized and having their domicile in States of this Union wherein at this time, by the law of such home State, such company or companies are required to deposit with officers within the home State securities covering the entire reserve upon the business transacted in that State and all other States, in such manner to secure equally all policy holders of such company, shall have two years after this act takes effect in which to comply with the provisions of Section 3 of this act. Provided, that the fact of such deposit in the home State shall be shown to the Commissioner of Insurance, Statistics and History of this State by a certificate under the hand and seal of the proper officer of the home State of such company or companies.

SEC. 7. That each insurance company doing business in this State and coming within the provisions of this act, shall within thirty days after the thirtieth day of June and thirty-first day of December of each year, file with the Commissioner of Insurance, Statistics and History of this State, a statement duly executed and sworn to by either the president or secretary of the company, showing the entire amount of the reserves on its entire business in force in this State on June 30 and December 31, respectively, and an itemized schedule of its investments in Texas property and Texas securities, which shall also be sworn to.

SEC. 8. That any insurance company coming within the provisions of this act, or the stockholders thereof, may, in addition to the deposit required by this act, at its or their option, deposit with the Treasurer of this State the capital stock or any part thereof, of such company, or securities covering such capital stock, and may, at their option, withdraw or substitute such stock or securities so voluntarily deposited; provided, that the substituted securities shall be approved by the Insurance Commissioner.

SEC. 9. That upon the deposit in the Treasury or any of the above mentioned depositories in this State of any securities or stock provided by this act, the Treasurer of this State or president of such bank shall execute to the company making the deposit a receipt therefor, giving such description of the said securities or stock as will identify the same, and stating that the same are held on deposit for the company depositing the same, and any company making such deposit and holding such receipt shall have the right to advertise such fact, or to print the same upon the policies it may issue.

SEC. 10. That the proper officers and agents of each insurance company making a deposit of securities, as provided by this act, shall be permitted at all reasonable times to examine its securities and to detach coupons therefrom, and to collect all interest thereon under such reasonable rules and regulations as may be prescribed by the Treasurer and the Commissioner of Insurance, Statistics and History of this State.

SEC. 11. It shall be the duty of the Commissioner of Insurance, Statistics and History of the State to cause the terms of this law to be enforced, and the deposit required hereby to be made and kept up at all times, so that the same, together with any investment in real estate, as hereinbefore provided, shall at all times be equal to at least the amount of the reserve, as provided by this act. But the Commissioner of Insurance, Statistics and History may, in his discretion, permit the withdrawal of any of such securities and the substitution of other like securities in their stead, so that the required amount be kept on deposit; and upon the failure of any insurance company to make the investments and deposits required by this act, the Commissioner of Insurance, Statistics and History shall report such failure to the Attorney General, who shall institute suit in the district court of Travis county, Texas, to forfeit the permit of such company to do business in this State.

SEC. 12. The provisions of this act shall not be held to apply to any benevolent association without capital stock, and doing business upon the assessment plan.

SEC. 13. The fact that there is no law in this State requiring the investment of the reserve apportioned or belonging to insurance policies upon the lives of citizens of Texas, in Texas securities, and the protection of such reserve by requiring them to be deposited in the treasury of this State, creates an emergency, and an imperative necessity exists that this act take effect and be in force from and after its passage, and it is so enacted.

Approved April 24, 1907.
Takes effect ninety days after adjournment.

UNITED STATES *v.* SOUTH-EASTERN UNDERWRITERS ASSOCIATION, ET AL.

APPEAL under the Criminal Appeals Act from a judgment sustaining a demurrer to an indictment for violation of the Sherman Antitrust Act.

Briefs were filed (1) on behalf of the States of Alabama, Arizona, Arkansas, Colorado, Connecticut, Delaware, Florida, Georgia, Indiana, Iowa, Kansas, Kentucky, Louisiana, Maine, Maryland, Minnesota, Mississippi, Nebraska, Nevada, New Hampshire, New Jersey, New Mexico, New York, North Dakota, Ohio, Oregon, Pennsylvania, South Dakota, Tennessee, Utah, Vermont, Washington, Wisconsin and West Virginia, and (2) on behalf of the State of Virginia, as *amici curiae*, urging affirmance.

Mr. Justice Black delivered the opinion of the Court.

For seventy-five years this Court has held, whenever the question has been presented, that the Commerce Clause of the Constitution does not deprive the individual states of power to regulate and tax specific activities of foreign insurance companies which sell policies within their territories. Each state has been held to have this power even though negotiation and execution of the companies' policy contracts involved communications of information and movements of persons, moneys, and papers across state lines. Not one of all these cases, however,

322 U.S. 533. Appeal from the District Court of the United States for the Northern District of Georgia. No. 354. Argued January 11, 1944. Decided June 5, 1944.

has involved an Act of Congress which required the Court to decide the issue of whether the Commerce Clause grants to Congress the power to regulate insurance transactions stretching across state lines. Today for the first time in the history of the Court that issue is squarely presented and must be decided. . . .

The record, then, presents two questions and no others: (1) Was the Sherman Act intended to prohibit conduct of fire insurance companies which restrains or monopolizes the interstate fire insurance trade? (2) If so, do fire insurance transactions which stretch across state lines constitute "Commerce among the several States" so as to make them subject to regulation by Congress under the Commerce Clause? Since it is our conclusion that the Sherman Act was intended to apply to the fire insurance business we shall, for convenience of discussion, first consider the latter question.

Ordinarily courts do not construe words used in the Constitution so as to give them a meaning more narrow than one which they had in the common parlance of the times in which the Constitution was written. To hold that the word "commerce" as used in the Commerce Clause does not include a business such as insurance would do just that. Whatever other meanings "commerce" may have included in 1787, the dictionaries, encyclopedias, and other books of the period show that it included trade: business in which persons bought and sold, bargained and contracted. And this meaning has persisted to modern times. Surely, therefore, a heavy burden is on him who asserts that the plenary power which the Commerce Clause grants to Congress to regulate "Commerce among the several States" does not include the power to regulate trading in insurance to the same extent that it includes power to regulate other trades or businesses conducted across state lines.

The modern insurance business holds a commanding position in the trade and commerce of our Nation. Built upon the sale of contracts of indemnity, it has become one of the largest and most important branches of commerce. Its total assets exceed $37,000,000,000, or the approximate equivalent of the value of all farm lands and buildings in the United States. Its annual premium receipts exceed $6,000,000,000, more than the average annual revenue receipts of the United States Government during the last decade. Included in the labor force of insurance are 524,000 experienced workers, almost as many as seek their livings in coal mining or automobile manufacturing. Perhaps no modern commercial enterprise directly affects so many persons in all walks of life as does the insurance business. Insurance touches the home, the family, and the occupation or the business of almost every person in the United States.

This business is not separated into 48 distinct territorial compartments which function in isolation from each other. Interrelationship, interdependence, and integration of activities in all the states in which they operate are practical aspects of the insurance companies' methods of doing business. A large share of the insurance business is concentrated in a comparatively few companies located, for the most part, in the financial centers of the East. Premiums collected from policyholders in every part of the United States flow into these companies for investment. As policies become payable, checks and drafts flow back to the many states where the policyholders reside. The result is a continuous and indivisible stream of intercourse among the states composed of collections of premiums, payments of policy obligations, and the countless documents and communications which are essential to the negotiation and execution of policy contracts. Individual policyholders living in many different states who own policies in a single company have their separate interests blended in one assembled fund of assets upon which all are equally dependent for payment of their policies. The decisions which that company makes at its home office—the risks it insures, the premiums it charges, the investments it makes, the losses it pays—concern not just the people of the state where the home office happens to be located. They concern people living far beyond the boundaries of that state.

That the fire insurance transactions alleged to have been restrained and monopolized by appellees fit the above described pattern of the national insurance trade is shown by the indictment before us. Of the nearly 200 combining companies, chartered in various states and foreign countries, only 18 maintained their home offices in one of the six states in which the S. E. U. A. operated; and 127 had headquarters in either New York, Pennsylvania, or Connecticut. During the period 1931–1941 a total of $488,000,000 in premiums was collected by local agents in the six states, most of which was transmitted to home offices in other states; while during the same period $215,000,000 in losses was paid by checks or drafts sent from the home offices to the companies' local agents for delivery to the policyholders. Local agents solicited prospects, utilized policy forms sent from home offices, and made regular reports to their companies by mail, telephone or telegraph. Special travelling agents supervised local operations. The insurance sold by members of S. E. U. A. covered not only all kinds of fixed local properties, but also such properties as steamboats, tugs, ferries, shipyards, warehouses, terminals, trucks, busses, railroad equipment and rolling stock, and movable goods of all types carried in interstate and foreign commerce by every media of transportation.

Despite all of this, despite the fact that most persons, speaking from common knowledge, would instantly say that of course such a business is engaged in trade and commerce, the District Court felt compelled by decisions of this Court to conclude that the insurance business can never be trade or commerce within the meaning of the Commerce Clause. We must therefore consider these decisions. . . .

In all cases in which the Court has relied upon the proposition that "the business of insurance is not commerce," its attention was focused on the validity of state statutes—the extent to which the Commerce Clause automatically deprived states of the power to regulate the insurance business. Since Congress had at no time attempted to control the insurance business, invalidation of the state statutes would practically have been equivalent to granting insurance companies engaged in interstate activities a blanket license to operate without legal restraint. As early as 1866 the insurance trade, though still in its infancy, was subject to widespread abuses. To meet the imperative need for correction of these abuses the various state legislatures, including that of Virginia, passed regulatory legislation. *Paul* v. *Virginia* upheld one of Virginia's statutes. To uphold insurance laws of other states, including tax laws, *Paul* v. *Virginia*'s generalization and reasoning have been consistently adhered to.

Today, however, we are asked to apply this reasoning, not to uphold another state law, but to strike down an Act of Congress which was intended to regulate certain aspects of the methods by which interstate insurance companies do business; and, in so doing, to narrow the scope of the federal power to regulate the activities of a great business carried on back and forth across state lines. But past decisions of this Court emphasize that legal formulae devised to uphold state power cannot uncritically be accepted as trustworthy guides to determine Congressional power under the Commerce Clause. Furthermore, the reasons given in support of the generalization that "the business of insurance is not commerce" and can never be conducted so as to constitute "Commerce among the States" are inconsistent with many decisions of this Court which have upheld federal statutes regulating interstate commerce under the Commerce Clause.

. . . It is settled that, for Constitutional purposes, certain activities of a business may be intrastate and therefore subject to state control, while other activities of the same business may be interstate and therefore subject to federal regulation. And there is a wide range of business and other activities which, though subject to federal regulation are so intimately related to local welfare that, in the absence of Congressional action, they may be regulated or taxed by the states. In marking out these activities the primary test applied by the Court is not the mechanical one of whether the particular activity affected by the state regulation is part of interstate commerce, but rather whether, in each case, the competing demands of the state and national interests involved can be accommodated. And the fact that particular phases of an interstate business or activity have long been regulated or taxed by states has been recognized as a strong reason why, in the continued absence of conflicting Congressional action, the state regulatory and tax laws should be declared valid. . . .

The precise boundary between national and state power over commerce has never yet been, and doubtless never can be, delineated by a single abstract definition. The most widely accepted general description of that part of commerce which is subject to the federal power is that given in 1824 by Chief Justice Marshall in *Gibbons* v. *Ogden*, 9 Wheat. 1, 189–190: "Commerce, undoubtedly, is traffic, but it is something more: it is intercourse. It describes the commercial intercourse between nations, and parts of nations, in all its branches. . . . " Commerce is interstate, he said, when it "concerns more States than one." *Id.*, 194. No decision of this Court has ever questioned this as too comprehensive a description of the subject matter of the Commerce Clause. To accept a description less comprehensive, the Court has recognized, would deprive the Congress of that full power necessary to enable it to discharge its Constitutional duty to govern commerce among the states.

The power confined to Congress by the Commerce Clause is declared in The Federalist to be for the purpose of securing the "maintenance of harmony and proper intercourse among the States." But its purpose is not confined to empowering Congress with the negative authority to legislate against state regulations of commerce deemed inimical to the national interest. The power granted Congress is a positive power. It is the power to legislate concerning transactions which, reaching across state boundaries, affect the people of more states than one;—to govern affairs which the individual states, with their limited territorial jurisdictions, are not fully capable of governing. This federal power to determine the rules of intercourse across state lines was essential to weld a loose confederacy into a single, indivisible Nation; its continued existence is equally essential to the welfare of that Nation.

Our basic responsibility in interpreting the Commerce Clause is to make certain that the power to govern intercourse among the states remains where the Constitution placed it. That power, as held by this Court from the beginning, is vested in the Congress, available to be exercised for the national welfare as Congress shall deem necessary. No commercial enterprise of any kind which conducts its activities across state lines has been held to be wholly beyond the regulatory power of Congress under the Commerce Clause. We cannot make an exception of the business of insurance. . . .

PRUDENTIAL INSURANCE CO. *v.* BENJAMIN INSURANCE COMMISSIONER

By an original proceeding in the Supreme Court of South Carolina, appellant challenged the validity under the Federal Constitution of a state statute which imposed a tax upon foreign insurance companies. The state court upheld the tax, 207 S. C. 324, 35 S. E. 2d 586, and an appeal was taken to this Court. . . .

Mr. Justice Rutledge delivered the opinion of the Court.

This case and *Robertson* v. *California, post*, p. 440, bring not unexpected sequels to *United States* v. *South-Eastern Underwriters Assn.*, 322 U. S. 533. In cycle reminiscent conversely of views advanced there and in *Paul* v. *Virginia*, 8 Wall. 168, claims are put forward on the basis of the *South-Eastern* decision to sustain immunity from state taxation and, in the *Robertson* case, from state regulation of the business of insurance.

The specific effect asserted in this case is that South Carolina no longer can collect taxes from Prudential, a New Jersey corporation, which for years prior to 1945 the state had levied and the company had paid. The tax is laid on foreign insurance companies and must be paid annually as a condition of receiving a certificate of authority to carry on the business of insurance within the state. The exaction amounts to three per cent of the aggregate of premium received from

328 U.S. 408. Appeal from the Supreme Court of South Carolina. No. 707. Argued March 8, 11, 1946. Decided June 3, 1946.

business done in South Carolina, without reference to its interstate or local character. No similar tax is required of South Carolina corporations.

Prudential insists that the tax discriminates against interstate commerce and in favor of local business, since it is laid only on foreign corporations and is measured by their gross receipts from premiums derived from business done in the state, regardless of its interstate or local character. Accordingly it says the tax cannot stand consistently with many decisions of this Court outlawing state taxes which discriminate against interstate commerce. South Carolina denies that the tax is discriminatory or has been affected by the *South-Eastern* decision. But in any event it maintains that the tax is valid, more particularly in view of the McCarran Act, by which it is claimed Congress has consented to continuance of this form of taxation and thus has removed any possible constitutional objection which otherwise might exist. This Prudential asserts Congress has not done and could not do.

The State Supreme Court has held the continued exaction of the tax not to be in violation of the commerce clause or affected by the ruling made in the *South-Eastern* case, 207 S. C. 324, 35 S. E. 2d 586. That holding presents the principal basis for this appeal.

The versatility with which argument inverts state and national power, each in alternation to ward off the other's incidence, is not simply a product of protective self-interest. It is a recurring manifestation of the continuing necessity in our federal system for accommodating the two great basic powers it comprehends. For this Court's part, from *Gibbons* v. *Ogden*, 9 Wheat. 1, no phase of that process has been more continuous or at times perplexing than reconciling the paramount national authority over commerce, created by Article I, § 8 of the Constitution, with appropriate exercise of the states' reserved powers touching the same or related subject matter.

The continuing adjustment has filled many of the great constitutional gaps of Marshall's time and later. But not all of the filling has been lasting. Great emphases of national policy swinging between nation and states in historic conflicts have been reflected, variously and from time to time, in premise and therefore in conclusion of particular dispositions. In turn, their sum has shifted and reshifted the general balance of authority, inevitably producing some anomaly of logic and of result in the decisions.

No phase has had a more atypical history than regulation of the business of insurance. This fact is important for the problems now presented. They have origin in that history. Their solution cannot escape its influence. Moreover, in law as in other phases of living, reconciliation of anomalous behavior, long continued, with more normal attitudes is not always easy, when the time for that adjustment comes.

Essentially the problems these case tender are of that character. It is not necessary to renew the controversy presented in *South-Eastern*. Whether or not that decision properly has been characterized as "precedent-smashing," there was a reorientation of attitudes toward federal power in its relation to the business of insurance conducted across state lines. Necessarily this worked in two directions. As the opinion was at pains to note, 322 U. S. 533, 545 ff., no decision previously had held invalid an Act of Congress on the ground that such business was beyond reach of its power, because previously no attempted exercise of that authority had been brought here in litigation. But from *Paul v. Virginia* to *New York Life Ins. Co. v. Deer Lodge County*, 231 U.S. 495, negative implication from the commerce clause was held not to place any limitation upon state power over the business, however conducted with reference to state lines. And correlatively this was taken widely, although not universally, to nullify federal authority until the question was squarely presented and answered otherwise in the *South-Eastern* case.

Whether *Paul v. Virginia* represented in its day an accommodation with or a departure from the preexisting evolution of commerce clause law and whether its ruling, together with later ones adhering to it, remained consonant with the subsequent general development of that law, may still be debated. But all may concede that the *Paul* case created for the business of insurance a special, if not a wholly unique, way of thinking and acting in the regulation of business done across state lines. See Ribble, State and National Power over Commerce (1937) 89, 186–187. The aegis of federal commerce power continued to spread over and enfold other business so conducted, in both general and specific legislative exertions. Usually this was with judicial approval; and, despite notable instances of initial hostility, the history of judicial limitation of congressional power over commerce, when exercised affirmatively, has been more largely one of retreat than of ultimate victory. The plain words of the grant have made courts cautious, except possibly in some of the instances noted, about nullifying positive exertions of Congress' power over this broad and hard to define field. At the same time, physical and economic change in the way commerce is carried on has called forth a constantly increasing volume of legislation exercising that power.

Concurrently with this general expansion, however, from *Paul* to *South-Eastern* the states took over exclusively the function of regulating the insurance business in its specific legislative manifestations. Congress legislated only in terms applicable to commerce generally, without particularized reference to insurance. At the same time, on the rationalization that insurance was not commerce, yet was business affected with a vast public interest, the states developed comprehensive regulatory and taxing systems. And litigation of their validity came to be freed of commerce clause objections, at any rate from *Deer Lodge* on to *South-Eastern*.

Due process in its jurisdictional aspects remained to confine the reach of state power in relation to business affecting other states. But the negative implications of the commerce clause became irrelevant, as such, for the valid exercise of state regulatory and taxing authority.

Meanwhile the business of insurance experienced a nation-wide expansion graphically depicted not only in the facts of the situation presented in the *South-Eastern* case but also in the operations of Prudential as described by its advocates in this cause. These divergent facts, legal and economic, necessarily were reflected in state legislation. States grappling with nation-wide, but nationally unregulated, business inevitably exerted their powers to limits and in ways not sought generally to be applied to other business held to be within the reach of the commerce clause's implied prohibition. Obvious and widespread examples are furnished in broad and detailed licensing provisions, for the doing of business within the states, and in connected or distinct taxing measures drawn in apparent reliance upon freedom from commerce clause limitations.

Now we are told many of these statutes no longer can stand. The process of read-justment began affirmatively with *South-Eastern*. Since the commerce clause is a two-edged instrument, the indicated next step, indeed the constitutionally required one, as the argument runs, is to apply its negative cutting edge. Conceptions so de-veloped with reference to other commerce must now be extended to the commerce of insurance in completion of the readjustment. This, it is confidently asserted, will require striking down much of the state legislation enacted and effec-tive prior to the *South-Eastern* decision. Particularly will this be true of all discriminatory state taxes, of which it is said South Carolina's is one. Moreover, those results must follow regardless of the McCarran Act's provisions. For by that Act, in Prudential's assessment, Congress neither intended to, nor could, validate such taxes.

It is not surprising that the attack is thus broad. When a decision is conceived as precedent-smashing, rightly or wrongly, the conception's invitation may be to greater backtracking than is justified, in spite of warning to proceed with care. 322 U. S. 533, 547 ff.

Prudential's misconception relates not to the necessity for applying, but to the nature and scope of the negative function of the commerce clause. It is not the simple, clean-cutting tool supposed. Nor is its swath always correlative with that cut by the affirmative edge, as seems to be assumed. For cleanly as the commerce clause has worked affirmatively on the whole, its implied negative operation on state power has been uneven, at times highly variable. More often than not, in matters more governable by logic and less by experience, the business of negative implication is slippery. Into what is thus left open for inference to fill, divergent ideas of meaning may be read much more readily than into what has been made explicit by affirmation. That possibility is broadened immeasurably when not logic alone, but large choices of policy, affected in this instance by evolving experience of federalism, control in giving content to the implied negation. In all our constitutional history this has become no more apparent than in commerce clause dispositions.

That the clause imposes some restraint upon state power has never been doubted. For otherwise the grant of power to Congress would be wholly ineffective. But the limitation not only is implied. It is open to different implications of meaning. And this accounts largely for variations in this field continuing almost from the beginning until now. They started with Marshall and Taney, went forward from Waite to Fuller, and have been projected in later differences perhaps less broad, but hardly less controversial. Consequently in its prohibitive, as in its affirmative or enabling, effects the history of the commerce clause has been one of very considerable judicial oscillation.

Moreover, the parallel encompasses the latest turn in the long-run trend. For, concurrently with the broadening of the scope for permissible application of federal authority, the tendency also has run toward sustaining state regulatory and taxing measures formerly regarded as inconsonant with Congress' unexercised power over commerce, and to doing so by a new, or renewed, emphasis on facts and practical considerations rather than dogmatic logistic. These facts are of great importance for disposing of such controversies. For in effect they have transferred the general problem of adjustment to a level more tolerant of both state and federal legislative action. . . .

In considering the issues raised by the McCarran Act and the question of its applicability, ground may be cleared by putting aside some matters strenuously argued in the State Supreme Court and here. First, it follows from what has been said that we are not required to determine whether South Carolina's tax would be valid in the dormancy of Congress' power. For Congress has expressly stated its intent and policy in the Act. And, for reasons to be stated, we think that the declaration's effect is clearly to sustain the exaction and that this can be done without violating any constitutional provision.

By the same token, we need not consider whether the tax, if operative in Congress' unilluminated silence, would be discriminatory in the sense of an exaction forbidden by the commerce clause, as Prudential categorically asserts, or not so, as South Carolina maintains with equal certitude. Much attention has been given both here and in the state court to these questions. But in the view we take of the case the controlling issues undercut them. Nor do we determine, as Prudential's argument seems to subsume, whether all of its business done in South Carolina and affected by the tax should be regarded as constituting interstate commerce so as to fall within the "in commerce" classification or, on the other hand, some of it may properly be considered as being only local or intrastate business. These questions we put to one side. And for present purposes we assume that the tax would be discriminatory in the sense of Prudential's contention and that all of its business done in South Carolina and affected by the tax is done "in" or as a part of interstate commerce.

It is not necessary to spend much time with interpreting the McCarran Act. Pertinently it is as follows:

> . . . the Congress hereby declares that the continued regulation and taxation by the several States of the business of insurance is in the public interest, and that silence on the part of the Congress shall not be construed to impose any barrier to the regulation or taxation of such business by the several States.
>
> SEC. 2. (a) The business of insurance, and every person engaged therein, shall be subject to the laws of the several States which relate to the regulation or taxation of such business.
>
> (b) No Act of Congress shall be construed to invalidate, impair, or supersede any law enacted by any State for the purpose of regulating the business of insurance, or which imposes a fee or tax upon such business, unless such Act specifically relates to the business of insurance. . . . 59 Stat. 33, 34; 15 U.S.C. §§ 1011–1015.

Obviously Congress' purpose was broadly to give support to the existing and future state systems for regulating and taxing the business of insurance. This was done in two ways. One was by removing obstructions which might be thought to flow from its own power, whether dormant or exercised, except as otherwise expressly provided in the Act itself or in future legislation. The other was by declaring expressly and affirmatively that continued state regulation and taxation of this business is in the public interest and that the business and all who engage in it "shall be subject to" the laws of the several states in these respects.

Moreover, in taking this action Congress must have had full knowledge of the nation-wide existence of state systems of regulation and taxation; of the fact that they differ greatly in the scope and character of the regulations imposed and of the taxes exacted; and of the further fact that many, if not all, include features which, to some extent, have not been applied generally to other interstate business. Congress could not have been unacquainted with these facts and its purpose was evidently to throw the whole weight of its power behind the state systems, notwithstanding these variations.

It would serve no useful purpose now to inquire whether or how far this effort was necessary, in view of the explicit reservations made in the majority opinion in the *South-Eastern* case. Nor is it necessary to conclude that Congress, by enacting the McCarran Act, sought to validate every existing state regulation or tax. For in all that mass of legislation must have lain some provisions which may have been subject to serious question on the score of other constitutional limitations in addition to commerce clause objections arising in the dormancy of Congress' power. And we agree with Prudential that there can be no inference that Congress intended to circumvent constitutional limitations upon its own power.

But, though Congress had no purpose to validate unconstitutional provisions of state laws, except insofar as the Constitution itself gives Congress the power to do this by removing obstacles to state action arising from its own action or by consenting to such laws, H. Rep. No. 143, 79th Cong., 1st Sess., p. 3, it clearly put the full weight of its power behind existing and future state legislation to sustain it from any attack under the commerce clause to whatever extent this may be done with the force of that power behind it, subject only to the exceptions expressly provided for.

Two conclusions, corollary in character and important for this case, must be drawn from Congress' action and the circumstances in which it was taken. One is that Congress intended to declare, and in effect declared, that uniformity of regulation, and of state taxation, are not required in reference to the business of insurance by the national public interest, except in the specific respects otherwise expressly provided for. This necessarily was a determination by Congress that state taxes, which in its silence might be held invalid as discriminatory, do not place on interstate insurance business a burden which it is unable generally to bear or should not bear in the competition with local business. Such taxes were not uncommon among the states, and the statute clearly included South Carolina's tax now in issue.

That judgment was one of policy and reflected long and clear experience. For, notwithstanding the long incidence of the tax and its payment by Prudential without question prior to the *South-Eastern* decision, the record of Prudential's continuous success in South Carolina over decades refutes any idea that payment of the tax handicapped it in any way tending to exclude it from competition with local business or with domestic insurance companies. Indeed Prudential makes no contrary contention on any factual basis, nor could it well do so. For the *South-Eastern* decision did not, and could not, wipe out all this experience or its weight for bearing, as a matter of the practical consequences resulting from operation of the tax, upon that question. *Robertson* v. *California, post,* p. 440.

Consequently Prudential's case for discrimination must rest upon the idea either that the commerce clause forbids the state to exact more from it in taxes than from purely local business; or that the tax is somehow technically of an inherently discriminatory character or possibly of a type which would exclude or seriously handicap new entrants seeking to establish themselves in South Carolina. As to each of these grounds, moreover, the argument subsumes that Congress' contrary judgment, as a matter of policy relating to the regulation of interstate commerce, cannot be effective, either "of its own force" alone or as operative in conjunction with and to sustain the state's policy.

In view of all these considerations, we would be going very far to rule that South Carolina no longer may collect her tax. To do so would flout the expressly declared policies of both Congress and the state. Moreover it would establish a ruling never heretofore made and in doing this would depart from the whole trend of decision in a great variety of situations most analogous to the one now presented. For, as we have already emphasized, the authorities most closely in point upon the problem are not, as appellant insists, those relating to discriminatory state taxes laid in the dormancy of Congress' power. They are rather the decisions which, in every instance thus far not later overturned, have sustained coordinated action taken by Congress and the states in the regulation of commerce.

The power of Congress over commerce exercised entirely without reference to coordinated action of the states is not restricted, except as the Constitution expressly provides, by any limitation which forbids it to discriminate against interstate commerce and in favor of local trade. Its plenary scope enables Congress not only to promote but also to prohibit interstate commerce, as it has done frequently and for a great variety of reasons. That power does not run down a one-way street or one of narrowly fixed dimensions. Congress may keep the way open, confine it broadly or closely, or close it entirely, subject only to the restrictions placed upon its authority by other constitutional provisions and the requirement that it shall not invade the domains of action reserved exclusively for the states.

This broad authority Congress may exercise alone, subject to those limitations, or in conjunction with coordinated action by the states, in which case limitations imposed for the preservation of their powers become inoperative and only those designed to forbid action altogether by any power or combination of powers in our governmental system remain effective. Here both Congress and South Carolina have acted, and in complete coordination, to sustain the tax. It is therefore reinforced by the exercise of all the power of government residing in our scheme. Clear and gross must be the evil which would nullify such a exertion, one which could arise only by exceeding beyond cavil some explicit and compelling limitation imposed by a constitutional provision or provisions designed and intended to outlaw the action taken entirely from our constitutional framework.

In this light the argument that the degree of discrimination which South Carolina's tax has involved, if any, puts it beyond the power of government to continue must fall of its own weight. No conceivable violation of the commerce clause, in letter or spirit, is presented. Nor is contravention of any other limitation. . . .

SECURITIES AND EXCHANGE COMMISSION *v.* NATIONAL SECURITIES, INC., ET AL.

Mr. Justice Marshall delivered the opinion of the Court. This case raises some complex questions about the Securities and Exchange Commission's power to regulate the activities of insurance companies and of persons engaged in the insurance business. The Commission originally brought suit in the United States District Court for the District of Arizona, pursuant to § 21(e) of the Securities Exchange Act of 1934, 48 Stat. 900, as amended, 15 U. S. C. § 78u (e). It alleged violations of § 10 (b) of the Act, 48 Stat. 891, 15 U. S. C. §78j (b), and of the Commission's Rule 10b–5, 17 CFR §240.10b–5 (1968). According to the amended complaint, National Securities and various persons associated with it had contrived a fraudulent scheme centering on a contemplated merger between National Life & Casualty Insurance Co. (National Life), a firm controlled by National Securities, and Producers Life Insurance Co. (Producers). The details of the alleged scheme are not important here. The Commission contended that National Securities purchased a controlling interest in Producers, partly from Producers' directors and partly in the form of treasury stock held by Producers. After taking control of Producers' board, respondents sought to obtain shareholder approval of the merger by sending communications to Producers' 14,000 stockholders. These communications, according to the

393 U.S. 453. Certiorari to the United States Court of Appeals for the Ninth Circuit. No. 41. Argued November 18–19, 1968. Decided January 27, 1969.

Commission, contained misrepresentations of material facts and omitted to state material facts necessary to make the statements which were made not misleading. Among other things, respondents allegedly failed to disclose their plan for the surviving company to assume certain obligations which National Securities had undertaken as part of the consideration for its purchases of Producers' stock. In plain language, Producers' shareholders were not told that they were going to pay part of the cost of National Securities' acquisition of control in their company.

The Commission was denied temporary relief, and shortly thereafter Producers' shareholders and the Arizona Director of Insurance approved the merger. The two companies were formally consolidated into National Producers Life Insurance Co. on July 9, 1965. Thereafter, the Commission amended its complaint to seek additional relief; the previously sought injunction forbidding further violations of Rule 10b–5 was to be supplemented by court orders unwinding the merger and returning the situation to the *status quo ante*, requiring respondents to make an accounting of their unlawful gains, and readjusting the equities of the various respondents in whatever companies survived the decree. The Commission also requested whatever further relief the court might deem just, equitable, and necessary. Respondents moved for judgment on the pleadings, and the trial court dismissed the complaint for failure to state a claim upon which relief could be granted. The court ruled that the relief requested was either barred by §2 (b) of the McCarran-Ferguson Act, 59 Stat. 34 (1945), as amended, 15 U. S. C. § 1012 (b), or was beyond the scope of §21 (e) of the Securities Exchange Act. 252 F. Supp. 623 (1966). The Ninth Circuit affirmed, relying on the McCarran-Ferguson Act. 387 F. 2d 25 (1967). Upon application by the Commission, we granted certiorari because of the importance of the questions raised to the administration of the securities laws. 390 U. S. 1023 (1968).

Insofar as it is relevant to this case, §2 (b) of the McCarran-Ferguson Act provides that "[n]o Act of Congress shall be construed to invalidate, impair, or supersede any law enacted by any State for the purpose of regulating the business of insurance . . . unless such Act specifically relates to the business of insurance. . . . " Respondents contend that this Act bars the present suit since the Arizona Director of Insurance found that the merger was not "[i]nequitable to the stockholders of any domestic insurer" and not otherwise "contrary to law," as he was required to do under the state insurance laws. Ariz. Rev. Stat. Ann. §20–731 (Supp. 1969). If the Securities Exchange Act were applied, respondents argue, these laws would be "superseded." The SEC sees no conflict between state and federal law; it contends that the applicable Arizona statutes did not give the State Insurance Director the power to determine whether respondents had made full disclosure in connection with the solicitation of proxies. Although respondents disagree, we do not find it necessary to inquire into this state-law dispute. The first question posed by this case is whether the relevant Arizona statute is a "law enacted . . . for the purpose of regulating the business of insurance" within the meaning of the McCarran-Ferguson Act. Even accepting respondents' view of Arizona law, we do not believe that a state statute aimed at protecting the interests of those who own stock in insurance companies comes within the sweep of the McCarran-Ferguson Act. Such a statute is not a state attempt to regulate "the business of insurance," as that phrase was used in the Act.

The McCarran-Ferguson Act was passed in reaction to this Court's decision in *United States* v. *South-Eastern Underwriters Assn.*, 322 U. S. 533 (1944). Prior to that decision, it had been assumed, in the language of the leading case, that "[i]ssuing a policy of insurance is not a transaction of commerce." *Paul* v. *Virginia*, 8 Wall. 168, 183 (1869). Consequently, regulation of insurance transactions was thought to rest exclusively with the States. In *South-Eastern Underwriters*, this Court held that insurance transactions were subject to federal regulation under the Commerce Clause, and that the antitrust laws, in particular, were applicable to them. Congress reacted quickly. Even before the opinion was announced, the House had passed a bill exempting the insurance industry from the antitrust laws. 90 Cong. Rec. 6565 (1944). Objection in the Senate killed the bill, 90 Cong. Rec. 8054 (1944), but Congress clearly remained concerned about the inroads the Court's decision might make on the tradition of state regulation of insurance. The McCarran-Ferguson Act was the product of this concern. Its purpose was stated quite clearly in its first section; Congress declared that "the continued regulation and taxation by the several States of the business of insurance is in the public interest." 59 Stat. 33 (1945), 15 U. S. C. §1011. As this Court said shortly afterward, "[o]bviously Congress' purpose was broadly to give support to the existing and future state systems for regulating and taxing the business of insurance." *Prudential Insurance Co.* v. *Benjamin*, 328 U. S. 408, 429 (1946).

The question here is whether state laws aimed at protecting the interests of those who own securities in insurance companies are the type of laws referred to in the 1945 enactment. The legislative history of the McCarran-Ferguson Act offers no real assistance. Congress was mainly concerned with the relationship between insurance ratemaking and the antitrust laws, and with the power of the States to tax insurance companies. See, *e.g.*, 91 Cong. Rec. 1087–1088 (remarks of Congressmen Hancock and Celler). The debates centered on these issues, and the Committee reports shed little light on the meaning of the words "business of insurance." See S. Rep. No. 20, 79th Cong., 1st Sess. (1945); H. R. Rep. No. 143, 79th Cong., 1st Sess. (1945). In context, however, it is relatively clear what problems

Congress was dealing with. Under the regime of *Paul* v. *Virginia, supra,* States had a free hand in regulating the dealings between insurers and their policyholders. Their negotiations, and the contract which resulted, were not considered commerce and were, therefore, left to state regulation. The *South-Eastern Underwriters* decision threatened the continued supremacy of the States in this area. The McCarran-Ferguson Act was an attempt to turn back the clock, to assure that the activities of insurance companies in dealing with their policyholders would remain subject to state regulation. As the House Report makes clear, "[i]t [was] not the intention of the Congress in the enactment of this legislation to clothe the States with any power to regulate or tax the business of insurance beyond that which they had been held to possess prior to the decision of the United States Supreme Court in the *Southeastern Underwriters Association* case." H. R. Rep. No. 143, 79th Cong., 1st Sess., 3 (1945).

Given this history, the language of the statute takes on a different coloration. The statute did not purport to make the States supreme in regulating all the activities of insurance companies; its language refers not to the persons or companies who are subject to state regulation, but to laws "regulating the *business* of insurance." Insurance companies may do many things which are subject to paramount federal regulation; only when they are engaged in the "business of insurance" does the statute apply. Certainly the fixing of rates is part of this business; that is what *South-Eastern Underwriters* was all about. The selling and advertising of policies, *FTC* v. *National Casualty Co.,* 357 U.S. 560 (1958), and the licensing of companies and their agents, cf. *Robertson* v. *California,* 328 U.S. 440 (1946), are also within the scope of the statute. Congress was concerned with the type of state regulation that centers around the contract of insurance, the transaction which *Paul* v. *Virginia* held was not "commerce." The relationship between insurer and insured, the type of policy which could be issued, its reliability, interpretation, and enforcement—these were the core of the "business of insurance." Undoubtedly, other activities of insurance companies relate so closely to their status as reliable insurers that they too must be placed in the same class. But whatever the exact scope of the statutory term, it is clear where the focus was—it was on the relationship between the insurance company and the policyholder. Statutes aimed at protecting or regulating this relationship, directly or indirectly, are laws regulating the "business of insurance."

In this case, Arizona is concerning itself with a markedly different set of problems. It is attempting to regulate not the "insurance" relationship, but the relationship between a stockholder and the company in which he owns stock. This is not insurance regulation, but securities regulation. It is true that the state statute applies only to insurance companies. But mere matters of form need not detain us. The crucial point is that here the State has focused its attention on stockholder protection; it is not attempting to secure the interests of those purchasing insurance policies. Such regulation is not within the scope of the McCarran-Ferguson Act.

Notes

1. Carlyle Buley, *The American Life Convention, 1906–1952: A Study in the History of Life Insurance* (New York: Appleton-Century-Crofts, 1953), p. xii.

QUESTIONS FOR REVIEW AND DISCUSSION

1. What is the purpose of governmental regulation of business?
2. Why has the insurance industry been excepted from the general rule of federal regulation?
3. Compare and contrast the development of both state controls and federal controls over both the railroads and the insurance industry. Include in the comparison the conflicts between state governments and the federal government over regulation. What are the similarities and differences in the kinds of business enterprise and in the physical or corporate structures of those businesses that are under governmental regulation?
4. Can the states regulate certain areas of commerce better than the federal government?
5. What have been the arguments for and against deregulation of the airlines?
6. Why would some businesses prefer state regulation, while others would prefer federal regulation? Why would some business prefer state regulation at one time and federal regulation at another time? Can you offer examples from the case study materials of times and circumstances when insurance companies have shown a preference for either federal or state regulation?
7. What were both the advantages and the disadvantages of a law such as the Texas insurance law of 1907 that excluded out-of-state life insurance companies from operating freely in Texas?

11

Adjusting to Technological Innovation

Innovation has been defined as applied invention. The innovator is the one who first makes an application of an invention which, until the application takes place, has little or no economic significance. Innovation also involves a willingness to take risks by introducing a new, untried technology or service. In some cases the risks may be quite high. How rapidly the innovation spreads, its rate of diffusion, depends upon the decision making of entrepreneurs who are, themselves, uncertain of its ultimate impact and effectiveness.

The risks of innovating may be reduced, however, by the friendly support of government. Such indeed was the situation when radio broadcasting first burst upon the national scene in the early 1920s. The case study that follows deals with the interaction of private broadcasters and public officials. Each group had its own motives for fostering the innovation called radio broadcasting, and together they created a major new industry in the United States.

A little background on the development of radio in general is probably in order to put the case in better perspective. Wireless electronic communication was the product of the cross-fertilization of the work of a score or more of inventors in Europe and in the United States. Among those Americans who can claim a share of the pioneering honors in the prehistory of broadcasting are Nathan B. Stubblefield, who may have transmitted the human voice as early as 1892 in a Murray, Kentucky, demonstration; Reginald A. Fessenden, who broadcast an impromptu program from his laboratory at Brant Rock, Massachusetts, in 1906; and Lee DeForest, who broadcast from the Eiffel Tower in 1908 and put Enrico Caruso and the Metropolitan Opera on the air in 1910.

Regularly scheduled broadcasting made its debut in the years following World War I. Historians of the broadcasting medium have never ceased disputing about which station, among a half-dozen contenders, can rightly call itself the nation's oldest; but most associate the birth of broadcasting with Westinghouse Electric's construction of station KDKA in Pittsburgh, Pennsylvania, in 1920. On the evening of November 2, 1920, from a shack on the roof of a factory building at the Westinghouse plant, KDKA first went on the air, broadcasting to a local audience of probably no more than a few hundred listeners the results of that day's presidential election between Warren G. Harding and James M. Cox. In the months that followed, broadcasting became a public passion in the United States. By the end of 1922, there were already almost 600 licensed stations in operation and an estimated 400,000 receiving sets in use.

The regulation of radio communication predates the broadcasting era that began in 1920. Regulation of radio communication has always been regarded as a federal matter, with state and local governments playing little role. The Radio Act of 1912 was the first general law that gave the federal government control of radio. It vested the power to license both stations and operators in the Department of Commerce and Labor (the Department of Commerce was formed in 1913). Of course, prior to 1920 the function of radio communication was confined to point-to-point communication only, that is, the sending of specific messages to individual recipients. The concept of broadcasting—communication intended for reception by the public at large—as a viable business opportunity did not become apparent until after KDKA paved the way. With the emergence of broadcasting, however, the need for a different form of federal regulation to deal with the new radio technology became apparent. It is with that need and the responses to it that this case study is concerned.

Philip T. Rosen

GOVERNMENT, BUSINESS, AND TECHNOLOGY IN THE 1920s: THE EMERGENCE OF AMERICAN BROADCASTING

Technological innovations, or innovative applications of existing technology, are likely to be perceived differently by different segments of society. Ordinary citizens may view such changes in terms of the prospective benefits to society at large or to themselves as consumers. Businesspeople generally view them in terms of the prospective effects upon their firms' profit-and-loss statements. Some would argue that governmental bureaucrats, by and large, regard neither the welfare of society nor the viability of business as their first concern because to them the prime reality is power. If true, then their perception of technological innovation, like their view of most other changes, would be shaped by the innovation's probable effects upon existing power relations and the opportunities it creates for enlarging their own share of power. This may be termed "the politics of innovation." The development of radio broadcasting affords us an excellent opportunity to test that thesis.

When radio station KDKA in Pittsburgh, Pennsylvania, broadcast the returns of the 1920 presidential election, a new application of a technology that had been in use for some time was introduced. Previously, radio had been employed only as a means of direct communication between sender and receiver, such as between ships at sea or between ships and shore installations. Certain power relations in

Washington, D.C., had been established on the basis of utilizing radio technology for direct communication, with the navy having gained virtual monopolistic control. Broadcasting—that is, transmitting signals to a random, anonymous, and potentially unlimited audience—undermined the navy's position and set off a bitter interdepartmental struggle among the navy, the Post Office, and the Department of Commerce for control of radio broadcasting. The outcome of that struggle defined the role of the federal government in regulating wireless communication, and it decisively affected both the survival of radio broadcasting and the course of its development.[1]

When Warren G. Harding assumed the presidency in 1921, the proponents and critics of the changing role of radio based their positions on their previous use of radio communication and on the needs and desires of their particular governmental departments. Prior to 1920, the history of radio had been largely shaped by naval policy. The navy disapproved of the growth of radio broadcasting and actively sought to curtail its development. The navy had always discouraged any competing radio service that might interfere with ship-to-ship and ship-to-shore traffic, and broadcasting was no exception. Naval officials opposed the erection of broadcasting stations and pressured the Department of Commerce, which had the legal authority to license stations and operators, to close down broadcasting facilities that interfered with maritime radio users. In short, the navy regarded radio as too valuable a natural resource to be wasted upon what H. L. Mencken later called "a long series of imbecile speeches by fifth-rate politicians and agitators, and an equally long series of stupid musical programmes done by fifth-raters."[2]

The Post Office and the Department of Commerce opposed the navy's plans on different grounds but for the same reason; namely, they each desired control for themselves. Under the direction of Will H. Hays, a new type of managerial politician, the Post Office advanced the general proposition that all means of electronic communication should be controlled by the federal government. Hays further contended that because of his department's interests in both wire service and wireless service the Post Office should assume jurisdiction over radio broadcasting. Hays was always a shrewd, if not overly scrupulous, advocate for his department's interests. Thus, he backed radio broadcasting as a means to attack naval control of communications, and he supported his subordinates who launched expansionist ventures. Moreover, he applauded the 1921 report by the Bureau of Efficiency that endorsed the Post Office's proposals for establishing a Bureau of Communications through which the postmaster general would supervise radio. Citing both the need to consolidate facilities for increased efficiency and the European example of delegating the regulation of radio to one agency (usually the postal service), the report considerably strengthened Hay's contention. The combination of Hay's extraordinary powers of reconciliation and his cordial relationship with President Harding made the Post Office chief and his agency formidable contestants in any intragovernmental struggle.[3]

The other serious challenger to the navy's hegemony over radio was the Department of Commerce. Under the direction of Herbert C. Hoover, a technological progressive and bureaucratic imperialist, the Department of Commerce was attempting to integrate the functions of numerous bureaus and agencies. Whether one sees Hoover as a forgotten Progressive, a Quaker humanitarian, or an economic nationalist, the underlying goal of his policies was to extend the power of the secretary of commerce. What had been previously said of Lloyd George—he did not seem to care which way he traveled providing he was in the driver's seat—was, in large measure, true of Hoover as well, with one important exception. Hoover not only wanted to be in the driver's seat, he demanded to plot the course.[4]

In the midst of a postwar depression, Hoover assumed control of the department in 1921. Ready with a program more appropriate for a president than a secretary of commerce, he combatted the economic slump by waging a "new war on waste." An important aspect of his campaign centered upon developing the new industries that had evolved as a result of the war. Radio broadcasting had an important place in his program, and Hoover wanted to control it. In the spring of 1921, he planned two decisive actions to insure the survival of broadcasting and to firmly establish his department's role in regulating radio broadcasting. First, he carefully marshalled a variety of interest groups, including broadcasters, commercial companies, amateurs, allies in government, engineers, and scientists, to support control of broadcasting under the Department of Commerce. Next, he chose to remain largely in the background while the rivalry between the navy and the Post Office for control of radio broadcasting threatened to erupt into a full-fledged conflict. In following this approach, Hoover maneuvered behind the scenes to create a constituency that would support the Department of Commerce's policies.[5]

The quarrel between the navy and the Post Office was intensified by the interests that various other governmental departments held in broadcasting. The quarrel revolved around the construction of additional Post Office radio stations and the decision to designate one department to perform broadcasting services for all governmental agencies that were interested in reaching the public. The navy's basic response referred to the 1904 Interdepartmental Board Report, which it claimed was "more sound and applicable today than when . . . it was written." The 1904 report had opted for naval domination of communications by recommending that the navy establish and operate a coastal radio system. The report had further recommended that commercial stations be restricted and that other governmental departments obtain the radio services they might require from the navy. President Theodore Roosevelt's approval of the 1904 report had given the navy complete control of radio communication in the United States. In 1921 Commander Stanford C. Hooper stated that any time the navy's views conflicted with other departments that were "trying to get the radio under their wings" the 1904 report should be used to establish the navy's prior claims. In effect, the navy argued that if additional radio functions were to be undertaken, the navy system of 183 shore stations and 500 ship installations could adequately handle the task.[6]

The Post Office used another technological innovation, the airplane, as a lever for dislodging the navy from its position of control. The navy's radio facilities, the Post Office declared, could not provide operations adequate to meet the needs of the Air Mail Service. In fact, the Post Office insisted, the navy's operations were so inferior that they endangered pilots' lives and delayed important messages. On that pretext, James C. Edgerton, supervisor of the Air Mail Service, moved aggressively to establish Post Office supremacy. In 1921 Edgerton supervised the opening of a nationwide postal radio system, extending from the District of Columbia to the Pacific Coast and operating as an auxiliary to the Air Mail Service. This system not only aided ground-to-air operations but also broadcast market reports and weather information to listeners in cooperation with the Department of Agriculture. Edgerton envisioned a postal radio network disseminating information and entertainment to the public. He believed that "once public demand is created for such a service, amplification of such a service would be automatically secured." These actions by the Post Office struck at the very heart of the 1904 report.[7]

The navy attracted its own supporters and allies in the contest. Groups on the West Coast, where communication facilities were limited, depended upon the navy for transmission of their press releases and commercial messages. Several shipping concerns, particularly those that found wireless companies unreliable and interference among radio users bothersome, actively supported the navy; and many scientists and engineers saw the navy as the key to developing the art of radio. The navy also had a strong potential ally in the Radio Corporation of America (RCA). After the role played by the Naval Communications Service in creating that company in 1919, a spirit of cooperation prevailed between RCA and the navy in the first year of operation. Not only was Rear Admiral William H. G. Bullard, director of naval communications, appointed to attend company meetings, but RCA also frequently consulted the navy before implementing company policies.[8]

In 1920 and 1921, however, two developments occurred that jeopardized this cozy relationship. First, there were problems with radio apparatus that RCA had constructed for the navy. Second, and more importantly, RCA began, on its own initiative, to construct coastal stations and radio facilities for commercial maritime traffic. The latter development threatened to undermine the navy's position that the government should control coastal communications. The navy's intense reaction to both developments stemmed from the Naval Communication Service's hostility to RCA's general manager, David Sarnoff. Sarnoff had tried to join the navy's radio bureau in World War I, but its director, Commander David W. Todd, characterized him as "distasteful" because of his Central European ancestry—in other words, because he was a Jew. When RCA began to construct its own commercial stations, the navy immediately labeled the corporation's policies as a Sarnoff innovation that would interfere with the navy's coastal stations.[9]

By 1921 Commander Stanford Hooper was charging Owen D. Young, chairman of the board of RCA, with breach of trust and RCA with trickery and deception. To defeat the RCA program, Hooper launched an emotionally laden political attack; exploiting a deep-seated American prejudice, he began lobbying in Congress against the RCA "monopoly" of radio communications. However, in Hooper's way of thinking, monopoly was not a monopoly if it was held by an agency of government. In any event, by December 1921, the special relationship between RCA and the navy had totally deteriorated, and the company gravitated toward the Department of Commerce in the interdepartmental struggle.

Nor was RCA alone in doing so, as most other industrial concerns with an interest in radio communications had already run afoul of the navy. American Telephone and Telegraph (AT&T), for example, had attempted to use wireless telephony as an extension of its land system, only to be thwarted by the navy on the basis that AT&T's undertaking would interfere with the navy's coastal system of stations. Under these circumstances, AT&T also turned to the secretary of commerce.

Hoover, seizing the opportunity, proposed that the private radio users join with the Department of Commerce to form an alliance opposing the navy and the Post Office. Accordingly, throughout the summer and fall of 1921, business and engineering representatives from Westinghouse, the Radio Corporation of America, General Electric, the Institute of Radio Engineers, American Telephone and Telegraph, the American Engineering Standards Committee, and the Radio Division of the Commerce Department held a series of meetings to plan their strategy. They opted for close cooperation with Secretary Hoover to develop a national radio policy that would use supervision by the Department of Commerce to protect private enterprise. Moreover, they argued that broadcasting, the most rapidly growing use of radio, should be encouraged and protected. Gradually, a common front began to emerge as the interests of the broadcasting industry and the Department of Commerce began to intersect. In effect, Hoover had made the Department of Commerce the champion of commercial radio broadcasting, in opposition to the positions of the navy and the Post Office; thereby, the way was cleared for broadcasting's unprecedented expansion.[11]

Commercial concerns and governmental departments were soon joined by other groups that were interested in who controlled radio. The amateur operators, whose ranks were increased by returning veterans who had received instruction in wireless communication during the war, constituted an important interest group in the contest for control of radio communication. Their most effective organization, the American Radio Relay League (ARRL), had almost six thousand members by 1921. Ever conscious of their influence, Hoover portrayed the Department of Commerce as the "patron saint" of the amateur. He actively solicited the views of amateurs on the best ways for the Department of Commerce to serve them and also made every effort to have his personnel attend their meetings to present the department's position on radio matters. Logically enough, when news of the Post Office's plans to administer radio communication became known, the ARRL turned to the Department of Commerce for information and aid to counteract the Post Office's scheme.[12]

As the Department of Commerce's program gained momentum, Hoover heard the call, from a variety of sources, for an "honest broker"—one who could rise above the conflict and arrive at a nonpartisan assessment. The Bureau of Standards went so far as to contend that American commercial and amateur interests, by relying upon the Department of Commerce, provided a unifying force in radio. The bureau went on to claim that the "department is the government representative of the commercial radio companies, the amateur radio operators, and those interested in technical development of radio communications"—a classification that covered just about everyone. As the department itself did not use radio for communication, it could be billed as an unbiased agency able to serve civic, commercial, and governmental interests. What appeared to be a groundswell of opinion urging the Department of Commerce to intervene was in reality a plan carefully orchestrated by Secretary Hoover.[13]

Against this background of interdepartmental strife, the Department of Commerce stepped forward to assume control. At Secretary Hoover's urging, President Harding called for governmental and private radio users to assemble in Washington, D.C., on February 22, 1922, for the First National Radio Conference. In what Secretary of State Charles Evans Hughes termed "the conference before the conference," the Department of Commerce, commercial companies, and amateurs met to plan their strategy. They aimed to bring legitimacy to broadcasting, to prevent domination by the navy or the Post Office, and to secure recognition under the Department of Commerce. Above all, Secretary Hoover strove to identify radio broadcasting as a service industry that would bring benefits to the public as great as those which radio already provided in maritime communications. Hoover limited the participation of the navy and the Post Office at the radio conference by relegating them to the status of mere radio users, thus further undermining their positions.[14]

From the beginning, the Department of Commerce molded and led the conference. Dr. S. W. Stratton, director of the Bureau of Standards, chaired the conference, and Secretary Hoover delivered the keynote address, personally presided at a number of sessions, and took a direct interest in every aspect of the meeting. In his keynote address, the secretary of commerce articulated the main issue before the conference—the definition and regulation of broadcasting. Throughout his speech, Hoover carefully identified broadcasting with the public's interest, the public's rights, and the public's welfare. His guiding principle was to preserve this new service by carefully connecting it with the general public good and to the Department of Commerce. By his active participation, Hoover created tremendous publicity for radio broadcasting and also defined the framework in which the delegates would operate at the conference.[15]

The various committees advanced proposals that closely followed Department of Commerce recommendations. Much to the chagrin of both the navy and the Post Office, the delegates concurred that legislation should be passed to amend the Radio Act of 1912 so that the secretary of commerce would have adequate authority to supervise the airwaves. The delegates also suggested that the secretary of commerce assemble a committee of governmental representatives to resolve the interdepartmental conflict. In short, the radio conference officially adopted the position held by Hoover.[16]

Almost immediately, Secretary Hoover began to carry out the recommendations of the First National Radio Conference. He invited the various governmental departments that were involved with radio communication to help form what would become the Interdepartmental Radio Advisory Committee (IRAC). Like the radio conference that preceded it, IRAC was under the Department of Commerce. Once again Dr. Stratton helped out and chaired IRAC, this time aided by J. H. Dellinger of the Bureau of Standards who acted as secretary. The appearance of this committee marked the first step toward resolving the fierce interdepartmental conflict that had characterized the initial phase of radio broadcasting.[17]

What followed could serve as an object lesson for all bureaucratic power struggles. The Post Office, refusing to recognize that it had been defeated, persisted in futile efforts to dominate the government's monopoly of radio and, thus, soon lost all control of radio. The navy, in contrast, adjusted to the new circumstances and, thereby, saved itself a piece of the pie. The Naval Communications Service, reluctantly conceding that "the policy it endeavored to maintain must be modified," endorsed IRAC's contention that the 1904 report was obsolete. In return, IRAC reciprocated by agreeing to the navy's assertion that "military control of radio communications in times of war is a proper objective." The committee also strove to emphasize those technical goals that had always been of primary importance for the navy, including elimination of static interference and standardization of radio apparatus. Secretary Hoover further agreed to support the Naval Communications Service's request to secure increased congressional appropriations for modernizing the navy's radio system. Thus, by displaying adaptability and by agreeing to limited objectives, the navy not only learned to live with the new policy but actually prospered from it.[18]

There remained, of course, the matter of obtaining congressional ratification of the settlements that had been reached on the bureaucratic battlegrounds. The next year, using his success in resolving the interdepartmental conflict as a springboard, the secretary of commerce advanced boldly into the legislative arena. On January 2–3, 1923, the Committee on Merchant Marine and Fisheries of the House of Representatives held hearings on House Resolution 11964, a measure introduced by Congressman Wallace White, a Republican from Maine. The chief provisions of the White bill revised sections of the Radio Act of 1912. The legislation strengthened Hoover's position by bestowing wide discretionary powers upon the Department of Commerce. In addition, the proposal placed federal radio stations, when transmitting commercial messages, under the jurisdiction of the secretary of commerce. White, reflecting the feeling of the House committee, contended that many public agencies had misused the wireless by appropriating desirable wavelengths, thereby disregarding the rights of the broadcast listener.[19]

In a statement calculated to further placate the private sector, David B. Carson, director of the Bureau of Navigation, assured businesspeople that the enactment of White's bill would allow the Department of Commerce to reallocate frequencies, thereby affording a wider distribution for broadcasting stations. In short, House Resolution 11964 was aimed directly at the navy: its provisions would place military outlets, when transmitting nongovernmental maritime messages, under civilian authority. In addition, it proposed to eliminate the government frequency range from 187.5 to 500 kHz. In effect, the passage of House Resolution 11964 would have placed the Department of Commerce in a position of supremacy.[20]

Throughout the hearings, the navy objected most vehemently to paragraph C of section 1, which remanded naval stations to the control of the secretary of commerce when they were engaged in the transmission of nongovernmental material. Hoover asserted that the navy, like any other group, should be regulated while undertaking commercial work. He declared that the moment the navy entered the private sector "it ought to yield" to the Department of Commerce's supervision. He further postulated that without such authority it would be impossible to set up any systematic control.[21]

The navy countered that it was often difficult to separate the official from the private part of its duties. It also complained that strict interpretation of the bill would necessitate the licensing of all naval personnel by the Department of Commerce. After numerous conferences with the secretary of the navy, Congressman White and Commander Hooper of the Naval Communications Service agreed to circumvent the problem. They accepted a navy proposal that the president, acting on the advice of IRAC, would assign channels to government stations, thus conforming to the general rules and guidelines developed by the secretary of commerce. By shrewd maneuvering and by involving IRAC in the regulatory process, the navy was able to avoid being placed directly under the Department of Commerce's jurisdiction.[22]

On January 11, 1923, White submitted to Congress a new bill, House Resolution 13773. It was similar to House Resolution 11964 but contained the necessary concessions to the navy. The measure passed the House of Representatives on January 31, 1923, and arrived before the Senate Committee on Interstate Commerce on February 8, 1923. The navy supported the resolution and urged Senate enactment. Because of the navy's backing, the Bureau of Navigation felt certain of the bill's success and prepared for Secretary Hoover a list of members to serve on the advisory committee, which would be created by the legislation. Secretary Hoover, however, took no chances: he drafted a letter, showing President Harding's support for the proposal, which President Harding was to send to various members of Congress.[23]

The White bill evoked a flood of correspondence advancing many partisan hopes and ideas. The American Radio Relay League continued to demand that the law define the amateur's domain and that it specify such matters as wavelengths and power. QST, the ARRL magazine, observed that even though the present "Secretary of Commerce and present Commissioner of Navigation are all friendly toward the amateur . . . they won't be in office always, and we ask you to imagine a Daniels as head of the Department of Commerce." At the same time, universities and colleges with broadcasting stations urged the lawmakers to give the academic outlets preferential treatment. Harry P. Davis, vice-president of Westinghouse, suggested a public service commission be established to regulate radio. In addition to these recommendations, groups such as IRAC, associations of citizens and listeners, and businesspeople preferred widespread support for the bill. The House committee concurred with the various witnesses and interest groups that the confusion in the airwaves could be relieved only through expanded and strengthened federal supervision.[24]

Yet, despite the seeming preponderance of support for White's legislation, the Senate Committee on Interstate Commerce took no action. Alabama Senator Oscar W. Underwood, like many of his colleagues, hesitated to move the bill out of committee, stating that the proposition was too important to be rushed through in the closing days of the session. The IRAC saw less innocent forces at work. The IRAC's subcommittee on policy and legislation observed that several business groups had opposed the plan in the Senate. The committee reported that, among others, RCA had urged Senator Underwood to proceed cautiously on the radio question. John W. Elwood, secretary of RCA, observed that legislative success is often dependent "upon timeliness." Despite the growing demand for congressional action to relieve the chaos in radio broadcasting, he was a firm believer "in letting things get worse so that you can make them better." Owen D. Young had affirmed that he would not object to supervision, but "regulation in advance of profits by people unfamiliar with the business . . . will assuredly result in no profits at all," a situation which he would indeed oppose. The lack of organization in radio broadcasting concerned both Young and Elwood. They argued that until radio broadcasting could be placed on a solid economic basis the industry could not be regulated properly.[25]

AT&T joined RCA in its objections to the bill. While admitting that the measure might improve conditions slightly, AT&T challenged several aspects of the plan. AT&T pointed out that the proposal did not provide sufficient protection for capital. Under the bill's provisions, a construction permit would be required to erect a station. Having obtained permission, construction could begin; but it was not mandatory that the Department of Commerce issue a license for operation, even if the company had adhered strictly to the provisions assigned to it. AT&T suggested that the secretary of commerce be required to follow through if all the stipulations of the permit had been fulfilled. Furthermore, AT&T opposed the wording of the clause on monopolies, which prohibited the secretary of commerce from approving applications for any corporation that engaged in a monopoly. The telephone company urged that the word "unlawful" be inserted into the clause. Finally, because no right to appeal the decisions of the secretary of commerce was provided, AT&T contended that the bill gave too much power to an administrative official and further stated that the measure was impossible to support. By the middle of February, Secretary Hoover regretfully conceded that the proposal would not become law. Accordingly, four years passed before legislation on radio broadcasting was forthcoming.[26]

Still smarting from his failure to achieve a legislative mandate, Hoover suffered a judicial setback. Two years earlier, on May 23, 1921, Assistant Secretary of Commerce Claudius H. Huston had revoked the license of the Intercity Radio Company for seriously menacing legitimate wireless activities by willfully interfering with government, commercial, and amateur stations in the vicinity of New York City. Intercity had taken the matter to court, and the Supreme Court of the District of Columbia had ruled in the firm's favor, ordering the secretary of commerce to reinstate the license. Secretary Hoover appealed the case; but in February 1923, the Court of Appeals also decided for Intercity and declared that while the secretary of commerce might designate the channels over which the corporation had to operate—that being left to administrative discretion by the Radio Act of 1912—the issuance of a license was mandatory. Hoover appealed the case to the U.S. Supreme Court, but after several delays the Intercity Radio Company went out of business, and the question remained moot.[27]

Secretary Hoover reacted to legal obstacles in a traditionally American way, namely, by going around them. Hoover simply refused to allow the law to stand in his way. A number of the policies that he implemented to regulate radio were either prohibited by the Radio Act of 1912 or fell outside his jurisdiction. In order to achieve his objectives, Hoover sought the compliance of his own department, the support of other governmental agencies, and the approbation of the press and the broadcasting industry.[28]

The Bureau of Navigation and the radio inspectors had long recognized that it would be desirable to reallocate frequencies and to allow businesspeople to use the government's broadcasting frequencies. But without new legislation, the secretary of commerce, hampered by court restrictions, could not reallocate frequencies. Sections 2 and 4 of the Radio Act of 1912 provided for definite wavelengths for commercial stations, specifically excluding them from the range of 187.5 to 500 kHz. Article 2 of the Service Regulations, which was affixed to the International Radio-Telegraph Convention and had been ratified by the United States on July 8, 1913, further protected the federal radio band by limiting private operators to frequency assignments outside the range of 187.5 to 500 kHz. In a memorandum to the secretary of commerce, Commissioner of Navigation David B. Carson observed that the clear intent of both the domestic act and the international convention was to restrict the use of that band of channels for military purposes.[29]

Throughout 1922, Commissioner Carson had worked for passage of the White bill that would have allowed private groups to use the federal range of radio frequencies. By December 1922, with congestion and interference prevalent above 500 kHz and no hope of congressional activity on the measure, Carson argued that it would be desirable to ignore the existing statutes and remove restrictions on the government band and to implement a general rearrangement of frequencies, even without new legislation. Without such drastic action, congestion and chaos would continue to hinder broadcasting.[30]

This change of attitude within the higher echelons of the Department of Commerce reflected the activities of radio inspectors in the field who were forced by their lack of legal authority to improvise when faced with many of the difficult situations and problems inherent in their task. The inspectors often "took the law in their own hands without consultation or due process." At virtually all levels within the Department of Commerce, extemporization became the norm in efforts to counter the chaos created by the broadcasting boom.[31]

Sure of support within the department, Secretary Hoover then turned to other governmental divisions. After the failure of the White bill, he received encouragement from other agencies to take action. Some officials, including James C. Gilbert of the Department of Agriculture, mentioned the need to revise the Department of Commerce's procedures, in spite of the failure of the congressional resolution. Captain H. P. Perrill of the Office of the Chief Coordinator of the Bureau of the Budget suggested that Secretary Hoover proceed as if the proposed legislation had been enacted.[32]

With the backing of these bureaucrats, Secretary Hoover moved to cement his relationship with the press. In the early years of his secretaryship, Hoover had developed ties with public relations personnel and the news media, while at the same time constructing an elaborate apparatus that could be utilized to manipulate popular opinion. As he moved to skirt the legal barriers to effective control of radio, Hoover's public relations machinery was placed in high gear. Skillfully utilizing personal conferences and his press contacts, Hoover began to interpret his department's new policy to the American people. To supplement these activities, the Department of Commerce issued a weekly summary to the press that included an impressive compilation of clippings that dealt with all aspects of communication. As the department implemented Hoover's plans, officials were instructed to send all incorrect or adverse commentaries directly to Hoover's personal secretary. Corrections and additional material concerning the Department of Commerce's plan were emitted continuously to clarify and prevent unfavorable or inaccurate reporting.[33]

Finally, to provide legitimacy for the extralegal measures implemented by the Department of Commerce, and as a finale to his press campaign, Secretary Hoover assembled the Second National Radio Conference in Washington, D.C., on March 20, 1923. The conference was convened to consider the chaos rampant in radio, which had become worse with the failure of White's bill and with the Intercity case. As it had dominated the first gathering, the Department of Commerce also painstakingly arranged every detail of the second one. Well before the delegates assembled in Washington, D.C., the department had carefully prepared the conference's agenda that would eventually become the conference's recommendations.[34]

The agenda considered the commercial use of the wavelengths between 187.5

and 500 kHz that were reserved for the government, the general reallocation of frequencies, reclassification of stations, and cessation of amateur activities during peak listening hours. The urgent demands of businesspeople for relief from static interference, however, monopolized the considerations. In order to resolve that issue, the department suggested rearranging the wavelengths and opening the military bands to private radio users. Secretary Hoover felt that in lieu of the required legal sanctions, the cooperation of these groups of radio users would ensure him the authority to achieve his aims.[35]

The Second National Radio Conference (closely following the Department of Commerce's agenda) urged a radical departure from past policies. Previously, all radio broadcasting had been conducted on 618.6, 750 and 833.3 kHz. The conference delegates advocated that the principle of allocating frequency blocs be applied to this service and that a band from 550 to 1365 kHz be established. In that scheme, stations would be classified according to their transmitting power, the character of the programs transmitted, and their general operating methods. The delegates urged that three groups of broadcasting stations be created: Class A, equipped to use power not exceeding 500 watts and assigned wavelengths from 999.4 to 1365 kHz; Class B, equipped to use from 500 to 1,000 watts and assigned wavelengths from 550 to 800 kHz and from 870 to 999.4 kHz; and Class C, placed at 833.3 kHz.[36]

The members advised the secretary of commerce that, because technological advances since World War I had widened the electromagnetic spectrum, those marine, mobile, and aircraft services which were displaced by the creation of the broadcast frequency band now could be allocated elsewhere. For example, ship-to-shore communications on 666.3 and 999.4 kHz could be moved to 429 kHz. Such a displacement raised the possibility of resistance from users in the maritime sector, of course. While maritime radio users rarely used the 999.4 kHz frequency assigned to them under the international convention, those same groups did rely heavily on the popular 666.3 kHz frequency. To encourage shippers to start using the 429 kHz frequency, the delegates proposed that all maritime traffic cease using 666.3 kHz between the hours of 7:00 P.M. and 11:00 P.M. and instead operate on frequencies between 375 and 500 kHz. A silent period during those hours on 666.3 kHz supposedly would cut down the static interference with commercial broadcasting programs.[37]

In addition, other spectrum blocs were designated for maritime and point-to-point communications, including 190, 235–85, 315–550, and 999.4 kHz. Radio compass and radio beacon stations were to conduct their essential maritime navigation functions on 300 and 375 kHz. Ground-to-air transmissions that were crucial for aircraft safety were to be carried on 375 to 550 and on 1300 to 1350 kHz. The convention at long last had begun to deal with some of radio broadcasting's more salient problems. Finally, the federal radio bands were to be opened to businesspeople.[38]

The delegates asserted that, in spite of judicial and legislative setbacks, the secretary of commerce had ample authority to implement the conference's agenda. They further believed that under the law he could rearrange stations, regulate hours and wavelengths, and revoke or withhold licenses. Secretary Hoover, while recognizing some potential difficulties in instituting the agenda, called its recommendations "a step in the ideal development of measures for the prevention of interference in public broadcasting." On May 15, 1923, he began to introduce the plan proposed by the conference. He assigned channels, although the Radio Act of 1912 neither made nor authorized any distribution of frequencies to individual stations. He placed commercial operators in the band from 187.5 to 500 kHz, although both domestic and international law protected that band for government use. He reallocated channels, although those same laws specified definite wavelengths for certain groups of radio users. As *Radio Broadcast* observed in an article entitled "Secretary Hoover Acts," the situation was "suddenly remedied" without the passage of the White bill.[39]

The Second National Radio Conference's recommendations and the Department of Commerce's implementation of them received widespread support. The acceptance by businesspeople and bureaucrats of these extralegal actions made them, in effect, law. Commercial broadcasters uniformly approved the creation of the band from 187.5 to 500 kHz and envisioned a reduction of static interference. In an attempt to coordinate federal services with civilian groups, IRAC announced that only those channels designated by the conference for public business would be assigned to government stations.[40]

The military also approved the new policies. The army agreed that since the electromagnetic spectrum had been enlarged by technological developments the maintenance of a government radio band in times of peace was unjustified. The Signal Corps added that the acceptance of this new plan would improve the army's reputation with broadcast listeners.[41]

Because it was the largest user of radio communication, the navy sacrificed much more than any other group by acquiescing to the creation of a commercial broadcasting band. The Naval Communications Service diplomatically agreed to what Stanford C. Hooper labeled the "sensible thing" and endorsed both the recommendations of the second conference and the IRAC policy.[42]

Although its actions might appear overly generous, the navy recognized that it no longer could justify maintaining the band reserved to the federal government. Under the new arrangement, naval fleet operations used the frequency ranges from 95 to 120 kHz, 190 to 230 kHz, 250 kHz, and 2,005 to 2,995 kHz. When necessary, frequency ranges from 1,030 to 1,285 kHz and 3,005 to 3,815 kHz were possible substitutes. In addition, shore facilities received authorization to operate either below 150 kHz or above 4,000 kHz. In sum, the navy utilized 75 specific frequencies allocated in the following manner: 5 low-frequency channels with low or high power; 14 medium-frequency channels with high power; 30 high-frequency channels with low power; 20 high-frequency channels with low power; and 6 high-frequency channels with low power. Equally important, the new arrangement revitalized naval programs that had been set aside because of post–World War I congressional cutbacks of military expenditures. In order to operate on the new frequencies, the department needed modern apparatus. Because of the new rules and procedures, the Naval Communications Service was able to justify replacing equipment that was inoperative at the new frequencies and receiving increased appropriations to facilitate the conversion. Again, by displaying adaptability the Navy actually prospered from the new policy.[43]

The RCA Annual Report for 1923 observed that "radio broadcasting promises permanency." To a large extent this promise resulted directly from the policies implemented by Secretary Hoover in the spring and summer of 1923. In spite of legislative inactivity and a judicial decision that undermined his authority, Hoover instituted several extralegal measures destined to establish the supremacy of the secretary of commerce. With the cooperation of bureaucrats and businesspeople, he created an informal pool whereby the business community and the Department of Commerce could combat the disorder and chaos that surrounded broadcasting.[44]

In addition, the Second National Radio Conference's recommendation to reallocate channels dealt effectively with the major difficulties that plagued radio users. Since its resolutions placed most amateur, ship, and land stations outside the commercial broadcasting band, static interference was drastically curtailed. Moreover, be creating a separate band of frequencies for commercial broadcasting outlets, the conference assured the continued development and survival of that medium. Indeed, under the protection of the secretary of commerce, the development of commercial broadcasting flourished. In the nine months after Herbert C. Hoover's appointment as secretary of commerce, the new industry blossomed into a rapidly expanding national craze. In December 1921, 23 stations were issued licenses by the Department of Commerce; another 8 were licensed in January 1922; 24, in February; 77, in March; 76, in April; and 97, in May. By 1923 there were 579 operational outlets in the United States. Not only had the secretary of commerce aided in the creation of a new industry, he had also identified the Department of Commerce with that industry's success. Hoover's policies had been so effective that Americans seemed, to many, to be preoccupied with nothing but crystal sets and radio programs.[45]

Notes

1. Elting E. Morison, *Men, Machines, and Modern Times* (Cambridge, Mass.: MIT Press, 1966), 9, 19; Lance C. Buhl, "Mariners and Machines: Resistance to Technological Change in the American Navy, 1865–1869," *Journal of American History*, 61 (Dec. 1974): 703–727.

2. "Selecting Wavelengths for Broadcasting, 1921–22," *History of Radio*, Vol. 1, Stanford C. Hooper Papers, Manuscript Division (MSS), Library of Congress (LC), Box 40, Misc.; Woodworth to Bagley, Mar. 4, 1919, National Archives Record Group (NARG) 38, Records of the Office of the Chief of Naval Operations, Director of Naval Communications (DNC), File 21, 7000–49; as quoted in LC Exhibit Commemorating 50th Anniversary of Radio, Features Papers of Pioneer Scientists and Broadcasters, n.d. Press Release No. 70-33, LC.

3. Will H. Hays, *The Memoirs of Will H. Hays* (New York: Doubleday, 1955), v, 278–280, 283, 288–289, 302–304; Francis Russell, *The Shadow of Blooming Grove: Warren G. Harding and His Times* (New York: McGraw Hill, 1968), 302, 359, 535; Memo for Secretary of Commerce, April 3, 1922, Herbert C. Hoover Presidential Library (HHPL), Box 444, Secretary of Commerce, Official File, Radio Correspondence, Press Releases.

4. Ellis W. Hawley, "Herbert C. Hoover, The Commerce Secretariat, and The Vision of an Associated State, 1921–1928," *Journal of American History*, 61 (June 1974): 121; *Minneapolis Star Tribune*, Sept. 8, 1925 (HHPL), Personal File, 1925.

5. White to Hoover, Mar. 7, 1921, Wallace White Papers, Manuscript Division, LC, Box 15, Dept. File, 66th Congress, Sec. of Commerce; West to Hooper, Feb. 15, 1922, Hooper Papers, MSS, LC, Box 4, Corresp., Feb.–Mar. 1922.

6. Hooper to Dodd, July 11, 1921, Hooper Papers, MSS, LC, Box 3, Corresp., May–Aug. 1921; Bureau of Engineering to Sec. of the Navy, July 25, 1921, NARG 80, General Records of the Navy Dept., Sec. of Navy, File 575403-600; Memo for Sec. of Navy, Chief of Naval Operations, Sept. 23, 1921, NARG 38, DNC, File 100.

7. "Government to Offer Radio Telephone Service," *Electrical World*, 80 (July 15, 1922): 138; Hays to Sec. of Navy, May 9, 1921, NARG 28, Post Office Dept., Postmaster General Letterbooks, Jan. 1, 1921 to June 30, 1921.

Concerning Edgerton's efforts, *see* Terrell, Memo for Files, Nov. 8, 1921, NARG 173, Records of the Federal Communications Commission, General Records, Radio Div., File 1474; James C. Edgerton, Report on Possibilities of the Air Mail Service, 1921, NARG 172, FCC, General Records Radio Div., File 1474; Hooper to Bullard, Mar. 17, 1927, Hooper Papers, MSS, LC, Box 8, Corresp., Mar. 1927.

8. Cooper to Naval Communications Service, Mar. 1, 1921, NARG 38, DNC, File 65022–49; Memo for Woodworth, District Communications Superintendent, 3rd Naval District, July 23, 1919, NARG 38, DNC, WHG Bullard Files, Box 1; Daniels to Chairman, Senate Committee on Naval Affairs, Feb. 27, 1920, NARG 38, WHG Bullard Files, Box 1.

For RCA-Navy cooperation, *see* Todd, Memo for Bullard, Mar. 12, 1919, NARG 38,

DNC, WHG Bullard Files, Box 1; Bullard to Young, Nov. 6, 1919, NARG 38, DNC, WHG Bullard Files, Box 1.

9. Jewett to Hooper, Mar. 8, 1921, Hooper Papers, MSS, LC, Jan. to April 1921; Hooper, "Survey of Radio Situation, 1921," *Journal of American Society of Naval Engineers*, Hooper Papers, MSS, LC, Box 44; Todd, Report of Telephone Conversation with Nally, April 2, 1917, NARG 38, DNC, Todd Files, Box 3.

10. Hooper, Memo re: Young, Nov. 11, 1921, Hooper Papers, MSS, LC, Box 3; Hooper to Johnson, June 6, 1921, Hooper Papers, MSS, LC, Box 3.

11. Carty to Bullard, Oct. 26, 1920, NARG 38, DNC, File 62467-20; *AT&T Annual Report*, 1920, 23–24; NARG 173, FCC, General Corresp., Radio Div., File 1–3A; Hoover to Goldsmith, Oct. 6, 1921, NARG 40, Records of the Dept. of Commerce, File 67032/3; Kennelly and Dellinger, to Hoover, Aug. 22, 1921 (HHPL), Sec. of Commerce, Official File, Box 437.

12. Hoover to Maxim, Aug. 30, 1921, NARG 167, Records of the Bureau of Standards, J. H. Dellinger Papers, Box 6; Hoover to Terrell, Aug. 29, 1921, NARG 173, FCC, General Records, Radio Div., File 460.

13. Chief Radio Inspector, Memo to Sec. of Commerce, Sept. 21, 1921, NARG 40, Dept. of Commerce, File 67032/7; Dellinger, Confidential Memo to Stratton, Oct. 18, 1921, NARG 167, JHD Papers, Box 39.

14. "Harding Moves to Limit Wireless Telephony; Asks Hoover to Call Conference of Experts," *New York Times*, Feb. 8, 1922, 1; Edward F. Sarno, Jr., "The National Radio Conferences," *Journal of Broadcasting*, 13 (Spring 1966): 189–191; Hoover to Begg, Mar. 6, 1922, NARG 173, FCC, General Records, Radio Div., File 1179.

15. "Hoover Set up American System for Radio," *Broadcasting*, reprint (HHPL); Hoover to McCutchen, Feb. 23, 1922, NARG 173, FCC, General Records, Radio Div., File 1179; Hoover Address, First National Radio Conference, Feb. 27, 1922 (HHPL), Sec. of Commerce, Official File, Box 437.

16. "Urges Federal Rule Over Radiophones," *New York Times*, Mar. 11, 1922, 9; "Report of the Radio Telephone Committee," *Radio Broadcast*, 1 (July 1922): 191–193; Summary of Preliminary Report of the Technical Committee of the Radio Telephone Conference (HHPL), Sec. of Commerce, Official File, Radio Conf.; Goldsmith to Stratton, n.d. Comments on Tentative Report (HHPL) Sec. of Commerce, Official File, Radio Conf.

17. "Inter-Departmental Radio Advisory Committee to Help Regulate All Government Radio," *Radio Broadcast*, 1 (Oct. 1922): 456–457; History of the IRAC, Mar. 27, Wheeler, Terrell, IRAC Meeting, n.d. NARG 173, FCC, IRAC Files, Box 77, Operation and Procedures.

18. Hooper Memo, April 25, 1922, Hooper Papers, MSS, LC, Box 4; Sec. of Navy, to Chief Coordinator, May 11, 1922, NARG 80, Sec. of Navy, File 12479, 1726; Report of IRAC Meeting, April 6, 1923, NARG 40, Dept. of Commerce, File 67032/32; IRAC Report, adopted Jan. 18, 1924, NARG 173, FCC, IRAC Files, Box 104.

On the intransigence of the Post Office, *see* Work to Hoover, April 28, 1922, NARG 173, FCC, IRAC Files, Box 206; Denby to Postmaster General, May 12, 1922, NARG

38, DNC, File 110; Work to Hoover, April 15, 1922, (HHPL) Sec. of Commerce, Official File, Radio Corresp., Press Releases.

19. "For Regulating Radio," *New York Times*, April 19, 1921, 23; "Wanted: An American Radio Policy," *Radio Broadcast*, 1 (May 1922): 29–33; Hoover to White, Aug. 12, 1922, White Papers, MSS, LC, Box 35; Hoover to Goldsmith, Jan. 18, 1922, NARG 40, Dept. of Commerce.

20. "Need for Law," *Literary Digest*, 76 (Jan. 13, 1923): 25–26; Carson, Memo for Secretary of Commerce, Jan. 8, 1923, NARG 173, FCC, General Records, Radio Div., File 1600; Klein to Hoover, Jan. 8, 1923, NARG 40, Dept. of Commerce, File 67032/32.

21. "Hoover for Radio Control," *New York Times*, Jan. 3, 1923; Ziegemeier, Memo for Chief of Naval Operations, Jan. 2, 1923, NARG 80, Sec. of Navy 1916–26, File 12479 (1957 to 1987); Memo for Secretary of Navy, Jan. 4, 1923, NARG 38, DNC, File 110 (1922–1923).

22. Carson, Memo for Secretary of Commerce, Jan. 9, 1923, NARG 173, FCC, General Corresp., Radio Div., File 1484; White to Godley, Oct. 25, 1922, White Papers, MSS, LC, Box 42, Dept. of Commerce File.

23. Glenn A. Johnson, "The First Regulator of American Broadcasting, 1921–28, Secretary of Commerce Herbert Hoover" (Ph.D. diss., University of Iowa, 1970), 114–115; U.S. Congress, House Bill to Amend an Act to Regulate Radio Communications, 67th Cong., 4th sess., Jan. 16, 1923, White Papers, MSS, LC, Box 64, Subject File, Radio; Tyrer, Memo for Herter, Feb. 8, 1923, HHPL, Sec. of Commerce, Official File, Box 447, Radio Legislation; Hoover to Harding, Jan. 31, 1923, HHPL, Sec. of Commerce, Official File, Box 235, President Harding; Brown, Memo for Huston, Feb. 20, 1923, NARG 173, FCC, General Corresp., Radio Div., File 67032/32.

Concerning navy support, *see* Denby to Henning, Jan. 22, 1923, NARG 38, DNC, File 110 (1922–23); "Naval Communications Service," Address by Admiral Ziegemeier, Army-Navy Club, Feb. 21, 1923, NARG 38, DNC, File 110–120 (1924–26).

24. George F. Gurghard, "Eighteen Years of Amateur Radio," *Radio Broadcast*, 3 (Aug. 1923): 290–298; "The Legislative Situation," *QST*, n.d., White Papers, MSS, LC, Dept. File, Merchant Marine and Fisheries Committee; Rogers to Hoover, May 3, 1922, HHPL, Sec. of Commerce, Official File, Radio Corresp., Press Releases; Carson, Memo for Secretary of Commerce, Mar. 1, 1922, NARG 173, FCC, General Records, Radio Div., File 1179; IRAC Report, Meeting of Feb. 2, 1923, NARG 173, IRAC Files, Box 1, IRAC Meeting, Government Radio Broadcasting.

25. "Hoover to Advise on Radio Control," *New York Times*, Feb. 10, 1922; Carl Dreher, "Is the Amateur at Fault?" *Radio Broadcast*, 4 (Feb. 1924); Maxim to Terrell, Oct. 24, 1922, NARG 173, FCC, General Records, Radio Div., File 1179; Supervisor of Radio, New York to Carson, Nov. 17, 1923, NARG 173, FCC, General Records, Radio Div., File 1109; "Interference Problems Are Being Solved," *Radio News Bulletin*, Feb. 29, 1924, NARG 173, FCC, General Records, Radio Div., File 570.

Concerning congressional inaction, consult "Incompetent Senate," *Outlook*, 133 (Mar. 7, 1923): 432–433; "News from the Capital," *Electrical World*, 81 (Feb. 24, 1923): 468; IRAC Report of Subcommittee on Policy and Legislation, Mar. 13, 1923, NARG 173, IRAC Files, Box 204, Policy and Legislation, 1923.

26. Notes of American Telephone and Telegraph Radio Conference (Confidential), New York City, Feb. 26 to Mar. 2, 1923, NAB.

27. Clarence C. Dill, *Radio Law Practice and Procedure* (Washington, D.C.: National Book 1938), 68–69; "Hoover Is Summoned in a Wireless Case," *New York Times*, Nov. 17, 1921; "Court Upholds Intercity Radio," *New York Times*, Nov. 19, 1921; Hoover to Solicitor General, Department of Justice, Feb. 17, 1923, NARG 40, Dept. of Commerce, File 80524; Report of Investigation of Interference Caused by Intercity Radio Station, Bureau of Standards, Mar. 6, 1922, NARG 173, FCC, General Records, Radio Div., File 1102; Intercity Radio Company File, NARG 173, FCC, General Records, Radio Div., File 1102.

28. F. C. James, *The Growth of Chicago Banks* (New York: Harper and Brothers, 1938), 3–4; Forrest McDonald, *The Torch is Passed: The United States in the 20th Century* (Reading, Mass.: Addison-Wesley, 1968), 4–7.

29. Carson, Memo for Secretary of Commerce, April 14, 1922, NARG 173, FCC, General Records, Radio Div., File 1179; Carson to Gates, May 29, 1922, NARG 173, FCC, General Records, Radio Div., File 307; Tyrer to Choate, Oct. 24, 1922, NARG 173, FCC, General Records, Radio Div., File 1600.

30. Terrell to Emmet, Dec. 28, 1922, HHPL, Sec. of Commerce, Official File, Box 447, Radio Legislation, 1922.

31. Carson to Hill, Nov. 10, 1922, NARG 173, FCC, General Records, Radio Div., File 1600; George Sterling, "Government in Broadcasting," 24 A (NAB).

32. IRAC Report, Mar. 2, 1923, NARG 40, Dept. of Commerce, File 67032/32; Carson to Chief Signal Officer, Nov. 10, 1922, NARG 173, FCC, General Corresp., Radio Div., File Com-3 (S–T); IRACGB Report of Feb. 16, 1923, NARG 173, IRAC Files, IRAC Meeting, Feb. 16, 1923; IRAC Report of April 24, 1925, NARG 173, IRAC Files, Box 1.

33. Emmet to Terrell, April 16, 1923, HHPL, Sec. of Commerce, Official File, Box 44, Radio: Corresp., Press Releases, 1923.

34. Walter B. Emery, *Broadcasting and Government: Responsibilities and Regulations* (Lansing: Michigan State University Press, 1961), 18; "Calls Radio Conference," *New York Times*, Mar. 7, 1923; Hoover to Secretary of Navy, Mar. 6, 1923, HHPL, Sec. of Commerce, Official File, Box 438, Radio: Conferences, Second National Radio Conference; Dept. of Commerce, Press Release, Mar. 6, 1923, HHPL, Secretary of Commerce, Official File, Box 444, Radio: Corresp., Press Releases, 1923; Hoover to White, Mar. 6, 1923, White Papers, MSS, LC, Box 35, Dept. File, Commerce Legislation, 67th Congress; Terrell, Memo for Secretary of Commerce, Feb. 23, 1923, NARG 173, FCC, General Records, Radio Div., File 1484.

35. Paul F. Godley, "A Kingdom for More Wavelengths," *Radio Broadcast*, 2 (Jan. 1923): 191–193; "Debate Plans to End Chaos in Radio," *New York Times*, Mar. 21, 1923; "Urge Wide Reform in Broadcasting," *New York Times*, Mar. 25, 1923; Chief Radio Inspector, Memo for Commissioner of Navigation, Mar. 17, 1923, HHPL, Secretary of Commerce, Official File, Box 438, Radio: Conferences; Carson, Memo for Davis, Feb. 19, 1924, NARG 173, IRAC Files Corresp. and Reports Commerce Dept., 1924.

36. Department of Commerce Press Release, April 2, 1923, HHPL, Sec. of Com-

merce, Official File, Box 438, Radio: Conferences: Lecture of S. C. Hooper, "Frequency Allocation," 1927, NARG 19, Bureau of Ships, File 1084; Carson, Memo for Secretary of Commerce, Jan. 27, 1923, NARG 173, FCC, General Records, Radio Div., File 1179; Amendments to Regulations of Bureau of Navigation, General Letter No. 247, April 2, 1923, NARG 173, FCC, General Records, Radio Div., File 1179/8.

37. "Recommendations of Radio Conference," *Electrical World*, 81 (Mar. 31, 1923): 765; Jack Binnis, "How Spark Interference Was Reduced," *Radio Broadcast*, 4 (Mar. 1924): 474; Carson to Supervisor of Radio, New York, Nov. 19, 1923, NARG 173, FCC, General Records, Radio Div., File 1600; Tyrer to Radio Corporation of America, Oct. 3, 1934, NARG 173, FCC, General Records, Radio Div., File 1600; Wilbur to Secretary of State, June 2, 1925, NARG 38, DNC, File 323-031; "Radio Laws and Regulations," 1926, National Radio Institute, NARG 173, FCC, Radio Div., File 1166.

38. Department of Commerce Release, Recommendations of the National Radio Conference, Mar. 24, 1923, HHPL, Sec. of Commerce, Official File, Box 438, Radio Conferences; McLean to Commander-in-Chief, U.S. Fleet, June 16, 1924, NARG 38, DNC, File 323-100; Tyrer to Orriss, April 11, 1923, NARG 173, FCC, General Records, Radio Div., File 1179; Report of Section 6, Division 1, Dept. of Commerce, June 30, 1923, NARG 167, JHD Papers, Box 4.

39. "Plans New Classes for Radio Stations," *New York Times*, April 2, 1923; "Department of Commerce Acts on Radio Recommendations," *Electrical World*, 81 (April 7, 1923): 794; "Wavelengths and Lighthouse Keepers," *Outlook*, 133 (April 11, 1923): 645–646; "Wavelengths for Class B Stations," *Radio Broadcast*, 3 (June 1923): 167; "Secretary Hoover Acts," *Radio Broadcast*, 3 (Aug. 1923): 277; Carson to Squier, Mar. 31, 1923, NARG 111, Chief Signal Officer, Box 337, National Radio Conference, Folder 1; Carson to Anderson, Jan. 15, 1923, NARG 173, FCC, General Records, Radio Div., File 1600; Bureau of Navigation, All Radio Supervisors, Mar. 27, 1924, NARG 173, FCC, General Records, Radio Div., File 2666.

40. President, RCA, to Hoover, April 4, 1923, HHPL, Sec. of Commerce, Official File, Box 438, Radio Conferences; Department of Commerce Radio Regulations, Bulletin No. 5, AT&T, July 30, 1923, NARG 173, FCC, General Records, Radio Div., File 5000; Carson to Starkey, Sept. 22, 1923, NARG 173, FCC, General Records, Radio Div., File 1600; IRAC Wave Frequency Assignments, Sept. 21, 1923, NARG 173, IRAC Files, Box 52.

41. Charles Saltzman, "The Radio Equipment Situation," *Infantry Journal*, 25 (Dec. 1924); "Conference Discusses Radio Chaos," *Electrical World*, 81 (Mar. 24, 1923): 708; Squier, Memo for Secretary of War, April 12, 1923, NARG 111, Chief Signal Officer, Box 337, National Radio Conference, Folder 1; IRAC Report of Subcommittee on Technical Problems, May 17, 1923, NARG 173, IRAC Files, Subcommittee on Technical Problems; Bender to IRAC, Aug. 4, 1924, NARG 173, FCC, IRAC Files, Box 107.

42. Hooper Tape Recordings, 312–13, Hooper Papers, MSS, LC, Box 37.

43. Concerning frequency allocation, *see* Hooper to McLean, July 15, 1924, Hooper Papers, MSS, LC, Box 6; "Naval Communications," Lectures delivered by Ridley

McLean, Naval War College, Oct. 31, 1924, Hooper Papers, MSS, LC, Box 6; Craven, Hooper Tape Recordings, 37 Hooper Papers, MSS, LC, Box 37; Chief of Naval Operations to Naval Force Europe, Special Service Squadron, Transportation Service, Sept. 23, 1923, NARG 38, DNC, File 323; Burgess to Smither, Sept. 28, 1923, NARG 173, IRAC Files, Box 106, Commerce Dept.; Bureau of Engineering to Chief of Naval Operations, Allocation of Radio Frequencies, June 23, 1925, NARG 173, IRAC Files, Corresp. and Reports, 1922–49.

On radio equipment, consult "Engineer Says Navy Needs More Up to Date Equipment," *New York Times*, Nov. 3, 1926; Tawresey, Memo for Bingham, Aug. 9, 1923, NARG 38, DNC, File 140–902; Chief of Naval Operations to Commander-in-Chief, U.S. Fleet, March 17, 1924, NARG 38, DNC, File 323-100; Secretary of Navy to Carlson, April 23, 1925, NARG 80, Sec. of Navy, 1916–26; File 12479 (2060-2098:1).

44. As quoted in Llewellyn White, *The American Radio* (Chicago: University of Chicago Press, 1947), 83–84; C. M. Jansky, "Contributions of Herbert Hoover to Broadcasting," *Journal of Broadcasting*, 3 (Summer 1957): 241–247; *Commerce Yearbooks, 1921, 1922, 1923* (Washington, D.C.: Government Printing Office, 1922, 1923, 1924); *Recent Social Trends in the United States*, Vol. 1 (New York: McGraw Hill, 1933), 153–156.

The radio aerial became a prominent feature of the American landscape, *see* William E. Leuchtenburg, *The Perils of Prosperity, 1914–1932* (Chicago: Univ. of Chicago Press, 1967), 196; Upton Close, *The Commentator's Story* (Palm Beach: Time for Truth Press, 1952), 2.

45. Upton Close, *The Commentator's Story*, 2; *Commerce Yearbook, 1922*, p. 418; Carson to Hogan, Dec. 1, 1922, NARG 173, FCC, General Records, Radio Div., File 1179.

QUESTIONS FOR REVIEW AND DISCUSSION

1. What factors that are important for the development of a technological innovation can you identify as being present in the development of radio broadcasting in the United States?
2. Identify the successful strategies that were used by the Department of Commerce in the governmental struggle to control radio.
3. What role did Herbert Hoover's character and personality play in shaping the government's policies toward commercial broadcasting?
4. How would you assess the role of the federal government in the development of commercial broadcasting in America?
5. Identify the social, economic and political implications of the Department of Commerce's victory in the struggle to control radio broadcasting.
6. Would the navy's or the Post Office's recommendations for controlling radio communications have worked in the United States had they been adopted in the first place?

12

Antitrust and American Public Policy, 1900–1945

In the half century between the passage of the Sherman Antitrust Act and America's entrance into World War II, both large-scale business enterprise and public policy toward it had become increasingly complex. The relatively simple corporate structures that George Rice and like-minded critics had railed against in the nineteenth century underwent a maturation process during the first five decades of the twentieth century—so too did the rather simple solutions that Rice and others had offered to what they had seen as the "trust problem" in America.

In 1900 big business in the United States was characterized by huge, vertically integrated companies. Even though only a small fraction of American businesses were organized in that form, that fraction dominated the nation's industrial landscape. By 1904 it was estimated that the so-called trusts controlled 40 percent of all manufacturing capital in the country.[1]

While the vertically integrated giants of the early 1900s performed various business functions besides manufacturing, those functions usually dealt with a single, related line of products. American Tobacco concentrated on tobacco items; Standard Oil, on petroleum products; and so on. The introduction of diversification of product lines as a management strategy did not appear to any significant extent until the 1920s. The firms that were the first to adopt diversification as a conscious policy were those that had not only the research facilities and experience to devote to the creation of new products but also the technological and marketing ability to manufacture and sell them successfully. Only the larger organizations had such resources, and so it was that big businesses again led the way in the American economy.

Diversification brought with it many necessary administrative changes. The transition from operating as a vertically integrated industry to operating in several different industries required a new approach to management. Under the vertically integrated framework, executives were either tied to one functional activity, such as production, marketing, or finance, or to one line of products. In such a framework, executives were unable to properly appraise the scope of their rapidly diversifying twentieth-century enterprises. After 1920, such leading companies as DuPont, General Motors, Sears Roebuck, and Standard Oil found an alternative to the old corporate structure in a new, decentralized, divisional corporate structure. Business historian Alfred D. Chandler, Jr. described this new corporate form: "In this type of organization, a general office plans, coordinates, and appraises the work of a number of operating divisions and allocates to them the necessary personnel, facilities, funds, and other resources."[2] The multidivisional structure made possible the further growth of the industrial giants as they aggressively pursued the policy of diversification.

Big business in twentieth-century America was also marked by the emergence of what Chandler has termed "managerial capitalism."[3] The administration of the new multidivisional entities came to be the province of salaried, career executives who held relatively little of the companies' stock. These executives replaced the earlier generation of owner-managers who, in many cases, had been the founders of their enterprises. The result of the new style of administration was a widening gap between the nominal authority that a firm's stockholders had and the real control of a firm's affairs which was in the hands of professional managers. Managerial capitalism also carried with it new implications for many facets of conventional business behavior including the venerable goal of maximization of profits and the relationships of business with government, labor, and society in general.

If the large business organizations of 1941 looked quite different from the Standard Oil Company of George Rice's and John D. Rockefeller's time, so too was the public policy toward them that had evolved. There was still considerable concern over the problem of bigness in the economy, but the policies that commentators advocated took different forms. The case study that follows traces the major approaches to the trust, or monopoly, question as it was propounded by both prominent governmental officials and by influential private citizens in the first half of the twentieth century. At that time, the trust question was one of the most hotly debated issues in American politics.

Notes

1. Clair Wilcox, *Competition and Monopoly in American Industry* (Washington, D.C.: U.S. Government Printing Office, 1940), 65.
2. Alfred D. Chandler, Jr., *Strategy and Structure* (Cambridge, Mass.: MIT Press, 1962), 2.
3. Alfred D. Chandler, Jr., "The United States: Seedbed of Managerial Capitalism," *Managerial Hierarchies*, ed. Alfred D. Chandler, Jr. and Herman Daems (Cambridge, Mass.: Harvard University Press, 1980), 14.

C. Joseph Pusateri

APPROACHES TO THE PROBLEM OF BUSINESS MONOPOLY FROM THEODORE ROOSEVELT TO THURMAN ARNOLD

In an essay tracing the history of the antitrust movement in the United States, historian Richard Hofstadter described the years from 1890 to 1914 as "the era of the founding fathers of antitrust."[1] In the front ranks of those founding fathers stands the prominent figure of Theodore Roosevelt. Probably no other single individual in the twentieth century drew quite as much public attention to the question of big business and its place in American society as did Roosevelt both during and after his years in the White House. He thrust the trust question into the center of American political debate, causing it to become for a time the dominating issue of his era.

Historians have continually pointed out that Theodore Roosevelt's actual views on the subject of business combinations were quite different from what his popular label of "trustbuster" would seem to imply. He believed that large-scale enterprise was a natural outcome of America's industrial growth and was indeed necessary if the nation was to retain its newly won economic leadership in the world. At the same time, however, he admitted the possibility of abuses of corporate power. He attempted to distinguish between the positive and the negative effects of concentrated corporate power, between what he saw as good trusts and bad trusts. He, therefore, sought to establish public policy that would accept the former and punish the latter. Whether Roosevelt's views were a sophisticated interpretation of a complex problem or simply evidence of his economic naiveté remains the basis of rousing disagreement among historians. In Roosevelt's own time, social satirist Finley Peter Dunne had his fictional comic character, Mr. Dooley, poke fun at Roosevelt's ambiguity on the trust issue. Mr. Dooley said the president believed the trusts were "heejous monsthers built up be th' inlightened intherprise iv th' men that have done so much to advance progress in our beloved counthry."[2]

Theodore Roosevelt's position on business monopoly was well summarized in his State of the Union message, December 3, 1907. In it (see Exhibit 12–1), he denied that his policies represented "any hostility to corporations as such."[3]

EXHIBIT 12–1. THEODORE ROOSEVELT, STATE OF THE UNION MESSAGE, DECEMBER 3, 1907

. . . On the contrary, it means a frank recognition of the fact that combinations of capital, like combinations of labor, are a natural result of modern conditions and of our National development. As far as in my ability, my endeavor is and will be to prevent abuse of power by either and to favor both so long as they do well. The aim of the National Government is quite as much to favor and protect honest corporations, honest business men of wealth, as to bring to justice those individuals and corporations representing dishonest methods. Most certainly there will be no relaxation by the Government authorities in the effort to get at any great railroad wrecker—any man who by clever swindling devices robs investors, oppresses wage-workers, and does injustice to the general public. But any such move as this is in the interest of honest railway operators, of honest corporations, and of those who, when they invest their small savings in stocks and bonds, wish to be assured that these will represent money honestly expended for legitimate business purposes. . . .

The antitrust law should not be repealed; but it should be made both more efficient and more in harmony with actual conditions. It should be so amended as to forbid only the kind of combination which does harm to the general public, such amendment to be accompanied by, or to be an incident of, a grant of supervisory power to the Government over these big concerns engaged in interstate business. This should be accompanied by provision for the compulsory publication of accounts and the subjection of books and papers to the inspection of the Government officials. A beginning has already been made for such supervision by the establishment of the Bureau of Corporations.

The antitrust law should not prohibit combinations that do no injustice to the public, still less those the existence of which is on the whole of benefit to the public. But even if this feature of the law were abolished, there would remain as an equally objectionable feature the difficulty and delay now incident to its enforcement. The Government must now submit to irksome and repeated delay before obtaining a final decision of the courts upon proceedings instituted, and even a favorable decree may mean an empty victory. Moreover, to attempt to control these corporations by lawsuits means to impose upon both the Department of Justice and the courts an impossible burden; it is not feasible to carry on more than a limited number of such suits. Such a law to be really effective must of course be administered by an executive body, and not merely by means of lawsuits. The design should be to prevent the abuses incident to the creation of unhealthy and improper combinations, instead of waiting until they are in existence and then attempting to destroy them by civil or criminal proceedings.

A combination should not be tolerated if it abuses the power acquired by combination to the public detriment. No corporation or association of any kind should be permitted to engage in foreign or interstate commerce that is formed for the purpose of, or whose operations create, a monopoly or general control of the production, sale, or distribution of any one or more of the prime necessities of life or articles of general use and necessity. Such combinations are against public policy; they violate the common law; the doors of the courts are closed to those who are parties to them, and I believe the Congress can close the channels of interstate commerce against them for its protection. The law should make its prohibitions and permissions as clear and definite as possible, leaving the least possible room for arbitrary action or allegation of such action, on the part of the Executive, or of divergent interpretations by the courts. Among the points to be aimed at should be the prohibition of unhealthy competition, such as by rendering service at an actual loss for the purpose of crushing out competition, the prevention of inflation of capital, and the prohibition of a corporation's making exclusive trade with itself a condition of having any trade with itself. Reasonable agreements between, or combinations of, corporations should be permitted, provided they are submitted to and approved by some appropriate Government body.

The Congress has the power to charter corporations to engage in interstate and foreign commerce, and a general law can be enacted under the provisions of which existing corporations could take out Federal charters and new Federal corporations could be created. An essential provision of such a law should be a method of predetermining by some Federal board or commission whether the applicant for a Federal charter was an association or combination within the restrictions of the Federal law. Provision should also be made for complete publicity in all matters affecting the public and complete protection to the investing public and the shareholders in the matter of issuing corporate securities. If an incorporation law is not deemed advisable, a license act for big interstate corporations might be enacted; or a combination of the two might be tried. The supervision established might be analogous to that now exercised over national banks. At least, the antitrust act should be supplemented by specific prohibitions of the methods which experience has shown have been of most service in enabling monopolistic combinations to crush out competition. The real owners of a corporation should be compelled to do business in their own name. The right to hold stock in other corporations should hereafter be denied to interstate corporations, unless on approval by the Government officials, and a prerequisite to such approval should be the listing with the Government of all owners and stockholders, both by the corporation owning such stock and by the corporation in which such stock is owned.

Roosevelt's call for the recognition of the inevitability of economic combinations and the use of government regulation to police them was strongly reiterated in his unsuccessful campaign to regain the presidency in 1912. His program of New Nationalism was vigorously opposed by a second founding father of the antitrust movement, Woodrow Wilson. A Princeton University scholar and former president of that university, Wilson was, in 1912, the governor of New Jersey and the Democratic party's candidate for president. He talked at length in that election year of emancipating business, of creating a New Freedom for all Americans economically, and of his implacable opposition to artificial monopolies.

Where for Roosevelt the Sherman Antitrust Act was a weapon of limited utility, for Wilson it was the lever by which monopolies could be overthrown and competitive conditions restored in the American economy. In the 1912 campaign, Wilson ran against Theodore Roosevelt, who was on the Progressive party ticket, and against the Republican nominee, William Howard Taft. Throughout the campaign Wilson expressed his own thoughts, mixed with those of Louis D. Brandeis, a lawyer and Wilson's closest economic advisor. As Arthur S. Link, Wilson's preeminent biographer, has written: "Brandeis was also probably the chief spokesman of the philosophy of regulated competition, unhampered enterprise, and'economic freedom for the small businessman. And it was Brandeis who clarified Wilson's thought and led him to believe the most vital question confronting the American people was preservation of economic freedom in the United States."[4]

As a result, Wilson's New Freedom speeches centered upon "the means by which business could be set free from the shackles of monopoly and special privilege." In one of those speeches (see Exhibit 12-2), Wilson explained at length his perception of the trust problem.[5]

EXHIBIT 12-2. WOODROW WILSON, THE NEW FREEDOM

I admit the popularity of the theory that the trusts have come about through the natural development of business conditions in the United States, and that it is a mistake to try to oppose the processes by which they have been built up, because those processes belong to the very nature of business in our time, and that therefore the only thing we can do, and the only thing we ought to attempt to do, is to accept them as inevitable arrangements and make the best out of it that we can by regulation.

I answer, nevertheless, that this attitude rests upon a confusion of thought. Big business is no doubt to a large extent necessary and natural. The development of business upon a great scale, upon a great scale of cooperation, is inevitable, and, let me add, is probably desirable. But that is a very different matter from the development of trusts, because the trusts have not grown. They have been artificially created; they have been put together, not by natural processes, but by the will, the deliberate planning will, of men who were more powerful than their neighbors in the business world, and who wished to make their power secure against competition.

The trusts do not belong to the period of infant industries. They are not the products of the time, that old laborious time, when the great continent we live on was undeveloped, the young nation struggling to find itself and get upon its feet amidst older and more experienced competitors. They belong to a very recent and very sophisticated age, when men knew what they wanted and knew how to get it by the favor of the government.

Did you ever look into the way a trust was made? It is very natural, in one sense, in the same sense in which human greed is natural. If I haven't efficiency enough to beat my rivals, then the thing I am inclined to do is to get together with my rivals and say: "Don't let's cut each other's throats; let's combine and determine prices for ourselves;

determine the output, and thereby determine the prices: and dominate and control the market." That is very natural. That has been done ever since freebooting was established. That has been done ever since power was used to establish control. The reason that the masters of combination have sought to shut out competition is that the basis of control under competition is brains and efficiency. I admit that any large corporation built up by the legitimate processes of business, by economy, by efficiency, is natural; and I am not afraid of it, no matter how big it grows. It can stay big only by doing its work more thoroughly than anybody else. And there is a point of bigness,—as every business man in this country knows, though some of them will not admit it,—where you pass the limit of efficiency and get into the region of clumsiness and unwieldiness. You can make your combine so extensive that you can't digest it into a single system; you can get so many parts that you can't assemble them as you would an effective piece of machinery. The point of efficiency is overstepped in the natural process of development oftentimes, and it has been overstepped many times in the artificial and deliberate formation of trusts.

A trust is formed in this way; a few gentlemen "promote" it—that is to say, they get it up, being given enormous fees for their kindness, which fees are loaded on to the undertaking in the form of securities of one kind or another. The argument of the promoters is, not that every one who comes into the combination can carry on his business more efficiently than he did before; the argument is: we will assign to you as your share in the pool twice, three times, four times, or five times what you could have sold your business for to an individual competitor who would have to run it on an economic and competitive basis. We can afford to buy it at such a figure because we are shutting out competition. We can afford to make the stock of the combination half a dozen times what it naturally would be and pay dividends on it, because there will be nobody to dispute the prices we shall fix.

Talk of that as sound business? Talk of that as inevitable? It is based upon nothing except power. It is not based upon efficiency. It is no wonder that the big trusts are not prospering in proportion to such competitors as they still have in such parts of their business as competitors have access to; they are prospering freely only in those fields to which competition has no access. . . .

Why? Why, with unlimited capital and innumerable mines and plants everywhere in the United States, can't they beat the other fellows in the market? Partly because they are carrying too much. Partly because they are unwieldy. Their organization is imperfect. They bought up inefficient plants along with efficient, and they have got to carry what they have paid for, even if they have to shut some of the plants up in order to make any interest on their investments; or, rather, not interest on their investments, because that is an incorrect word,—on their alleged capitalization. Here we have a lot of giants staggering along under an almost intolerable weight of artificial burdens, which they have put on their own backs, and constantly looking about lest some little pigmy with a round stone in a sling may come out and slay them.

For my part, I want the pigmy to have a chance to come out. And I foresee a time when the pigmies will be so much more athletic, so much more astute, so much more active, than the giants, that it will be a case of Jack the giant-killer. Just let some of the youngsters I know have a chance and they'll give these gentlemen points. Lend them a little money. They can't get any now. See to it that when they have got a local market they can't be squeezed out of it. Give them a chance to capture that market and then see them capture another one and another one, until these men who are carrying an intolerable load of artificial securities find that they have got to get down to hard pan to keep their foothold at all. I am willing to let Jack come into the field with the giant, and if Jack has the brains that some Jacks that I know in America have, then I should like to see the giant get the better of him, with the load that he, the giant, has to carry—the load of water. For I'll undertake to put a water-logged giant out of business any time, if you will give me a fair field and as much credit as I am entitled to, and let the law do what from time immemorial law has been expected to do,—see fair play. . . .

The regulated monopoly espoused by Theodore Roosevelt and the regulated competition advocated by Wilson and Brandeis were two differing approaches to the problem of concentration of economic power. They were not, however, the only approaches being offered at the time.

The business community itself put forward an approach based upon the concept of industrial self-government. This concept included as its basic principles the elimination of price competition, the development of trade associations, and friendly governmental cooperation. One source for these ideas can be found in the activities of executives in the steel industry during the first decade of the twentieth century. The United States Steel Corporation, unable to forcibly eliminate price-setting competition in the industry despite its awesome size, sought to achieve stability through mutual agreement with its competitors.

In 1907, Judge Elbert H. Gary, U.S. Steel's chairman of the board, inaugurated a series of regular dinners at which steel producers met and arrived at mutually acceptable decisions on prices. Even though the dinners were abandoned after a few years, they pointed the way to even more sophisticated techniques for avoiding the rigors of price-setting competition. The philosophy behind achieving acceptable prices was expounded by Gary himself in his 1910 presidential address to the newly organized American Iron and Steel Institute. According to Gary:

> Real, hearty, cheerful and continued cooperation on the part of the members will secure results which should be entirely satisfactory. Frank and friendly intercourse; full disclosure of his business by each to the others; recognition by all of the rights of each; a disposition to assist and benefit each other so far as practicable and proper; conduct founded on the belief that healthy competition is wiser and better than destructive competition; all these are desirable and necessary and will be effective.[6]

Two years later, in 1912, Gary's endorsement of "healthy competition" was broadened into a new interpretation of business competition. Arthur J. Eddy, a Chicago lawyer whose specialty was the establishment of industrial trade associations, authored a lengthy treatise advocating the elimination of price warfare. Calling his concept the New Competition, Eddy denounced the Sherman Antitrust Act's champions as hopeless reactionaries and asked for the repeal of antitrust legislation. In its place Eddy called for laws that would legalize industrial trade association activities, such as price and output fixing, and that would be overseen by the federal government.

Eddy's arguments foreshadowed the policy that was pursued by Herbert Hoover in the 1920s as secretary of commerce during the Harding and Coolidge administrations (see Chapter 11). Hence Eddy, writing in 1912, was the quasi prophet of the relationship between business and government that developed in the 1920s. Eddy's book, *The New Competition*, contained a very forceful argument (see Exhibit 12–3).[7]

EXHIBIT 12–3. ARTHUR J. EDDY,
FROM *THE NEW COMPETITION*, 1912

Competition is a fetish that men ignorantly worship, but the cult has had its day, the sanctity of the god is being assailed, the people are waking up and asking:

"What is this competition and why should it be hedged about and preserved?"

The country merchant asks himself: "Why is it a good thing for me to undersell the man across the way and try to drive him out of business?

Why is it a good thing for him to undersell me and try to drive me out of business?"

If either succeeds, will not a stranger take the loser's place?

The country mechanic asks himself: "Why should I work for less than others in the foolish effort to starve them out of the village? Why should they try to take the bread from my mouth by working for less than I must have to support my family? What gain is there in that sort of competition?"

The labor union says to its members: "You shall not compete one against another by offering to work for lower wages or longer hours, that sort of competition is dead."

The tendency with the unions is to go a step further and say: "You shall not even compete in the amount of work you do per day, but each man shall do so much and no more." A crude solution of a pressing problem; a very curt answer to the proposition, "Competition is the life of trade. . . ."

Times are changing and, with the times, business methods. Secrecy is yielding to publicity, men are coming out into the open and dealing more fairly with one another. As an inevitable result competition is undergoing a change, the old is giving way to a new, true competition is taking the place of the false.

The country feels that things are happening, but they are happening so fast it does not quite comprehend. The people do not understand the new competition that is slowly but surely taking the place of the old, courts do not understand it, legislatures do not understand it, therefore they oppose it and vainly try to preserve the old and vicious order of things—try to make men fight when they no longer wish to fight, to make them destroy one another industrially and commercially when they are striving to establish industrial and commercial peace.

The old cry, "Competition is the life of trade," is yielding to the new cry, "Cooperation is trade." The old cry is the echo of primitive and barbaric conditions; it never did mean competition on terms of fairness and equality, it meant the relentless suppression of the weak, the merciless triumph of the strong, it meant methods so questionable they are now condemned as criminal.

The old, with its unfair advantages, its secret prices and rebates, its conspiracies to ruin competitors, help favored parties, localities, towns, at the expense of others, is passing; the new is taking its place, is winning its way in spite of ignorant clamor, regardless of legislative enactments, in the face of hampering decisions; it is winning its way because, fundamentally, it is right—it is progress. . . .

The first step toward the development of the new competition in any given industry is to bring the hostile units together, make them acquainted, allay their distrust, induce them to abandon the played-out policy of secrecy, and to agree to exchange information along the lines enumerated—in short, to do business on a frank and straightforward basis.

To the small or the isolated manufacturer this sort of cooperation is of far greater importance than to the large concern centrally located. In many industries the time is at hand when the small producer will be able to exist only in cooperation with the large.

The new competition helps the small producer by giving him the benefit of information and valuable data possessed by the large; it shows him where he can rightfully and successfully compete, it marks out the field that is legitimately his.

It is not easy to get rival manufacturers to agree to file for the benefit of all interested the bids and prices they make, but it has been tried, and the new competition works better than the old.

It is not easy to make men who have habitually referred to competitors as rascals and liars admit that they are not—but it has been done, and herein is the new competition better than the old. . . .

Of all the peoples on the face of the globe the American people ought to be the least fearful of mere size.

But we are—or rather have been, for fear of size is passing. We have framed laws aimed not at methods but at magnitude. We passed the Sherman Act which is aimed at size, and for many years the courts applied that act to combinations irrespective whether the things they did were fair and reasonable or not, but of late a change has come over the country, our eyes are becoming accustomed to magnitude, no longer do we jump at the sight of a trust like a small boy at a shadow in the dusk; we are beginning to see that size has its advantages as well as its disadvantages; that it enables men to do things on a scale commensurable with the wealth, the resources, the power of the country—in short that the much feared, much hated trust may have its place in the economy of national and international trade.

While those opposing philosophies on big business were being expounded, the machinery of public authority also was responding to the challenge of big business. Part of that machinery was judicial—more specifically the Supreme Court of the United States. The Court was responsible for determining the meaning of legislation passed by Congress—in this case the Sherman Antitrust Act of 1890.

The Sherman Antitrust Act, according to the legislators who had devised it, was based on the tradition of English common law. Prohibitions existed in common law against both contracts and combinations whose effect tended to be the restraint of trade and commerce. On the surface, therefore, it appeared that the Sherman Antitrust Act had simply codified the common law prohibitions and added specific legal penalties.

Matters were not quite that clear-cut, however. English precedent recognized a distinction between contracts that, because of their scope or other special circumstances, could be regarded as reasonable and contracts that could not. These variables, however, did not seem to be reflected in the words of the Sherman Antitrust Act, which stated that "every contract, combination in the form of trust or otherwise, or conspiracy, in restraint of trade" was illegal. Had the Congress really intended to outlaw *every* such combination, or was its intention simply to move against those always considered illegal under the common law?

After some false starts, the Supreme Court offered an answer in 1911 in *Standard Oil Company of New Jersey* v. *United States*. While the Court did order the dissolution of the Standard Oil Trust, it also laid down what came to be known as "the rule of reason." Speaking through Chief Justice Edward D. White, the Supreme Court inserted into the antitrust law the doctrine that, while the Sherman Antitrust Act prohibited "every" combination in restraint of trade, those words should be understood to mean only those combinations that "unreasonably" restrain trade. Reasonable monopolies were thus presumably legal, and judges had the responsibility to determine which ones were in the public interest, according to the circumstances of each case and whatever other criteria the courts might feel in the mood to apply.

In actuality, White's rule of reason was simply the Supreme Court's formal version of Theodore Roosevelt's distinction between good trusts and bad trusts. If the judiciary seemed to be supporting Roosevelt, a plurality of Americans did otherwise in the following year when they elected Woodrow Wilson president. Soon after taking office, Wilson saw his views on business monopoly embodied in legislation authored by Representative Henry Clayton of Alabama, the chairman of the House Judiciary Committee. Clayton's final bill, however, proved less fearsome than many antimonopoly reformers had wished it to be. The provisions that outlawed specific business practices did so only when their effect was to "substantially" lessen competition. Thus, interpretation was still required, and the courts continued to play a key role in formulating antitrust policy. The Clayton Antitrust Act of 1914, while broadening the Sherman Antitrust Act, did not void the rule-of-reason doctrine.

The permanence of that doctrine was insured by the Supreme Court's decision in a case involving the U.S. Steel Corporation, the nation's largest industrial enterprise at that time. Although the decision was announced in 1920, prosecution of the steel giant had begun almost a decade before that, during the administration of President Taft. The ruling of the Court, written by Justice Joseph McKenna, left little doubt that mere bigness, in and of itself, was not to be considered a violation of the antitrust laws. On that point, McKenna's opinion read:

> The corporation is undoubtedly of impressive size, and it takes an effort of resolution not to be affected by it or to exaggerate its influence. But we must adhere to the law, and the law does not make mere size an offense, or the existence of unexerted power an offense. It, we regret, requires overt acts, and trusts to its prohibition of them and its power to repress or punish them. It does not compel competition, nor require all that is possible.[8]

Richard Hofstadter, who had characterized the years before 1914 as the era of the founding fathers of antitrust, termed the two decades after the passage of the Clayton Antitrust Act as antitrust's "era of neglect."[9] Statistics would seem to bear out that description. Prosecutions instituted by the Justice Department fluctuated between a low of only 3 in some years to a high of just 22. These numbers were considerably short of the 29 prosecutions begun in 1912, when antitrust feelings reached their pre–World War I high, and of the 85 begun in 1940 during Thurman Arnold's tenure as head of the Justice Department's Antitrust Division.

The Wilson administration's need of support from the business establishment in the war effort against Germany was accompanied on the economic front by a retreat in the battle against trusts. Following the return of the Republicans to the White House in 1921, the ties between business and government were strengthened all the more. The prosperity that the United States enjoyed in the 1920s was credited to American business, and the government was not ungrateful. The government's lack of concern for the issue of trusts was shown in Calvin Coolidge's 1926 State of the Union message. Coolidge's reference to regulation of business was only one-third as long as his discussion of the nation's overseas insular possessions. Thus far had the public policy of antitrust fallen.

The onset of the Great Depression in 1929 and the election of Franklin Delano Roosevelt (FDR) in 1932 brought no immediate change in public policy toward trusts or monopolies. Despite the fact that FDR's inaugural address in March 1933 was marked by references to "unscrupulous money changers" and to the "rulers of the exchange of mankind's good" who had failed the nation "through their own stubbornness and their own incompetence," it was not the new president's intention to establish an antibusiness administration.[10] Rather, he borrowed more from Theodore Roosevelt and Arthur J. Eddy than he did from the statesman he claimed to most admire, Woodrow Wilson. The essence of the early New Deal was to achieve the rehabilitation of the nation through a coordinated partnership of all sectors in the economy.

The FDR of 1933 had faith that a united effort of business, labor, and government could be forged, and sacrificing impediments to cooperation, such as
antitrust laws, was not too high a price to pay. The National Industrial Recovery
Act (NIRA) of 1933 was the primary instrument of the early New Deal program.
The NIRA established the National Recovery Administration (NRA), which was
to supervise the preparation of "codes of fair competition." The codes, drawn up
by businessmen from various industries, might have been regarded at other times
as illegal price-fixing and collusion. The NRA, however, gave the codes its bless-
ing. In a "fireside chat" on the evening of May 7, 1933, President Roosevelt
explained and defended the NRA's approach (see Exhibit 12–4).[11]

EXHIBIT 12–4. FRANKLIN DELANO ROOSEVELT, FIRESIDE CHAT, 1933

It is wholly wrong to call the measures that we have taken Government
control of farming, control of industry, and control of transportation. It is
rather a partnership between Government and farming and industry and
transportation—not partnership in profits, for the profits would still go to
the citizens, but rather a partnership in planning and partnership to see
that the plans are carried out.

Let me illustrate with an example. Take the cotton-goods industry. It is
probably true that 90 percent of the cotton manufacturers would agree to
eliminate starvation wages, would agree to stop long hours of
employment, would agree to stop child labor, would agree to prevent an
overproduction that would result in unsalable surpluses. But, what good is
such an agreement if the other 10 percent of cotton manufacturers pay
starvation wages, require long hours, employ children in their mills, and
turn out burdensome surpluses? The unfair 10 percent could produce
goods so cheaply that the fair 90 percent would be compelled to meet the
unfair conditions.

Here is where Government comes in. Government ought to have the
right and will have the right, after surveying and planning for an industry,
to prevent, with the assistance of the overwhelming majority of that
industry, unfair practice and to enforce this agreement by the authority of
Government.

The so-called "antitrust laws" were intended to prevent the creation of
monopolies and to forbid unreasonable profits to those monopolies. That
purpose of the antitrust laws must be continued. But these laws were

never intended to encourage the kind of unfair competition that results in long hours, starvation wages, and overproduction.

The same principle applies to farm products and to transportation and every other field of organized private industry.

We are working toward a definite goal, which is to prevent the return of conditions which came very close to destroying what we call modern civilization. The actual accomplishment of our purpose cannot be attained in a day. Our policies are wholly within purposes for which our American constitutional Government was established 150 years ago.

The hopeful and even enthusiastic atmosphere in which the NRA's effort began in 1933 soon gave way to bickering, controversy, and disillusionment. When the Supreme Court in 1935 unanimously declared the National Industrial Recovery Act unconstitutional, the NRA had already outlived its usefulness as a vehicle for recovery. Five years later, Clair Wilcox, an economist at Swarthmore College, in summarizing the NRA's record for a congressional study, related that record to the American antitrust tradition (see Exhibit 12-5).[12]

EXHIBIT 12-5. CLAIR WILCOX, FROM *COMPETITION AND MONOPOLY IN AMERICAN INDUSTRY*, 1940

The "codes of fair competition" which governed American industry during the life of the N.R.A. were exempt from the prohibitions of the anti-trust laws. Violation of any of their provisions was made an unfair method of competition subject to action by the Federal Trade Commission, and a misdemeanor punishable by a fine of $500 for every day in which it occurred. These codes were originated, almost without exception, by trade associations. The code authorities which were set up to administer them were largely composed of or selected by trade associations. The personnel and the policies of these authorities were controlled by trade associations. In three cases out of four, the code authority secretary and the trade association secretary bore the same name and did business at the same address. . . . The program thus involved a virtual delegation to trade associations of the powers of government, including in many cases the power to tax.

The N.R.A. undertook, in the words of its own declaration of policy, "to build up and strengthen trade associations throughout all commerce and industry." It conferred new powers and immunities on strong associations, invigorated weak associations, aroused moribund associations, consolidated small associations, and called some eight hundred new associations into life. It sought to employ these agencies as instruments in the promotion of industrial recovery. But many of the provisions which it permitted them to write into their codes were ill designed to achieve this end. . . .

Of the first 677 codes, 560 contained some provision for the direct or indirect control of prices. Of these, 361 provided for the establishment of standard costing systems; 403 prohibited sales below "cost"; 352 forbade members to sell below their individual "costs"; and 51 forbade them to sell below some average of the whole industry's "costs." Thirty-nine standard costing systems were approved by the N.R.A. In many cases, the adoption of a common formula for use in the determination of individual "costs" led to the establishment of an arbitrary minimum price. . . .

Some 200 codes provided for the establishment of minimum prices in the event of an "emergency." When a code authority found that "destructive price cutting" had created an "emergency," it was empowered to determine the "lowest reasonable costs" of producing the goods involved and to fix prices which would cover these costs. These concepts were never clearly defined. "An emergency," it was said, "is something that is declared by a code authority." According to spokesmen for the retail solid fuel trade, "We have always had an emergency in retail solid fuel. . . . " "Emergencies" were also declared among manufacturers of agricultural insecticides and fungicides, cast iron soil pipe, and mayonnaise and salad dressing, and among dealers in ice, lumber and timber products, tires, tobacco, and waste paper. Such declarations afforded members of these trades an opportunity to arrive at "cost determinations" which could be used to justify high minimum prices. The history of the N.R.A. gives evidence that they made the most of this opportunity. . . .

The codes were invalidated by the decision of the Supreme Court in the Schechter case in 1935. But their provisions are still significant. They had their origin in the activities carried on by trade associations prior to 1933. They have persisted, in large measure, in the activities carried on by such associations since 1935. . . . The movement toward "self government in industry" has been checked, but not reversed. The logical outcome of this movement, as it is revealed by the contents of codes, is the collective determination of prices, the curtailment of output, the allocation of markets, and production, and the enforcement of these arrangements by the imposition of penalties; in short, the complete cartelization of American business.

The period of neglect for antitrust activity ended in 1938 when the economy, which until the final quarter of 1937 appeared to be on the road to recovery, showed a sudden downturn. This new crisis in the economy thrust the advocates of vigorous antitrust action into leadership positions within FDR's administration. Actually, the disciples of Wilson's New Freedom crusade of 1912 had never accepted FDR's national planning approach of the early New Deal. Cheered on by antitrust leaders such as Robert Jackson, Thomas Corcoran, and Harold Ickes in the executive branch and by populists such as William E. Borah of Idaho and Joseph C. O'Mahoney of Wyoming in the Senate, FDR signaled his change of direction policy on antitrust in a special message to Congress on April 29, 1938 (see Exhibit 12–6). His emphasis then, unlike five years before, was on the dangers of concentrated corporate power.[13]

EXHIBIT 12–6. FRANKLIN DELANO ROOSEVELT, MESSAGE TO CONGRESS, APRIL 29, 1933

Among us today a concentration of private power without equal in history is growing.

This concentration is seriously impairing the economic effectiveness of private enterprise as a way of providing employment for labor and capital and as a way of assuring a more equitable distribution of income and earnings among the people of the nation as a whole.

Statistics of the Bureau of Internal Revenue reveal the following amazing figures for 1935:

Ownership of corporate assets:

Of all corporations reporting from every part of the nation, one-tenth of 1 per cent of them owned 52 per cent of the assets of all of them; and to clinch the point:

Of all corporations reporting, less than 5 per cent of them owned 87 per cent of all the assets of all of them.

Income and profits of corporations:

Of all the corporations reporting from every part of the country, one-tenth of 1 per cent of them earned 50 per cent of the net income of all of them;

and to clinch the point:

Of all the manufacturing corporations reporting, less than 4 per cent of them earned 84 per cent of all the net profits of all of them.

The statistical history of modern times proves that in times of depression concentration of business speeds up. Bigger business then has larger opportunity to grow still bigger at the expense of smaller competitors who are weakened by financial adversity.

The danger of this centralization in a handful of huge corporations is not reduced or eliminated, as is sometimes urged, by the wide public distribution of their securities. The mere number of security-holders gives little clue to the size of their individual holdings or to their actual ability to have a voice in the management. . . .

Private enterprise is ceasing to be free enterprise and is becoming a cluster of private collectivisms: masking itself as a system of free enterprise after the American model, it is in fact becoming a concealed cartel system after the European model.

We all want efficient industrial growth and the advantages of mass production. No one suggests that we return to the hand loom or hand forge. A series of processes involved in turning out a given manufactured product may well require one or more huge mass production plants. Modern efficiency may call for this. But modern efficient mass production is not furthered by a central control which destroys competition among industrial plants each capable of efficient mass production while operating as separate units. Industrial efficiency does not have to mean industrial empire building. . . .

The traditional approach to the problems I have discussed has been through the anti-trust laws. That approach we do not propose to abandon. On the contrary, although we must recognize the inadequacies of the existing laws, we seek to enforce them so that the public shall not be deprived of such protection as they afford. To enforce them properly requires thorough investigation not only to discover such violations as may exist but to avoid hit-and-miss prosecutions harmful to business and government alike. To provide for the proper and fair enforcement of the existing anti-trust laws I shall submit, through the budget, recommendations for a deficiency appropriation of $200,000 for the Department of Justice.

But the existing anti-trust laws are inadequate—most importantly because of new financial economic conditions with which they are powerless to cope.

The Sherman Act was passed nearly forty years ago. The Clayton and Federal Trade Commission Acts were passed over twenty years ago. We have had considerable experience under those acts. In the meantime we have had a chance to observe the practical operation of large-scale industry and to learn many things about the competitive system which we did not know in those days. . . .

No man of good faith will misinterpret these proposals. They derive from the oldest American traditions. Concentration of economic power in the few and the resulting unemployment of labor and capital are inescapable problems for a modern "private enterprise" democracy. I do not believe that we are so lacking in stability that we shall lose faith in our own way of living just because we seek to find out how to make that way of living work more effectively.

Roosevelt's message to Congress in 1938 might be regarded as the overture to a new era in antitrust history. In the same year, he appointed Thurman Arnold, a colorful, voluble, and energetic professor in Yale's law school, assistant attorney general to head the Antitrust Division of the Justice Department. Arnold, as the new assistant attorney general, more than quadrupled the number of attorneys in his division, added economists to the staff for the first time, and made sure that the activities of his division were given considerable publicity. The case level of the Antitrust Division soon reached over 50 per year and climbed even higher, as Arnold further modernized the Antitrust Division.

Prosecuting several industries at a time, Arnold focused particularly on pro-tecting consumers and on increasing their purchasing power. He instituted cases against firms in the aluminum, automobile, construction, movie, petroleum, and shoe industries. Unlike many antitrust partisans, however, he found nothing es-sentially holy about small-scale enterprises and also prosecuted small firms that violated the antitrust laws. His approach to enforcement was more pragmatic than ideological. Arnold was a puzzle to many observers. One magazine article said of him: "He enjoys the distinction of being the only New Dealer who is also an Elk, and very likely the only Elk who is also an iconoclast."[14]

Arnold was not predictable. As one historian has written of him: "Just when big business was convinced of his unquenchable hostility, Arnold launched a massive suit against labor unions with the same intensity that he demonstrated in his direc-tion of the proceedings against the petroleum industry." He regarded the Sherman Antitrust Act as an imperfect but workable instrument that only re-quired a willingness to use it on the part of the responsible public authorities. Hence, he emphasized enforcing the Sherman Antitrust Act and obtained dra-matic results.

Arnold's administration of the Antitrust Division was the first one to be con-sumer oriented. He told a group of Oregon lawyers in 1939: "The idea of antitrust laws is to create a situation in which competition compels the passing on to the consumers the savings of mass distribution and production." One of Arnold's books, *The Bottlenecks of Business*, has been called "an economic and political platform for the consumer."[15] Certainly the consumer movement that rose to prominence in the 1960s was foreshadowed by Thurman Arnold's work in the Justice Department two decades before.

Arnold eventually resigned his post at the Justice Department in 1943 when he accepted a presidential appointment to the United States Circuit Court of Appeals. Arnold's new appointment was recommended by leading members of FDR's administration who had come to believe that Arnold's antitrust campaign was interfering with the war effort. Although Arnold argued strenuously that antitrust suits could aid wartime mobilization by preventing profiteering, FDR's advisors, led by Secretary of War Henry Stimson, accused Arnold of impeding production by frightening the business community. Several years later, Arnold, still bitter over being eased out of the Antitrust Division, stated: "FDR, recognizing that he could have only one war at a time, was content to declare a truce in the fight against monopoly."[16]

Ironically, Arnold's most important single legal victory came in *United States v. Aluminum Company of America*, which was not settled until 1945—two years after he had taken his seat on the federal bench. Alcoa (Aluminum Company of America), formed in 1888, was the sole domestic producer of aluminum ingots when it was prosecuted 50 years later. The U.S. government charged that Alcoa's monopolistic position was in itself a violation of the Sherman Antitrust Act. Alcoa, on the other hand, contended that it was not a monopoly because it had never earned extortionate profits or engaged in predatory behavior.

The case was decided by the distinguished jurist, Learned Hand, in the Court of Appeals for the Second Circuit because the Supreme Court was unable to muster a quorum of six justices to hear the case. Hand's ruling was thus regarded as the equivalent of a Supreme Court decision. In an elegantly written opinion, Judge Hand rejected Alcoa's plea that it was a well-behaved, natural monopoly and thus not in violation of the Sherman Antitrust Act (see Exhibit 12–7).[17]

EXHIBIT 12–7. UNITED STATES v. ALUMINUM COMPANY OF AMERICA, JUDGE LEARNED HAND, 1945

Was this a monopoly within the meaning of Section 2? The judge found that, over the whole half century of its existence, "Alcoa's" profits upon capital invested, after payment of income taxes, had been only about ten percent, and, although the plaintiff puts this figure a little higher, the difference is negligible. . . . This assumed, it would be hard to say that "Alcoa" had made exorbitant profits on ingot, if it is proper to allocate the profit upon the whole business proportionately among all its products—ingot, and fabrications from ingot. A profit of ten percent in such an industry, dependent, in part at any rate, upon continued tariff protection, and subject to the vicissitudes of new demands, to the obsolescence of plant and process—which can never be accurately gauged in advance—to the chance that substitutes may at any moment be discovered which will reduce the demand, and to the other hazards which attend all industry; a profit of ten percent, so conditioned, could hardly be considered extortionate. . . .

. . . But the whole issue is irrelevant anyway, for it is no excuse "for monopolizing" a market that the monopoly has not been used to extract from the consumer more than a "fair" profit. The Act has wider purposes. Indeed, even though we disregarded all but economic considerations, it would by no means follow that such concentration of producing power is to be desired, when it has not been used extortionately. Many people believe that possession of unchallenged economic power deadens initiative, discourages thrift and depresses energy; that immunity from competition is a narcotic, and rivalry is a stimulant, to industrial progress; that the spur of constant stress is necessary to counteract an inevitable disposition to let well enough alone. Such people believe that competitors, versed in the craft as no consumer can be, will be quick to detect opportunities for saving and new shifts in production, and be eager to profit by them. In any event the mere fact that a producer, having command of the domestic market, has not been able to make more than a "fair" profit, is no evidence that a "fair" profit could not have been made at lower prices. . . . True, it might have been thought adequate to condemn only those monopolies which could not show that they had exercised the highest possible ingenuity, had adopted every possible economy, had anticipated every conceivable improvement, stimulated every possible demand. No doubt, that would be one way of dealing with the matter, although it would imply constant scrutiny and constant supervision, such as courts are unable to provide. Be that as it may, that was not the way that Congress chose; it did not condone "good trusts" and condemn "bad" ones; it forbade all. Moreover, in so doing it was not necessarily actuated by economic motives alone. It is possible, because of its indirect social or moral effect, to prefer a system of small producers, each dependent for his success upon his own skill and character, to one in which the great mass of those engaged must accept the direction of few. These considerations, which we have suggested only as possible purposes of the Act, we think the decisions prove to have been in fact its purposes.

The government's victory in the Alcoa case was a limited one for the antitrust advocates, however. Because very few, if any, companies ever approached the dominance of an industry as Alcoa had, Hand's ruling was of restricted value. The rule of reason had been modified, not repealed outright, and industrial monopolies that lacked any domestic competition would continue.

For a variety of reasons, a vigorous program of antitrust litigation did not develop following the conclusion of World War II. Business managers took greater care to avoid possible antitrust law violations; the Justice Department was frequently willing to settle matters out of court; and new forms of business combinations—particularly conglomerates that resulted from mergers—seemed to be outside the scope of existing legislation. Furthermore, with the development of the Cold War, the federal government tended to regard industry as a partner in building the nation's defense system. Thus the departure of Thurman Arnold from the Justice Department represented the end of an era—an era in which government's role in the control of business was among the central issues in American politics.

Notes

1. Richard Hofstadter, "What Happened to the Antitrust Movement?" *The Business Establishment*, Earl F. Cheit, ed. (New York: John Wiley & Sons, 1964), 115.

2. William F. Harbaugh, *The Life and Times of Theodore Roosevelt*, new rev. ed. (New York: Oxford University Press, 1975), 154.

3. U.S. Congress, Senate, *Congressional Record*, 60th Cong., 1st sess., December 3, 1907.

4. Arthur S. Link, *Woodrow Wilson and the Progressive Era, 1910–1917* (New York: Harper & Row, 1954), 20–21.

5. Woodrow Wilson, *The New Freedom* (New York: Doubleday, Page & Co., 1913), 164–191.

6. *American Iron and Steel Institute Yearbook* (1910), pp. 33f.

7. Arthur J. Eddy, *The New Competition* (New York: D. Appleton & Co., 1912), 339–342.

8. United States v. United States Steel Corporation et al., 251 U.S. 417 (1920).

9. Hofstadter, 115.

10. *The Public Papers and Addresses of Franklin D. Roosevelt* (New York: Random House), vol. 2, 11–12.

11. U.S. Congress, House, *Congressional Record*, 73rd Cong., 1st sess., May 8, 1933.

12. Clair Wilcox, *Competition and Monopoly in American Industry*, Monograph 21, Temporary National Economic Committee (Washington, D.C.: U.S. Government Printing Office, 1940), 259–267.

13. U.S. Congress, Senate, *Congressional Record*, 75th Cong., 3rd sess., April 29, 1938.

14. Joseph Alsop and Robert D. Kintner, "Trust Buster—the Folklore of Thurman Arnold," *Saturday Evening Post*, August 12, 1939, 5.

15. Gene M. Gressley, "Thurman Arnold, Antitrust, and the New Deal," *Business History Review* (Summer 1964): 214–231.

16. Thurman Arnold, "Must 1929 Repeat Itself?" *Harvard Business Review* (January 1948): 43.

17. United States v. Aluminum Company of America 148 F. 2d 416 (2d Cir. 1945).

QUESTIONS FOR REVIEW AND DISCUSSION

1. Contrast the arguments of Theodore Roosevelt and Woodrow Wilson on the issue of public policy toward big business. Who offered the more logical and reasonable case for an effective policy?

2. What difficulties, if any, would the U.S. economy have encountered had the policy advocated by Arthur J. Eddy been pursued by the nation?

3. Is the public policy of the United States today towards large-scale business enterprise always consistent with its public rhetoric on the subject? If it is not, why not?

4. In terms of how Americans today feel about big business, do they seem to favor the ideas of Theodore Roosevelt, Woodrow Wilson, Arthur J. Eddy, or Thurman Arnold? Of those leaders, who has had the greatest influence on contemporary antitrust policy?

5. Can a private business exercise monopolistic power in an industry and still be operating in the public interest? If this is possible, explain why it is.

13

Free Competition and Private Decision Making

In 1776, besides the signing of the Declaration of Independence, another event of lasting significance took place—Adam Smith's *The Wealth of Nations* was published. Smith's classic treatise forms the basis for much of modern economic theory. In it, Smith marveled at the beneficial economic effects wrought by the "invisible hand" of free competition. According to Smith, individual economic decision makers while pursuing their own private self-interests are guided by this invisible hand to work for the public good as well. Adam Smith, however, was describing a freely operating competitive marketplace, and in the real world such a condition of pure competition seldom exists. As one economist, Paul Samuelson, has written, "A cynic might say of perfect competition what Bernard Shaw said of Christianity: The only trouble with it is that it has never been tried."[1]

Business behavior, like human behavior in general, is diverse. Much of it promotes competition, while some business behavior is aimed at restricting or even eliminating competition altogether, especially in the area of pricing. The practice defined as illegal cooperation, collusion, or conspiracy, aims to restrict competition. Actually, it is a form of quasi monopoly because the conspirators reap the rewards of monopolistic power without having to take the formal steps, such as in a merger, that are necessary to establish a monopoly. One recent study summarized the effect of business collusion: "Done secretly, the collusion provides market power, and its fruits, higher prices and profits, beneath a surface illusion of competition."[2]

Collusion, particularly in its most blatant form of price-fixing, is so clearly and historically illegal that it is treated in the law under a so-called "per se rule." Price-fixing is illegal per se, and the government need only show at a trial that the defendants attempted to engage in the practice to secure conviction. The motive behind the attempt or whether the objective was ever achieved is not relevant. The conspiracy, if it is proved to exist, is illegal by itself.

The case study that follows traces the history, investigation, and prosecution of the largest and possibly one of the most shocking examples of business collusion in the twentieth century—an intricate conspiracy among the makers of heavy electrical equipment. The conspiracy was extraordinary not only for its complexity but also for its duration. In 1961 more than two dozen companies were found guilty of misconduct and, as rarely happens, seven corporate executives served brief jail sentences. Those convictions represented the largest criminal antitrust action in the history of the Sherman Antitrust Act. The companies involved paid fines totaling almost $2 million, and by pleading guilty, they opened themselves to civil damage suits filed by overcharged customers. Eventually, over $400 million was paid as a result of those damage suits.

The paradox, of course, lay in the fact that the top officials of the indicted companies publicly adhered to the timeless virtues of free competition while, at the same time, key members of those organizations worked assiduously to eliminate the uncertainties of competitive pricing. The question inevitably must be answered—was the conspiracy in the electrical industry only an exceptional case of corporate misconduct, or did it reveal a more endemic problem? Simply put, how real is the American business executive's commitment to the free enterprise principles that are the sum and substance of modern capitalism?

Notes

1. Paul A. Samuelson, *Economics*, 9th ed. (New York: McGraw-Hill Book Company, 1973), 43.

2. William G. Shepherd and Clair Wilcox, *Public Policies Toward Business*, 6th ed. (Homewood, Ill.: Richard D. Irwin, Inc., 1979), 195.

Richard Austin Smith

THE INCREDIBLE ELECTRICAL CONSPIRACY

As befitted the biggest criminal case in the history of the Sherman Act, most of the forty-five defendants arrived early, knocking the snow of Philadelphia's Chestnut Street from their shoes before taking the elevator to federal courtroom No. 3. Some seemed to find it as chill inside as out, for they kept their coats on and shifted from one foot to the other in the corridor, waiting silently for the big mahogany doors to open. On the other side of those doors was something none of them relished: judgment for having conspired to fix prices, rig bids, and divide markets on electrical equipment valued at $1,750,000,000 annually. The twenty indictments, under which they were now to be sentenced, charged they had conspired on everything from tiny $2 insulators to multimillion-dollar turbine generators and had persisted in the conspiracies for as long as eight years.

As a group, they looked like just what they were: well-groomed corporation executives in Ivy League suits, employed by companies ranging in size from Joslyn Manufacturing & Supply Co., whose shop space is scarcely larger than the courtroom itself, to billion-dollar giants like General Electric and Westinghouse. There was J. E. Cordell, ex-submariner, sales vice president of Southern States Equipment Corp., pillar of the community in a small Georgia town, though his

Richard Austin Smith, "The Incredible Electrical Conspiracy," *Fortune*, April 1961, pp. 132–137, 170–180, and May 1961, pp. 161–164, 210–224.

net worth never exceeded $25,000, and urbane William S. Ginn, G.E. vice president at $135,000 a year, a man once thought to be on his way to the presidency of the corporation. There was old, portly Fred F. Loock, president of Allen-Bradley Co., who found conspiring with competitors quite to his taste ("It is the only way a business can be run. It is free enterprise."), and G.E.'s Marc A. deFerranti, who pocketed his repugnance on orders from his boss. There was M. H. Howard, a production manager of Foster Wheeler, who found it hard to stay in the conspiracy (his company's condenser business ran in the red during two years of it), and C. H. Wheeler Manufacturing's President Thomas, who found it hard to quit—he'd been told his firm couldn't survive if he left the cartel.

At nine-thirty the courtroom doors opened and everyone trooped in. It was a huge room, paneled in mahogany with carved pilasters that reached up thirty feet or more to a white ceiling; yet big as it was it very soon filled with tension. What the defendants were thinking of was not hard to guess: the possibility of prison; the careers ruined after decades of service; the agile associates who weren't there, the ones who had saved their hides by implicating others.

Shortly after ten o'clock, Judge J. Cullen Ganey, chief judge of the U.S. District Court, entered the courtroom. He had earned a reputation in his twenty years on the bench for tolerance and moderation. But it was clear almost immediately that he took a stern view of this conspiracy: "This is a shocking indictment of a vast section of our economy, for what is really at stake here is the survival of the kind of economy under which this country has grown great, the free-enterprise system." The first targets of his censure were the twenty-nine corporations and their top management. He acknowledged that the Justice Department did not have enough evidence to convict men in the highest echelons of the corporations before the court, but in a broader sense the "real blame" should be laid at their doorstep: "One would be most naive indeed to believe that these violations of the law, so long persisted in, affecting so large a segment of the industry and finally involving so many millions upon millions of dollars, were facts unknown to those responsible for the corporation and its conduct. . . . " Heavy fines, he said, would be imposed on the corporations themselves.

Next he turned a cold blue eye on the forty-five corporation executives who had not escaped the nets of Antitrust. Many of the individual defendants he saw "torn between conscience and an approved corporate policy . . . the company man, the conformist, who goes along with his superiors and finds balm for his conscience in additional comforts and the security of his place in the corporate setup." The judge said that individuals "with ultimate responsibility for corporate conduct, among those indicted," were going to jail.

By midafternoon of that first day E. R. Jung, Clark Controller vice president, was ashen under a thirty-day prison sentence and a $2,000 fine. Gray-haired Westinghouse Vice President J. H. Chiles, Jr., vestryman of St. John's Episcopal Church in Sharon, Pennsylvania, got thirty days in prison, a $2,000 fine; his colleague, Sales Manager Charles I. Mauntel, veteran of thirty-nine years with the corporation, faced thirty days and a $1,000 fine; Ginn of G.E. (indicted in two conspiracies), thirty days and a $12,500 fine; G.E. Divisional Manager Lewis Burger, thirty days plus a $2,000 fine; G.E. Vice President George Burens, $4,000 and thirty days. "There goes my whole life," said this veteran of forty years with G.E., waving his arm distractedly as he waited to telephone his wife. "Who's going to want to hire a jailbird? What am I going to tell my children?"

By lunchtime the second day it was all over. The little game that lawyers from G.E. and Westinghouse had been playing against each other—predicting sentences and total fines—was ended. G.E. had "lost," receiving $437,500 in total fines to Westinghouse's $372,500. All told, $1,924,500 worth of fines were levied, seven jail sentences and twenty-four suspended jail sentences handed down. But sentencing, far from closing the case, has raised it to new importance.

The Problems of Predominance

No thoughtful person could have left that courtroom untroubled by the problems of corporate power and corporate ethics. We live in a corporate society. Big business determines institutionally our rate of capital formation, technological innovation, and economic growth; it establishes the kind of competition that is typical of our system and sets the moral tone of the market place. The streets of every city in the U.S. are crowded with small businesses that take their cue from great corporations, whether it trickles down from what some executive tells a crop of college graduates about free enterprise or the way he himself chooses to compete. Their lawyers pleaded that the way the electrical-equipment executives did compete was not collusion at its *worst*. To be sure, it wasn't so vulgar as the strong-arm price fixing of the Gulf Coast shrimpers or the rough stuff employed by a certain Philadelphia linen-supply company. But by flouting the law, the executives of the great companies set an example that was bound to make small companies feel they had similar license, and never mind the kid gloves. As Robert Bicks, then head of Antitrust, declared early in the proceedings, "These men and companies have in a true sense mocked the image of that economic system which they profess to the world."

This being so, it is highly important to understand what went wrong with the electrical-equipment industry and with General Electric, the biggest company of them all and the one without which the conspiracies could not have existed.

"Security, Complacency, Mediocrity"

When Ralph Cordiner took over the presidency of G.E. from Charles E. Wilson in December of 1950, it was clear from the outset that the corporation was in for some teeth-rattling changes. Cordiner had spent the previous five years working up a reorganization plan that would give G.E. the new plants, the new additions to capital and the new management setup he thought essential to the revitalization. Moreover, he had long made plain his distaste for running any big company the way G.E. had been run by his predecessors, with authority tightly concentrated in the president's office. Decentralization was a thing with him: he had never forgotten how the "layers of fat" in a centralized G.E. had slowed his own incessant drive for recognition to a point where he'd once quit to take the presidency of Schick. The simple fact was that intellectually and temperamentally a centralized organization went against his grain, whether it be run with Electric Charlie Wilson's relaxed conviviality or the clockwork autocracy of Gerard ("You have four minutes") Swope.

The corporation at large learned almost immediately what the new boss had in store for it and from Cordiner himself. Within six weeks he rode circuit from New York to Bridgeport, Chicago, Lynn-Boston, Schenectady, spreading the word to some 6,000 G.E. executives. The gist of his message could be divided into three parts. First, G.E. was in sorry shape. It was dedicated principally to "security, complacency, and mediocrity." Second, decentralization and rewards based on performance were going to be relied on in the rapid transformation of this "sinecure of mediocrity" into a dynamic corporation. G.E. would be split into twenty-seven autonomous divisions comprising 110 small companies. The 110 would be run just as if they were individual enterprises, the local boss setting his own budget, even making capital expenditures up to $200,000. But with authority and responsibility would go accountability and measurement, measurement by higher, harder standards. Third, G.E.'s new philosophy of decentralized management specifically prohibited meeting with competitors on prices, bids, or market shares. Charlie Wilson's General Instruction 2.35 on compliance with the antitrust laws, first issued in 1946 and re-issued in 1948 and 1950, would remain very much in force.

There was good reason for stressing this last point. Antitrust was then a very sore subject at G.E. In the decade just ended (1940–50), the corporation had been involved in thirteen antitrust cases, the offenses ranging from production limitation and patent pooling to price fixing and division of markets. Moreover, G.E. had long been something of a battleground for two divergent schools of economic thought. One school was straight Adam Smith and dedicated to the classical concept that corporate progress, like national progress, was best secured by freedom of private initiative within the bonds of justice. Its advocates believed that nothing was less intelligent than entering into price restrictions with competitors, for this just put G.E. on a par with companies that had neither its research facilities nor its market power. Ralph Cordiner, the company's most articulate advocate of this viewpoint, prided himself on the fact that it was at his insistence that the three G.E. employees implicated in illegal price-fixing got the sack in 1949; his philosophy, at its most eloquent, was simply: "Every company and every industry—yes, and every country—that is operated on a basis of cartel systems is liquidating its present strength and future opportunities."

The second school of thought held that competition, particularly price competition, was for the birds. Getting together with competitors was looked on as a way of life, a convention, "just as a manager's office always has a desk with a swivel chair." It was considered easier to negotiate market percentages than fight for one's share, less wearing to take turns on rigged bids than play the rugged individualist. Besides, the rationale went, they were all "gentlemen" and no more inclined to gouge the consumer than to crowd a competitor. Admittedly, all of them knew they were breaking the law—Section 1 of the Sherman Act is as explicit as a traffic ordinance. Their justification was on other grounds. "Sure, collusion was illegal," explained an old G.E. hand, "but it wasn't *unethical*. It wasn't any more unethical than if the companies had a summit conference the way Russia and the West meet. Those competitor meetings were just attended by a group of distressed individuals who wanted to know where they were going."

One important reason for the strength of G.E.'s anticompetition school was a change that occurred in the electrical industry after World War II. Smaller companies were becoming bigger and they were broadening their product lines. Customers had a wider choice of heavy electrical equipment, alike in quality and design. Price, consequently, became the decisive selling point. To turn this situation to their best advantage, buyers adopted a new technique: the competitive bid. When the utilities took it up, it became so prevalent that some manufacturers came to believe certain types of equipment would be treated like commodities with prices expected to fluctuate from day to day. This produced serious instability in the market and made profit planning difficult. The conspiracies proliferated at G.E. and elsewhere because the manufacturers lacked the gumption to shift the buyers' attention from price to higher quality, better service, and improved design.

Precisely what numerical strength the anticompetition school commanded at the time Cordiner took office in 1950 is of course a controversial point. G.E. prefers to talk of it as "a pocket," while the collusionists themselves like to think nine G.E. executives out of ten shared their point of view. A fact to keep in mind is that thirty-two G.E. executives implicated themselves before the grand juries in addition to those general managers and vice presidents, clearly involved, but not called to testify. There can be no doubt that the collusionists' influence was formidable and pervasive. And now, despite what Cordiner said about over-all company policy on cartels, under his decentralization plan the head of each of the 110 units comprising the company was being given power to set his own marketing policies and to raise or lower prices as he saw fit. Under the circumstances, anyone might have foreseen the results.

A Way of Life for Clarence Burke

One of the more attentive listeners to what the incoming president had to say about antitrust was Clarence Burke, a hard-driving, tenacious executive in his middle forties (who was to become the $42,000-a-year general manager of the High Voltage Switchgear Department and one of fifteen G.E. executives sentenced in Philadelphia). Burke had come to the heavy-equipment end of G.E. in 1926, fresh from the Georgia Institute of Technology (B.S. in electrical engineering), and his entire corporate life had been spent there. The heavy-equipment division was more than just the group that accounted for some 25 per cent of G.E. sales; it was the oldest division, and the foundation upon which the whole company had been built. Moreover, it was the stronghold of the collusionists. All of the nineteen indictments to which G.E. pleaded either guilty or no contest in Philadelphia sprang from price fixing, bid rigging, market division in heavy equipment.

Burke's introduction to the heavy-equipment conspiracies was [as] easy as falling off a log. It occurred when he reported to Pittsfield, Massachusetts, on June 1, 1945, as sales manager of distribution transformers. A month or so after Burke's arrival, H. L. "Buster" Brown, sales manager of the whole Transformer Department, called the new man in and told him he'd be expected to attend a Pittsburgh meeting of the transformer section of the National Electrical Manufacturers' Association. It was a regularly scheduled affair, held during OPA days, in what is now the Penn-Sheraton Hotel, and it was attended by thirty or forty industry people plus the N.E.M.A. secretaries from New York. But after adjournment—when the N.E.M.A. secretaries had departed—the company men reassembled within the hour for a cozier meeting. The talk this time was about prices, OPA-regulated prices, and how the industry could best argue Washington into jacking up the ceilings. Burke didn't consider this illegal, and he took part in several subsequent monthly meetings before OPA was abolished.

The convenient price klatches following the regular N.E.M.A. meetings continued after OPA's demise. But instead of discussing pricing under government controls, the conspirators turned to fixing prices among themselves. "In that conspiracy," Burke recalled this winter, "we didn't try to divide up the market or prorate the sealed-bid business. We only quoted an agreed-upon price—to the penny." Nor did the post-OPA agreements seem to some of the participants like Burke to put them any more outside the law than agreements under the OPA. "We gradually grew into it. Buster Brown assured us that [the company's antitrust directive] didn't mean the kind of thing we were doing, that Antitrust would have to say we had *gouged* the public to say we were doing anything illegal. We understood this was what the company wanted us to do."

For a while this comfortable rationale sustained Burke and any conspirators who had qualms about the matter, but in 1946 it was demolished by the company lawyers. Teams of them made the rounds of G.E. departments, no doubt in response to federal probings that were to result in the successful antitrust prosecutions of G.E. two years later. The lawyers put everyone in G.E. on notice that it certainly was illegal to discuss prices with competitors, whether the public was gouged or not. Then the head office followed this up by barring anybody who had anything to do with pricing from attending N.E.M.A. meetings. Engineering personnel were substituted for people like Buster Brown and Clarence Burke. The G.E. conspirators called such enforced withdrawal from active participation "going behind the iron curtain." This situation continued for about nine months, during which everyone received a copy of Electric Charlie's antitrust admonition and during which G.E.'s competitors kept the Pittsfield shut-ins informed by telephone of their own price agreements. Then, abruptly, the iron curtain was raised.

"Word came down to start contacting competitors again," Burke remembers. "It came to me from my superior, Buster Brown, but my impression was that it came to him from higher up. I think the competitive situation was forcing them to do something, and there were a lot of old-timers who thought collusion was the best way to solve the problems. That is when the hotel-room meetings got started. We were cautioned at this time not to tell the lawyers what we were doing and to cover our trails in our expense-account reports." Part of Burke's camouflage: transportation entries never showed fares to the actual city where the meeting was held but to some point of equivalent distance from Pittsfield.

The conspiracy operated, although sporadically, for the next several years of Burke's Pittsfield assignment (he was reassigned February 1, 1950). Every so often, the G.E. participants would retire behind the iron curtain, until it seemed necessary to bring about some general price increases. Then there would be a resumption of quiet talks with the men from other major manufacturers like Westinghouse. The antitrust-compliance directives they had all initialed? "When anybody raised a question about that, they would be told it doesn't apply now."

"I Was Adept at This Sort of Thing"

By 1951, however, at the time Burke was listening to Ralph Cordiner's antitrust exhortations, the Pittsfield conspiracy had closed down—to make matters simpler if, as everyone correctly suspected, Cordiner was going to clamp down on such cabals. But bigger and better conspiracies were in the offing. In September, 1951, not very long after the Cordiner meeting, Clarence Burke walked into a new job at G.E.—and into membership in probably the oldest conspiracy then extant. The conspiracy was in circuit breakers and it had been operative over the span of a quarter-century. Burke's new job was manager of all switchgear marketing, which included circuit breakers, switchgear, and other items of heavy electrical equipment. This particular spot was open because the previous incumbent had been troubled ever since signing a restatement of Charlie Wilson's "Policy Concerning the Antitrust Laws" the year before. As Burke got the story from Robert Tinnerholm, who interviewed him for the job: "I was to replace a man who took a strictly religious view of it; who, because he had signed this slip of paper [the Wilson directive] wouldn't contact competitors or talk to them—even when they came to his home." Burke got the job, an important step up the G.E. ladder, because he had become something of a conspiratorial wheel by then: "They knew I was adept at this sort of thing. I was glad to get the promotion. I had no objections." No objections then or subsequently, as it turned out, for he had found it easy to persuade himself that what he was doing in defiance of the letter of the antitrust directive was not done in defiance of its spirit.

Burke's boss when he first went to switchgear in 1951 was Henry V. Erben, to whom Buster Brown had reported in the cozy old days at Pittsfield. Erben had risen to the No. 3 spot in G.E.—executive vice president, Apparatus Group—and as Burke recalls, "he was saying then that he had talked to Cordiner about this policy, that Cordiner was not pleased with [the idea of getting together with competitors] but that he, Erben, had said he would do it in a way that would not get the company into trouble. And I'd been told by others that Erben had said things like this earlier than that."

Burke's initial assignment in Philadelphia was to get to know the local marketing executives of Westinghouse, Allis-Chalmers, and Federal Pacific, and then to see [that] they met the other new members of G.E.'s switchgear management. (This department had been restaffed in anticipation of being split into three parts, the separate companies called for by Cordiner's decentralization plan.) He was also expected to take a hand at indoctrination in conspiracy. "Erben's theory had been live and let live, contact the competitors. He gave us that theory at every opportunity and we took it down to other levels and had no trouble getting the most innocent persons to go along. Mr. Erben thought it was all right, and if they didn't want to do it, they knew we would replace them. Not replace them for that reason, of course. We would have said the man isn't *broad* enough for this job, he hasn't grown into it yet."

One man, ironically enough, who had not yet "grown" into the job was George Burens, the new boss of the whole switchgear operation. Burens had started out in G.E. as a laborer; he had the additional disadvantage of being a junior-high-school man in a corporate world full of college men, but during the next thirty years he had steadily risen by sheer competitive spirit. Part of his zest for competition had been acquired in the Lamp Division, where he had spent the bulk of his career. Lamps had long been noted as the most profitable of G.E. divisions and the most independent, a constant trial to Gerard Swope in the days when he tried to centralize all administrative authority in G.E.'s New York headquarters. But most of Burens' competitive spirit was simply in the nature of the man. "He had grown up hating competitors," was the way a colleague put it. "They were the enemy."

"This Is Bob, What Is 7's Bid?"

Burens arrived on the scene in September of 1951 and busied himself solely with the job of splitting switchgear into three independent companies (high, medium, and low voltage), each with a general manager and himself as general manager of the division. Once decentralization was accomplished, he was content for a time to let his new departmental general managers like Clarence Burke run the conspiracy. And some conspiracy it was.

Some $650 million in sales was involved, according to Justice Department estimates, from 1951 through 1958. The annual total amounted to roughly $75 million and was broken down into two categories, sealed bids and open bids. The sealed-bid business (between $15 million and $18 million per year) was done with public agencies, city, state, and federal. The private-sector business was conducted with private utilities and totaled some $55 million to $60 million per annum.

The object of the conspiracy, in so far as the sealed-bid business was concerned, was to rotate that business on a fixed-percentage basis among four participating companies, then the only circuit-breaker manufacturers in the U.S. G.E. got 45 per cent, Westinghouse 35, Allis-Chalmers 10, Federal Pacific 10. Every ten days to two weeks working-level meetings were called in order to decide whose turn was next. Turns were determined by the "ledger list," a table of who had got what in recent weeks, and after that the only thing left to decide was the price that the company picked to "win" would submit as the lowest bid.

Above this working-level group was a second tier of conspirators who dealt generally with the over-all scheme of rigging the sealed bids but whose prime purpose was maintenance of book prices (quoted prices) and market shares in the yearly $55 million to $60 million worth of private-sector business. Once each week, the top executives (general managers and vice presidents) responsible for carrying out the conspiracy would get the word to each other via intercompany memo. A different executive would have the "duty" over each thirty-day period. That involved initiating the memos, which all dealt with the same subject matter: the jobs coming up that week, the book price each company was setting, comments on the general level of equipment prices.

The conspiracies had their own lingo and their own standard operating procedures. The attendance list was known as the "Christmas-card list," meetings as "choir practices." Companies had code numbers—G.E. 1, Westinghouse 2, Allis-Chalmers 3, Federal Pacific 7—which were used in conjunction with first names when calling a conspirator at home for price information ("This is Bob, what is 7's bid?"). At the hotel meetings it was S.O.P. not to list one's employer when registering and not to have breakfast with fellow conspirators in the dining room. The G.E. men observed two additional precautions: never to be the ones who kept the records and never to tell G.E.'s lawyers anything.

Where to Cut Throats

But things were not always smooth even inside this well-oiled machine, for the conspirators actually had no more compunction at breaking the rules of the conspiracy than at breaching the Sherman Act. "Everyone accused the other of not living up to the agreement," Clarence Burke recalled "and the ones they complained about tried to shift the blame onto someone else." The most constant source of irritation occurred in the sealed-bid business, where chiseling was difficult to detect. But breaks in book price to the utilities in the open-bid business also generated ill will and vituperation. Indeed, one of the many ironies of the whole affair was that the conspiracy couldn't entirely suppress the competitive instinct. Every so often some company would decide that cutthroat competition outside was preferable to the throat-cutting that went on in the cartel; they would break contact and sit out the conspiracy for a couple of years.

What prompted their return? Chronic overcapacity, for one thing, overcapacity that put a constant pressure on prices. Soon after he went to Washington as defense mobilization chief in 1950, Electric Charlie Wilson announced that the nation's electric-power capacity needed to be increased 30 per cent over the next three years. The equipment industry jumped to match that figure, and added a little more as well. Thus an executive, who ebulliently increased capacity one year, a few years later might join a price conspiracy to escape the consequences of that increase. "This is a feast or famine business," summed up Clarence Burke. "At one time everybody was loaded with orders, and ever since they wanted to stay that way. When utilities decide they need more generating capacity, they start buying and we have three years of good business—and then three years of bad. The decision to build capacity was delegated down to the managers [under decentralization]."

A more human explanation of why the conspiracy snarled on for eight years was corporate pressure, the pressure to perform. "All we got from Lexington Avenue," said Burke, "was 'get your percentage of available business up, the General Electric Co. is slipping.'" Cordiner himself has remarked: "I would say the company was more than slightly nervous in 1951–52–53."

Certainly corporate pressure no more exculpates an executive who enters into an illegal conspiracy than the relatively low pay of a bank clerk justifies his dipping into the till. But that is not to say it didn't carry weight with the conspirators from G.E. For the company was not only experiencing the increased pressure that goes with new presidents but was adjusting to a whole new organizational setup. Said one observer of the scene, Vice President Harold Smiddy, G.E.'s management expert: "Some thought . . . that he was going too fast. But Cordiner's asset is stretching men. He can push them and he did." Said another observer, G.E. director Sidney Weinberg: "If you did something wrong, Cordiner would send for you and tell you you were through. That's all there would be to it."

Down the line, where the pressure must have been intense, Clarence Burke had this to say of it as a factor in continuing the conspiracy: "We did feel that this was the only way to reach part of our goals as managers. Each year we had to budget for more profit as a per cent of net sales, as well as for a larger percentage of available business. My boss, George Burens, wouldn't approve a budget unless it was a 'reach' budget. We couldn't accomplish a greater per cent of net profit to sales without getting together with competitors. Part of the pressure was the will to get ahead and the desire to have the good will of the man above you. He had only to get the approval of the man above *him* to replace you, and if you wouldn't cooperate he could find lots of other faults to use to get you out."

Cordiner Takes the Plunge

By May of 1953, Clarence Burke had been promoted to general manager of one of the three new switchgear departments (high voltage), a post that made him in effect the president of a small company with some $25 million worth of sales. He felt he had a bellyful of the cartel because "No one was living up to the agreements and we at G.E. were being made suckers. On every job some one would cut our throat; we lost confidence in the group." So he got out.

The G.E. boycott of that cartel continued on through 1954. To be sure, Westinghouse, Allis-Chalmers, and the other competitors would still call Royce

Crawford, Burke's marketing man, to tell him the prices that the high-level group had decided on, and express the heartfelt hope he would honor it. Crawford did honor it pretty much, though maintaining a free hand to go after all the business available.

This was the situation when, in mid-September 1954, Ralph Cordiner replaced the Wilson directive of antitrust compliance with a stronger one of his own. Far more explicit than Wilson's directive, Cordiner's Directive Policy 20.5 went beyond the compliance required by law and blanketed the subject with every conceivable admonition.

But 1954 was a bad year for the industry and for G.E. The company's sales slumped for the first time since Cordiner had taken the helm, dropping almost $176 million. Moreover, profits as a per cent of sales were still well below the 8 per cent achieved by Charlie Wilson in 1950. The result was that Cordiner and Robert Paxton, executive vice president for industrial products, began putting more heat on one division after another.

"We were told," as one general manager remembered it, "that G.E. was losing business and position because our prices weren't competitive." Then, in the latter part of 1954, Paxton heard a report that moved him from words to the action his blunt Scottish temperament favored. Westinghouse had beaten G.E. out of a big turbine order and had done it at considerably off book price. Determined that no more of the big ones were going to get away, Paxton decided he'd instruct the fieldmen personally. Thus, when the next big job came along, a $5-million affair for transformers and switchgear with Ebasco, the New York district manager knew he was not to let the competition underbid him. But Westinghouse and the others were hungry too, and the price breaks came so fast it was difficult to keep track of them: one day the price was 10 per cent off book, the next 20 per cent, finally 40 per cent.

So began the celebrated "white sale" of 1954–55. Before it was over, the electrical industry was discounting price as much as 40 to 45 per cent off book. Delivery dates began stretching out, [and they] got as far as five years away from date of sale. This of course meant that the impact of 1955's giveaway prices was not confined to that one year; the blight they put on profits persisted down to 1960.

Mixing Conspiracy with Golf

General Electric, with its broad product lines, was not hit as hard by the "white sale" as some of its smaller competitors, but it was just as anxious as anyone else to call a halt. The word went out from headquarters on Lexington Avenue that prices had to be got back up, and stability restored. Sales responsibility was being returned to the general managers. They certainly welcomed the news, for all during the period that Paxton had taken over sales nobody had relieved the general managers of the companion responsibility of turning in the profit demanded. Now with power over sales restored, they could strike a better balance between the irreconcilables of getting more market and getting more profit.

At the Switchgear Division, the pressure was so great that George Burens, the lifelong believer in tough competition, underwent a remarkable conversion. He called department manager Clarence Burke into his office and told him the old cartel was going to be cranked up again. More than that, Burens was going to do the job of re-establishing it himself. Shortly thereafter, he and Burke trotted off to mix in a little conspiracy with a little golf in Bedford Springs, Pennsylvania. Burens and Burke formed a foursome with Landon Fuller and J. B. McNeill, key men in sales at Westinghouse. They concluded that it might take more than the combined market power of G.E. and Westinghouse (some 70 to 75 per cent) to get things back to normal; other companies would have to be brought in. Fuller agreed to contact Allis-Chalmers and Burens agreed to get in touch with I-T-E Circuit Breaker—but only at a high level. Everyone was concerned at the danger of low-level contacts and rightly so, for, as Burke remembers what happened subsequently: "It got so that people who worked for people who worked for me knew about pricing arrangements."

About January, 1956, another high-level meeting was held in Cleveland. Fuller's call on Allis-Chalmers had been successful; he had Joseph W. McMullen in tow. But at I-T-E, George Burens, trying to keep the contact at a high level, apparently hadn't got to the right man. Joe McMullen, however, had his eye on somebody in I-T-E (Harry Buck, as it turned out) and volunteered to bring him into camp. Then there was a round of golf and a couple of rounds of drinks and the conspirators went their separate ways, after agreeing to keep in touch by memorandums. Every month that year one company conspirator would initiate a memorandum to the others (who now included I-T-E's Buck), listing every pending job whether sealed bid or open and stating what the calculated book price would be. Then the conspirators would reassemble and compare calculations to forestall any chiseling from the agreed-upon book. There were nine such meetings in 1956, held in various hotel suites. These and the memorandums worked fairly well, until the first part of 1957. Then a one-man gang named McGregor Smith lit the fuse that blew them up.

The Malign Circle

"Mac" Smith, chairman of the Florida Power & Light Co., personally handled some of the buying for his dynamic utility. As he went marketing for equipment, it struck him that the manufacturers had set artificially high profit goals for them-selves, had priced their products accordingly, and then had got together to see that the prices stuck. In other words, a malign circle of manufacturers was short-circuiting what Ralph Cordiner liked to call the "benign circle of power producers and power consumers." Smith was buying a lot of transformers, switchgear, and other equipment in 1957, but the manufacturers were defending book price as if life depended on it and, despite heavy pressure from Mac Smith and his purchasing agents, were giving little in the way of discounts.

Then one Monday, Smith closed his transformer purchases with a number of companies, including G.E. and Westinghouse; on Tuesday Clarence Burke got a worried report from one of his switchgear salesmen in Miami: Westinghouse had proposed to Florida Power that it add all its circuit-breaker order (about a mil-lion dollars worth) to its order for Westinghouse transformers. In return, Westinghouse would take 4 per cent off circuit-breaker book and hide the dis-count in the transformer order. Telling his man to be sure of the facts first, Burke gave him authority to meet the Westinghouse terms. A grateful Mac Smith then decided to split the circuit-breaker order, half to Westinghouse, which had bro-ken the price, and half to G.E., which had matched the break.

This unexpected turn of the wheel brought the Westinghouse salesman boil-ing into Florida Power's executive suite. There he raised Mac Smith's hackles to a point where the latter called G.E. and asked it to do him the favor of taking the whole order. G.E. naturally obliged.

Retaliation was not long coming. "Westinghouse went to Baltimore Gas & Electric," says Burke, shaking his head in recollection of the chaos that ensued, "and said they'd give them 5 per cent off on switchgear and circuit breakers, and a week later Allis-Chalmers gave Potomac Electric 12 per cent off. A week after *that*, Westinghouse gave Atlantic City Electric 20 per cent off, and it went on down to much worse than the 'white sale'—in the winter of 1957–58 prices were 60 per cent off book."

That was the end of that cartel. It did not, of course, mean the end of the other conspiracies G.E. was involved in. Far from it. Each general manager of a divi-sion or department took a strictly personal view of his participation in any cartel. Thus while circuit breakers was at daggers drawn, industrial controls was enjoying an amiable conspiracy. Indeed, W. F. Oswalt, general manager of G.E.'s industrial-control department, seems to have accomplished the neat trick of ful-filling the purpose of that conspiracy—to fix prices—while at the same time remaining true to Cordiner's antitrust directive, in a fingers-crossed sort of way. He regularly attended meetings from 1953 to 1955, then stopped upon receiving the assurance of the other conspirators that they would keep him informed of what went on. In August of 1956, for example, Oswalt was lounging comfortably in his cabin at North Bay, Ontario, physically removed from the cabin down the road where the cartel was busy hammering out a price rise. Nevertheless, the resultant 10 per cent boost in prices was really his contribution: a representative of one of the smaller companies had panted back and forth between him and "the boys," carrying his strong recommendations to that effect.

Cordiner's "Pieces of Paper"

G.E. was involved in at least seven other conspiracies during the time the circuit-breaker cartel was inoperative. The one in power transformers (G.E. Vice President Raymond W. Smith) was going, for G.E. had yet to develop the "black box" (a design breakthrough using standard components to produce tailor-made transformers), which two years later would enable it to take price leadership away from Westinghouse. The one in turbine generators (G.E. Vice President William S. Ginn) was functioning too. In the fall of 1957 it was agreed at the Barclay Hotel to give G.E. "position" in bidding on a 500,000-kilowatt TVA unit.

The question that naturally arises, the cartels being so numerous, is why didn't G.E.'s top management stop them? Cordiner has been criticized within the company, and rightly so, for sitting aloofly in New York and sending out "pieces of paper"—his 20.5 antitrust directive—rather than having 20.5 personally handed to the local staff by the local boss. But there was also a failure in human relations. A warmer man might have been close enough to his people to divine what was going on. According to T. K. Quinn (*I Quit Monster Business*), the G.E. vice president who had helped him up the ladder, Ralph Cordiner, was "first class in every aspect of management except human relations."

After the conspiracy case broke, the question of top-level complicity came up. G.E. hired Gerhard Gesell of the Washington law firm of Covington & Burling to come to a conclusion one way or another as to whether Cordiner, Paxton, or any other member of the Executive Office had knowledge of the cartels. No corroborated evidence ever came to light that Cordiner knew of them; quite the opposite. As Clarence Burke put it last month: "Cordiner was sincere but undersold by people beneath him who rescinded his orders."

Robert Paxton, however, is something else again. The fifty-nine-year-old G.E. president, who resigned this February for reasons of health, was in the unenviable position of having worked most of his corporate life in those vineyards of G.E. where cartels thrived. He was in switchgear for twenty-one years, five of them as works manager, went to Pittsfield with his close friend Ray Smith (later one of the convicted conspirators), and eventually became manager of the Transformer and Allied Product Division there. A conspiracy had started before he got to Pittsfield and one was operating (first under Ginn, then under Smith) after he left. Paxton was not then *responsible* for marketing, as G.E. points out, but he has always shown a lively interest in the subject: "I found myself, even as a very young engineer working for General Electric, dealing with the very practical daily problem of how to minimize cost and how to maximize profit."

Gesell discovered there was violent disagreement within G.E. about Paxton and the cartels: "Things were said about his having knowledge. I interviewed Ray Smith and made every effort to pin down what he thought he had, but it was always atmospheric. The government investigated and didn't have any better luck."

Judge Ganey, however, expressed a more definite view: "I am not naive enough to believe General Electric didn't know about it and it didn't meet with their hearty approbation." In Ganey's opinion, Directive 20.5 was "observed in its breach rather than in its enforcement." To say the least, there was a serious management failure at G.E.

Cold Turkey and the Pressure for Profits

In 1958 the circuit breaker–switchgear conspiracy started up again. George Burens and his three departmental general managers, Burke, H. F. Hentschel, and Frank Stehlik, were all dead set against resumption. But the pressure was too great. Pressure had already produced some profound changes in Burke. "He used to be hail fellow well met," said a colleague who witnessed the transformation over the years, "until he was put under that great pressure for profits. Then he simply shrank into himself; everything got to be cold turkey with him—without any warmth at all." Now the pressure was redoubling, as it always did after the market went to pieces. Burens and some of the other apparatus executives were summoned to New York in 1958 for a talk with the boss, Group Executive Arthur F. Vinson. This affair became known to Burens' subordinates as the "Beat Burens" meeting, for at it were aired angry complaints by G.E.'s customers that, with switchgear selling at 40 to 45 per cent off book, other G.E. departments should be offering their products at substantial discounts. The solution: stabilize switchgear prices; in other words, get back in the cartel.

Burens returned to Philadelphia, battered but unshaken in his resolve to keep clear of the cartel. He expected to do it by keeping up quality and efficiency, and by pricing the product so that there was a fair profit. Ironically enough, in view of his subsequent indictment, he was firmly of the belief that, given six-months time, he could bring prices up in the free market without messing around with any conspiracy. But at the annual business-review meeting of apparatus people, held on July 30 and 31 in Philadelphia, he underwent a further hammering from other divisional general managers about the way switchgear prices were hurting them. He seemed morose at the following banquet, held in a private dining room at the Philadelphia Country Club; indeed, he got into a heated argument about prices with Paxton, who had succeeded Ralph Cordiner as president that April.

What happened next to change George Burens' mind about getting back into the conspiratorial rat race is a matter of great controversy. It concerns whether he got a direct order to rejoin the cartel from Arthur Vinson. If Vinson did so instruct Burens, and others, then General Electric's complicity extended to the highest corporate level, for Vinson was a member of the fifteen-man Executive Office, a group that included Cordiner and Paxton. . . .

Suffice it to say here that Burens did rejoin and was confronted by a delicate problem of face. He didn't want to have to crawl back, particularly after having given everyone such a hard time when he quit. But as matters turned out, G.E. was holding its quadrennial Electric Utility Conference in California that fall and there Burens ran into Fischer Black, the amiable editor of *Electrical World*. Black reported that a lot of people in the industry were sour on G.E. in general and Burens in particular because Burens had refused to go along with new pricing agreements. To end this insalubrious state of affairs, Black would be happy to set up a meeting—if Burens would just attend. The latter agreed.

On October 8, 1958, the cartel set gathered at the Astor Hotel in New York. The G.E. contingent was there, headed by Burens and Burke, Landon Fuller for Westinghouse, Harry Buck for I-T-E Circuit Breaker, Frank Roby for Federal Pacific. L. W. "Shorty" Long had called in to say he couldn't make it but anything they decided was O.K. with Allis-Chalmers. Black himself popped in to chirp that he was paying for the suite and to be sure and order up lunch. Then he left them to business. Not much of it was transacted. There was a lot of crape-hanging over what had happened in the past and a number of hopeful ideas for the future were discussed. The net of it was that everybody agreed to go home, check their records, and come up with proposals on November 9, at the Traymore hotel in Atlantic City.

A Party for Burens

Whatever watery cordiality prevailed at the Astor vanished into the steam of conflict at the Traymore. Circuit-breaker prices had been dropping alarmingly ever since September, so much so that G.E., Westinghouse, Allis-Chalmers, and Federal Pacific extended options to some utilities to purchase large numbers of circuit breakers at 40 to 55 per cent below book. Moreover, I-T-E Circuit Breaker had got into the business . . . and wanted a slice of the sealed-bid market. Federal Pacific had a slice but wanted a fatter one.

Deciding what to do about prices was not particularly trying; an agreement was reached to keep them substantially identical at book. The real trouble came over changing the percentages of sealed-bid business. G.E., Westinghouse, and Allis-Chalmers knew that anything done to accommodate the demands of Federal Pacific and I-T-E would have to come out of their hides. But at the end of ten hours of angry argument they decided the only way to get the cartel going again was to submit to the knife: General Electric's percentage was sliced from 45 to 40.3, Westinghouse's from 35 to 31.3, Allis-Chalmers from 10 to 8.8. I-T-E was cut in for 4 per cent and Federal Pacific got a 50 per cent boost, its percentage of the market was raised from 10 to 15.6.

So began the final circuit-breaker cartel, born in recrimination and continued in mistrust. George Burens struggled with it for the next three months, a round of meetings at the old hotels and some swanky new places. Circuit-breaker prices inched up. Then in January, 1959, Burens was promoted out. It was a gay party that celebrated his departure to head up G.E.'s Lamp Division, and nobody was gayer than Burens, the tough competitor returning to free competition. Paxton was on hand with an accolade; the Lamp Division, he said, needed Burens' admirable talents to get it back where it belonged.

But there was no gay party for the incoming general manager of switchgear. Lewis Burger was simply told his job was "at risk" for the next two years. If he performed, he could keep it and become a vice president to boot. If he was found wanting, he wouldn't be able to go back to his old job. He'd just be out. Burger promptly joined the circuit-breaker conspiracy. But the day was not far off, indeed it was only nine months away, when a phone call would set in motion the forces that would shatter the conspiracy and send Burger along with Burens off to prison.

Shortly before ten o'clock on the morning of September 28, 1959, an urgent long-distance call came in to G.E.'s vast Transformer Division at Pittsfield, Massachusetts. It was for Edward L. Dobbins, the divisional lawyer, and the person on the line was another attorney, representing Lapp Insulator Co. He just wanted to say that one of Lapp's officers had been subpoenaed by a Philadelphia grand jury and was going to tell the whole story. "What story?" said Dobbins pleasantly, then listened to an account that sent him, filled with concern, into the office of the divisional vice president, Raymond W. Smith.

At that time, Vice President Smith was a big man in G.E., veteran of twenty-eight years with the corporation, and one of President Robert Paxton's closest personal friends; he was also a big man in Pittsfield, where the Transformer Division employs 6,000 people out of a population of 57,000, director of a local bank, active member of the hospital building board. Smith heard Dobbins out, his six-foot-five frame suddenly taut in the swivel chair and a frown deepening on his forehead; he got up and began pacing back and forth. "It's bad," he said, "very bad." Then he added, shaking his head grimly, "You just don't know how bad it is!"

The story Dobbins had, which the man from Lapp was about to spill before a Philadelphia grand jury, was that Paul Hartig, one of Ray Smith's departmental general managers, had been conspiring with Lapp Insulator and a half-dozen other manufacturers to fix prices on insulators. Such news was unsettling enough to any boss, but Smith's alarm had its roots in something deeper than the derelictions of a subordinate. He was himself "Mr. Big" of another cartel, one involving $210 million worth of transformers a year, and he didn't need the gift of prescience to sense the danger to his own position. Nevertheless, Smith concluded that he had no choice but to report the trouble to Apparatus Group Vice President Arthur Vinson, in New York.

That very night Vinson flew up to Pittsfield. A cool, dynamic executive, boss of G.E.'s nine apparatus divisions, Vinson was used to hearing the word "trouble" from his general managers, but the way Smith had used it permitted of no delay, even for a storm that made the flight a hazardous one. He had dinner with the Smiths at a nearby inn, and then, back in Smith's study, heard the story. Vinson's concern centered immediately on the extent of G.E.'s involvement. His recollection today is that after discussing Hartig, he asked Ray Smith whether the Transformer Division was itself involved in a cartel and received assurances to the contrary. Hartig's case appeared to be just that of a young manufacturing executive whose inexperience in marketing matters had got him compromised.

By sheer coincidence, G.E. Chairman Ralph Cordiner showed up in Pittsfield the next day. He had come, ironically enough, to hear an account of the new market approach by means of which Smith's Transformer Division expected to beat the ears off the competition, foreign and domestic. G.E. had worked out a method of cutting the formidable costs of custom-made transformers by putting them together from modular (standard) components. Westinghouse, long the design and cost leader in the transformer field, had been put on notice only the previous month that new prices reflecting the 20 per cent cost reduction were in the making.

Told of Hartig's involvement in the insulator cartel, Cordiner reacted with shock and anger. Up until then he had reason to think his general managers were making "earnest efforts" to comply with both the spirit and the letter of the antitrust laws; he had so testified in May before a congressional antitrust subcommittee. When the Tennessee Valley Authority had complained that it was getting identical bids on insulators, transformers, and other equipment, and the Justice Department had begun to take an active interest in this charge, he had sent G.E.'s amiable trade-regulation counsel, Gerard Swope, Jr., son of the company's former chief executive, to Pittsfield. Swope considered it his mission to explore "a more dynamic pricing policy to get away from the consistent identity of prices." He had, however, ventured to say, "I assume none of you have agreed with competitors on prices," and when nobody contested this assumption, he came away with the feeling that any suspicion of pricing agreements boiled down to a competitor's voicing a single criticism at a cocktail party. Cordiner had been further reassured by a report from G.E.'s outside counsel, Gerhard Gesell of Covington & Burling, who had burrowed through mountains of data and couldn't find anything incriminating. Gesell's conclusion, accepted by the top brass, was that G.E. was up against nothing more than another government attack on "administered" prices such as he and Thomas E. Dewey had beaten off earlier that year in the Salk vaccine case.

It was no wonder, then, that Cordiner was upset by what he heard about the insulator department. And this was only the beginning. G.E.'s general counsel, Ray Luebbe, was brought into the case, and within a matter of days Paul Hartig was in Luebbe's New York office implicating Vice President Ray Smith. Smith made a clean breast of things, detailing the operation of the transformer cartel (bids on government contracts were rotated to ensure that G.E. and Westinghouse each got 30 per cent of the business, the remaining 40 being split among four other manufacturers; book prices were agreed upon at meetings held everywhere from Chicago's Drake Hotel to the Homestead at Hot Springs, Virginia; secrecy was safeguarded by channeling all phone calls and mail to the homes, destroying written memoranda upon receipt).

Then Smith implicated a second G.E. vice president, William S. Ginn. Head of the Turbine Division at forty-one, Ginn was considered a comer in the company. Unfortunately for him, he was just as much of a wheel in conspiracy, an important man in *two* cartels, the one in transformers, which he had passed on to Ray Smith, and the one in turbine generators, which only the year before had aroused the suspicions of TVA by bringing about some very rapid price increases.

The involvement of divisional Vice Presidents Smith and Ginn put G.E.'s whole fifteen-man Executive Group—a group including Cordiner and Paxton—in an understandable flap. By now, the corporation was plainly implicated in four cartels, and an immense number of questions had to be answered, questions of how to ferret out other conspiracies, what legal defense to make, whether there was any distinction between corporate and individual guilt. For the next few weeks—from early October to late November—the executive office was to devote itself almost exclusively to searching for dependable answers.

Big Fish in Small Companies

The Justice Department was also looking for answers. It had got started on the case because of TVA's suspicions and because Senator Estes Kefauver had threatened an investigation of the electrical industry, putting the executive branch of government on notice that if it didn't get on with the job, the legislative branch would. Robert A. Bicks, the most vigorous chief of Antitrust since Thurman Arnold, certainly had plenty of will to get on with the job but the way was clouded. The Antitrust Division had once before—in 1951-52—tried to find a pattern of collusive pricing in the maze of transformer bids, but had wound up with no indictments. Now, as Bicks and William Maher, the head of the division's Philadelphia office, moved into the situation, proof seemed just as elusive as ever.

The tactics of the Antitrust Division were based on using the Philadelphia grand jury to subpoena documents, and then, after study of these, to subpoena individuals—the corporation executives who would logically have been involved if a conspiracy existed. The ultimate objective was to determine whether the biggest electrical manufacturers and their top executives had participated in a cartel, but the approach had to be oblique. As Maher put it: "Even if we had proof of a meeting where Paxton [president of G.E.] and Cresap [president of Westinghouse] had sat down and agreed to fix prices, we would still have to follow the product lines down through to the illegal acts. You have to invert it, start with what happened at a lower level and build it up step by step. The idea is to go after the biggest fish in the *smallest* companies, then hope to get enough information to land the biggest fish in the biggest companies."

In mid-November a second Philadelphia grand jury was empaneled, and Justice Department attorneys began ringing doorbells across the land. As more of these rang and the trust busters took more testimony (under grand-jury subpoena), a sudden shiver of apprehension ran through the industry. The grapevine, probably the most sensitive in American business, began to buzz with talk that the feds were really on to something—moreover, that jail impended for the guilty. Everyone by then was only too well aware that an Ohio judge had just clapped three executives behind bars for ninety days for participating in a hand-tool cartel.

Cordiner's Command Decision

Back at G.E., meanwhile, Cordiner had issued instructions that all apparatus general managers, including those few who so far had been implicated, were to be interviewed by company attorneys about participation in cartels. Most of the guilty lied, gambling that the exposures would not go any further than they had. Cordiner, accepting their stories, began to formulate what he thought would be G.E.'s best defense. It would have two principal salients: first, the company itself was not guilty of the conspiracies; what had occurred was without the encouragement or even the knowledge of the chairman, the president, and the Executive

Office. G.E.'s corporate position on antitrust compliance was a matter of record, embodied in Directive 20.5, which Cordiner had personally written and promulgated five years before. Furthermore, illegal conduct of any individuals involved was clearly beyond the authority granted to them by the company, and therefore the company, as distinguished from the individuals, should not be held criminally responsible. Second, those employees who had violated Directive 20.5 were in for corporate punishment. "Stale offenses" were not to be counted, but a three-year company "statute of limitations" would govern liability (the federal limitation: five years).

Punishment of necessity had to go hand in hand with a corporate not-guilty stance. If G.E.'s defense was to be that the conspiracies had taken place in contravention of written policy (Directive 20.5), then unpunished offenders would be walking proof to a jury that 20.5 was just a scrap of paper. On the other hand, here was a clear management failure on the part of the Executive Office—a failure to detect over a period of almost a decade the cartels that were an open secret to the rest of the industry. As G.E. was to learn to its sorrow, lots of people who approved of punishment for the offenders did not think this permitted G.E. to wash its hands of responsibility. Westinghouse's president, Mark W. Cresap, Jr., spoke for many executives both inside the industry and out when he stated his position this January: "Corporate punishment of these people . . . would only be self-serving on my part . . . this is a management failure."

But aside from the moral question, the legal basis of G.E.'s not-guilty stance was shaky to say the least. Its lawyers felt bound to inform the Executive Office: "The trend of the law appears to be that a business corporation will be held criminally liable for the acts of an employee so long as these acts are reasonably related to the area of general responsibility entrusted to him notwithstanding the fact that such acts are committed in violation of instructions issued by the company in good faith. . . . " Under the decentralization policy, distinguishing between an "innocent" corporation and its "guilty" executives would be tough, for Cordiner himself had given the general managers clear pricing powers.

The Cordiner position had another weakness: it was based on the assumption that G.E. was involved in only four cartels—at the most. Yet wider involvement could reasonably have been expected. That very month general counsel Luebbe (who retired on October 1, 1960) had been warned by one of the general managers who had confessed that collusion would be found to have spread across the whole company front. ("I tried to tell Luebbe to stop the investigation," reflected the general manager, "and try to make a deal with the government. I told him in November, 1959, that this thing would go right across the board. He just laughed at me. He said, 'You're an isolated case—only you fellows would be stupid enough to do it.'") Thus when wider involvement actually did come to light—the four cartels multiplied into nineteen and accounted for more than 10 per cent of G.E.'s total sales—the company found itself in the ludicrous position of continuing to proclaim its corporate innocence while its executives were being implicated by platoons.

The Ax Falls

But vulnerable or not, G.E.'s posture was officially established in November, and management moved to put it into effect. Ray Smith was summoned to Arthur Vinson's big, handsome office and told he was going to be punished. His job was forfeit and his title too. There was a spot for him abroad, at substantially less money, if he wanted to try to rebuild his career in General Electric. Smith was stunned. Once implicated, he had leveled with the company to help it defend itself, and there'd been no hint of punishment then or in the succeeding two months. He decided he'd had it, at fifty-four, and would just take his severance pay and resign.

It was probably a wise move. Those conspirators who didn't quit on the spot had a very rough go of it. Initial punishment (demotion, transfer, pay cuts) was eventually followed by forced resignation, as we shall see. But the extra gall in the punishment was the inequality of treatment. William Ginn had been implicated at the same time as Ray Smith, and his case fell well within G.E.'s statute of limitations. Yet he was allowed to continue in his $135,000 job as vice president of the Turbine Division—until he went off to jail for that conspiracy, loaded with the biggest fine ($12,500) of any defendant.

Widespread resentment over this curious partiality to Ginn and over the meting out of discipline generally was destined to have its effect: willing G.E. witnesses soon began to turn up at the trust busters' camp; among them was an angry Ray Smith, who claimed he had been acting on orders from above. His mood, as a government attorney described it, was that of a man whose boss had said: "I can't get you a raise, so why don't you just take $5 out of petty cash every week. Then the man gets fired for it and the boss does nothing to help him out."

There was, however, an interval of some three months between Smith's resignation in November and his appearance in Philadelphia with his story. And eventful months they were. The first grand jury was looking into conspiracies in insulators, switchgear, circuit breakers, and several other products. The second grand jury was hearing four transformer cases and one on industrial controls. With a score of Justice men working on them, cases proliferated, and from December on lawyers began popping up trying to get immunity for their clients in return for testimony. Scarcely a week went by that Bicks and company didn't get information on at least two new cases. But what they still needed was decisive data that would break a case wide open. In January, 1960, at just about the time Ralph Cordiner was making an important speech to G.E.'s management corps ("every company and every industry—yes, and every country—that is operated on a basis of cartel systems is liquidating its present strength and future opportunities"), the trust busters hit the jackpot in switchgear.

"The Phases of the Moon"

Switchgear had been particularly baffling to the Antitrust Division, so much so that in trying to establish a cartel pattern in the jumble of switchgear prices the trust busters got the bright idea they might be in code. A cryptographer was brought in to puzzle over the figures and try to crack the secret of how a conspirator could tell what to bid and when he'd win. But the cryptographer was soon as flummoxed as everyone else. One of the government attorneys in the case, however, had made a point of dropping in on a college classmate who was the president of a small midwestern electrical-equipment company. This executive didn't have chapter and verse on the switchgear cartel but what he did have was enough for Justice to throw a scare into a bigger company, I-T-E Circuit Breaker. Indicating that subpoenas would follow, antitrust investigators asked I-T-E's general counsel, Franklyn Judson, to supply the names of sales managers in specific product lines. Judson decided to conduct an investigation of his own. When the subpoenas did come, a pink-cheeked blond young man named Nye Spencer, the company's sales manager for switchgear, was resolutely waiting—his arms loaded with data. He had decided he wasn't about to commit another crime by destroying the records so carefully laid away in his cellar.

There were pages on pages of notes taken during sessions of the switchgear conspiracy—incriminating entries like "Potomac Light & Power O.K. for G.E." and "Before bidding on this, check with G.E."; neat copies of the ground rules for meetings of the conspirators: no breakfasting together, no registering at the hotel with company names, no calls to the office, no papers to be left in hotel-room wastebaskets. Spencer, it seems, had been instructed to handle some of the secretarial work of the cartel and believed in doing it right; he'd hung onto the documents to help in training an assistant. But the most valuable windfall from the meticulous record keeper was a pile of copies of the "phases of the moon" pricing formula for as far back as May, 1958.

Not much to look at—just sheets of paper, each containing a half-dozen columns of figures—they immediately resolved the enigma of switchgear prices in commercial contracts. One group of columns established the bidding order of the seven switchgear manufacturers—a different company, each with its own code number, phasing into the priority position every two weeks (hence "phases of the moon"). A second group of columns, keyed into the company code numbers, established how much each company was to knock off the agreed-upon book price. For example, if it were No. 1's (G.E.'s) turn to be low bidder at a certain number of dollars off book, then all Westinghouse (No. 2), or Allis-Chalmers (No. 3) had to do was look for their code number in the second group of columns to find how many dollars they were to bid *above* No. 1. These bids would then be fuzzed up by having a little added to them or taken away by companies 2, 3, etc. Thus there was not even a hint that the winning bid had been collusively arrived at.

With this little device in hand, the trust busters found they could light up the whole conspiracy like a switchboard. The new evidence made an equally profound impression on the grand juries. On February 16 and 17, 1960, they handed down the first seven indictments. Forty companies and eighteen individuals were charged with fixing prices or dividing the market on seven electrical products. Switchgear led the list.

A Leg Up from Allis-Chalmers

These initial indictments brought about two major turning points in the investigation. The first was a decision by Allis-Chalmers to play ball with the government. This move came too late to save L. W. (Shorty) Long, an assistant general manager—he was one of the eighteen already indicted—but the trust busters were willing to go easier on Allis-Chalmers *if* the company came up with something solid. It did. Thousands upon thousands of documents were turned over to the government. Further, the testimony of Vice President J. W. McMullen, and others was so helpful (attorney Edward Mullinix had coached them many hours on the importance of backing up allegations with receipted hotel bills, expense-account items, memorandums, telephone logs, etc.) that a number of new cases were opened up. Only two of those first seven indictments retained their Justice Department classification as "major" cases. To them were added five new major indictments—power transformers, power switching equipment, industrial controls, turbine generators, and steam condensers—culled from thirteen to follow that spring and fall.

The second major turning point came through a decision in March by Chief Federal Judge J. Cullen Ganey, who was to try all the cases. That decision concerned whether the individuals and companies involved in the first seven indictments would be permitted to plead *nolo contendere* (no contest) to the charges. The matter was of vital importance to the companies, which might well be faced by treble-damage suits growing out of the conspiracies. (A G.E. lawyer had advised the Executive Office: "If a criminal case can be disposed of by a *nolo* plea, the prospective damage claimant is given no assistance in advancing a claim;

it must be built from the ground up.") The matter was also of great importance to a determined Robert Bicks, who argued that *nolo* pleas would permit the defendants "the luxury of a 'Maybe we did it; maybe we didn't do it' posture. 'Oh, yes, technically before Judge Ganey we admitted this, but you know we weren't guilty. You know we didn't do this.'"

Actually, in the opinion of one veteran antitrust lawyer, everybody in the industry and 99 per cent of the government thought the court would accept *nolos*. Indeed, the Justice Department was so worried about the matter, and so anxious to forfend such a development, that for the first time in the history of the department an attorney general sent a presiding judge an affidavit urging rejection of *nolos*.

"Acceptance of the *nolo* pleas tendered in these cases," William Rogers deposed to Judge Ganey, "would mean [that] . . . insistence on guilty pleas or guilty verdicts would never be appropriate in any antitrust case—no matter the predatory nature of the violation or the widespread adverse consequences to governmental purchasers. This result would neither foster respect for the law nor vindicate the public interest. These interests require, in the cases at bar here, either a trial on the issues or pleas of guilty."

But Judge Ganey didn't need to be impressed with the seriousness of the cases. He ruled that *nolo contendere* pleas were inacceptable (unless, of course, the Justice Department had no objections). The corporations and individuals would either have to plead guilty or stand trial. At the arraignment in April, Allis-Chalmers and its indicted employees promptly plead "guilty"; most others, including G.E. and its employees, pleaded "not guilty." They intended at that time to take their chances before a jury, no matter how bleak the prospects.

The Trails to Arthur Vinson

Around the time of Judge Ganey's eventful decision, Bicks and company got what seemed to be another windfall: two potential leads to the very summit of power at G.E. The first came from Ray Smith. He and a St. Louis lawyer registered at a Philadelphia hotel that February and got in touch with the local Justice Department office. The attorneys there refused to see Smith personally—he was on the way to being indicted in the transformer conspiracy and they were afraid that talking to him might be construed as pressure—but he did get his story to them via a series of notes, with the St. Louis lawyer as the go-between. The gist of it was eye-popping. In June of 1958 two top officials of G.E. and two from Westinghouse had got together during the Electrical Equipment Institute convention in Boston. The meeting had taken up the matter of stabilizing prices in transformers, among other products. That cartel was not only to be kept alive; it was to be revitalized.

At first blush Smith's charge looked like the answer to a trust buster's dream. But under careful checking some serious flaws arose: Smith could only attest to what Arthur Vinson, allegedly one of the two G.E. officials at the Boston meeting, had told him of the top-level get-together. Any account by Vinson to Smith of what the other parties had said or done was hearsay. Moreover, in the face of Vinson's expected denial that any such meeting had ever occurred it would be just Smith's word against Vinson's—unless, of course, corroborating evidence might come to light in the course of the investigation. None ever did, apparently, for nothing came of the charge.

The second lead to top-level executives, however, was based on the evidence not of one man but four. Vice President George Burens, head of G.E.'s Switchgear Division, and his three departmental general managers (Clarence Burke, H. F. Hentschel, and Frank Stehlik)—all of whom had been indicted in switchgear that February—trooped down to Washington and claimed the government had missed the key man: their boss, again Group Executive Arthur Vinson.

Needless to say, Antitrust was fascinated. On top of Smith's charges, here were four of the company's general managers, one a vice president, now prepared to swear that Vinson had authorized them to rejoin a price-fixing conspiracy sometime in the third quarter of 1958. Moreover, their story was a clear-cut account, with few of the ambiguities the Justice Department had come to expect from G.E. witnesses.

The Luncheon in Dining Room B

The story, as Clarence Burke told it to the Justice Department, to the grand jury, and, last month, to *Fortune*, began with a 1958 visit by Vinson to the Philadelphia works. Burens had been under heavy fire from other apparatus general managers, because, they said, his cut-rate switchgear prices were bringing complaints from their customers, who considered they should be getting similar discounts on other G.E. equipment. Now, according to Burke, Vinson himself was taking up the cudgels to get a reluctant Burens to raise switchgear prices by reactivating the cartel.

This is Burke's account of the episode: "I got a call from Burens to drop by his office [in Philadelphia]. Arthur Vinson was there and Burens, looking like the wreck of the Hesperus. Burens said 'Tell Art your experience contacting competitors, particularly Westinghouse,' So I said, 'Art, we've been in and out and we've tried it so much but they only try to make monkeys out of us, particularly

Westinghouse. They get us to agree to book prices and then they chisel.' Art said that that wouldn't take place any more, that it had all been squared away. I said I had heard that before, then they say they hadn't had enough control over their field. Vinson said, 'I have assurance of it from Montieth [Westinghouse vice president]; they don't want to be leaders, they just want to make money.' Burens said, 'See, that confirms it—we don't have to be in.' Vinson said (with some vehemence), 'I told you I've got it all set up.' So Burens said, 'All right, we'll re-establish contacts.' Then he said something like 'I know you're in a hurry, Art. I've called the two other managers and we'll have a quick lunch.'

"As we came out of Burens' office, I saw Stehlik coming down the corridor toward us and noticed that he wouldn't reach the turn which led down to dining room B, so I dropped back and waited for him. He remembers this, and on the way down to the dining room I briefed him on Art's having ordered us to re-establish contacts.

"All during lunch we talked about price stability and I tried to get Art to say the same thing he had in Burens' office, but he wouldn't volunteer anything. Finally, I said, Art, these competitors of ours have been calling us up recently.' He looked as if he could have hit me, and Burens said quickly, 'Yes, Art, what do you think we ought to do?' Vinson said again we ought to talk to them, but he said don't let it get below the general managers' level."

Burke's best recollection was that the Vinson order occurred between the end of July and September 13, 1958. In independent testimony, Burens set it in August or September; Stehlik, between mid-August and October; Hentschel, the latter part of August. The dates were highly important, in view of subsequent events; they were also highly illuminating. They fitted in nicely with Ray Smith's story of the top-level Boston meeting that June, the meeting reported to him by Vinson where Westinghouse and G.E. had allegedly decided to bury the hatchet and get together again on prices.

As a result of this information, Vinson was indicted. Clarence Burke's name was dropped from the new switchgear indictment in consideration of his testimony against Vinson, although he continued to be charged for conspiracy in circuit breakers. Then a few weeks later the government chestily filed a Voluntary Bill of Particulars, which included Cordiner, Paxton, and the board of directors among those charged with the illegal switchgear actions. In the same bill the government volunteered the time and place of Vinson's alleged instruction of Burens, et al. to reactivate the switchgear cartel "in or about July, August, or September, 1958, at General Electric's plant in Philadelphia."

The Bill of Particulars had been intended as a tactical move to impress G.E. with the strength of the switchgear case and influence the corporation to change its not-guilty plea. It had just the opposite effect. The company lawyers realized that if Group Executive Vinson went down, their whole corporate defense (no authorization) would collapse at the same time. Moreover, they were by then familiar with "the Vinson lunch," having got wind of it in April during some re-interviews with Burke and others. Vinson had denied the whole affair. More than that, he had come up with records of his whereabouts during 1958. Now that the government had particularized the time, place, and individuals, all Vinson had to do was prove he'd never even been in Philadelphia during July, August, and September of 1958.

A Talk with Bicks

Necessarily, the Vinson case had a vital bearing on how G.E. would plead on its own indictments, but the issue was also important to the other corporate defendants. The one thing nobody wanted was a trial where the dirty linen of the conspiracies would be washed every day in the public press. If one company, or even an employee of one company, chose to stand trial, everyone else might just as well too, for all the juicy details of their involvement would surely come out. But the problem of settling the case without trial was complicated by the fact that the companies involved were of different sizes and degrees of guilt. Five companies, for example, had had no part in any conspiracy save steam condensers; they were understandably opposed to any package deal on the twenty indictments that committed them to a guilty plea instead of the *nolo* plea they might otherwise have been allowed to make.

G.E. and Westinghouse, however, were both convinced by now that rapid settlement was essential. G.E.'s own hopes of a successful not-guilty plea had been trampled to death under the parade of grand-jury witnesses, and were interred by a decision in the Continental Baking case that summer. Moreover, Bicks and company still had the grand juries going full blast; at the rate these were taking testimony any delay in settling might dump a half-dozen additional indictments on top of the twenty already handed down. Judge Ganey was certainly willing to speed up the proceedings and suggested all defendant companies have an exploratory talk with Robert Bicks.

On the thirty-first of October the lawyers of almost all the affected companies crowded into a Justice Department conference room and from nine in the morning till seven that night worked at hammering out a package of guilty and *nolo* pleas. On thirteen "minor" cases, where only corporations had been indicted, Bicks was willing to accept *nolos*, but he insisted on guilty pleas in the seven major cases. And he wanted pleas (guilty or *nolos*) on all twenty indictments at the same time. But one thing stood in the way of the package deal: G.E.'s insistence on trial or dismissal of the Vinson indictment in switchgear, a major case.

Early the next month Vinson himself made a move that for cool nerve commanded the respect of even Justice Department attorneys. He offered to let the government see the evidence supporting his alibi. If the evidence failed to convince Bicks that his indictment should be dismissed, then he'd be at a serious disadvantage, having given the government that much more time to poke holes in his alibi. Bicks accepted the offer with alacrity; in his office on Sunday night, November 6, the curtain rose on one of the strangest incidents of the whole affair.

Eight Fateful Days

Vinson's attorneys had got recapitulations of the testimony about the luncheon in the Philadelphia plant from the executives concerned. That luncheon allegedly took place in company dining room B, so it had to occur on a working day. There were fifty-odd working days in July, August, and September, but only eight when Burens, Burke, Hentschel, and Stehlik were all at the plant between the hours of eleven and one. For those eight days, said Vinson's lawyers, his expense accounts showed no Philadelphia trip, and Vinson was a man who put the smallest items on that account. There was no entry in the company-plane log showing a Philadelphia flight for Vinson on the eight days, though he was an inveterate flyer, nor any such entry in the executive-limousine log. On one of the eight days the head of a fund-raising committee at Michigan State had a toll slip on a telephone call to Vinson in New York at close to noon, eastern standard time. On another, a Manhattan banking transaction had been stamped at a late morning hour. For two days Vinson could prove he had been with some Little Cabinet officers in Washington. There was a Pinnacle Club luncheon check testifying he'd had a noon meal in New York with an executive from another company and other checks from G.E.'s executive dining room, consecutively numbered and countersigned by the waitress. And so it went.

Bicks was impressed. The next day the expense-account records of the Four (Burens, Burke, Hentschel, and Stehlik) were examined and Bicks made a disquieting discovery. There was no item showing a group luncheon with Vinson in the records of the Four. Vinson had been indicted without an expense-account item to help corroborate the conspiratorial meeting. This led Bicks to wonder whether the whole Vinson charge might not be a self-serving fabrication, to support a plea of corporate coercion. He summoned the Four to Washington, and they volunteered there to go through lie-detector tests.

It was a grueling experience, considering the perjury charges hanging on the outcome, but certainly a dramatic one. The procedure was to establish the "lie pattern" of each individual by recording his uncertainties under casual questions and then compare this pattern with his response to sudden queries about the

Vinson lunch. Clarence Burke's lie pattern was established early when he hesitated on being asked if he'd ever been arrested ("I was wondering if 'arrest' meant being nabbed by a traffic cop"). Then the FBI man asked unimportant things like where he'd lived and worked and sensitive things like whether he'd ever cheated on his income tax (he said he had) and whether Vinson was in Philadelphia between July 31 and September 13 (he reiterated that Vinson was). The machine showed Burke to be telling the truth; Burens, Hentschel, and Stehlik also came through their lie-detector tests with flying colors.

There was now no doubt in the minds of the trust busters about the veracity of the Four. But corroborative evidence, not lie-detector tests, was needed to demolish the Vinson alibi. The government promptly assigned a score of agents to that job.

The Impregnable Alibi

As the weeks ticked off, FBI men poked Vinson's picture at Philadelphia cab drivers to see if anyone remembered driving him to the switchgear plant, examined notebooks for erasures, interviewed scores of individuals. The most likely day of their meeting, Justice figured, was September 12. Vinson's alibi for that day consisted of some phone calls and a bank deposit in New York; but G.E. records couldn't pin down the time of the phone calls and the bank deposit had been made after two o'clock. But then the investigation turned up a G.E. man who had written a detailed memorandum of his activities during that day, and they included a meeting with Vinson in the New York office just before lunch.

All weekend December 3 and 4 Bicks pondered the Vinson case. He was of half a mind to press for Vinson's trial anyhow, banking that corroborative evidence might turn up then or proof be forthcoming that the incident with the Four had occurred earlier, say in 1957, at the time Vinson became vice president of the Apparatus Group. On the other hand, Vinson's alibi had stood up like a rock; it seemed certain to get him off the hook and might even win jury sympathy for the other switchgear defendants. Bicks decided to drop the charges.

In a carefully worded statement, government attorneys informed Judge Ganey they couldn't "argue convincingly to a jury of Vinson's guilt of the specific charges contained in the Bill of Particulars." At the same time, they set aside the charge in the Bill of Particulars that Cordiner, Paxton, and G.E.'s board of directors had authorized the switchgear conspiracy, and stated that the government did not now claim any of them "had knowledge of the conspiracies . . . nor that any of these men personally authorized or ordered commission of any of the acts charged."

So the curtain rang down on the Vinson case, and then went up on the last act of the drama. With Vinson's involvement no longer at issue, G.E. pleaded "guilty" to all the major indictments against it, and with the government's consent, *nolo contendere* to the thirteen "minor" ones. The other major companies followed suit. The way thus cleared, judgment was swift in coming. On February 6, executives from every major manufacturer in the entire electrical-equipment industry sat in a crowded courtroom and heard Judge Ganey declare: "What is really at stake here is the survival of the kind of economy under which this country has grown great, the free-enterprise system." Seven executives went off to a Pennsylvania prison; twenty-three others, given suspended jail sentences, were put on probation for five years; and fines totaling nearly $2 million were handed out.

Twenty-nine companies received fines ranging from $437,500 for G.E. down to $7,500 each for Carrier Corp. and Porcelain Insulator Corp. The others, for the record, were: Allen-Bradley Co., Allis-Chalmers Manufacturing Co., A. B. Chance Co., Clark Controller Co., Cornell-Dubilier Electric Corp., Cutler-Hammer, Inc., Federal Pacific Electric Co., Foster Wheeler Corp., Hubbard & Co., I-T-E Circuit Breaker Co., Ingersoll-Rand Co., Joslyn Manufacturing & Supply Co., Kuhlman Electric Co., Lapp Insulator Co., McGraw-Edison Co., Moloney Electric Co., Ohio Brass Co., H. K. Porter Co., Sangamo Electric Co., Schwager-Wood Corp., Southern States Equipment Corp., Square D Co., Wagner Electric Corp., Westinghouse Electric Corp., C. H. Wheeler Manufacturing Co., and Worthington Corp.

Is the Lesson Learned?

So ended the incredible affair—a story of cynicism, arrogance, and irresponsibility. Plainly there was an egregious management failure. But there was also a failure to connect ordinary morals and business morals; the men involved apparently figured there was a difference.

The consent decrees now being hammered out by the Justice Department are partial insurance that bid rigging and price fixing won't happen again. Yet consent decrees are only deterrents, not cures. The fact is that the causes which underlay the electrical conspiracies are still as strong as they ever were. Chronic overcapacity continues to exert a strong downward pressure on prices. The industry's price problem—outgrowth of an inability to shift the buyer's attention from price to other selling points like higher quality, better service, improved design—could hardly be worse: many items of electrical equipment are currently selling for less than in the ruinous days of the "white sale." Corporate pressure is stronger than ever on executives, who must struggle to fulfill the conflicting demands of bigger gross sales on the one hand and more profit per dollar of net sales on the other. These are matters that require careful handling if conspiracy is not to take root again in the electrical-equipment industry.

The antitrust laws also confront the largest corporations with a special dilemma: how to compete without falling afoul of Section 2 of the Sherman Act, which makes it unlawful to "monopolize, or attempt to monopolize." It will take plenty of business statesmanship to handle this aspect of the law; one way, of course, is simply to refrain from going after every last piece of business. If G.E. were to drive for 50 per cent of the market, even strong companies like I-T-E Circuit Breaker might be mortally injured.

Has the industry learned any lessons? "One thing I've learned out of all this," said one executive, "is to talk to only one other person, not to go to meetings where there are lots of other people." Many of the defendants *Fortune* interviewed both before and after sentencing looked on themselves as the fall guys of U.S. business. They protested that they should no more be held up to blame than many another American businessman, for conspiracy is just as much "a way of life" in other fields as it was in electrical equipment. "Why pick on us?" was the attitude. "Look at some of those other fellows."

This attitude becomes particularly disturbing when one considers that most of the men who pleaded guilty in Judge Ganey's court (to say nothing of the scores given immunity for testifying before the grand juries) are back at their old positions, holding down key sales and marketing jobs. Only G.E. cleaned house; out went Burens, Burke, Hentschel, and Stehlik, plus ten others, including the heretofore unpunished William S. Ginn. (Although the confessed conspirators at G.E. had been assured that the transfers, demotions, and pay cuts received earlier would be the end of their corporate punishment, this was not the case. In mid-March they were told they could either quit or be fired, and were given anywhere from a half hour to a few days to make their decision.)

Disjointed Authority, Disjointed Morals

But top executive officers of the biggest companies, at least, have come out of their antitrust experience determined upon strict compliance programs and possessed now of enough insight into the workings of a cartel to make those programs effective. Allis-Chalmers has set up a special compliance section. G.E. and Westinghouse, without which cartels in the industry could never endure, are taking more elaborate preventive measures. Both are well aware that any repetition of these conspiracies would lay them open to political pressure for dismemberment; size has special responsibilities in our society, and giants are under a continuous obligation to demonstrate that they have not got so big as to lose control over their far-flung divisions.

This case has focused attention on American business practices as nothing else has in many years. Senator Kefauver says he intends to probe further into the question of conspiracy at the top levels of management. Justice Department investigations are proliferating. Said Attorney General Robert Kennedy this April: "We are redoubling our efforts to convince anyone so minded that conspiracy as 'a way of life' must mean a short and unhappy one."

The problem for American business does not start and stop with the scofflaws of the electrical industry or with antitrust. Much was made of the fact that G.E. operated under a system of disjointed authority, and this was one reason it got into trouble. A more significant factor, the disjointment of morals, is something for American executives to think about in all aspects of their relations with their companies, each other, and the community.

QUESTIONS FOR REVIEW AND DISCUSSION

1. How would you have responded to the statement that follows, made by one of the corporate presidents who was quoted in the case study regarding the conspiracy: "It is the only way a business can be run. It is free enterprise."

2. Can a business practice be "illegal" but not "unethical," as one General Electric executive maintained in defending the conspiracy?

3. What could or should Ralph Cordiner of General Electric have done beyond the steps he had taken to prevent his company from being involved in activities that violated the Sherman Antitrust Act?

4. Since General Electric's top management suffered no personal penalties, should the General Electric executives who were involved in the conspiracy have been fired or forced to resign, as they were?

5. Were the Justice Department's and the court's actions severe enough? What do you think the penalties should have been?

6. Do you think that conspiracies between competing companies still occur in the business community despite the precedent of the 1961 convictions?

J. B. COWDEN.
PROVISIONS.
903
COWDEN'S CASH CORNER.
CORNER.
WHITE CLOUD

14

The Coming of the Conglomerates

During the decades of the 1950s and 1960s, a major wave of mergers swept through the business community in the United States. It was the third such wave in the twentieth century, but it differed from its two predecessors in that it lasted longer and was characterized by a new corporate phenomenon, mergers by conglomerates. The parties who were involved in those mergers were neither direct competitors nor did they have a supplier-customer relationship. The organizations that resulted from these mergers were combinations of firms—usually eight or more—with totally unrelated products. Mergers of conglomerates accounted for over 50 percent of all business mergers in the 1950s and more than 60 percent in the following decade.

These conglomerates were frequently the creations of aggressive, individualistic entrepreneurs such as Harold S. Geneen (International Telephone and Telegraph), Charles "Tex" Thornton (Litton Industries), and James Ling (Ling-Temco-Vought). Such managers believed that they could apply their general business expertise to companies in any industry with equal success. They also believed in the concept of synergism, that is, the potential for profits of the merged conglomerates would far exceed that of each firm operating separately. Expressed in numerical shorthand, these corporate empire-builders were convinced that $2 + 2 = 5$.

During the difficult days of the 1970s, the glamour wore off of the conglomerates. The number of such mergers declined sharply from over seven hundred in the late 1960s to less than two hundred by the mid-1970s. Governmental criticism as well as poor profit records accounted for the conglomerate's temporary fall from grace. Questions arose as to whether conglomerates were adding anything of real significance or permanence to the productive capacity of American industry. Was the nation better off or worse off as a result of these corporate manipulations? One critic argued: "The new conglomerate managers did not discover new management techniques, but rather a seemingly endless number of tax, accounting, and financial gimmicks that favored merger over internal growth."[1]

With the advent of a benign Reagan administration in Washington, D.C., and a galloping stock market in New York, the 1980s, however, have seen the century's fourth great wave of mergers develop. Heated discussions about corporate takeovers, some engineered by financial raiders, fill the columns of the business press. Many of the same questions that plagued the issue of conglomerates in the 1960s are being debated once more. In the following case study, the growth of one conglomerate, the Beatrice Corporation, is traced. While not one of the more volatile or controversial conglomerates, the development of Beatrice provides a good example of the role that the conglomerate should and often does play in the American economy.

Notes

1. Willard F. Mueller, *The Structure of American Industry*, 5th ed. (New York: Macmillan Publishing Co., 1977), 453.

Harry C. McDean

BEATRICE: THE HISTORICAL PROFILE OF AN AMERICAN-STYLED CONGLOMERATE

Ask a friend about Beatrice and the most likely response you will get is, "Isn't that the company that makes almost everything?"

Of course, your friend is right. In recent years, Beatrice, the 36th largest industrial corporation in America, manufactured over 8,000 product lines and marketed them under more than 200 widely recognized brand names.[1]

Like Mexican food? Buy Beatrice's Rosarita products. Prefer Chinese? Then pick up its La Choy brand. Want good old American food instead? How about a Butterball Turkey or one of the other Swift processed food products manufactured by Beatrice. Want to pan fry that meat? Use its Wesson oil. Need to spice up that meat with catsup or barbecue sauce? Try any one of its Hunt's products. Hate regular food and like candy instead? Buy one of its Clark candies, such as Holloway Milk Duds. Want something to quench the thirst that follows? Buy some Tropicana juices or Coca-Cola from one of the bottling companies that Beatrice owns. Prefer milk? Then buy Meadow Gold milk, one of Beatrice's best-known milk labels. Do you thirst for pure, clean water instead? Call your friendly Culligan (Beatrice) man, or go to the store and buy bottled Arrowhead. Need a lamp for the living room? Buy a Stiffel that Beatrice produces. Interested in intimate apparel? Then try its Playtex line. Need a suitcase? Try Samsonite, Beatrice's line of luggage. And if you simply want to escape from it all, call Avis and rent one of its cars.

Beatrice, of course, does not want to produce everything. If you bought Hart skis in the mid-1970s, then you bought Beatrice. But not so, if you bought them recently. Beatrice has gotten out of the ski business, and out of many other businesses as well. For example, Beatrice no longer owns Dannon yogurt, Harmon-Khardon stereo speakers, Mothers cookies, STP automobile additives, or Airstream travel trailers. Moreover, when Beatrice acquired other conglomerates, it did not acquire all their products. Some of those product lines were sold by the parent companies just prior to their acquisition by Beatrice. For example, Esmark, which Beatrice acquired in 1984, had sold several of its nationally traded brands just months before it was acquired by Beatrice. And to make this scenario even more intriguing, Norton Simon, which Beatrice acquired when it bought Esmark (Esmark had bought Norton Simon in 1983), had sold its Swift Fresh Meats Division in 1981, which explains why Beatrice does not own Swift Meats while it does own Swift Foods.

Does this checkerboard of businesses and business mergers confuse you? Welcome to the world of "The American-Styled Conglomerate." It is a world that appears, on the surface, to be a montage: one that is contrived, patched together with the bits and pieces of various product lines, but one that has no apparent design and purpose. This surface appearance of the conglomerate world often determines what its critics—journalists and scholars alike—have to say about it. Their most common judgment is that America's conglomerates, like Beatrice, have been created by a generation of managers who suffer from "merger mania," an apparent psychosis that has led them on a relentless and blind acquisitions' binge.[2] In reality, a conglomerate is a company formed from the merger of several business enterprises producing different goods and services, in order to protect itself against the dangers of product specialization and to make possible the advantages of superior management and economies of scale.[3]

To comprehend this montage of the conglomerate world, however, one must look beneath the surface and examine the economic, political, and social background in which they developed. This brief case study approaches the development of Beatrice by looking beneath the surface to the broader forces of American history that helped create and then continually restyled Beatrice. Beatrice's managers did not operate in a vacuum, but rather were buffeted by the processes of historical change. They sought to reshape Beatrice so that it would fit into that process of change. Far from being a patchwork, Beatrice reflects, and in fact is, the image of institutional change in twentieth-century America.

During its formative years in the 1890s, Beatrice reflected the historical environment that produced it. Life in general was simple in the nation's midwestern farm belt in the 1890s, and so was Beatrice. As was the case with most midwestern businesses in the late nineteenth century, Beatrice was run initially by its owners, not by managers. Unlike many such companies, however, Beatrice was named for a town—Beatrice, Nebraska—not for its founders. There, in Beatrice, Nebraska, two small businesses—one that marketed cream and another the butter and eggs of local farmers—had opened and closed their doors during the 1880s. They were bought in 1894 by two former employees, George E. Haskell and William W. Bosworth, who formed a partnership called Beatrice Creamery Company.[4]

As was true of nearly all businesspeople in the late nineteenth century, Haskell and Bosworth had neither a college education nor any professional training in business. Few people who intended to go into business in the 1860s and 1870s went to college; there were no schools of business in the nation's universities. People such as Haskell and Bosworth achieved what they did in business, not as a result of formal training, but rather because they perceived more clearly than did others the processes of historical change.[5]

Haskell and Bosworth correctly saw in the 1890s that a new trend was underway in American farming. In the 1880s and 1890s, major universities in the Midwest, such as Iowa State and the nearby University of Nebraska, had founded schools of agriculture in which were organized research programs to help educate farmers. These programs, together with those sponsored by the federal government under its newly formed Experiment Stations, encouraged midwestern farmers to grow *silage crops*—crops that could be stored in silos and fed to farm animals during the winter. By diversifying their operations, farmers no longer tied their incomes to the prices that a single crop fetched on the commercial market. Farmers were not only raising hogs to sell on the market, but now also had milk from their cows and eggs from their chickens to sell, as well.[6]

Midwestern towns, just as midwestern farms, were undergoing changes of historic moment. Omaha, Nebraska, boomed as a result of the railroad lines that converged in it. Omaha's population doubled between 1880 and 1885, then doubled again by 1888 to exceed 120,000 residents. The decision to locate the state university in Lincoln, Nebraska, just south of Beatrice, caused Lincoln's population to double between 1885 and 1887. By the early 1890s, it too was expected to exceed the 100,000 mark. Beatrice, Nebraska, itself was proclaiming by the early 1890s that its population soon would exceed 50,000.[7]

The market for farm products expanded in these and in other burgeoning midwestern cities. There was an increased demand by the growing urban population for fresh farm products. Farmers, however, faced several problems in meeting that demand.

Even though urban customers were not as knowledgeable about farm products as were the farmers, they soon realized the marked differences in the quality and character of milk products and eggs. In fact, so concerned were most urban residents about the quality of fresh milk that few grocers were interested in selling it. At that time milk was dipped from large milk cans and poured into individual containers in the store. Contamination often occurred and milk-related epidemics were common. Butter, the most common milk product, was also suspected of being contaminated. Exploiting these reasonable fears, Haskell and Bosworth determined to eliminate their customers' fears by grading butter, eggs, and poultry. They designed special protective wrappings and packages; printed their brand name, Beatrice Creamery Company, on their cream and butter labels; and distributed their products to grocery stores and restaurants in their own covered wagons with the name Beatrice on the sides.[8]

Thus was formed one of the cornerstones upon which Beatrice's success was built—brand identification, or, in the terminology of economists, product differentiation. As early as the 1890s, Beatrice found that urban customers could be taught to prefer certain brands of basically homogeneous products, such as butter. Once the urban customer became accustomed to differentiating a product by its brand name, then a market for that product was established. Based on this initial discovery by businesspeople like Haskell and Bosworth, economic research eventually confirmed that once the market share of a brand name was established in the manufacturing of food products, it was difficult for new entrants to cut into that market.[9] Thus, Beatrice Creamery—as the first entrant into Nebraska's packaged, brand name labeled, butter business—was assured success.

Haskell and Bosworth also enjoyed initial success because they solved another problem that midwestern farmers faced in the late nineteenth century—that of transporting their goods to market. Farmers could not afford the risk and the expense involved in transporting their perishable products in horse-drawn buggies over rough country roads to urban markets.[10] Recognizing the problem, Haskell and Bosworth developed a marketing strategy that not only became a hallmark of Beatrice's marketing system in the years to come, but also provided one of the cornerstones upon which Beatrice's marketing success was built.

Haskell and Bosworth decentralized their operations by establishing branch offices. These offices were strategically located and were responsible for conducting Beatrice's business in a specific area. In the 1890s, however, using branch offices was far simpler than it is today. Initially, local farmers delivered their eggs, produce, cream, and butter—freshly collected that day on the farm—to the branch offices. Soon, however, Haskell and Bosworth faced what virtually every company, including the Beatrice organization, has faced from that day until the present: the *old* structure would not work in the *new* economic environment. In modern jargon, a *restructuring* was needed. Restructuring is another practice that has occurred with such regularity at Beatrice that it too has become a hallmark of its operations.

Faced with an exploding demand for their packaged and labeled butter, Haskell and Bosworth located *skimming stations*—places where the cream was skimmed from the milk—at strategic points along less-traveled roads in Nebraska. This strategy gave Beatrice access to farmers who were unable to reach the branch offices. Soon, Beatrice made even this operation more efficient by selling newly designed cream separators to the farmers, so they could separate the cream from the milk themselves on their farms. The benefit was mutual: Beatrice lowered its operating and overhead costs at the skimming stations, and the farmers not only used the skimmed milk to feed their farm animals but also more easily delivered their cream to Beatrice's stations. Before long Beatrice had sold more than 50,000 separators to Nebraska's farmers.[11]

This early restructuring of Beatrice affected its ownership also. At the turn of the century, Haskell assumed sole ownership of the Beatrice Creamery Company, and Bosworth received a settlement that allowed him to establish his own produce business within Beatrice. Both were pleased with the new arrangement. This settlement, however, contained two lessons for future changes at Beatrice.

First, the business environment of the early twentieth century was such that disputes over business strategy were easily resolved. In the case of Beatrice, the business merely was split so that one of the principals could pursue his own special interests which did not compete with those of the other. Much later, however, sharp changes in Beatrice's historical environment eventually prevented it from so easily resolving disputes that its managers had over business strategy. Those kinds of disputes, we shall learn, helped to erode the strength of Beatrice in the 1970s and 1980s.

Second, the fact that Haskell's Beatrice Creamery Company went on to become nationally prominent while Bosworth's produce company withered away illustrates a widely held belief among marketers: while consumers differentiate among brands within certain homogeneous product lines, they will not necessarily do so in others. Unfortunately, Bosworth learned through the demise of his own business the lesson that failure can be caused by an inexplicable unwillingness of consumers to differentiate among certain types of brand name products.[12] Marketing experts today still cannot adequately explain why consumers will differentiate by brand name among some homogeneous products and not others. Beatrice itself eventually was plagued by deadly, wrenching debates among its managers over which products were likely to succeed in the marketplace.

In the early period of Beatrice's history, of course, the solution to such marketing problems was resolved very simply. While Bosworth's business waned, Haskell's business grew as a result of the willingness of consumers to differentiate his brand name—Meadow Gold—from that of others. So great was the demand for Meadow Gold Butter that Haskell soon had more than 350 cream-receiving stations operating throughout Nebraska. These stations delivered so much cream to Beatrice that in 1904 Haskell installed a newly designed churn in Lincoln, which produced more than ten million pounds of butter in its first year of operation.[13]

This new installation, together with construction of cold storage facilities, needed to store the products, pushed Haskell into America's world of high finance. When Haskell and Bosworth had incorporated in 1898 in Nebraska, they had done so simply to take advantage of that state's limited liability laws. The two men jointly had been able to handle the $100,000 capitalization of Beatrice. But Haskell's financial needs changed when he reached a settlement with Bosworth to end their partnership, installed the new churn at Lincoln, and built new cold storage warehouses.

Those financial needs led Haskell across the border into Des Moines, Iowa, where financial markets were more fully developed. There in 1905 he acquired new funds and reincorporated. Beatrice's capitalization was brought to $3,000,000. At this point, Beatrice went public to secure funds for further capitalization and to construct additional plants in Topeka, Kansas; Oklahoma City, Oklahoma; Pueblo, Colorado; and Chicago, Illinois. Going public meant that Beatrice sold shares of its stock to investors through the financial brokers in Des Moines.[14]

Yet in spite of this move, Beatrice remained a closely held company, even after Haskell's death in 1919. As shall be seen, the dramatic changes in financial markets and corporate structures that swept the country during the 1920s profoundly affected Beatrice. To cope with these changes, Beatrice in 1924 went public in the classic meaning of the term; that is, Beatrice incorporated in the state of Delaware. Delaware's laws permitted companies to exist in the state on paper only, to raise capital through the sale of stock, and to exchange stock in any fashion they chose for the stock of other companies. From that point forward, Beatrice would be shaped by the forces that work in the stock market.[15]

That Beatrice sought new states in which to incorporate under more permissive laws merely reflected what was happening in the dairy business. Just as Haskell had found that he could differentiate Meadow Gold Butter in the minds of consumers, so others had discovered they could do the same for their dairy products (e.g., Borden for canned milk, Carnation for dried milk, Kraft for cheese). Companies such as Borden, Carnation, and Kraft formed corporations to help finance the construction of plants that they needed to enter new markets.[16] Yet Beatrice, cognizant of the potential competition Meadow Gold Butter might face from those corporations, was careful not to fan their competitive spirits.

Hence, in the early twentieth century, Beatrice entered geographic markets where it posed no threat to the emerging national dairy corporations. In other words, Beatrice entered markets where its flagship product—Meadow Gold Butter—has little if any competition. Beatrice did not challenge the flagship dairy products, such as cheese and canned milk, sold by the leading dairy companies—especially the fast growing national companies like Kraft, Borden, Carnation, and Foremost. Beatrice knew fully well that the dairy products of those companies were differentiated in the minds of consumers, and thus it would be a mistake for Beatrice to attempt to compete with them.

Moreover, Beatrice found that those national companies seemed reluctant to enter their own brands of butter into competition with Meadow Gold. There were solid economic reasons behind that reluctance for the national companies knew that Beatrice had a network of farmers throughout the Midwest that provided it with inexpensive cream. Thus Beatrice had a decisive advantage over most of the urban-based dairy product companies in the manufacturing of creamery products.[17]

To further discourage the competition, even that of local creameries, Beatrice employed a highly successful marketing strategy. By wrapping its butter in airtight packages, labeled elegantly with the Meadow Gold trademark, Beatrice's urban consumers were guaranteed that their butter was made from cream pasteurized by the nation's largest, most advanced technology. Available in handy one-pound packages, Meadow Gold Butter became the first dairy product to be advertised in nationally distributed magazines, beginning in 1912. Soon thereafter, Beatrice launched a national newspaper advertising campaign, mailed promotional fliers, and placed Meadow Gold posters on the counters of grocery stores.[18]

Thus, by the time Haskell died in 1919, Meadow Gold Butter lead the nation in sales. Those who worked for Haskell had learned lessons that encouraged them in future years to venture into and out of various businesses in accordance with changes in consumer interests. First, they had learned from Bosworth's experience that some products cannot be differentiated between in the minds of consumers. Second, when a brand name product can be differentiated from others, it is comparatively easy to enter a new market if that brand name product is widely recognized and nationally advertised. Third, entry into new markets is easiest when potential competitors have as yet failed to manufacture a similar brand name product. Finally, it is best to enter new markets with flagship products only. That strategy diminishes the threat to other corporations that sell closely related products in a geographic area (e.g., canned milk and fresh milk) and thereby serves to blunt any hostile or competitive reactions.

Those lessons explain why Beatrice employed history far more than logic in devising its business strategy in the 1920s. History taught Beatrice lessons that defied logic, as well as the emerging economic theories. Theories in economics

during the 1920s encouraged "economies of scale"—corporations were instructed to integrate virtually all the operations that were related to their product line.
Such integrations both horizontal and vertical would help managers cut their
overhead and operating costs.[19]

Yet, because of the aforementioned lessons in marketing strategy, Beatrice was
slower than most to integrate. Like most corporations in the 1920s, Beatrice incorporated in Delaware to take advantage of the array of securities options that
Delaware's laws provided. But unlike other corporations, Beatrice was cautious.
Many companies issued new securities and often traded them for securities in
other firms that they wanted to integrate into their own. Beatrice traded securities
selectively—even after the stock market crash of 1929 abruptly drove down stock
prices, thus making it cheap to buy stock in companies that had formerly had expensive stock.

Several historical observations encouraged Beatrice's caution. One very obvious observation, although many outsiders failed to understand it then as well as
today, was that *reverse* integration in the dairy business was unthinkable. Even
during the height of its financial flurries during the 1920s, Beatrice never considered *buying backwards*, or reverse integration, to obtain its own herds of dairy
cows, milking equipment, dairy farms, and the like. Knowledgeable dairy-
products manufacturers knew from observation that because dairy operations
were only a part of the diversified activities of midwestern farmers, no sophisticated business manager could restructure a company to produce milk cheaper than
the farmers could. In addition, Beatrice's decentralized field operations educated
its managers on the complex economies inherent in modern commercial farming. They recognized that these economies would forever make American
farming a high-risk capitalist enterprise.[20]

A second observation persuaded Beatrice to avoid the rush to integrate. Its own
history provided solid testimony about the potential hostility or competitive reactions that might be generated should Beatrice integrate *forward*. While many
corporations bought companies that marketed their goods, Beatrice did not. Nor
did it attempt to build its own sales stores. Beatrice never became involved in the
fast-paced growth of grocery store chains—like Safeway, A&P, and Kroger.[21] Instead, Beatrice continued to sell its butter as it always had—at the wholesale level
through its network of jobbers and refrigerated warehouses. To enter competition
at the retail level would invite hostility from the chains, perhaps resulting in the
introduction of store-label butter to replace that of Meadow Gold.

For similar reasons, Beatrice integrated horizontally with great caution during
the 1920s. Not wishing to encourage competition for its butter, Beatrice wisely
expanded operations only in creamery-products plants down through 1929. As it
did so, it tested new creamery-product lines that faced little, if any, competition.

The result was that Beatrice found ways to process, package, and label a new product—Meadow Gold Ice Cream—that could be differentiated from other ice creams in the consumer's mind.

Beatrice's entry into the ice cream market dated back to 1907 at its Topeka creamery. Served on cones at soda fountains located in pharmacies, the ice cream did not sell well because product differentiation was impossible to establish. The consumers did not always know what brand of ice cream was on their cone. As late as 1927, Beatrice sold less than five hundred thousand gallons. By 1931, however, it was producing more than ten million gallons annually.

Such a dramatic increase in ice cream production occurred because Beatrice had invested heavily in a new piece of ice cream technology called Vogt Continuous Freeze. Installed for the hefty price tag of $600,000, the new technology permitted Beatrice to manufacture a new brand name—Meadow Gold Smooth Freeze—in attractive half-gallon packages.[22]

Beatrice had good reasons for making the investment. It perceived several changes in the ice cream market that the new technology could exploit. To begin with, it soon became clear that during times of social upheaval—such as an economic depression—people enjoyed frivolous, small delights, which included an ice cream treat. More important, the by then obvious success of the chain stores, equipped with large freezers that displayed frozen products (beginning in 1930), provided a new, stable market for conveniently packaged, nationally advertised ice creams.[23]

For somewhat similar reasons, Beatrice slowly entered the fresh milk market. In 1927, it owned only four fresh milk plants, which, as in the case of its ice cream, were strategically located so as not to invite competition. Beatrice's production of fresh milk was an experiment to determine the extent to which one brand of fresh milk could be differentiated from others in the consumer's mind through packaging, labeling, and advertising. Although Beatrice's efforts in the fresh milk market were largely unsuccessful in the 1920s, market conditions changed in the 1930s. Beatrice began a program of rapid expansion—financed mostly by trading stock as allowed under Delaware's laws of incorporation—that resulted in the acquisition of more than seventy fresh milk plants by 1950.

The most obvious change in the dairy food market came from the rapid rise of grocery store chains. The chains had the ability to store and to market packaged and labeled milk products. Yet even that market was difficult to develop because consumers continued to fear the possibility of buying contaminated milk. Consumer resistance to fresh milk products was finally overcome through a combination of technical, political, and marketing innovations. The initial step came in the 1920s with the production and sale of both commercial and home refrigeration units, which greatly extended the shelf life of milk products. Next, sanitary packaging of milk was facilitated in the late 1920s with the design of rapid-fill machinery for bottled milk, and in 1935 with the introduction of machinery that packaged milk in paper containers. Those technologies made the mass production of contained fresh milk feasible.[24]

Perhaps most important, several sanitation measures relieved consumers' fears of milk contamination. Beginning in 1930, the U.S. Public Health Service actively promoted milk ordinances and codes in the states. By the mid-1950s, most states and local communities had adopted the U.S. Public Health Service's "Grade 'A' Model Code." Milk could receive the "A" grade only if it was processed through very expensive equipment, called "Triple 'A' Standard Equipment," which included, among other technologies, stainless steel refrigerated trucks at the farm and high temperature, short-time processing equipment at the plant.[25]

Beatrice itself participated only tangentially in developing these innovations. Nor was Beatrice responsible for most of the efforts to introduce modern milk technologies into existing fresh milk plants. Rather, Beatrice's strategy was to purchase fresh milk plants once they were firmly established, with their own market share carved out. There were several reasons for this strategy.

The president of Beatrice offered one reason in his testimony during the Federal Trade Commission's hearings in 1965 into Beatrice's acquisitions. He contended that it made no sense to construct new plant facilities when Beatrice was offered opportunities to purchase standing, modernized plants. Maintaining that many dairy manufacturers had wanted to retire at the same time that Beatrice had entered the fresh milk-products business, he noted that such owner-operators were anxious to exchange their businesses for stock in Beatrice. Since Beatrice— under the laws of Delaware—could simply issue stock to owner-operators in exchange for their assets, everyone came away happy.[26]

A second reason, although not enunciated at the hearings, nonetheless became obvious to anyone present. Beatrice thought it unwise to compete directly in market areas that had been well established by local fresh milk firms. Beatrice knew well the edge that first entrants in a market had in winning brand-name recognition for their products. For that reason alone, entry in the fresh milk market might be suicidal. If Beatrice had been unable to carve out a market share of at least 1,500 gallons daily in a local area, its plants would have operated at a loss. Moreover, direct entry in the fresh milk market was certain to spawn hostility and competitiveness from other established producers, who might then diversify so they could compete directly with Beatrice's flagship products.[27]

The hearings revealed yet a third reason for Beatrice's acquisitions. Beatrice say "buys" that it could not pass up. Many of the companies that Beatrice bought had been in the fresh milk business for several decades. Although they might have been good dairy manufacturers, the finances involved in the process of modernization progressively became too complex. To expand operations, they routinely bought the plants of other producers at market value when they should have paid book value. Or, to modernize, they borrowed money at high interest rates when it would have been far wiser to issue stock. In either case, they raised their debts-to-assets ratios, driving down their owner equity. If the company was held publicly, those actions depressed their stocks' value. When the value of that stock became so low that both investors and bankers balked at providing the needed operating capital, dairy company managers in the 1930s and 1940s believed they had no choice but to sell out to a national dairy food company. So the national companies that had been unusually cautious in financing expansion, such as Beatrice, or those that had worked out sophisticated financial ties, like Foremost and Borden, were in good positions to take over the depressed companies at below book, or liquidation, value.[28]

Typical of such "buys" for Beatrice in the 1950s was Creameries of America. Based in Los Angeles, Creameries typified dairies that, beginning in the 1920s, had extended their markets through aggressive acquisitions programs. As a result, by World War II, Creameries had bought dairies in cities such as Los Angeles, Pasadena, Bakersfield, and San Jose in California, as well as in cities in other western states, such as El Paso, Texas, Albuquerque, New Mexico, Salt Lake City, Utah, and Boise, Idaho. Creameries even owned a dairy in Honolulu. As with many dairies, the financing of Creameries' acquisitions suffered from bad timing. Many facilities had been bought just before the stock market prices crested in the late 1920s. Moreover, these and subsequent plants that it acquired needed modernization. Creameries incurred new debts to do so, and as time progressed, its debts deepened while interest rates increased. When Creameries needed $11 million to modernize in the early 1940s, the banks balked. When Creameries sold public stock to raise the capital, it could generate only one-third of the needed funds. To get the rest, Creameries agreed to what in effect was a suicide note—an agreement to set aside cash earnings to liquidate the new debt rapidly. When news of that agreement became public, Creameries' stock dropped to $11.00 a share on the stock market. With a book value in excess of $17.00 a share, Creameries sought out Beatrice as a buyer.

Beatrice's response to Creameries' offer was based, as it was in other takeovers, on its time-tested policy of avoiding hostility and competitiveness in the business environment. That policy may well have encouraged Creameries' managers to appeal to Beatrice, for it was widely known that the company did not pursue hostile takeovers—ones achieved over the opposition of the other company's management. Beatrice's approach was to leave intact the management of the companies it acquired. Meanwhile, of course, the company taken over had its finances restructured. In the case of Creameries, Beatrice issued a two-tiered stock

swap for the stock and debt securities of Creameries. One tier was a swap of
Beatrice common stock for Creameries common stock at market value. The
other tier was a trade for a new issue of Beatrice preferred stock in exchange for
Creameries' secured debts, dollar for dollar. A final accounting shows that
Beatrice exchanged $11 million of its stock to acquire Creameries , whose assets
totaled $17,753,763 and whose depreciated book value was $11 million.[29]

Although the initial phase of Beatrice's acquisitions program was marked by
this judicious approach, it was not long until prudence was seemingly abandoned
for what appeared to be missionary zeal. In one brief ten-year spurt of acquisitions
between 1951 and 1961, Beatrice bought 175 concerns. By 1961, it owned milk
and creamery operations in 42 states that sold more than $311 million in dairy
products.[30]

A change in the historic environment of the dairy products industry prompted
those acquisitions. Because of a Supreme Court decision reached in 1951—
Dean Milk Co. v. City of Madison—it suddenly became possible for national
dairy companies to realize economies of scale that heretofore had been unthinkable. That decision prompted further court actions during the 1950s that struck
down municipal ordinances that prevented the sale of dairy products imported
from distant manufacturing and distribution centers. The impact of these decisions on dairy manufacturing was far reaching and complex.[31]

In the first place, the 1951 decision made it obvious to national and local dairy
product manufacturers alike that the competition for markets would intensify. This
realization had a dual effect on the industry. Fearing that the nationals would penetrate their markets, many local dairy operators saw the wisdom of selling to the
national companies rather than competing with them. Similarly, stockholders in
local or regional dairy products industries worried about the value of their investments. So even financially healthy dairy products concerns suddenly experienced
sharp drops in the market value for their stocks. These otherwise healthy dairy companies then too became good buys for the national companies.[32]

These developments in the investment climate, however, provide only a partial explanation for Beatrice's vigorous acquisitions program. Beatrice acted out
of desperation. Beatrice feared that if it failed to acquire the assets of existing,
technologically advanced, financially sound local dairies, other national companies would. Should Beatrice permit that to happen, other national companies
would gain toeholds in new market areas, giving them a competitive edge. The
other nationals would realize new economies of scale through the distribution
network that new acquisitions provided, and they would achieve savings by
broadening the reach of their national advertising campaigns.[33]

None of these possibilities became reality because in the late 1950s, the Federal Trade Commission (FTC) took steps to end the intense competitive struggle

in which the national dairies were caught. It issued a string of complaints against the nationals, including Beatrice, that, beginning in 1965, not only blocked most future acquisitions, but forced the divestiture of many acquisitions that had been made in the 1950s. In the case of Beatrice, the FTC argued that Beatrice's acquisitions allowed it to deploy ten marketing and distribution tactics that violated the Clayton Antitrust Act and had "the effect of substantially lessening competition or tending to create a monopoly. . . . " The bill of particulars stated that it made "loans of equipment and facilities in substantial amounts to its customers and potential customers"; it charged "favored customers and potential customers discriminatory prices"; and it expended "substantial sums to promote its various brands through advertising and other promotions."[34]

Obviously, these charges forced Beatrice to reorient its acquisitions program. But there were other forces of historic moment that encouraged Beatrice to move in the direction it took. One came from the new marketing strategies that were devised by the nation's grocery store chains. In the 1960s Safeway, Kroger, and A&P each began to introduce their own private labels to compete with those sold in their stores by the national food manufacturers. Because the chains had control over shelf space in their stores and could, in other ways, alter a store's environment to encourage consumers to purchase one item over others, they were positioned to bargain openly or secretly for special treatment from manufacturers of both brand name and other private label food products.[35]

For example, in 1961-1962, Kroger—operating 1,424 retail grocery stores in twenty-four states—clearly was positioned to offer its own private label milk. Because of the nation's aforementioned milk laws, Kroger decided against buying its own dairy concerns. Instead, it played Beatrice off against other national dairy concerns to negotiate a price break from Beatrice on the production of Kroger-labeled milk.[36]

The FTC in 1965 issued a complaint against both Beatrice and Kroger for reaching this agreement. Even though a final decision in 1969 exonerated Beatrice from any wrongdoing and prevented Kroger from pressuring Beatrice (or any one else) into making similar agreements, the experience taught Beatrice a lesson—a change had occurred in the dairy market environment.[37] It appeared then that some dairy products, especially fresh milk, might not lend themselves any longer to name brand labeling and to product differentiation. It seemed that chain stores like Kroger, A&P and Safeway could employ new sets of marketing tactics to create consumer demands for their own private label of dairy products. As a result, Beatrice began to question its ability to expand, or even to hold, its market share in dairy products.[38]

Contributing to this concern was the growing success of dairy farmers' cooperatives. Faced with overhead costs that continued to mount as the expense of new milking technologies and sanitation equipment grew, dairy farming became progressively more specialized in the 1960s. Unable to reach what they considered satisfactory agreements with the national dairy companies, some dairy farmers formed cooperatives. These were unique marketing institutions, owned and operated by participating dairy farmers, that employed legalized pools through which dairy products were sold. By the 1960s, cooperatives such as Land-O-Lakes were enjoying considerable success, cutting into the market share of national companies like Beatrice.[39]

These challenges to Beatrice's market share in dairy products were joined by an even greater threat in the 1960s—one that hit the dairy industry as a whole, and with it, Beatrice in particular. Evidence began to mount that the animal fats in dairy products were a major contributor to heart disease. This revelation struck the dairy food industry like a sledgehammer, threatening to flatten it altogether.[40]

All the aforementioned historic forces of the 1960s—the FTC decisions, the new marketing developments both in the chain stores and among dairy farmers, and the connection made between dairy foods and heart disease—seriously jeopardized Beatrice's future in the dairy products industry. For a corporation whose history was one of continuous growth through acquisitions, its future success now hinged on its ability to look beyond the dairy products industry for new products to manufacture and sell.

While Beatrice could have altered its historic course of growth through acquisitions by choosing to develop its own products, it never considered doing so. Obviously, its history dictated against it: Beatrice's history was not rooted in developing either personnel or institutions for creating new products. It was far more expeditious for Beatrice to do what it had always done—grow through acquisition. Only now, this process of growth would have a new goal, that of product diversification.

Although this reorientation of its strategy led Beatrice to become one of the nation's first conglomerates, it was not the only company that sought to diversify in the 1960s. Other national dairy product companies did so, as did many other food manufacturing firms and an array of other manufacturers. Beatrice soon found its diversification strategy buffeted by the greatest wave of mergers in the nation's history. In 1968 a record-setting 2,407 mergers were reached. The vast majority of these mergers (75 to 80 percent) were designed to achieve product diversification.[41]

Beatrice's own diversification strategy was complicated by the wild speculative forces that were unleashed by these other mergers. Nevertheless, during the 1960s Beatrice attempted to draw on its history to guide it through these tumultuous events and continued the practice of never acquiring a company against the wishes of that company's management. Beatrice had learned through its long history that the best managers often were those who were currently running the newly acquired company. They usually knew the company's strengths and weaknesses. More often than not, those managers needed only the "deep pockets" of Beatrice to relieve their company of its financial mistakes. Beatrice not only kept original managers in the newly acquired companies but also sought to assimilate them into the larger structure of Beatrice, which it did by searching for managers who could be promoted to corporate level positions in Chicago.[42]

Beatrice solved yet other problems by drawing on its history. It knew the important role that brand names played in product differentiation. After acquiring companies that had established brand name products, Beatrice made no attempt to replace their logos with its own.

From its history in the milk products industry, Beatrice also realized that the market for differentiated products could change. For example, the company knew that consumer attitudes toward animal fats would shake up the market shares for the brand name fats used in cooking. Therefore, acquisitions of brand name vegetable fats was preferable to animal-based ones.[43]

Beatrice also had learned the importance of convenience packaging. Although its early packaging of creamery products helped shape this attitude, Beatrice had acquired, during World War II, La Choy Foods, a small nondairy product business that made convenience-packaged Chinese foods which were sold in grocery stores. The skyrocketing demand for La Choy products prompted Beatrice to watch the markets closely for convenience products and encouraged Beatrice to expand its line of convenience foods. By the 1960s, when McDonald's hamburgers and Swanson's TV dinners were competing with home-cooked meals, Beatrice decided that modern consumers preferred products that had built-in maid service over those that did not. It therefore sought to acquire companies whose brand names were strong in that area. Hence, companies like Rosarita Mexican Foods, Mother's Cookies, and Gebhardt Foods fit well in Beatrice's plan.[44]

Beatrice gradually began to expand the scope of products included in its strategy for convenience products. Nonfood convenience products were progressively included in its acquisitions. This new practice stemmed from Beatrice's realization that it had achieved economies of scale by renting or leasing extra capacity in its warehouses, refrigeration plants, and distribution facilities. Now, with its new acquisitions program in convenience products, it could realize the same sorts of economies of scale by buying companies whose products fit into that marketing structure. It, therefore, made sense to buy Tip Top Brushes, a company whose do-it-yourself household painting device lent itself to sales in grocery stores.[45]

Although Beatrice's goal was to acquire companies whose products fit into its historic system of distribution, marketing, and advertising, that proved difficult to attain, for the mergers of the 1960s helped shape a new financial environment that forced Beatrice to acquire many misfits.

Influenced by the theories of Nobel Prize-winning economist Franco Modigliani, an investment climate evolved which required that "a company manager should not maximize annual profits but maximize the value of shares on the stock market." Irrespective of the theoretical implications of Modigliani's work in the academic community, its popular conceptualization encouraged managers to develop business methods that one commentator—Harvard Business School Professor Robert Reich—labeled "paper entrepreneurialism."[46]

Reich found that unlike earlier entrepreneurs who ascended the corporate managerial ladder by providing their businesses with product innovations and cost-cutting measures, the mergers in the late 1960s had bred a new type of managerial entrepreneur who exercised growing influence in the corporate economies of the 1970s and 1980s. These managerial entrepreneurs made paper innovations—ones that made their companies attractive on paper to stockholders and to stock analysts, with the goal of raising a stock's value on the stock market.

By the late 1960s and early 1970s, these managerial paper shufflers discovered an array of possible innovations each time they acquired another company. They could deploy teams of skilled accountants to design new accounting methods that would demonstrate to the Wall Street investors how the recent acquisitions had strengthened the parent company. Or similar accounting innovations could be employed to show the managerial wisdom of buying another company and then selling off many of its parts.

Although Reich provides an extensive list of the paper games that managers played in an effort to raise stock prices in the 1970s and 1980s, suffice it to say that these games made it difficult for Beatrice to acquire companies that were good marketing fits: good fits often were held by a company that might also own dozens of other, unrelated businesses.

Sometimes those companies were more like Beatrice and less like those that Reich described; that is, they diversified their product lines in order to diminish the impact that the loss of a market for a product might have on the company as a whole. Other companies may have started out acquiring other companies for the same reasons that Beatrice did, but they rapidly came to act more like those run by the paper shufflers. For example, in 1972 Swiss Foods (originally incorporated at about the same time that Beatrice was founded) was reincorporated as Esmark to reflect its new strategy of product diversification. Soon thereafter, its president, Donald P. Kelly, announced that the new company was in the business of making money by acquiring and selling businesses—and no business that it owned was sacred. Kelly said that Esmark would sell Swiss Foods because "we haven't anything that isn't for sale."[47]

Thus, by the 1970s, three different types of business entities appeared to be playing the game of acquiring and selling companies. One was the true conglomerate, like Beatrice. Another was the paper shuffler, as described by Reich. A third group was made up of companies like Esmark that may have begun as conglomerates but then appeared to be buying and selling other companies for profit. Because some of the aforementioned businesses did not play the acquisitions and divestiture game well, they were bought by others who were better players, thus compounding the complexity of the corporate environment.

These conditions made it progressively more difficult for Beatrice to make acquisitions that fit in its overall plan. This problem might have been resolved successfully in a less volatile investment climate. The continual changes that took place in the nation's investment institutions in the 1970s and 1980s, however, severely tested Beatrice's ability to operate either as prudently or with the same sense of fair play as it had in the past. In addition, Beatrice began to be compared, at least from the vantage point of stockholders, with other companies that were actually more successful at takeovers.

The ability of shareholders to compare Beatrice with other takeover companies was encouraged by the appearance in the 1970s of investors' advisory institutions like Moody's Investor's Services. Although services like Moody's at first developed merely to educate investors on the comparable worth of a company to its stockholders, soon corporate managers found that if they did not closely watch their stock ratings, they might become vulnerable to a takeover by a firm that did scrutinize the rankings.[48] While Beatrice fared well in the ratings during most of the 1970s, the end of the decade saw its position slipping. Several criteria employed by the advisory institutions indicated that Beatrice was not as effective as were other firms that played in the acquisitions and divestiture game. By focusing on Beatrice's comparatively low return on assets, the analysts could explain why the market value of its stock was low compared with that of other takeover firms. This widely publicized revelation abruptly transformed Beatrice into a candidate for a takeover early in the 1980s.

Although there were several reasons for Beatrice becoming a takeover candidate, perhaps it is ironic that each stemmed from the firm's ongoing efforts to retain the time-tested methods of acquiring and managing other companies. While many firms that specialized in takeovers either abruptly fired personnel in the companies they bought or rapidly reorganized and sold the new companies, Beatrice did as it always had: it made every effort to keep both the companies and the managers that it acquired. Only when such companies or managers proved to be misfits did Beatrice dispose of them.[49]

By the early 1980s it became clear that this judicious approach and sense of fair play would cost Beatrice its existence. In desperation, Beatrice began to treat its acquired companies and their managers with the same ruthlessness as did other firms that specialized in takeovers. Yet even that decision backfired, for unlike the personnel in companies taken over by firms who specialized in hostile takeovers, the personnel in the companies that Beatrice acquired expected to be treated fairly. When they were not treated in that way, they became vengeful. To fully comprehend these difficulties, however, requires a close examination of Beatrice's efforts to deal with them in the mid-1970s and in the 1980s.

These efforts began with Chairman William Karnes's decision to restructure Beatrice in the mid-1970s. Karnes recognized that Beatrice's acquisitions program brought companies and managers aboard that might not fit the firm's historic system of marketing and distribution. Rather than abruptly firing, or selling, the apparent misfits, Karnes restructured Beatrice so that the marketplace in time would, as it always had, decide the fates of both the managers and the products that their companies produced.

Utilizing Beatrice's central office as a hub, Karnes created lines of authority that reached out like spokes to profit-center managers. By 1976 Beatrice had 397 profit-center managers who were each given autonomy and authority to determine their own marketing strategy. This strategy was designed so that the needs of the profit centers—not fights among Beatrice's many product-line managers—would determine, with the passage of time, which of Beatrice's diverse products were good fits and which were not and, therefore, should be divested. So well did these profit centers appear to work in 1977 that *Dun's Review* picked Beatrice as one of America's five best-managed corporations.[50]

Beneath the surface, however, these changes were increasing the stress within Beatrice's management structure. Because the profit centers focused on and met the needs of local consumers, the demand from the profit centers for certain product lines often conflicted. Thus, these conflicts added to the biases of managers who had different views about which product lines should be expanded or contracted and which should be kept or divested. Ensuing debates soon deepened existing splits within Beatrice's management.[51]

Welling up from this turmoil was an amorphous group of managers who were held together by a common view that they all shared: Beatrice needed to centralize all planning in its corporate headquarters. That group sensed that its position would get a hearing when Karnes announced his retirement and Wallace Rasmussen was installed temporarily as chief executive officer (CEO) in 1977. Rasmussen, however, showed no inclination toward reform and instead sought to entrench himself by demoting opposing managers and working to make his position a permanent one.[52]

The result was that this fissure in management erupted so violently that non-management members of the board of directors resigned and made public their reasons for doing so. By early 1979, the heat of the debate was so intense that it not only made good copy for journalists, but resulted in lawsuits among managers and board members. Beatrice appeared to be a suffocating giant. To breathe fresh air into it, Beatrice was reorganized in 1980 so that a new board of directors—composed of a majority of outsiders—was elected.[53]

Meanwhile, James E. Dutt replaced Rasmussen as CEO. Selected by Beatrice's Board of Directors because he appeared to best represent the group of managers whose vision for good marketing and distribution fits had suffered the least from the stressful conditions of the 1970s, Dutt was expected to prudently sort out the product lines that were misfits and divest them. He was also to avoid acquiring conglomerates or other giant business entities that owned a range of diverse industries. Clearly, such acquisitions had been the cause of Beatrice's problems and should be avoided.[54]

What was expected of Dutt was not what he delivered, for Dutt found that business conditions in the 1980s were so volatile that he had to take radically different steps to avoid a takeover. One would not have expected such an outcome in 1980. Even as Rasmussen was being eased out, Beatrice began a prudent and systematic evaluation of which businesses it wanted to spin off and which it wanted to keep. It also began to look for product lines that it wanted to acquire. A few examples reveal the initial caution and selectivity of Dutt for Beatrice.

By the late 1970s, it was clear that some brand name food products did better than others. For example, all nondairy beverages grew faster than did staple foods. Therefore, it appeared likely that Beatrice would acquire nondairy beverage companies. Adhering to its long-standing policy of acquiring brand name product lines, Beatrice in 1978 bought Tropicana, which held 30 percent of the nation's market share in frozen orange juice (only Coca-Cola's Minute-Maid was a competitor). By merely holding its market share, Beatrice expected to enjoy increased profits as the market for citrus juices grew in the 1980s. In 1981 Dutt topped off acquisitions in this product area when he made the largest bottling company acquisition in the nation's history—Northwest Industry's 22 soft drink bottling companies. Included in this package were several of the nation's leading brand name bottling companies, including Coca-Cola of Los Angeles. As usual, the management personnel in these companies was maintained.[55]

In an effort to offset the debts that Beatrice incurred in these and similar acquisitions, Dutt sold off product lines that had proved over time that they did not fit. Some were obvious misfits, such as farm machinery, skis, travel trailers, and stereo equipment. Less obvious were food products that either had failed to develop as recognized national brand names or were ones where consumer demand waned. For example, because demand for all candies except chocolates fell, Beatrice began to divest all but its chocolate candies. Similarly, because its local bakeries' products failed to indicate they could establish a national market for themselves, they too were sold. Altogether, by 1982 Dutt had sold 56 companies that accounted for about one-eighth of Beatrice's total sales.[56]

All the while contending that this streamlined acquisition-and-divestiture-strategy would increase Beatrice's earnings on its assets, Dutt simultaneously sought to encourage plant managers to introduce cost-cutting efficiencies. Launched in 1981 as Beatrice's "UnCommon People, UnCommon Goals" program, it sought to increase productivity in plants without investment in new equipment. Utilizing a variety of communication and information techniques, workers were taught to believe "You Make the Difference." And some did. Beatrice's earnings were helped by La Choy Food products which boosted its production rate 16.6 percent in 1981 and by Fisher Nut which saved $130,000 by packaging the nuts in tin containers on the recommendation of workers.[57]

But neither Dutt's acquisition-and-divestiture strategy nor his "You Make the Difference" program could offset problems in the 1980s. First of all, Beatrice learned that it was less prepared than it thought to compete in the sale of certain new product lines. For example, no sooner was Tropicana acquired than Beatrice had to face what others in the commodities futures market had long known about the historic cycles of citrus fruit. A disaster hit the citrus industry in the form of a severe frost in Florida. The freeze wrecked Tropicana's ability to compete nationally with Minute Maid. To maintain its original market share against Coca-Cola, which increased its advertising campaign to take advantage of Tropicana's plight, Beatrice had to reach deep into its own pockets to double the advertising expenses of Tropicana.[58]

Moreover, Beatrice had incurred heavy short-term debts to make some of its acquisitions. Because the loans had been obtained when commercial interest rates approached historic highs, they sharply decreased the earnings of those companies that Dutt had acquired.[59]

In some cases, the ability of newly acquired companies to earn good profits was checked by another problem. Many analysts pointed out that the price that Beatrice had paid for many of its acquisitions was excessive. The fact that Dutt revealed his acquisitions' strategy by targeting the products he wanted may have combined with several other factors to drive up the price Beatrice paid for its acquisitions. One such factor was that food and tobacco companies like Borden, Philip Morris, and General Mills were potential competitors for many of the companies that Beatrice wanted.[60]

Dutt's problems were small, however, in comparison with the one that had befuddled Karnes and Rasmussen and intensified as the 1980s wore on. In the 1970s Beatrice had to play the acquisition game in an environment increasingly dominated by conglomerates and paper shufflers, or variations thereof. In the

1980s, investment institutions, formed for the express purpose of buying existing corporations, started to play the game with even greater ferocity and apparent viciousness.

The new entrants in the acquisition game assumed a variety of disguises. They often were headed by a recognized "raider," such as Carl Icahn, and had as their objective either to *greenmail* a company's managers, that is, require them to buy back at a hefty premium the stock the raider held or face a hostile takeover that would result in them being fired, or to take over the company solely for the purpose of selling its subsidiaries. On other occasions, the investment institutions were formed almost overnight by discontented managers who, after having been shoved out of their corporate offices in an earlier takeover, wanted to buy a company so they could be managers again. In any case, such takeover institutions found the nation's banks ready to loan them the money they needed to buy out targeted companies. The takeover institutions merely issued to the banks *junk securities*, which were secured against the assets of the targeted company that was yet to be bought, in exchange for the cash they needed to buy the stock of the targeted company.[61]

Called *leveraged buy outs*, such takeovers became common in the mid-1980s, making more intense than ever the speculative competition of corporations that were either susceptible to or hopeful for a takeover. Hence, as the 1980s wore on, the prices that the true conglomerates paid for targeted companies were driven higher and higher.

While these speculative forces were just beginning to mount in 1982, Dutt nonetheless had found bidding in 1981 for Northwest Industries—Beatrice's largest acquisition to that time—so intense that he had paid a premium of $450 million over book value for the company. That price staggered the analysts' calculations, for it was twice what had been paid for the company only two years earlier. In fact, Wall Street analysts doubted that even Beatrice was capable of waving a magic marketing wand that could generate earnings sufficient to make a profit on such overvalued assets.[62]

Because of such acquisitions, Dutt faced close scrutiny by the investors' services in 1982–1983. The analysts began to look at Beatrice's long-standing acquisitions policies as a detriment to its stockholders. Noting that the earnings of Beatrice's stock had been in a rut for more than a decade, they homed in on the company's inability—irrespective of who was managing it—to raise its substandard 13 percent earnings on assets. What the analysts suggested was that Beatrice's many parts were worth more than the whole.[63]

These reviews merely strengthened the information which already warned Dutt that Beatrice itself was a target of the takeover specialists.[64] Regardless of Dutt's original plans for Beatrice, he had to set those plans aside and pursue others to avert a takeover. Of the many strategies available to Dutt, he selected one that was designed to hide its real purpose beneath the mystique of modern managerial wizardry.

Announcing in late 1983 that he was imposing a two-year timetable on Beatrice, Dutt said that Beatrice would be restructured to move it away from both its long-standing strategy of growth through acquisitions and its decentralized operations. To implement the new plan, Dutt eliminated the once prize-winning profit centers, which by 1983 had grown to number more than 450. Replacing them were 30 centralized divisions. These, in turn, were organized beneath six new operating groups: (1) grocery, (2) beverage, (3) refrigerated goods, (4) consumer goods, (5) international brands, and (6) industrial/chemical businesses. A new vice-president would head each of these groups.[65]

In the process of restructuring, Dutt made it clear that none of the companies in any group was safe from divestiture. For that matter, neither was any of the six groups. Dutt made that clear when he announced plans to sell the entire industrial/chemical group. Contending that Beatrice would earn a better return on assets with convenience products than by remaining in the capital-intensive chemical business, Dutt took steps in early 1984 to sell the entire group.[66]

The sale of those product lines and of others that were capital intensive had an obvious goal—generating cash liquidity. Liquidity in itself would raise the price of Beatrice's stock, thereby making a takeover more difficult. In addition, Beatrice's new liquidity would permit it to buy back 10 percent of its publicly held stock, thus further strengthening the company's position in the marketplace.[67]

To help head off takeover plans, Dutt announced in 1983 that beginning with advertising in connection with the 1984 Olympics the company would launch an advertising campaign to make the world aware of Beatrice's product lines. No doubt the ensuing campaign did help make the public aware of its many product lines. Beginning late in 1984, a new Beatrice logo began to appear atop those of the many brand name products it sold—from Rosarita Beans to Arrowhead Water.[68]

Although Beatrice's advertising personnel contended that the campaign was created to enhance consumer interest in its lesser-known brand name products, and in spite of the fact that sales and marketing labeled the campaign as "the most radical shift in marketing strategy every perpetrated,"[69] stock analysts recognized it for what it was —a ploy to make Beatrice a more costly firm to take over.[70]

But Dutt pushed on. To aid him in bringing about what one respected business journal called "the most difficult overhaul in American business history," Dutt sharply upset a Beatrice tradition—he hired outsiders to help him do the job. In fact, Beatrice soon was in the news for its own raids—ones on high-level managers of its competitors. Dart and Kraft, itself facing wrenching internal problems generated by the rash of takeovers that was breaking out across the food industry in the 1980s, was a favorite target and provided Beatrice with some of its top officers in 1984.[71]

Dutt's tactics achieved at least a temporary victory for him. Beatrice's stock rose about 35 percent during the course of the year. Thus the time was right for Dutt to deploy his final tactic of his strategy: to take over Esmark—the company that rumors indicated wanted to take over Beatrice.

Headed by Donald P. Kelly, Esmark, in late 1983, set its sights on a good mix of products, which the acquisition of Beatrice would have made possible.[72] Unfortunately for Kelly, however, analysts were questioning how the acquisition of Norton Simon in early 1983 could possibly benefit Esmark's stockholders. When a swing in the price of Esmark's stock began to suggest that Esmark was a likely target for a takeover, Kelly and other Esmark executives—in an effort to avert a possible takeover—negotiated with a leveraged buy out institution to purchase Esmark's stock and take the company private. Of course, part of the packaged buy out plan included retention of Esmark's executives or *golden parachutes*—high-cost severance or retirement settlements for them.[73]

Dutt, who recognized not only the value of Esmark but also the opportunity to end Esmark's threat to Beatrice, entered the bidding for Esmark's stock in the spring of 1984. Within a few weeks, Esmark's stock went from $40 a share to $60 a share, with Beatrice winning ownership of Esmark at the latter price.[74] Unfortunately for Dutt, however, he miscalculated both the value of Esmark in the eyes of the stockholder's advisory services and the ability of Esmark's top executives to rebound after being fired by Dutt.

Stock analysts moved swiftly to critique Beatrice, as they had Esmark a year earlier when it had acquired Norton Simon. Focusing on Esmark's $1.3 billion debt that Beatrice would assume and on Beatrice's total debt of $5 billion (thereby more than doubling its debts-to-assets ratio from 32 percent to 65 percent), analysts labeled Beatrice's recent acquisition "a gamble." And a risky one at that. Its debt was so great that major Beatrice/Esmark businesses faced "the immediate need for their sale," which "may force prices for them down." These analysts feared that Beatrice's stock would thus fall back into a rut.[75]

In any event, Beatrice's stock fell below $30 a share, in spite of assets whose value should have put the price of a share somewhere around $50 to $55, and hung there for months. Suddenly in the fall of 1985 the price of its stock took off as a result of rumors that Beatrice would be taken over.

The source of those rumors reaches back to Dutt's shifts in management. As a company that throughout its history had taken pride in a policy that promised lifetime careers for its managers, Beatrice under Dutt seemed to be on a managerial head hunt. The pace of the hunt heightened with the acquisition of Esmark. Even successful, time-tested executives, like International Playtex's President Walter Bregman, were told in one curt telephone conversation with Dutt that they were fired. To further the suspense among management, in early 1985 Dutt fingered some of his high management personnel—like William Mowry, Jr., Anthony Luiso, and Frank Grezelecki—to be fired if the performance of their groups did not improve.[76]

By mid-1985, key executives were leaving Beatrice in droves. Soon it was apparent that former Esmark President Donald P. Kelly would have considerable help from departed Beatrice personnel in supporting a bid he was making to take over Beatrice. Beatrice's Board of Directors had no choice but to fire Dutt in September 1985. Although the board claimed that the new administration of William W. Grangers, Jr., "won't be caretakers," analysts correctly perceived that Beatrice's life in the American economy had reached a "crucial juncture."[77]

By late October 1985, it was clear that Donald Kelly was hooked in with Kohlberg, Kravis and Roberts, a firm that specialized in leveraged buy outs. That firm had been organized in 1976 to buy out publicly held companies by borrowing funds from participating banks—funds secured by the assets of the company that was about to be acquired—and using them to purchase the stock. Kohlberg Kravis announced that it had offered Beatrice $45 a share for its 109 million shares of outstanding stock. Kohlberg Kravis's bid contained guarantees that the jobs of managers who were outside of Beatrice's corporate headquarters would be secure, even though Kelly would be named president and many of its nonfood lines would be spun off. In addition, many of Beatrice's corporate executives would enjoy the benefits of golden parachutes. For example, Dutt would get a severance package worth at least $1.5 million.[78]

As October drew to a close, Beatrice's executives who did not have golden parachutes scrambled to find their own leveraged buy out firm to make a counter offer against Kohlberg Kravis. For even though it was uncertain as to which Beatrice products would be retained, it was clear that Beatrice soon would be owned by someone other than its current stockholders. As the *Wall Street Journal* reported in October 1985, Beatrice's board was "pressured to accept some offer in light of the recent rise in the company's stock price." Why were they pressured? Because "the directors would be vulnerable to shareholder lawsuits if they didn't accept an offer and the stock price fell."[79]

On November 14, 1985, the announcement was made that Beatrice's shareholders had anxiously awaited. The board had accepted a $50 per share buy out bid from Kohlberg, Kravis and Roberts. As everyone expected, it also was announced that Donald P. Kelly would become the new chairman and chief executive officer of Beatrice. The company, now wholly owned by Kohlberg,

Kravis and Roberts, was expected to replace the current administration in the Chicago office with a new set of executives, many of whom would be former Esmark managers.[80]

Notes

1. "The Fortune 500: The Largest U.S. Industrial Corporations," *Fortune*, April 29, 1985, 266.

2. Federal Trade Commission, Staff Report, *Economic Report on Corporate Mergers* (Washington, D.C.: U.S. Government Printing Office, 1969), 1–224. U.S. Congress, Senate, Subcommittee on Antitrust and Monopoly, Committee on the Judiciary, *Economic Concentration, Hearings*, 91st Congress, 1st session, pt. 8, 1969, 1–4450.

3. Harold S. Sloan and Arnold J. Zurcher, *Dictionary of Economics* (New York: Barnes and Noble, 1970), 93.

4. *The Beatrice Foods Story*, (Chicago: Beatrice Foods, 1978), not paginated (hereafter cited as BFS).

5. Thomas C. Cochran, *Business In American Life: A History* (New York: McGraw-Hill, 1972), 170–191.

6. Allan G. Bogue, *From Prairie to Farm Belt: Farming on the Illinois and Iowa Prairies in the Nineteenth Century* (Chicago: University of Chicago Press, 1955), 1–293; Fred A. Shannon, *The Farmer's Last Frontier: Agriculture, 1860–1897* (New York: Farrar and Rinehart, 1945), 1–434; Earl D. Ross, *History of the Iowa State College of Agriculture and Mechanic Arts* (Ames, Iowa: Iowa State College Press, 1942), 1–56.

7. James C. Olson, *History of Nebraska* (Lincoln, Neb.: University of Nebraska Press, 1966), 200–204.

8. Thomas R. Pirtle, *History of the Dairy Industry* (Chicago: Mojonnier, 1926), 1–645.

9. John M. Connor and Ronald W. Ward, eds. *Advertising and the Food System*, Monograph No. 14 (Madison, Wis.: University of Wisconsin Press), 1–129; Richard Schmalensee, "Product Differentiation Advantage of Pioneering Brands," *American Economics Review* 72: 349–365.

10. Seymour Dunbar, *A History of Travel in America* (Indianapolis: Bobbs-Merrill, 1915), vols. 2 and 3; Earl D. Ross, *Iowa Agriculture: An Historical Survey* (Iowa City: State Historical Society of Iowa, 1951), 1–86; Carl Frederick Kraenzel, *The Great Plains in Transition* (Norman, Okla.: University of Oklahoma Press, 1955), 137–149.

11. BFS.

12. John M. Connor, et. al., *The Food Manufacturing Industries* (Lexington, Mass.: D.C. Heath and Co., 1985), 77–101.

13. BFS.

14. Ibid.

15. Simon Kuznets, *Capital in the American Economy: Its Formation and Financing* (Princeton, N.J.: Princeton University Press, 1961); Herman E. Krooss and Martin R. Blyn, *A History of Financial Intermediaries* (New York: Random House, 1971); George

Soule, *Prosperity Decade, From War to Depression: 1917–1929* (New York: Harper and Row, 1947); John Kenneth Galbraith, *The Great Crash 1929* (Cambridge, Mass.: Houghton Mifflin Company, 1961).

16. Pirtle, *History of the Dairy Industry*, 458–645.

17. Ibid.

18. BFS.

19. Joseph Dorfman, *The Economic Mind in American Civilization*, Vol. IV, 1918–1933 (New York: Viking Press, 1959), 48–56.

20. Henry C. and Anne Dewees Taylor, *The Story of Agricultural Economics in the United States, 1840–1932* (Ames, Iowa: Iowa State College Press, 1952).

21. R. J. Martin, *The Supermarket: An Analysis of Growth, Development, and Change* (Pulman, Wash.: Washington State University Press, 1963),

22. BFS.

23. John T. Bowen, "Refrigeration in the Handling, Processing and Storing of Milk and Milk Products," *Miscellaneous Publication No. 138* (Washington, D.C.: United States Department of Agriculture, 1932), 1–38; Charles D. Dahle, "Majority of Ice Cream Manufacturers Are After Package Business," *Ice Cream Review* 12 (no. 9):52; Sheldon W. Williams and Vaid A. Vose, *Organization and Competition in the Midwest Dairy Industries* (Ames, Iowa: Iowa State University Press, 1970), 35–45.

24. Gerald D. Scott, "Development of Paper Milk Containers," Agricultural Economics Publication 2939 (Urbana, Ill.: Department of Agricultural Economics, University of Illinois, 1953), 1–25; Roland W. Bartlett, *The Milk Industry* (New York: The Ronald Press, 1946), 8–62.

25. National Committee on Food Marketing, *Organization and Competition in the Dairy Industry*, Technical Study No. 3 (Washington, D.C.: Government Printing Office, 1966), 1–409.

26. Federal Trade Commission Decisions, Findings, Opinions, and Orders, vol. 67, Jan. 1, 1965, to June 30, 1965, "In the Matter of Beatrice," Docket 6653 (Washington, D.C.: Government Printing Office, 1970), 483–533 (hereafter cited as FTCD—6653).

27. Ibid., 473–734.

28. Ibid., 500–691.

29. Ibid., 501–569.

30. Ibid., 500–691.

31. D. H. Carley and T. L. Cryer, "Flexibility of Operations in Dairy Manufacturing Plants: Changes 1944–1961" (Washington, D.C.: United States Department of Agriculture, Economic Research Services and Statistical Reporting Services, 1961), 1–44.

32. National Committee on Food Marketing, *Organization and Competition in Food Retailing*, Technical Study 7 (Washington, D.C.: Government Printing Office, 1966), 1–568.

33. Ibid.; U.S. Congress, Senate, Judiciary Committee, Subcommittee on Antitrust and Monopoly, *Concentration Ratios in Manufacturing Industry*, 87th Congress, 2nd session, pt. 1, 1–452.

34. FTCD—6653, 650–734.

35. Joel B. Dirlam, "The Food Distribution Industry," *The Structure of American Industry*, Walter Adams, ed. (New York: Macmillan, 1977), 40–85.

36. The Federal Trade Commission Decisions, Findings, Opinions, and Orders, vol. 76, July 1, 1969, to Dec. 31, 1969, "In the Matter of Beatrice Foods Co. and The Kroger Co., Inc." (Washington, D.C.: U.S. Government Printing Office, 1973), 719–829.

37. Ibid.

38. D. C. Arms and W. T. Butz, *Subdealers in the Milk Industry: Problems and Prospects* (University Park, Pa.: Pennsylvania State University Cooperative Extension Services, 1960), 1–32; E. S. Harris, "Price Wars in City Milk Markets," *Agricultural Economics Report No. 100* (Washington, D.C.: United States Department of Agriculture, Economic Research Services, 1966), 1–95; Norman Myrick, "Private Labels in the Milk Business," *American Milk Review* 22 (no. 2): 32–37.

39. Norman Reeder, "Giant New Co-ops Aim For More Market Power," *Farm Journal* 93 (no. 5): 20–33.

40. United States Department of Agriculture, Economic Research Services, *The Dairy Situation* (Washington, D.C.: Government Printing Office), May 1965, DS–305, March 1966, DS–313, Nov. 1966, DS–313.

41. Bureau of Economics, Federal Trade Commission, Economic Papers, 1966–69 (Washington, D.C.: Government Printing Office, 1970), 1–287.

42. "Corporate Traffic Managers Help Employees Avoid The Transfer Blues," *Administrative Management* 38 (October 1977): 49–50.

43. L. G. Martin, "How Beatrice Foods Sneaked Up On $5 Billion," *Fortune*, April 1976, 119–129; Robert Buzzell and Robert E. M. Nourse, "The Product Life-Cycle," *Grocery Manufacturing in the United States*, Gary A. Marple and Harry B. Wissmann, eds. (New York: Frederick A. Praeger Publishers, 1968), 39–83.

44. Ibid.; BSF; "Beatrice Foods Is Growth Through Management," *U.S. Investorastern Banker* 85 (June 3, 1974): 153–155; Federal Trade Commission Decisions, Findings, Opinions, and Orders, vol. 81, July 1, 1972 to Dec. 31, 1972, "In the Matter of Beatrice Foods Co.," Docket 8814 (Washington, D.C.: Government Printing Office, 1973), 481–539.

45. Ibid.; Federal Trade Commission Decisions, Findings, Opinions, and Orders, vol. 86, July 1, 1975 to Dec. 31, 1975, "In the Matter of Beatrice Foods," Docket 8864 (Washington, D.C.: Government Printing Office, 1976), 1–76.

46. Robert Reich, *The Next American Frontier* (New York: Harper and Row, 1983), 1–286.

47. "Esmark," *Everybody's Business: The Irreverent Guide to Corporate America*, Milton Moskowitz, Michael Katz and Robert Levering, eds. (New York: Harper and Row, 1980), quote on p. 28; W. Smith Greig, *The Economics of Food Processing* (Westport, Conn.: The Avi Publishing Co., 1971), 54–60.

48. *Moody's Handbook of Common Stocks* (New York: Moody's Investor's Service, Inc., 1970 to date); *The Corporate Merger*, William W. Alberts and Joel E. Segall, eds. (Chicago: University of Chicago Press, 1974); David Stone, *An Economic Approach to Planning the Conglomerate of the 70s* (Princeton: Auerbach Publishers, 1970).

49. Federal Trade Commission Decisions, *see* notes 2, 26, 36, 44, and 45.

50. "The Five Best-Managed Companies," *Dun's Review* 110 (December 1977): 47–61; "Beatrice Food's Karnes Takes Marketer of Year Award," *Marketing News* 9 (May 7, 1976): 8; "Food Firm Finds Recipe for Success in Specialties," *Chemical Week* Sept. 5, 1979, 71.

51. *World Food Report*, June 15, 1978, 3; *Wall Street Journal*, Nov. 3, 1980, 33; "The Man Who Came to Dinner," *Forbes*, Feb. 19, 1979, 86–88.

52. "The War of the Succession," *Forbes*, April 30, 1979, 43; "By Beatrice Ousted a Gruff Boss," *Business Week*, April 9, 1979, 36–37.

53. *Wall Street Journal*, March 22, May 7, May 9, May 10, May 21, 1979.

54. *Wall Street Journal*, June 16, July 21, July 31, 1980; *Chemical Week*, Dec. 3, 1980; 41–44.

55. "Beatrice Foods: Aiming to Quench a New Thirst for Beverages," *Business Week*, Industrial Edition, Dec. 21, 1981, 102–103; *Wall Street Journal*, Dec. 1, 1980, 2; "Suddenly Northwest Is Selling, Not Buying" *Business Week*, Nov. 23, 1981, 46–47.

56. *Wall Street Journal*, Sept. 3, 1980, June 4, 1981, July 6, 1981, Dec. 7, 1981; *Dairy Record* 84 (April 1983): 24; Merrill Brown, "Merger Mania Yields to Divestiture: Fever," *Washington Post*, March 3, 1983; *Business Week*, Industrial Edition, Dec. 21, 1981, 102–103; *Candy Industry*, September 1983, 18; *Advertising Age*, Aug. 29, 1983, 60.

57. *Quick Frozen Foods*, Sept. 1981, 26–28.

58. *Business Week*, Industrial Edition, Dec. 21, 1981, 102–103; *Wall Street Journal*, Dec. 1, 1980, 2.

59. Ibid.

60. Ibid.; Winston Williams, "Beatrice Foods in Shift," *New York Times*, Feb. 17, 1983; Geoffrey Colvin, "The Bigness Cult's Grip on Beatrice Foods," *Fortune*, Sept. 20, 1932, 122–125.

61. *Wall Street Journal*, Oct. 22, 31, Nov. 8, 1985.

62. *Business Week*, Industrial Edition, Nov. 23, 1981, 46–47, Dec. 21, 1981, 102–103; "Beatrice Foods' CEO J. L. Dutt Appears to be Returning to the Old Strategy of Growth at Expense of Profits . . . ," *Fortune*, Sept. 20, 1982, 122–129.

63. Ibid.; *Wall Street Journal*, February 17, 1983, September 27, 1983; Colvin, "The Bigness Cult's Grip on Beatrice Foods," 122–184; B. S. Moskal, "A Face Lift for Beatrice," *Industry Week*, Nov. 28, 1983, 20–21; T. Olson, M. Bremer and J. K. Jensen, "Beatrice Foods Co. Productivity Activities," *A.I.I.E. Proceedings*, 1982 Conference (May 23–27, 1982), 744–748.

64. *Wall Street Journal*, Feb. 22, 1984, 20, 58; Barbara Kallen, "Prime-Time Defense," *Forbes*, April 23, 1984, 86.

65. L. K. Jereski, "Beatrice Make-Over," *Marketing and Media Decisions*, May 1984, 74–77; A. Urbanski, "Beatrice Says Goodbye to the Bean Counters," *Sales and Marketing Management*, Feb. 6, 1984, 30–33; Moskal, "A Face Lift for Beatrice," 20–21; "Beatrice Foods: The Remaking of a Giant Marketer," *Forum* 4 (June 1983): 25–30.

66. Laura Jereski, "The Thick and Thin of Beatrice," *Marketing and Media Decisions*, September 1984, 156–168; "The New Food Giants," *Business Week*, Industrial Edition, Sept. 24, 1984, 132–138.

67. "Beatrice to Purchase Own Stock," *Processed Prepared Foods*, Jan. 1984, 34.

68. "Beatrice Foods Will Launch a Corporate Ad Campaign in an Effort to Integrate Marketing Functions," *Advertising Age*, June 13, 1983, 58.

69. *Sales and Marketing Management*, Feb. 6, 1984, 30–33.

70. "Prime-time Defense."

71. "Overhauling a $9-Billion Giant," *Advertising Age*, Feb. 27, 1984, 4–5; "Dart and Kraft Sues Beatrice Foods . . . ," *Advertising Age*, Jan. 30, 1984, 10.

72. "Prime-time Defense"; *Wall Street Journal*, Feb. 22, 1984.

73. K. Blanton, "Makes Tender Offer for Shares: Buy-Out Fund Alters Tack," *Pensions and Investment Age*, June 25, 1984, 3, 58; *New York Times*, May 22, 1984, pp. 29N, D1L, May 23, pp. 27N, D1L.

74. *New York Times*, May 25, 1984, PP 29N, D3L.

75. *New York Times*, Dec. 30, 1984, p. f4; Brian S. Moskal, "Can Dutt Do It?" *Industry Week*, June 11, 1984, 20–21; Jereski, "The Thick and Thin of Beatrice"; "Why Esmark Might Give Beatrice Foods Indigestion," *Business Week*, Industrial Edition, June 4, 1984, 30.

76. Sarah E. Moran, "Beatrice Struggles for Control," *Advertising Age*, March 11, 1985, 3, 88; David W. Gibson, "Stability in Transition for Beatrice Chemical," *Chemical Week*, Feb. 27, 1985, 22; John A. Byrne, "The Anatomy of a Sacking," *Forbes*, August 12, 1985, 100–102, 106.

77. *Wall Street Journal*, Aug. 5, Aug. 9, 1985.

78. *Wall Street Journal*, Oct. 2, Oct. 17, Oct. 18, Oct. 21, Oct. 22, 1985.

79. Ibid.

80. *Los Angeles Times*, Nov. 15, 1985.

QUESTIONS FOR REVIEW AND DISCUSSION

1. Why did the demand for Beatrice's butter grow so rapidly from 1896 to 1920?

2. Why did Beatrice expand slowly into other products in the dairy industry?

3. What were the reasons for the development of Beatrice's diversification strategy, 1945–1960?

4. Examine the historical forces that encouraged Beatrice to acquire "misfits" in the 1960s and 1970s.

5. How did Beatrice's managers try to deal with the problems of running a conglomerate in the 1970s and 1980s?

6. If you had been the chief executive officer of Beatrice, 1976–1985, what would you have done differently?

15

The Social Responsibility of Modern Business

It goes without saying that no corporate executive would ever claim to be socially irresponsible. Yet, there is no doubt that different conceptions have existed within the business community as to the meaning of the term *social responsibility*. As one prominent authority on the subject, Clarence C. Walton, has written, some managers still believe "a firm best serves the public interest when it best serves its own private interests through effective service to consumers, adequate profits to stockholders, fair working conditions for employees, and scrupulous observance of the law. To go beyond these commitments is folly."[1]

However, there has also been, particularly in the last 25 years, a growing conviction on the part of many corporate officials that their organizations do have an obligation to concern themselves with problems such as racial tension, urban decay, cultural development, and the overall quality of life. Walton describes that new attitude: "In short, the new concept of social responsibility recognizes the intimacy of the relationships between the corporation and society and realizes that such relationships must be kept in mind by top managers as the corporation and the related groups pursue their respective goals."[2] One company president, Kenneth Mason of Quaker Oats, phrased it this way: "Corporations that control the use of socially important assets have the responsibility to use those assets in a way that makes social sense."[3]

But, in fact, the difficult question is not whether managers and their firms should behave responsibly in the abstract. The real challenge lies in deciding what the socially responsible course of action is when the corporation is faced with a concrete problem or crisis situations. Such a decision must take into consideration the legitimate rights of the organization's management, its stockholders, and its employees.

The case study that follows deals with Union Carbide Corporation's response to the leak of poisonous gas from its plant in Bhopal, India, in 1984. Few companies have ever been faced with a crisis in social responsibility as severe as that encountered by Union Carbide. Even as this introduction is being written in 1986, the terms of Union Carbide's settlement with the survivors of Bhopal remain unclear.

The Bhopal accident raises a number of issues for debate and discussion. Who was responsible for what happened in Bhopal? Was the immediate response of Union Carbide's officials adequate and appropriate? What kind and what amount of compensation do the people of India have a right to expect from Union Carbide? What should a Union Carbide stockholder expect the corporation to do in negotiating the damage settlement? What will the cost of the Bhopal tragedy be to the future of Union Carbide as a viable enterprise?

Notes

1. Clarence C. Walton, *Corporate Social Responsibilities* (Belmont, CA: Wadsworth Publishing Co., Inc., 1967), vii.

2. *Ibid.*, p. 18.

3. Frederick D. Sturdivant, *Business and Society* (Homewood, Ill.: Richard D. Irwin, Inc., 1981), 5.

Jimmy Anklesaria

BHOPAL: THE UNION CARBIDE CORPORATION IN INDIA

DECEMBER 3, 1984, 4:30 A.M.

The last person anyone wants to receive a phone call from at 4:30 in the morning is a reporter. But the call that Edward Van Den Ameele, Union Carbide's manager of press relations, received in Connecticut was not an ordinary phone call. A reporter from CBS radio was on the line with news from India—as many as 75 people had been killed by poisonous gas leaking from a Union Carbide pesticide plant in Bhopal, India, a city of more than 700,000 people, situated 360 miles south of New Delhi. As Van Den Ameele listened in shocked disbelief, new reports came in that raised the number of dead to 200. "And it just kept going up and up," he said. "It felt like I was in a continuous long-running nightmare—only I wasn't asleep" (*Fortune*, January 7, 1985, p. 50).

On the other side of the world in Bhopal, the nightmare was even more horrifying. Thousands of men, women, and children were scurrying madly in the dark, twitching and writhing like the insects for whom the poisonous chemical was intended. This chemical, methyl isocyanate, is used by Union Carbide to produce pesticides sold under the Temik and Sevin brand names. The gas had escaped when a malfunction of a pressure valve caused water to enter a tank holding the deadly vapor, thus triggering a runaway reaction.

DECEMBER 10, 1984

A week after the fateful night of December 3, the crisis slowly, agonizingly, began to abate. The cloud of poisonous gas had long since dispersed, leaving over 2,000 dead and tens of thousands suffering from partial blindness, lung or liver damage, loss of family members, or destruction of cattle or other belongings. While medical aid poured into Bhopal, so did many American lawyers, who busily signed up plaintiffs among the injured and the relatives of the deceased to seek billions of dollars in damages from Union Carbide. On Wall Street the chemical giant's stock price fell by more than eleven points, to around $37 a share, an overall loss in market value of nearly $900 million (*Fortune*, January 7, 1985).

A string of management problems faced the company's executives: how to best aid the victims, how to be sure that what had happened at Bhopal did not happen again somewhere else, how to keep up the employees' morale, how to assure investors that the corporation was financially stable, how to protect the company from excessive legal liabilities, what would the future of Union Carbide in India and in other third-world nations be, and what would be the fate of the Union Carbide Research and Development Center south of Bhopal.

History

Union Carbide and Carbon Corporation was incorporated in New York on November 1, 1917 by a group of midwestern utility men. Backed by Cornelius Kingsley Garrison Billings, a Chicago utility heir, Union Carbide and Carbon acquired four technically related companies and their subsidiaries.

1. Linde Air Products Company, incorporated in Ohio in 1907, used acetylene and made oxygen for oxyacetylene welding.
2. National Carbon Company, Inc., incorporated in New York in 1917, was a manufacturer of electrodes that were used in Union Carbide's furnaces as well as in electric arc lamps that were used in streetlights.
3. Prest-O-Lite Company, Inc., incorporated in New York in 1913, used calcium carbide to make acetylene for portable lamps.
4. Union Carbide Company, incorporated in Virginia in 1898, made calcium carbide. (*Moody's 1985 Industrial Manual*, p. 4550.)

While Union Carbide and Carbon grew larger and more complex, its subsidiaries continued to enjoy a great deal of autonomy. No serious attempt was made to install control over them. As Gilbert Burck observed in *Fortune*:

The fifteen operating companies were practically autonomous, with their own presidents and policies; some even had boards of directors. Secrecy, jealousy, and duplication, not to say multiplication of effort, were the order of the day. No two divisions used the same code for a customer's name; it took days to find out how much Union Carbide sold to, say, U.S. Steel. (*Fortune*, December 1965, p. 148.)

The real change in the organization occurred when Morse Dial became president in the early 1950s. He established a four-man capital appropriations committee that operated from a corporate, rather than a subsidiary, point of view. Dial's emphasis on corporate culture resulted in the establishment of a personnel policy of shifting individuals from division to division in order to reduce loyalty to a subsidiary or division and to develop more commitment to the corporation. On May 1, 1954, the company's name was officially changed to Union Carbide Corporation, and many divisions lost their former names.

In May 1963, Dial's key assistant and executive vice-president, Birney Mason, Jr., was appointed chief executive officer (CEO). Mason immediately began a major reorganization and centralization effort because "the old organization wasn't working well. The company had been a collection of decentralized, walled in, highly individual operations that almost automatically put their welfare ahead of the corporation's" (Burck 1965, p. 147).

In 1971, Mason retired and was succeeded by F. Perry Wilson. Like Mason, Wilson consolidated the position of Union Carbide by diversifying its operations through mergers and acquisitions. In 1977, William S. Sneath replaced Wilson as chairman and CEO. Sneath had worked for Union Carbide since 1950 when he received an M.B.A. from the Harvard Business School. His leadership between 1977 and 1981 reshaped Union Carbide Corporation. Apart from relocating the company headquarters from New York City to the rural setting of Danbury, Connecticut, Sneath focused on the profitability of Carbide's core business. Rather than seek growth in revenue, Sneath strove to increase profits; rather than make heavy cash investments in new high-growth prospects, Sneath chose first to support the company's fundamental businesses in plastics, industrial gases, lightweight carbon fibers, and batteries (*Wall Street Journal*, May 4, 1982, p. 10).

In keeping with the new strategy, Union Carbide divested itself of about $1 billion in assets from 1974 to 1981. It withdrew from 27 "infant businesses" and from 12 "established Carbide businesses" because of unacceptable returns. Among the discontinued operations was a European plastics and chemicals unit that had annual revenue of over $300 million. It was sold to British Petroleum for $200 in cash and British Petroleum's assumption of about $200 million of Union Carbide's debt (*Forbes*, April 28, 1980, pp. 97–101).

On January 1, 1982, William Sneath retired as chairman but continued to serve on the board of directors. He was succeeded by Warren M. Anderson, employed by Union Carbide in 1945 and currently chairman and CEO of the corporation. By 1984, Union Carbide was the 3rd largest chemical manufacturer and 37th largest industrial corporation in America, with a net income of $323 million in sales of $9.51 billion. The book value of the firm's assets was $10.52 billion, according to reports filed with the Securities and Exchange Commission. The outlook for the company before December 3, 1984 was bright.

Union Carbide Corporation's Involvement in India

Union Carbide India Limited was one of Union Carbide's many operating units around the world (see EXHIBIT 15-1). Union Carbide Eastern, Inc., a wholly owned subsidiary of Union Carbide Corporation, owned 50.9 percent of the Union Carbide India stock. Although Union Carbide owned a majority of shares in the Indian plant, it was essentially an Indian operation. Most of the investors were Indian, as were all the managers and workers. According to William Lutz, chairman of Union Carbide Eastern, Inc., which was the division responsible for operations in Asia, "though Carbide provided the specifications for the plant, it was designed and built in India, at the insistence of the Indian government. Danbury never had a copy of the blueprints" (*Fortune*, January 7, 1985). Questions about whether the plant was built properly, whether workers were adequately trained, and whether the plant had adequate safety provisions would become crucial in fixing responsibility for the Bhopal accident and in judging whether Union Carbide's management had been doing its job in the years before the accident.

The Bhopal plant, operating at one-third capacity, was a chronic money loser. Production lost in Bhopal, however, could quite easily be made up from production at similar plants in Institute, West Virginia; Woodbine, Georgia; Cubatao, Brazil; and Beziers, France. Union Carbide was not disturbed, therefore, by the Bhopal plant's poor revenues and profit. Instead, it was concerned about the future of the company's Research and Development Center a few miles south of Bhopal.

The Research and Development Center

By far the largest of its kind in India, Union Carbide's Research and Development Center was the only one in the country engaged in the development of new pesticides. Before establishing the center in 1975, Union Carbide had been influenced by the fact that all pesticide discoveries had taken place in the United

States, Europe, or Japan and had been tested on crops and pests in temperate or cold climates whose conditions varied greatly from those of tropical climates.

Union Carbide wanted to have a well-equipped center in India for two reasons.

1. New pesticides could be discovered and tested under local conditions.
2. New pesticides that were developed in the corporation's research center at Raleigh, North Carolina, could be tested under tropical conditions.

Discovery of pesticides was not the center's only occupation. Work on an insect screen for pesticide testing started in 1978, and molecular synthesis came in 1980. The importance of the Research and Development Center to Union Carbide was evident as the number of scientists at the center increased from 25 in 1975 to about 60 by 1985. Millions of dollars had been spent on equipment which included nuclear magnetic resurgence, infra-red spectrophotometers and chromatograms.

Two weeks after the Bhopal accident, media attention shifted from the plant in Bhopal to the Research and Development Center. A report of the Delhi Science Forum urged the Indian government to investigate the work at the Research and Development Center. In stressing the urgent need to institute effective mechanisms for monitoring foreign collaborations in research and development, the report also demanded an investigation into "the grey area between peaceful application and biological warfare" (*India Today*, January 15, 1985, p. 60).

Scientists at the center were deeply hurt by these allegations. Said B. P. Srivastava, research and development manager:

> Because an unfortunate accident occurred, to suggest that we are engaged in antinational activities is grossly unfair. We are not criminals. These reckless allegations have deeply hurt all of us scientists. We are Indians too. We have regularly had scientists from the Indian Council of Agricultural Research and from universities coming to work here. The facilities are always open to inspection by the government. How come no one made any of these allegations earlier? If we were carrying on secret work, would we be so open to outsiders?"

Union Carbide was thus faced with a dilemma. If the Bhopal plant was shut down, what would be the future of the Research and Development Center? The equipment could be moved easily, but what about the scientists, most of whom were Indian? If the Research and Development Center remained in Bhopal, would it continue to serve its purpose without the plant? Said one scientist: "The advantage of having the plant was that we were constantly forced to think in commercial terms. We were in constant touch with the production people there. Without it, we may be reduced to mere academics like numerous government research institutions—doing work without thought to applicability" (*India Today*, January 15, 1985, p. 60).

Plagued both by uncertainty as well as by controversy, some of the center's top scientists were already talking about seeking jobs elsewhere.

Events Leading to the Poisonous Gas Leak

Based on interviews with plant employees and its own tests, Union Carbide recreated the scenario of events leading up to the methyl isocyanate leak at the Bhopal plant. Union Carbide's scenario was published in the *Wall Street Journal* on March 21, 1985, and is summarized as follows:

DECEMBER 2, 1985

10:20 P.M. The plant's second shift is ending. About 11,290 gallons of methyl isocyanate are stored in Tank 610.

11:00 P.M. Following the shift change, a control-room operator checks the tank's pressure gauge. Unaware that the pressure has risen since the earlier shift, he apparently is unconcerned because it is within normal range. A chemical leak is reported, but the source isn't detected.

DECEMBER 3, 1985

12:15 A.M. Another leak is reported. Pressure on the tank's gauge rises rapidly, exceeding the instrument's scale. An operator hears rumbling in the tank and the sound of concrete cracking is heard in the control room. The scrubber, a safety device which has been turned off since October, is switched on. A meter shows that it isn't working. A flare tower, another safety device that has been turned off for months while awaiting maintenance, also isn't working.

12:20 A.M. The plant's superintendent is informed of the gas leak. He arrives five minutes later and finds large amounts of methyl isocyanate in the area.

1:00 A.M. Alarms are sounded at the plant. Workers try to knock down escaping gas by spraying water on it.

1:30–2:30 A.M. Pressure in the tank subsides and the safety valve closes. An estimated 60 percent of the chemical stored in the tank has escaped.

Who Is Responsible?

THE COMPANY'S REACTION

If there is one area where the management of Union Carbide has changed its stand on the Bhopal accident, it is on who was responsible for the disaster. Recalling that fateful day, Union Carbide chairman and chief executive officer, Warren Anderson, remarked: "My first reaction was disbelief. As the day went on, and that number crept up and up, I almost felt that if I went back to sleep and woke up, all this would disappear. It's a shattering experience" (*Business Week*, December 24, 1984, p. 53).

Shattering as it was, the news from India warranted a swift, sweeping response and demanded immediate decisions from Union Carbide's management. A high-powered committee was set up that included William Lutz, chairman, Union Carbide Eastern, Inc.; Robert Oldford, president, Agricultural Products Division; Edward Van Den Ameele, manager of press relations; and Jackson Browning, director of health, safety and environment. The committee's first reaction was to send help to India—medical supplies, respirators, doctors with extensive knowledge of the effects of methyl isocyanate, and a team of technical experts to examine the plant. The next day Chairman Anderson was on a plane to India, perhaps to express his sympathy on behalf of the company. However, on arrival, he was arrested, held briefly before being released on $2,500 bail, and then sent to New Delhi where foreign ministry officials told him to leave the country for his own good. Anderson did accept some personal responsibility by saying: "The balance of my professional career will be associated with having to sort out this accident." He also said that the company would pay "fair" compensation and that a decision on compensation should be reached quickly. "I don't want this turning into an asbestos-type thing where no one gets paid after years of litigation" (*Business Week*, December 24, 1984, p. 56).

Four months later, however, Union Carbide Corporation blamed the tragedy squarely on the management of the Indian facility saying: "Safety is the responsibility of the people who operate our plants." All that Union Carbide conceded was that in May 1982, an inspection at the Bhopal site took place "under an agreement" between the parent and its subsidiary. The inspection disclosed lack of preventive maintenance, ill-trained employees, and possible hazardous conditions caused by poorly maintained utility outlets. Since the blame for the accident had now been shifted to the subsidiary, Union Carbide's management felt that any liability should be borne by the Indian company. Union Carbide Corporation, however, did make a $1 million donation and paid $2 million for emergency services. It also offered $5 million in cash, which was rejected by the Indian government because the company insisted on quarterly reports on the use of the funds. In addition, the employees of Union Carbide contributed $120,000 to a trust for voluntary relief organizations (*Business Week*, November 25, 1985, p. 96).

Union Carbide's employees certainly regretted that the accident in Bhopal had occurred. However, they felt no personal responsibility for it. According to some employees, the company was a victim of circumstances. Said one, "We're bitter.

A few incompetent, casual Indians put a black mark on my name." Ethically, agreed another, the disaster "is about equivalent to an airplane crash."

Almost a year after the accident, Chairman Anderson confirmed that the company's attitude had changed dramatically. "I overreacted," he recalls. "The early days were traumatic, but then you step back. It's gotten to be manageable and nonemotional. Life goes on. I've got a big company here" (*Business Week*, November 25, 1985, p. 98).

In early 1986, Union Carbide issued a Fact Sheet (see Exhibit 15–2) that highlighted the company's immediate, intermediate, and long-term relief efforts, as well as its commitment to health, safety and environmental protection.

THE INDUSTRY'S REACTION

The views of other chemical producing companies varied on the issue of the responsibility of multinational companies for assuring safety in their overseas plants. While some insisted on annual safety inspections of their foreign subsidiaries, others felt that safety audits should be conducted every three years. Some companies say that a corporate parent cannot place the ultimate responsibility for a plant's safety on their foreign subsidiaries. Others agree with Warren Anderson about local responsibility.

The Chemical Manufacturers Association in the United States does not recommend a specific cycle for plant audits. However, it does call for a different level of concern by U.S. companies for their overseas plants due to poor enforcement of regulations by third world governments. Geraldine V. Cox, the Chemical Manufacturers Association's technical director, suggested that responsibility for safety permeates many corporate layers, from workers to plant managers to corporate executives. "From the very top to the very bottom, everyone has a responsibility" (*Wall Street Journal*, April 5, 1985, p. 15).

Of the large chemical manufacturers in the United States, DuPont Company, Wilmington, Delaware, conducts a major safety audit of each of its foreign plants every 12 to 22 months. Monsanto Company, St. Louis, Missouri, inspects its foreign plants annually, except for those in the Far East which are audited every two years. American Cyanamid Company, Wayne, New Jersey, sends safety teams overseas once every three years, and Hercules Inc., inspects roughly on an annual basis.

The question of responsibility is a major factor in the litigation that inevitably follows an industrial accident. Authorities in India placed the responsibility for the disaster solely on the parent company. An investigation report mentioned: "There just were no safety procedures adequate to deal with the disaster, and we have plenty of documentation to substantiate that Danbury, Conn. knew exactly what was happening at the Bhopal plant" (*Christian Science Monitor*, March 31, 1985).

As the months elapsed, Union Carbide's stand hardened. From a position of compromise in December 1984, management has taken an increasingly combative stand. Anderson said: "Maybe they, early on, thought we'd give the store away. [Now] we're in a litigation mode. I'm not going to roll over and play dead" (*Business Week*, November 25, 1985, p. 96).

The Legal Battle

When a disaster occurs, especially one that is termed the worst industrial accident in history, litigation is bound to follow. So, it was not surprising to see American lawyers buzzing around in Bhopal, looking for material to file compensation suits in U.S. courts on behalf of the Bhopal victims. Their initial appearance sent hope soaring among the victims. That was short lived. Soon, strong doubts began to fill the minds of the victims, many of whom were illiterate slum dwellers. Could these lawyers be trusted? What was their game? What papers had the lawyers made them sign? Was the money they were promised only a mirage? Comments from some residents of Jayaprakash Nagar, a slum locality near Union Carbide's Bhopal plant, follow (*India Today*, January 15, 1985, p. 60):

> Ram Gopal Sharma, a mechanical fitter: "No one told me that there was any question of giving a percentage of the claim to the lawyers. I can read Hindi, but most of the forms were in English."
> Kamta Prasad Vishwakarma, another local resident: "A few days ago we started questioning one of the lawyers. We asked him for a receipt as proof of the fact that we had given him the power of attorney. He kept avoiding, and when we grew insistent, he fled."
> Bangal Soni, a dairy worker: "I signed whatever they asked me to. I hope it won't get me into trouble. I couldn't believe that a stranger would fight my case in America. But everyone was filing them, so did I. Greed got the better of me."

In its editorial on December 12, 1984, the *Wall Street Journal* severely chastised leading American lawyers, including Melvin M. Belli, for what it called "ambulance chasing." Belli's response as well as those of others to the editorial, are included in Exhibit 15–3.

Jurisdiction

Before the issue of responsibility or damages can be resolved, the question of whether American courts have jurisdiction over damages in an accident that took place in India has to be decided.

The management of Union Carbide is challenging the jurisdiction of U.S. courts to hear the cases, and is seeking to shift the cases instead to Indian courts, which are known to award lower damages. More important, from the company's standpoint, is the fact that there is no system of punitive damages in India. Substantial punitive damages awarded in the U.S. could wreck the company and its Indian subsidiary. Union Carbide's insurance does not cover punitive damages. Even if the cases are heard in the United States, most legal experts believe that the courts would apply Indian law, since it is the law of the place where an incident occurs, not the law of the place where the court is located, that matters. Union Carbide will probably face similar rules for setting monetary value on death, blindness, or diseases. In this respect, Indian law adheres to a 100-year-old-English precedent that those who keep a dangerous substance, such as poisonous gas, on their property are liable for any damages it may cause—even if no one is at fault (*Business Week*, December 24, 1984, p. 55).

The Indian government, which has undertaken to file a suit on behalf of all the victims, and American lawyers, who are representing thousands of clients, are pressing for the case to be heard in the United States. According to K. V. Rathee, an Indian lawyer: "A parent, or holding company, is fully liable for the actions or inactions of the subsidiary company, even if the subsidiary is located outside the U.S. Legal action can be filed either inside or outside the U.S." One of the major precedents that is being cited is a recent Supreme Court opinion that victims must get "meaningful relief." Lawyers representing the Bhopal victims argue that the Indian legal system, slow and poorly equipped as it is for mass tort litigation, would deprive the victims of "meaningful relief" (*India Today*, January 15, 1985, p. 63).

Compensation

With $10.6 billion in assets, Union Carbide is being sued for compensation and damages two times greater than that amount. Focusing on the value of earnings lost from death or injury, the company is confident that the claims could be handled with its existing resources. Since an Indian foreman earns less than $100 a month, the total value of such awards is unlikely to be massive. The Indian and American lawyers, however, argue that compensation should be determined by U.S. standards. As one Indian newspaper reports: "If the U.S. company thinks it can take shelter under the weak compensation [system] in India and escape payment of full compensation to the victims, it is mistaken. Think of a five-year-old child who loses both parents. The value of that loss is the same whether it's in America or in India." Exhibit 15–4 shows a list of recent major liability cases decided in the United States.

With claims for compensation running into billions of dollars, Union Carbide's strategy is to seek a negotiated settlement, perhaps with the government of India and the state of Madhya Pradesh, where the accident occurred.

The company has offered to pay $230 million to a specific trust over a period of 20 years. That money could be used to pay the heirs of Bhopal victims 100 years' annual income in Indian wages, and could pay the seriously injured 20 years' annual income in Indian wages. Any funds left over could be used to compensate all other people who were affected and be used for various medical programs.

To show its good intentions the company offered to build an orphanage, to save jobs by converting the Bhopal plant to nonchemical manufacturing, and to donate nearly one million dollars. In June 1985, at the request of Federal District Judge John F. Keenan, Union Carbide offered a further $5 million in emergency aid, which was, like the earlier offer, rejected by the Indian government. The company feels that "from the first day, Union Carbide's offers of help in every possible way have been spurned" (*New York Times*, June 20, 1985, p. 15).

The Indian response to Union Carbide's offer has been strong. The government's top legal official, law minister Ashoke K. Sen, says: "Union Carbide's offer is based on a total lack of appreciation of the magnitude of the problem, so is hardly worth considering because it is spread over 20 years." The government of India claims that more than 2,000 died from the leak of methyl isocyanate and that 17,000 people are permanently disabled, largely from lung ailments. Doctors have treated 200,000 — a quarter of Bhopal's population. In rejecting Union Carbide's $230 million offer, Mr. Sen says that India does not plan to make a counter offer. He feels Union Carbide must name a figure. "We view this as a human problem, not a merchant problem" (*New York Times*, June 20, 1985, p. 15).

Major Events in 1985

On August 11, 1985, barely eight months after the Bhopal accident, Union Carbide was hit by another poisonous gas leak. This one at its Institute, West Virginia, plant. Toxic gas leaked from one of the storage tanks, affecting 135 people in the vicinity. Once again legal suits against the company have been filed. What is disturbing about the Institute accident is the disclosure in a Union Carbide investigation report on the accident whereby the company blames its own employees and equipment for that gas leak. The report reveals that ten days before the August 11 accident, 32 employees had been in a position to know that gas might escape from a chemical tank. Safety alarms were out of service, a broken gauge had not been fixed, and basic safety procedures were ignored (*New York Times*, August 26, 1985, p. 1).

The Institute gas leak, though not as devastating as that in Bhopal, seems to highlight the need for protective measures in the U.S. Says Edward J. Bergin, a senior policy advisor in the U.S. Department of Labor: "Chemical companies here try to perpetrate the myth that it can't happen here, that it's always going to happen to the other guy. But in truth, we're living in a chemical nightmare. . . . What I'm saying is that the burden of proving that chemicals are safe — through adequate testing — should be shifted to the industry" (*India Today*, January 31, 1985, pp. 54–55).

On August 28, 1985, Union Carbide's chairman, Warren Anderson, announced a seven-point program aimed at improving Union Carbide's financial position. Some of the main features of this reorganization are:

- Modification of its bylaws and pension plan.
- Simplification of its corporate structure.
- Shedding of 4,000 white-collar workers, with expected savings of $250 million, or $62,500 per employee.
- Raising $500 million through divestiture of nonprofitable units.
- Buying back up to 10 million shares of stock, with $500 million to be taken from an employee pension plan.
- Charging $990 million against 1985 earnings.
- Shortening depreciation periods.

"This is a short-term program," says Anderson, "aimed at improving the company's profitability for 1986." But Union Carbide's employees are preoccupied with the disruptions in their own lives. Says one manager: "The employees have a lot of pressure on them, and they're depressed and angered. Morale is dismal." Another asked: "How do I know that someone with seniority, whose job has been axed, won't be moved into my job?" (Later that day he was laid off.) Many Union Carbide employees are looking for jobs because they have lost faith in the company's future. One former employee said: "I don't know where Carbide's going, but I sold my stock the day I quit."

In spite of its troubles, Vice-Chairman Alec Flamm is confident that Union Carbide is moving full speed toward financial health. Others wonder if the company is mortgaging its future to please Wall Street analysts. Questions regarding the cost of compensating the victims in Bhopal and in Institute, sagging employee morale, future safety at its chemical plants, and the stigma attached to the company still nag Union Carbide. Until those questions are answered, the company's future remains precarious (*Business Week*, November 25, 1985, p. 98).

EXHIBIT 15-1. UNION CARBIDE CORPORATION

Operating Units

Union Carbide Corporation's business worldwide is conducted through the divisions and subsidiaries listed in boldface type below. Major affiliates owned by the Corporation as of March 1, 1982 which were actively producing during 1981 or which were scheduled as of March 1, 1982 to begin production during 1982, are listed beneath the division or subsidiary having management responsibility for them. Subsidiaries and affiliates are 100% owned by the Corporation unless otherwise indicated.

Agricultural Products Division
Union Carbide Agricultural Products Company, Inc.

Battery Products Division

Carbon Products Division

Coatings Materials Division

Electronics Division

Engineering and Hydrocarbons Division
(An affiliate company)

Engineering Products Division

Einde Division

Ethylene Oxide Derivatives Division

Ethylene Oxide/Glycol Division

Films-Packaging Division

Home and Automotive Products Division

Medical Products Division

Metals Division

Nuclear Division

Polyolefins Division

Silicones and Urethane Intermediates Division

Solvents and Intermediates Division

Specialty Chemicals and Plastics Division

Union Carbide Africa and Middle East, Inc.

EGYPT
Union Carbide Egypt S.A.E.—75%

GHANA
Union Carbide Ghana Limited—66.67%

IVORY COAST
Union Carbide Cote d'Ivoire

KENYA
Union Carbide Kenya Limited—65%

NIGERIA
Union Carbide Nigeria Limited—60%

SAUDI ARABIA
*Carbide Hashim Industrial Gases
Company—25%*

SUDAN
*Union Carbide Sudan
Limited—84%*

**Union Carbide
Canada Limited—74.72%**

Union Carbide Eastern, Inc.

AUSTRALIA
*Chemos Industries Pty.
Limited—60.02%
Union Carbide Australia
Limited—60.02%*

HONG KONG
*Sonea Industries Limited
Union Carbide Asia Limited*

INDIA
*Union Carbide India
Limited—50.9%*

INDONESIA
*P. T. Agrocarb Indonesia—70.7%
P. T. Union Carbide Indonesia*

JAPAN
*Nippon Unicar Company
Limited—50%
Union Showa K.K.—50%
Sony-Eveready, Inc.—50%
Union Carbide Services Eastern
Limited*

KOREA
*Union Gas Company
Limited—86.15%*

MALAYSIA
*Union Carbide Malaysia Sdn.
Bhd.—80%*

Union Polymers Sdn. Bhd.—60%

NEW ZEALAND
*Union Carbide New Zealand
Limited—60.02%*

PHILIPPINES
Union Carbide Philippines, Inc.

REPUBLIC OF SRI LANKA
*Union Carbide Ceylon
Limited—60%*

SINGAPORE
*Metals and Ores Pte. Limited
Union Carbide Singapore Pte.
Limited*

THAILAND
Union Carbide Thailand Limited

Union Carbide Europe, Inc.

BELGIUM
*Union Carbide Benelux N.V.
Indugas N.V.—50%*

FRANCE
*La Littorale S.A.—99.95%
Union Carbide France S.A.
Viscora, S.A.—50%*

GERMANY (WEST)
*Ucar Battenen G.m.b.H.
Union Carbide Deutschland
G.m.b.H.
Union Carbide Industriegase
G.m.b.H.*

GREECE
*Union Carbide Hellas Industrial
and Commercial S.A.*

ITALY
*Elettrografite Meridionale S.p.A.
Uniliq S.p.A.
Union Carbide Italia S.p.A.*

SPAIN
Argon, S.A.—50%
Union Carbide Iberica, S.A.
Union Carbide Navarra, S.A.

SWEDEN
Unifos Kemi AB—50%
Union Carbide Norden AB

SWITZERLAND
Union Carbide Europe S.A.

UNITED KINGDOM
Union Carbide U.K. Limited
Viskase Limited—50%

Union Carbide Pan America, Inc.

ARGENTINA
Union Carbide Argentina
S.A.I.C.S.—99.99%

BRAZIL
Eletro Manganes Lida.—55%
Tungstento do Brasil Minerios e
Metais Lida.
S.A. White Martins—50.14%
S.A. White Martins
Nordeste—50.14%
Union Carbide do Brasil Lida.

COLOMBIA
Union Carbide Colombia, S.A.

COSTA RICA
Union Carbide Centro Americana,
S.A.

ECUADOR
Union Carbide Ecuador C.A.

MEXICO
Union Carbide Mexicana, S.A. de
C.V.—45.70%

VENEZUELA
Union Carbide de Venezuela,
C.A.

**Union Carbide
Puerto Rico, Inc.**

Union Carbide Caribe, Inc.
Union Carbide Films—Packaging,
Inc.
Union Carbide Grafito, Inc.

**Union Carbide
Southern Africa, Inc.**

REPUBLIC OF SOUTH AFRICA
Elektrode Maatskappy Van Suid
Afrika (Eiendoms)Beperk—50%
Tubatse Ferrochrome (Proprietary)
Limited—49%
Ucar Chrome Company (S.A.)
(Proprietary) Limited
Ucar Minerals Corporation

ZIMBABWE
Unconsolidated subsidiaries
Zimbabwe Mining and Smelting
Company (Private) Limited
Union Carbide Zimbabwe
(Private) Limited

EXHIBIT 15–2. FACT SHEET

Much has been said and printed regarding what has happened since the tragedy in Bhopal. Union Carbide believes it is relevant and important to know what has transpired since then. Shortly after the incident, Union Carbide Chairman Warren M. Anderson said that the company assumed moral responsibility for the tragedy. Since that time, Union Carbide Corporation has endeavored to alleviate the suffering resulting from the December 3 episode.

The information below is factual and relevant, but does not in any way represent Union Carbide's total commitment to helping the people of Bhopal. UCC is committed to determining the exact nature of the needs in Bhopal related to the tragedy and to seeing that just and effective measures are taken to deal with those needs.

UCC and UCIL's Immediate Responses

Union Carbide Corporation (UCC) and Union Carbide India Limited (UCIL) undertook immediate relief efforts to alleviate the consequences of the tragedy. Specifically, efforts immediately taken by UCC included:

- Warren M. Anderson's trip to India on December 4, 1984, to provide relief and compensation to victims;
- Within days following the Bhopal incident, UCC sponsored trips to India of internationally recognized pulmonary and eye experts;
- Within days after the incident, Union Carbide dispatched a five-person medical relief and technical investigation team to Bhopal to determine the immediate health and safety needs connected with the Bhopal plant, the cause of the incident, and as it developed, to dispose of the remaining methyl isocyanate (MIC) stocks;
- Prime Minister Ghandi's Bhopal Relief Fund accepted UCC's $1 million contribution on December 18, 1984;
- Madhya Pradesh state government declined to accept UCIL's offer of $840,000 to assist in providing immediate relief in early December 1984; this offer still stands;
- The State of Madhya Pradesh accepted UCIL's contributions of medicine, medical equipment, blankets, and clothing in December 1984;
- UCIL provided all available information on acute and short-term effects of MIC to Indian authorities and government agencies;
- UCIL's plant dispensary treated 6,000 persons immediately following the Bhopal incident;

- UCIL made a pledge in December 1984, to the State of Madhya Pradesh to establish an orphanage in Bhopal. This was not accepted as all orphaned children were taken in by Indian families. The pledge stands if families are unable to keep the children.

Intermediate Response

After the initial effects of the incident were addressed to the extent that UCC and UCIL were able to, further efforts to alleviate the needs of those in Bhopal were undertaken:

- UCC's Employee Relief Fund collected $120,000 which was distributed to organizations with relief efforts in Bhopal;
- UC Canada employees donated $5,000 to Operations Eyesight Universal, part of a larger Royal Commonwealth Society for the Blind donation for a Bhopal eye center;
- UCIL Employee's Relief Trust collected funds, made donations of food, medicine, clothing, grants for individuals, and support for community rebuilding projects;
- UCC supported trips to India for assessing medical needs by ophthalmic surgeon Dr. Robert Gorsich of Chicago; ophthalmologist Dr. G. Peter Halberg, Professor of Clinical Ophthalmology of New York Medical School; Dr. Hans Weill, Professor and Chairman of Pulmonary Medicine of Tulane University's School of Medicine; and Dr. Thomas Petty, Professor of Medicine and Co-Head, Division of Pulmonary Sciences of the University of Colorado's School of Health Sciences, and Director, Webb-Waring Lung Institute. UCC offers to supply advanced medical equipment were rebuffed;
- UCIL offers which were declined or ignored by the Madhya Pradesh state government include proposals to establish:
  —fully equipped medical care and research centers;
  —facilities for rehabilitation, vocational education and job training;
  —purchase of mobile medical van for local medical college;
  —educational scholarships for poor and handicapped students;
- UCIL paid full wages for 630 hourly and 200 staff workers of the Bhopal plant for seven months until the plant closed on July 11, 1985. UCIL recently announced that it will pay an additional $900,000 in compensation, plus normal benefits for termination of employment for workers. The plant closing followed the state government's refusal to renew the plant license, take over its formulating operations, or allow UCIL to set up and operate a nearby battery plant.

Current Long-Term Relief Efforts

Currently, UCC and UCIL have several long-term efforts underway which they are convinced will do much to meet the health and welfare needs of Bhopal.

- District Court Judge John Keenan has approved a plan for the Indian Red Cross to disburse $5 million contributed by UCC to assist survivors of the incident. The plan was submitted by the Executive Committee and Liaison Council for plaintiffs' lawyers, and developed jointly by the Indian Red Cross and the American Red Cross;
- UCC is working with American entrepreneur John Barrington O'Gilvie of New York on a project for establishing a prototype factory in Bhopal to manufacture low cost prefabricated housing. The plan will be submitted to Indian authorities in December 1985;
- UCIL proposed in mid-1985 to build module dwellings for 500 residents with a job training center, "headstart" school and community center. This project is currently pending Madhya Pradesh state government approval;
- UCC forwarded an initial grant of $50,000 to Sentinelles (a Swiss philanthropic foundation) on September 1985 for assessment of humanitarian needs in Bhopal and for disbursal as it deemed appropriate;
- UCC is working with Arizona State University on a project to establish a Bhopal Technical and Vocational Training Center. The Center would provide on an ongoing basis marketable basic vocational skills and rehabilitation for thousands of Bhopal area residents. It is hoped that the Center's activities can be structured in conjunction with an Indian government economic development zone. UCC has pledged $2 million to Arizona State University to carry out the project; the project is pending government approval. This pledge has been made without regard to subsequent compensation.

In addition to these and other efforts currently underway, UCC and UCIL are cooperating in pledging $10 million for establishing a hospital in the city of Bhopal to ensure that modern and appropriate health care is permanently available to those affected by the tragedy.

We believe this approach, modeled on the United States government's creation of Veterans Administration hospitals to treat consequences of combat injuries, will assure that all those adversely affected from a health perspective in Bhopal are provided adequate care.

Commitment to Health, Safety and Environmental Protection

Union Carbide is committed to the health, safety, and environmental protection of the communities in which it has facilities. UCC's commitment reflects the corporation's concern for residential neighborhoods, the public-at-large, and employees to know about the products manufactured in our plants, possible production or product hazards, and to ensure maximum protection for communities.

- A total of $220 million is earmarked for improved safety standards in 1985;
- Inventories of 25 of the most toxic chemicals at major installations are down 79 percent since December 4, 1984;
- Risks are being and have been reduced by consolidating plants and shipping points;
- Many toxic compounds are being and have been converted to less toxic derivatives before they leave the plant;
- The Union Carbide Policy Committee on Risk Assessment has created a centralized data base on hazardous and toxic materials and initiated a comprehensive review and revision as needed of Carbide policies and procedures on safety, health, and environmental protection affairs;
- Ongoing communications with local officials concerning emergency response programs are being and have been intensified;
- Special training programs are being and have been undertaken for emergency response personnel;
- UCC is committed to having updated emergency response programs in place at all plant locations that require them.

Union Carbide is convinced that it has made every reasonable effort to address the problems created by the tragedy at Bhopal and will continue to do so. Further, it recognizes its responsibilities to its customers, its neighbors, its employees, and the societies in which it operates.

If there are any further details you would like regarding Union Carbide's response to the Bhopal incident or our commitment to being an ethical and competent corporate member of society, please write us.

Union Carbide Corporation
39 Old Ridgebury Road
Danbury, CT 06817-0001
Attention: R. S. Wishart—E4

EXHIBIT 15-3. LETTERS TO THE EDITOR

Lawyers in Bhopal; Legal Eagles or Vultures?

Your Dec. 12 editorial on the unseemly spectacle of Melvin Belli and the like trooping into Bhopal and its probable ramifications was right on target. As an Indian, I was shocked and saddened by the tragedy. I also quite simply believe that Union Carbide has to cough up (and I am not talking paltry compensation here). The question that is truly important, however, is how and how fast.

This is where a quick settlement through prioritized treatment of the case in Indian courts comes in, preceded, if necessary, by good-faith negotiations between the Government of India and Union Carbide—they owe it to the victims to speed things up.

The last thing that one would want is for the case to drag on for years, at the end of which the lawyers get to keep the gold and the victims are lucky if they get the pot (if they are still alive), a la Manville and Agent Orange.

ANANT K. SUNDARAM

New Haven, Conn.

* * *

Your editorial was grossly inaccurate. You can criticize me and lawyers in general all you want, but please, please do your homework first.

First, I'm not the "self-proclaimed King of Torts." This was the accolade Life Magazine gave me in a feature interview in 1954.

Second, you state that speedy justice can be obtained in the Indian courts. It cannot. It takes 14 years to get to trial in the Indian courts and then a huge bond must be posted.

You state that our courts frown on "jurisdiction shopping." On the contrary, the American courts welcome it.

I think you should read for your own enlightenment the case of In Re Air Crash in Bombay, India, 1978 in 531 Fed. Supp. 1175 (1982), Holmes v. Syntex Laboratories, Inc., 802 Cal. Rplr. 773 (1983), and also Piper Aircraft Co. v. Reyno, 484 U.S. 235 (1981), which latter case expressly disavows Piper by the United States Supreme Court and sets a pattern for trying cases such as the Bhopal disaster in the United States.

The last inaccuracy is with reference to punitive damages. You won't get them in India.

You might also read Reylands v. Fletcher from the English High Court, 1883, which holds that one does not have to show negligence in a case such as Bhopal, that res ipsa loquitur, or the happening of the event is sufficient. Indeed, it goes beyond res ipsa loquitur and advises that absolute liability prevails in a case such as Bhopal.

Why are all you commercial enterprises and communication media and American businessmen against American lawyers? Have we done something to you personally?

Take away the American plaintiffs trial lawyer and you'll no longer have any right of privacy or jury trial or a constitutional guarantee or justice of any kind, for that matter.

Read the authorities I've cited and you'll see how errant you were, and you'll have to correct your article because "justice cannot be done in India!" India really is Ruritania as far as justice and the little guy is concerned.

MELVIN M. BELLI

San Francisco

* * *

I am apparently the only non-lawyer in the U.S. who entirely approves of the so-called "ambulance chasing" taking place in connection with the Bhopal tragedy. My interests are quite straightforward: I do not wish to die from poison gas leaks, and my feeling is that any company that manages to kill 2,000 people in this manner should be severely chastised. I am not in the least disturbed by the idea of Union Carbide being destroyed in the process of settling claims against it. Such a result will do more for a safe environment than the reams of environmental law and regulation on the books. This is precisely what the legal system is here for, and if that's ambulance chasing, I'm for it.

GREGOR OWEN

New York

* * *

It is as disgusting to most trial lawyers as to the WSJ to observe a small handful of lawyers picking through the bones uttering vague platitudes and rationalizing their conduct with self-serving, sophistic manifestos. It is patent that those trial lawyers, like Union Carbide, are in India for profit. And, as you correctly state, none of them legitimately wears the mantle of "brave knight." Their unfortunate conduct speaks so loudly as to drown out their self-righteous excuses.

Nevertheless, you needlessly and inaccurately attribute this greedy over-reaching to the contingency-fee system. Assuming that an Indian victim does not have the funds to hire a first-rate trial lawyer nor the resources with which to gather evidence to prove his case, what is he to do? Paying a few rupees to the corner lawyer, will hardly be adequate for the duel with corporate lawyers backed with unlimited capital. The contingency fee is the only weapon available to injured people whose cases must confront defense arsenals built and maintained by insurance companies and corporate giants.

G. DANA HOBART

Marina del Rey, Calif.

*　*　*

India is not just another developing country. It is the tenth largest industrial economy on earth, whose engineers design and build nuclear power plants, space satellites and sophisticated telecommunications equipment. It has a well developed industrial infrastructure and an oversupply of graduate engineers. In the ongoing Indian election campaign and thereafter everything possible will be done to deflect the Indian responsibility onto Union Carbide, and to portray it as the multinational which came into a poor, underdeveloped, third-world country and put an unsafe plant in it without concern for anything but profits. This is simply not so. Yes the company must share in the blame, but it seems to me the Indian Central and State Governments are the ones who ought to be held accountable first. It is also revealing that in the world's largest democracy no law suit was filed immediately in Indian courts against the Indian Governments involved which licensed the plant's construction and under whose laws the plant was maintained and operated.

SARWAR A. KASIIMOI

New York

Source: *The Wall Street Journal*, Monday, Dec. 31, 1984.

EXHIBIT 15-4

The Price Tag in Major Liability Cases

Company	Number of Claims	Cause	Cost
Manville	52,700*	Claims from asbestos-related injuries	$2 Billion*
A. H. Robins	7,700 cases resolved to date	Allegations that Robins' intrauterine contraceptive, the Dalkon Shield, caused illness and injury	$259 Million
7 Chemical Companies**	40,000 to 50,000	Class action by veterans claiming injuries from Agent Orange, the defoliant used by the U.S. military in Vietnam	$180 Million
Merrill Dow	800	Allegations that Bendectin, an antinausea drug for pregnant women, caused birth defects	$120 Million***
MGM Grand Hotels	84 deaths, hundreds of injuries	Las Vegas hotel fire on Nov. 21, 1980	$100 Million
Stouffer	26 deaths, 14 injuries	Harrison (N.Y.) hotel fire on Dec. 4, 1980	$50 Million

*Manville estimates of claims and costs by year 2001 prior to filing Chapter 11 in August, 1982
**Dow Chemical, Monsanto, Hercules, T. H. Agriculture & Nutrition, Diamond Shamrock, Uniroyal, Thompson Chemical
***Tentative Settlement   Data: BW Estimates

Source: *Business Week*, December 24, 1984.

QUESTIONS FOR REVIEW AND DISCUSSION

1. What is the overriding problem that Union Carbide is facing? How can the company overcome it?
2. Who is morally responsible for the damage caused by the gas leak at the Union Carbide plant in Bhopal? Who is legally responsible?
3. Should the case for damages be tried in India or in the United States? What should be considered fair compensation for the victims?
4. What lessons can be learned from the Bhopal accident regarding the social responsibility of multinational chemical companies in third world countries?
5. What are Union Carbide's chances of surviving the liability suits? Should Union Carbide's survival be an issue in determining the amount of compensation to the victims?
6. If you had been chairman of Union Carbide and were informed of the accident in Bhopal, what would your strategy have been for handling the case?

American Business History: Case Studies was copyedited by Patricia K. Kummer. Production editor was Brad Barrett. Martha Kreger and Martha M. Urban proofread the copy. The map on page 65 was rendered by James A. Bier. The text was typeset by Compositors, Inc., and printed and bound by Edwards Brothers, Inc.

The cover and text were designed by Roger Eggers.